Workshop Manual MG Midget TC TD TF & TF1500

A Floyd CLYMER Publication by:
www.VelocePress.com
Copyright 2017 Veloce Enterprises

IMPORTANT ADVICE

Where appropriate, information relating to the TC series is separated from the TD, TF and TF1500 series. However, TC owners are encouraged to read the TD/TF section, as much of the information is also relevant to the TC. Obviously, TD, TF and TF1500 owners are likewise encouraged to read the appropriate TC section.

INTRODUCTION

Welcome to the world of digital publishing ~ the book you now hold in your hand, was printed using the latest state of the art digital technology. The advent of print-on-demand has forever changed the publishing process, never has information been so accessible and it is our hope that this book serves your informational needs for years to come. If this is your first exposure to digital publishing, we hope that you are pleased with the results. Many more titles of interest to the classic automobile and motorcycle enthusiast, collector and restorer are available via our website at www.VelocePress.com. We hope that you find this title as interesting as we do.

NOTE FROM THE PUBLISHER

The information presented is true and complete to the best of our knowledge. All recommendations are made without any guarantees on the part of the author or the publisher, who also disclaim all liability incurred with the use of this information.

TRADEMARKS

We recognize that some words, model names and designations, for example, mentioned herein are the property of the trademark holder. We use them for identification purposes only. This is not an official publication.

INFORMATION ON THE USE OF THIS PUBLICATION

This manual is an invaluable resource for those interested in performing their own maintenance. However, in today's information age we are constantly subject to changes in common practice, new technology, availability of improved materials and increased awareness of chemical toxicity. As such, it is advised that the user consult with an experienced professional prior to undertaking any procedure described herein. While every care has been taken to ensure correctness of information, it is obviously not possible to guarantee complete freedom from errors or omissions or to accept liability arising from such errors or omissions. Therefore, any individual that uses the information contained within, or elects to perform or participate in do-it-yourself repairs or modifications acknowledges that there is a risk factor involved and that the publisher or its associates cannot be held responsible for personal injury or property damage resulting from the use of the information or the outcome of such procedures.

WARNING!

One final word of advice, this publication is intended to be used as a reference guide, and when in doubt the reader should consult with a qualified technician.

INDEX

ENGINE TC
Cylinder Head, Valves, Valve Guides	1
Pistons, Connecting Rods, Piston Rings	5
Engine & Gearbox – Remove & Replace	7
Camshaft – Cam Timing, Ignition Timing	8
Engine Fault Diagnosis	32

ENGINE TD—TF—TF1500
Lubrication System, Oil Pump	11
Cylinder Head, Rocker Shaft, Vales & Guides	19
Pistons, Connecting Rods, Bore Sizes	22
Timing Chain, Chain Tensioner	24
Camshaft Bearings – Remove & Replace	25
Engine & Gearbox – Remove & Replace	27
Crankshaft & Big End Bearings	28
Ignition, Distributor, Ignition Timing	28
Engine Mount, Control Link	29
Modifications	31
Engine Fault Diagnosis	32

FUEL SYSTEM TC—TD—TF—TF1500
Carburettor – Description & Operation	35
Carburettor – Adjustments	38
Carburettor – Troubleshooting	41
Carburettor – Service & Adjustments	44
Fuel Pump – Service & Adjustments	48
Fuel Pump – Test	52
Fuel Pump – Location	52
Fuel Pump – Troubleshooting	52
Fuel System Fault Diagnosis	54

COOLING SYSTEM TC—TD—TF—TF1500
Radiator – Remove & Replace	55
Water Pump – Service & Adjust Fan Belt	55
Cooling System Fault Diagnosis	58

CLUTCH TC—TD—TF—TF1500
Description & Operation	59
Clutch Pedal Adjustment	59
Clutch – Service & Adjustments	60
Modifications	63
Clutch Fault Diagnosis	64

GEARBOX TC
Disassembly	65
Reassembly	67
Gearbox Fault Diagnosis	77

GEARBOX TD—TF—TF1500
Disassembly	69
Reassembly	74
Modifications	74
Gearbox Fault Diagnosis	77

PROPELLER SHAFT
Description & Operation	74
Lubrication	74
Service – Universal Joint Replacement	75
Propeller Shaft Fault Diagnosis	78

REAR AXLE TC
Remove & Replace	79
Differential Disassembly & Reassembly	80
Crownwheel & Pinion – Adjustment	80
Rear Wheel Bearings	81
Rear Axle Fault Diagnosis	92

REAR AXLE TD—TF—TF1500
Description & Operation	81
Remove & Replace	82
Brake Hub & Drum	82
Brake Plate – Remove & Replace	84
Axle Shaft – Remove & Replace	84
Differential – Service & Adjustments	84
Modifications	92
Rear Axle Fault Diagnosis	92

STEERING TC
Steering Ball Joints – Maintenance & Service	94
Steering Gearbox – Service & Adjustments	94
Steering Drop Arm – Remove & Replace	95
Steering Column – Removal	96
Steering Fault Diagnosis	100

STEERING TD—TF—TF1500
Steering Wheel & Column – Removal	96
Steering Gearbox – Service & Adjustments	96
Steering Ball Joint – Service	97
Steering Rack Damper – Service	97
Modifications	99
Steering Fault Diagnosis	101

FRONT AXLE TC
Wheel Bearings & King Pins – Service	102
Front Road Springs – Service	103
Front Axle Fault Diagnosis	111

FRONT AXLE TD—TF—TF1500
Suspension – Service & Repair	103
Hub & Brake Drum – Remove & Replace	107
Front Coil Spring – Remove & Replace	108
Lower Wishbone Bushes – Replace	108
Lubrication	109
Modifications	110
Front Axle Fault Diagnosis	111

INDEX

REAR SUSPENSION TC
Rear Road Springs & Shackles	113
Rear Suspension Fault Diagnosis	115

REAR SUSPENSION TD—TF—TF1500
Rear Road Springs & Shackles	113
Rear Suspension Fault Diagnosis	115

BRAKES TC—TD—TF—TF1500
Description & Operation	116
Maintenance	116
Master Cylinder – Description	116
Brake Adjustments – Pedal & Shoes	118
Master Cylinder – Service & Repair	119
Wheel Cylinders – Service & Repair	121
Handbrake – Adjustment	122
Brake Shoe Assemblies – Service	122
Brake Fault Diagnosis	124

WHEELS & TYRES TC—TD—TF—TF1500
Wheels – Remove & Replace	126
Tubed Tyres – Remove & Replace	127
Tubeless Tyres – Remove & Replace	127
Tyre Wear Diagnosis	130

ELECTRICAL SYSTEM TC—TD—TF—TF1500
Description	132
Battery – Service	132
Generator – Test & Service	133
Starter – Test & Service	137
Regulator – Test & Service	139
Horn – Adjustment	141
Flashing Direction Indicators – Service	141
Windshield Wiper Motor – Service	142
Electrical System Fault Location & Remedy	143
Distributor – Service & Ignition Timing	144
Spark Plugs & HT Leads – Service	147
Wiring Diagram TC	148
Wiring Diagram TD—TF—TF1500	151
Electrical Fault Diagnosis	152

APPENDIX
Body – All Models	156
Maintenance & Lubrication – All Models	163
Torque Wrench Settings – All Models	165
Technical Specifications TC	166
Technical Specifications TD—TF—TF1500	174
Performance Tuning TC—TD	183
Performance Tuning TF—TF1500	191

ENGINE TC SERIES

1. CYLINDER HEAD

TO DECARBONISE

(1) First of all drain the water system by opening the tap at the bottom of the radiator and the small tap immediately behind the exhaust manifold.

(2) Remove the bonnet altogether after taking out the two screws at the rear end of the bonnet hinge.

(3) Detach the high-tension cables from the sparking plugs, unclip the distributor head; this permits the high-tension wiring to be taken away complete.

(4) Now take out the sparking plugs, being careful not to break the porcelain centres.

(5) Next remove the petrol pipe, the throttle controls and mixture control, and uncouple the exhaust pipe from the manifold.

(6) Disconnect the petrol pipes from the petrol pump and remove the petrol pump from the toolbox.

(7) Remove the carburettor float-chamber overflow pipes and air cleaner, unbolt the carburettors from the induction manifold, when the induction and exhaust manifold can be removed.

(8) The radiator must then be removed as follows:

(a) Remove the bolts securing the headlamp brackets to the radiator, also the radiator stays from the radiator header tank.

(b) Slacken the water hoses by loosening the clips securing the rubber hose to the bottom radiator pipe, and also the uppermost clips securing the rubber hose above the thermostat.

(c) The two nuts securing the radiator to the cross member can then be removed and the radiator lifted clear of the car.

(9) Remove the oil feed pipe to the rocker gear from the cylinder head.

(10) It is necessary also to slacken the fume pipe and inspection cover. If the gasket is damaged a new one must be fitted before the engine is run.

(11) Remove the valve cover and rocker gear from the cylinder head, when the push rods can be removed.

(12) After removing the cylinder head holding-down nuts, the cylinder head can be lifted clear.

The copper asbestos gasket is not difficult to remove, providing that it is lifted squarely with the cylinder head studs. If lifted at an angle, it will catch on them. As the copper either side of the asbestos is very thin and soft, it is easily damaged and the gasket rendered useless.

(13) After the cylinder head has been removed, stuff the open ends of the cylinders with clean rag

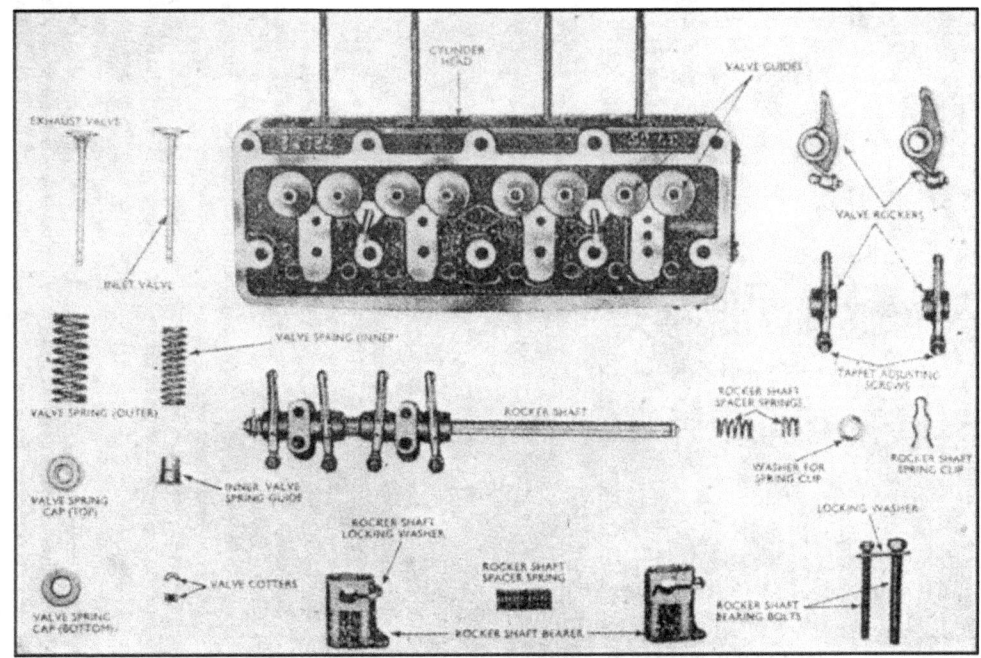

Relative Positions of All Parts of Rocker Gear.

to prevent the possibility of damage to the cylinder walls. The cylinder head can then be dealt with.

(14) The valve springs are secured by means of split cotters, and to remove each valve the cylinder head should be placed on a bench, combustion chambers downwards, with a wood block or suitable packing piece fitted in the combustion space below the valves which are being dealt with.

(15) Depress the valve spring from above and remove the two cotter halves and lift away the spring and its cap from the valves, which can be withdrawn from below. On the valve stem will be found a small synthetic rubber oil seal ring which can be easily slipped off.

TO INSTALL VALVE GUIDES

New valve guides should not be hammered in, so that if a press is not available it is advisable to have this work carried out by a qualified repairer. On earlier TD models the measurement between the arrows is .945 inch. On engines from Nos. XPAG.TD2.27867 and XPAG.TD3.27996 the measurement is .964 inch. It should be noted that the inlet valve guides are $\frac{7}{32}$ inch longer than the exhaust valve guides, but project the same distance above the head.

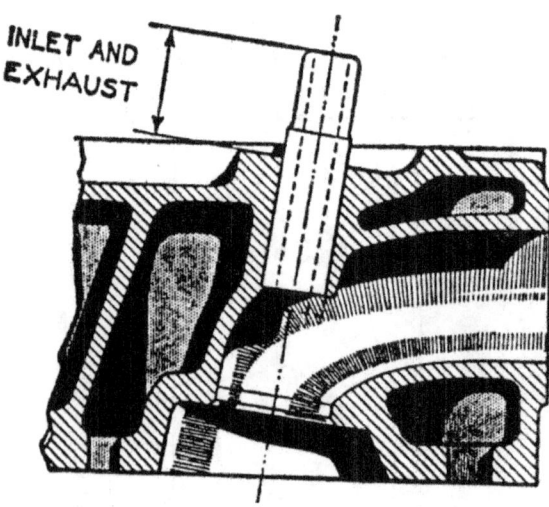

Position of the valve guide in the cylinder head.

Note: The correct clearance between the valve guide and the valve stem is .003″. After new valve guides have been fitted, it will be necessary to true-up the valve seatings to ensure that they are concentric with the new valve guides.

KEY TO INTERNAL ENGINE COMPONENTS

1 Mounting rubber—engine front
2 Engine control link—L H thread
3 Cup—link
4 Link cup rubber
5 Adjuster
6 Engine control bracket
7 Cylinder block complete
8 Plug—oil feed hole
9 Plug—oil hole by-pass
10 Oil seal cover
11 Gasket—oil seal cover
12 Bolt—cover
13 Studs—cylinder head
14 Water drain tap
15 Washer—drain tap
16 Stud—tappet cover
17 Tappet inspection cover
18 Joint—cover
19 Nut—cover stud
20 Washer—cover stud
21 Breather pipe
22 Bracket—breather pipe
23 Bolt—breather pipe bracket
24 Nut—breather pipe bracket
25 Clip—breather pipe
26 Bolt—breather pipe clip
27 Nut—clip bolt
28 Spring—oil filter—by-pass
29 Ball—oil filter—by-pass
30 Guide—ball
31 Seat—ball
32 Timing chain case assembly
33 Packing—chain case
34 Joint—chain case to plate
35 Bolt—long-chain case to block
36 Bolt—short—chain case to block
37 Bearer plate—front
38 Joint (studded) with guides
39 Bolt—plate to block
40 Bolt—plate to case
41 Bracket—plate
42 Bolt
43 Nut
44 Spring washer
45 Cylinder head (studded) with guides
46 Stud—cover
47 Stud—manifold
48 Rear cover—cylinder head
49 Joint—rear cover-plate
50 Screw—rear cover-plate
51 Water outlet pipe
52 Stud—thermostat
53 Bolt—water outlet pipe
54 Joint—water outlet pipe
55 Gasket—cylinder head
56 Nut—securing cylinder head
57 Cylinder head cover assembly
58 Oil filler cap
59 Joint—cylinder head cover
60 Nut—cylinder head cover
61 Washer—cylinder head cover
62 Stud—exhaust manifold flange
63 Nut—stud
64 Joint—exhaust manifold
65 Clamp—exhaust manifold
66 Nut—exhaust manifold clamp
67 Oil sump
68 Drain plug—sump
69 Washer—drain plug
70 Plug—oil hole
71 Packing
72 Joint—sump oil suction pipe
73 Bolt—sump—front
74 Bolt—sump—long
75 Bolt—sump—short
76 Dipstick
77 Suction filter assembly
78 Filter gauze
79 Spring—oil suction pipe
80 Fibre washer
81 Washer
82 Joint—flange
83 Bolt
84 Oil pipe assembly (filter to block).
85 Oil pipe assembly (pump to filter)
86 Bolt—banjo
87 Washer—small
88 Washer—large
89 Oil filter
90 Support bracket for oil filter
91 Bolt—bracket
92 Strap—oil filter bracket
93 Bolt—strap
94 Oil pump (bushed)
95 Bush—oil pump body
96 Oil pump cover with valve seat
97 Bolt—cover (long)
98 Bolt—cover (medium)
99 Bolt—cover (short)
100 Lock washer
101 Oil pump shaft and gear
102 Gear—driving
103 Key—driving gear
104 Circlip—driving gear
105 Oil pump gear (driven) with bush
106 Bush—oil pump gear
107 Spindle—driven gear
108 Guide—relief valve ball
109 Relief valve ball
110 Spring—relief valve
111 Cover plug—relief valve
112 Washer—cover plug
113 Joint—oil pump body
114 Oil pipe (gallery to head)
115 Screw (banjo to head)
116 Screw (banjo to block)
117 Washer—screw
118 Bracket—engine control link
119 Engine control link (RH thread)
120 Rubber bush
121 Cup washer
122 Air cleaner
123 Clip—air cleaner
124 Wing nut—air cleaner stud
125 Breather hose—air cleaner
126 Clip—breather hose
127 Pipe to air cleaner
128 Joint—pipe to carburetter
129 Bracket—generator
130 Bolt—generator bracket
131 Swivel bolt—short—generator
132 Adjusting link
133 Bolt—link
134 Nut—swivel bolt
135 Pulley—generator
136 Flexible connection—oil gauge
137 Connector—oil pipe
138 Oil pump body—integral filter head
139 Joint—oil pump body
140 Cover—oil pump
141 Pipe—oil pump cover
142 Washer—oil pump cover plug
143 Bolt—pump cover (medium)
144 Washer—pump cover bolt
145 Bolt—pump cover (short)
146 Bolt—pump cover (long)
147 Sump assembly—filter
148 Filter element

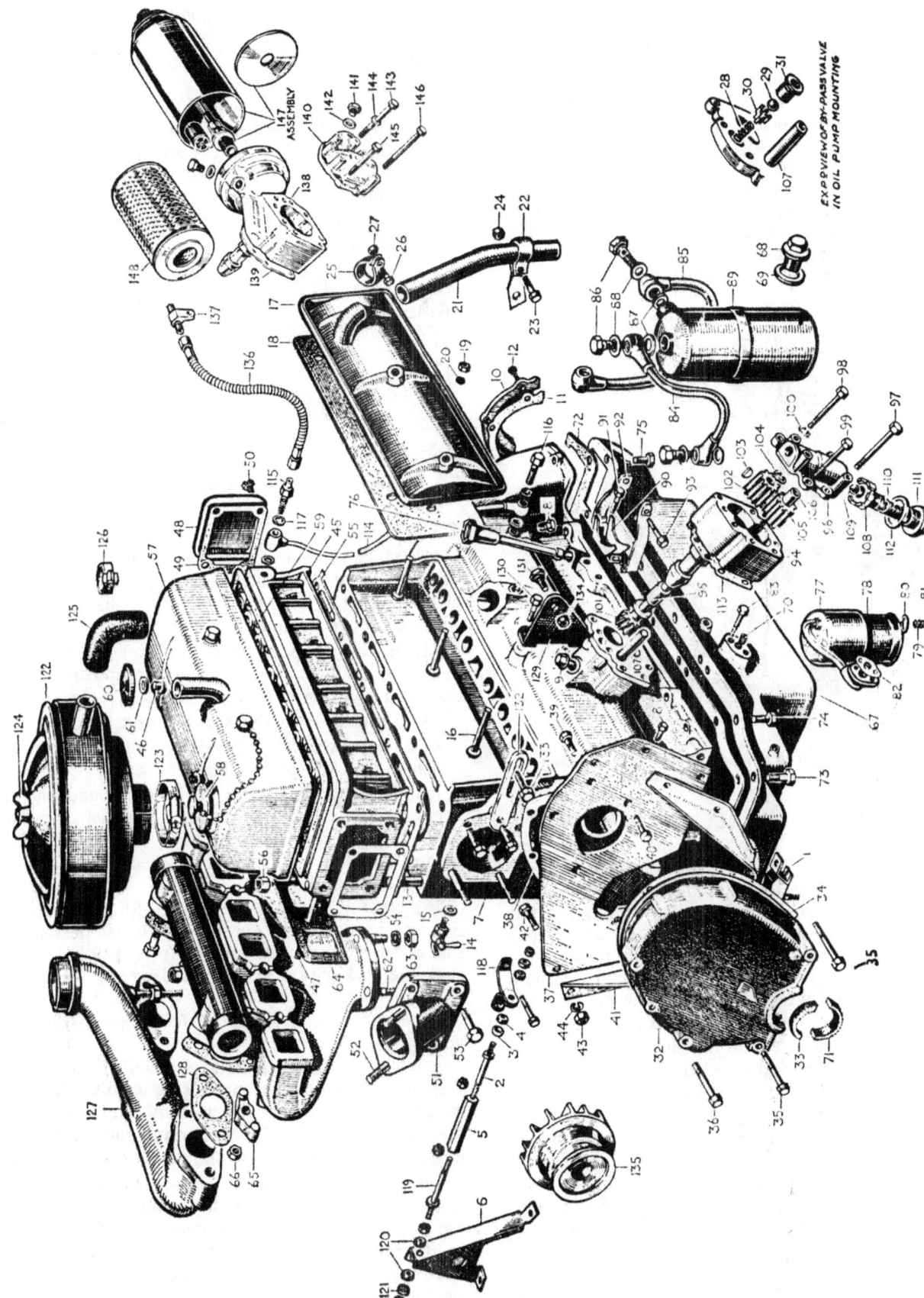

An exploded view of the external engine components. (On later engines, parts numbered 138-148 replace Nos. 28-31 and 84-93)

3

TO INSTALL VALVES

When refitting valves, lightly smear the stems with clean engine oil. Fit the springs with the closed coils against the head as shown. Note: It is essential to fit new neoprene sealing rings. Compress the springs by the same method as used in removal and insert the split cotters or collets, **making quite sure they remain in their groove as the spring is slowly released. Failure of the cotters to hold can allow the valve to go through the piston crown when the engine is running.** Valve springs should be checked for conformity with the dimensions given in the Appendix.

If any are unserviceable it is advisable to renew the complete set.

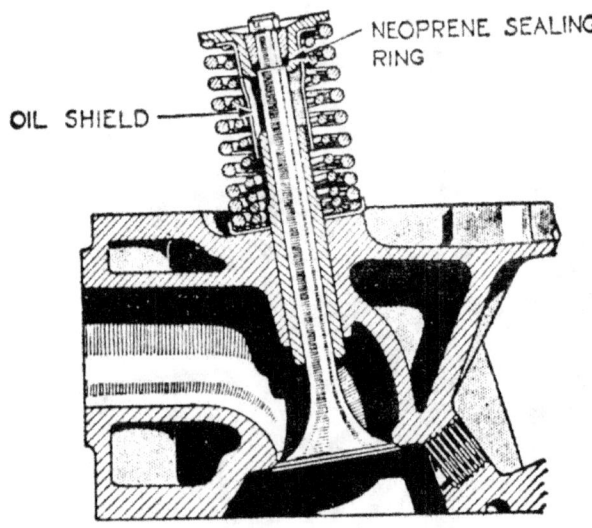

Valve assembly. The closed coils of the springs should always be against the cylinder head

TO REMOVE AND INSTALL ROCKER GEAR

Should it be desired to examine the rocker bushes, the rocker-shaft may be detached complete with its holding brackets by unscrewing the bolts which hold them to the cylinder head. It will be noticed that while all the rocker-shaft holding brackets are slotted and that distance pieces are inserted in these slots, the two middle brackets are fitted with washers which engage with Woodruff keyways in the rocker-shaft to prevent it turning. These washers may be picked or shaken out, and when the hair-pin retaining springs are removed the rockers, silencing springs, distance tubes and holding brackets may be drawn off the rocker-shaft one after the other. The end brackets being slotted allow a slight pinch on the shaft.

Before reassembling the rocker gear the cylinder head should be installed and the push rods inserted.

When installing the rocker-shaft, particular care must be taken of the following points:

(a) That the correct holding bracket is put on the rear end of the shaft. This bracket has a hole drilled up its centre to convey oil to the hollow rocker-shaft.

(b) That the washers engage properly with the keyways cut in the shaft.

(c) The tab plates which lock the holding-down bolts should be carefully inspected for any sign of cracking where they have been bent up round the bolt heads and straightened out again. If one of the bent-up corners of these plates should break off it is likely to find its way by one of the oil return passages into the sump.

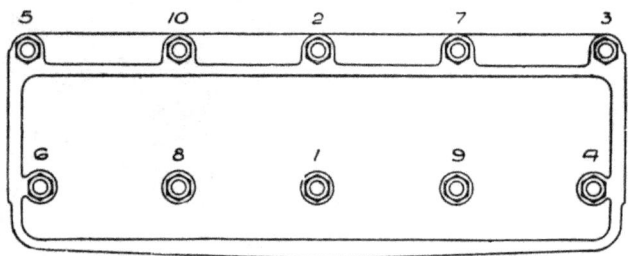

Order of Tightening Cylinder Head Nuts.

TO INSTALL

(1) Make sure the surfaces of both the cylinder block and cylinder head are clean; it is not necessary to use a jointing compound for the gasket, but it may with advantage be smeared with grease.

(2) Having slipped the gasket over the studs, next lower the cylinder head into position and fit the cylinder head securing nuts finger tight.

(3) Tighten down the securing nuts.

(4) The push rods should be installed next, after which the rocker gear is reassembled.

(5) Since the valves have been ground in, it is necessary to check the tappet adjustments to make sure there is a clearance; this, of course, will be readjusted after the engine has been completely reassembled and run.

(6) Now fit the valve cover, not forgetting the cork gasket, the gasket is not very wide so be sure that the cover fits squarely on it. It is advantageous to stick the cork gasket to the cylinder head with jointing compound, but not to the valve cover.

(7) Next, reconnect the oil feed pipe to the rocker gear.

(8) Now install the exhaust and induction manifolds complete with the carburettor assembly. As far as installation is concerned, this is quite a straightforward operation. The securing nuts holding the manifold and carburettors should be tightened evenly.

(9) All the major items are now installed, and attention should be turned to the smaller points; connect the mixture control, throttle controls and exhaust pipe to the manifold. Do not forget the gasket when connecting the exhaust pipe to the exhaust flange, and pull up the three nuts evenly on the flange.

2. PISTONS AND CONNECTING RODS

TO REMOVE

(1) The first operation is to drain the sump. Then the car should be raised at the front on trestles.

(2) After having drained the sump, the drag-link must be removed to allow the sump to drop.

(3) After the split pins and nuts are removed from the big-end bolts, the bottom caps can be withdrawn. It is advisable to replace the big-end caps and nuts on their own connecting rods and, of course, since the white metal bearing is held in a very thin shell, this also must be replaced in the correct position.

(4) When separating a piston from its connecting rod, special care will have to be exercised when undoing the pinch bolt in the small-end of the connecting rod. It will have to be removed entirely as it fits in a groove in the gudgeon pin. It is inadvisable to hold the connecting rod in a vice while the pinch bolt is undone, as a procedure of this sort is liable to distort the connecting rod. The correct method is to employ end pads which can be inserted into the open ends of the gudgeon pin and which extend beyond the sides of the piston and can be gripped in the vice without fear of damage.

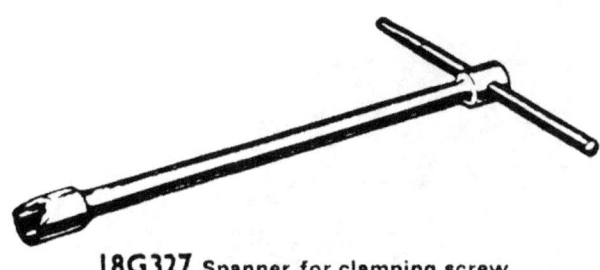

18G327 Spanner for clamping screw

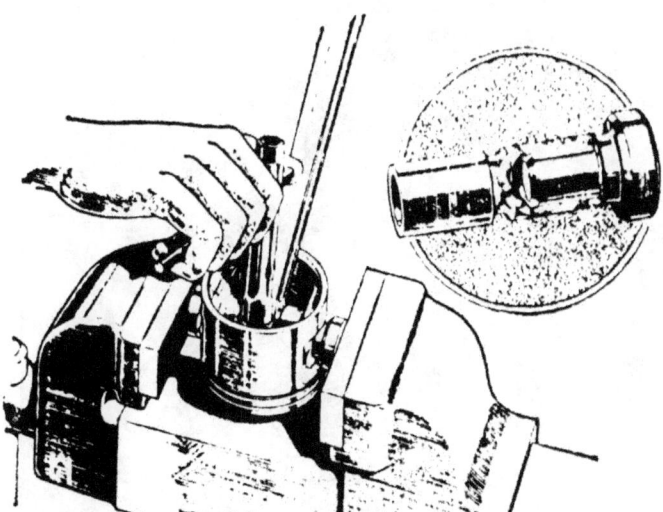

Method of holding piston using shouldered plugs (inset) when removing clamping screw

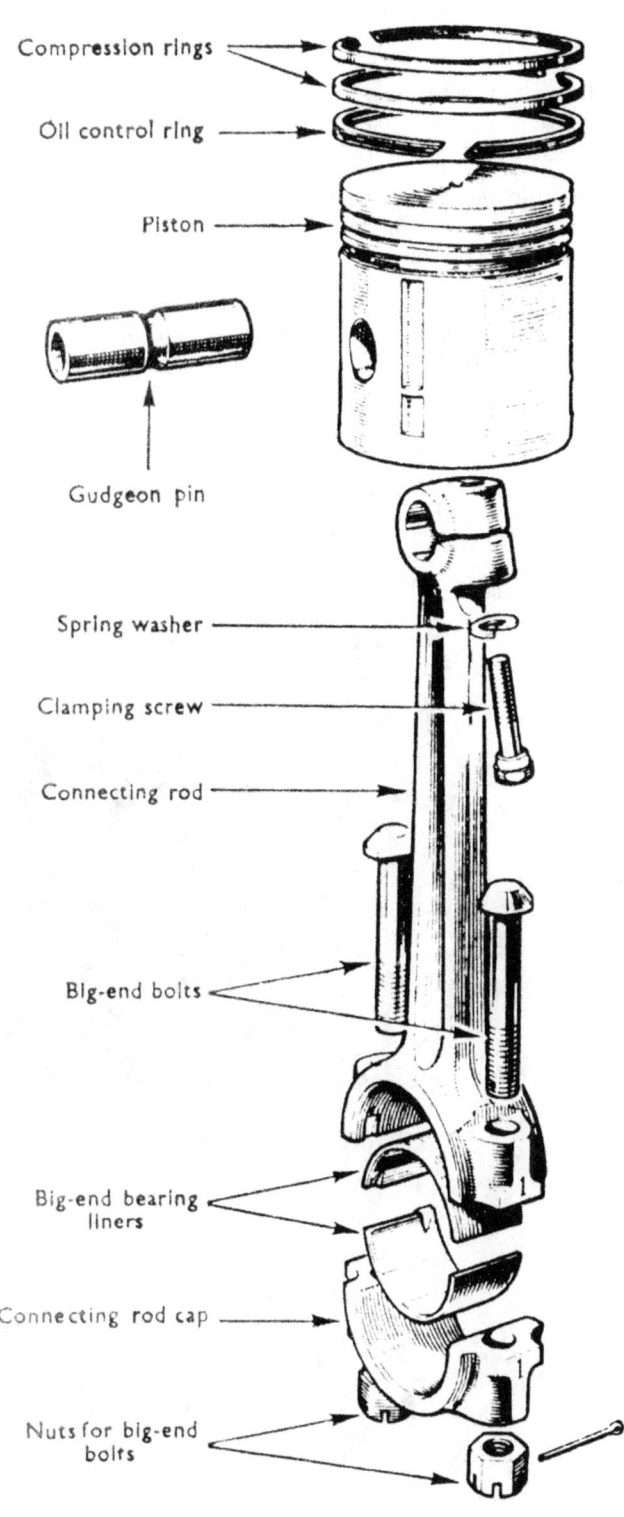

Piston and connecting rod assembly in XPAG engines.

TO INSTALL RINGS

Should it be necessary to replace or refit the pistons, the correct clearance between the piston and the cylinder wall below the piston rings and at 90° to the gudgeon pins, is .0015" to .0025".

The piston is fitted with three rings. The two upper rings are perfectly plain, being simple compression rings; the third is an oil control ring.

When installing the new rings of either type, the gap measured when they are compressed in the cylinder (without the piston, of course) should be .006" to .010".

NOTE: It is important when installing the piston rings to see that their gaps are equally spaced around the circumference of the piston and that no two gaps are opposite one another. This would defeat their object in preventing oil from travelling straight up into the combustion space.

TO INSTALL PISTONS AND CONNECTING RODS

The latest pistons are marked with the bore size in millimetres stamped on the top.

Take care when installing a piston and connecting rod to see that the gudgeon pin pinch bolt is towards the off-side of the engine, the reason for this being that the oil spray hole above the big-end bearing must be in a position to lubricate the cylinder walls correctly.

When tightening the big-end bolts, care should be taken not to overtighten them and stretch the bolts; even so, they should be sufficiently tight. Do not forget to replace the split pins.

The connecting rods are fitted with loose thin steel backed white metal bearings which, if renewed, do not require any special fitting except to ensure that the register locates properly in its groove in the rod and cap.

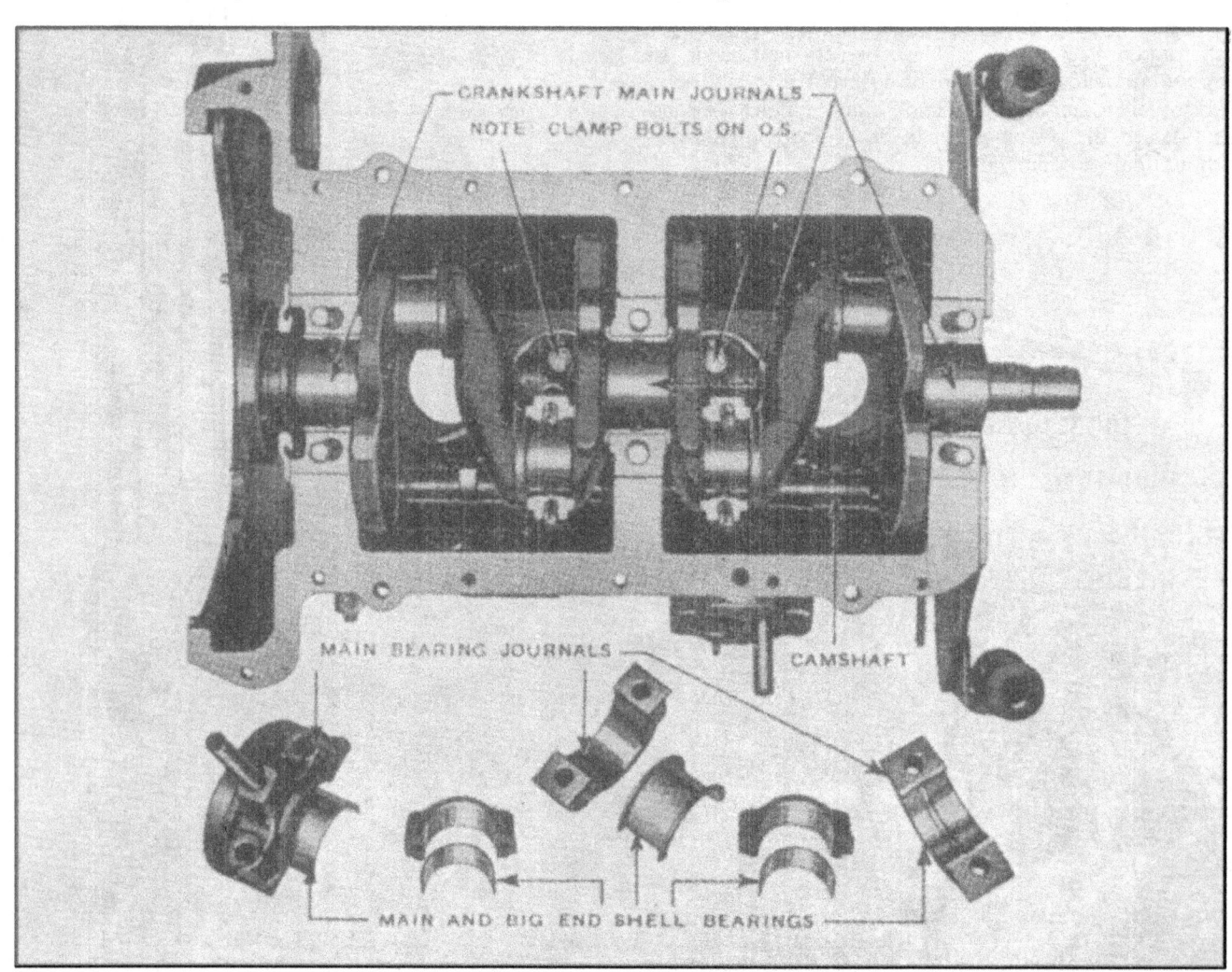

Details of Crankshaft and Bearings.

3. ENGINE AND GEARBOX ASSEMBLY

TO REMOVE

(1) After the radiator and bonnet have been removed, remove the seats, carpets, rubber gearbox cover or gearbox carpet and the floorboards.

(2) Undo the rubber muff where the steering column passes through the dash, and slide it, and its securing plate, down the column.

(3) Disconnect the battery and uncouple the harness cables from the ramp plate, also the cables from the generator.

(4) Uncouple the clutch operating chain from the pedal.

(5) Remove the clutch and brake pedals by extracting the split pin at the outer end of the pedal pivot pin and pushing this pin inwards through its bracket.

(6) Remove the accelerator pedal gear.

(7) Undo the screws which secure the ramp plate to the dash and lift the panel out.

(8) Remove the two leads from the starter motor terminal and the Bowden wire from the starter motor switch.

(9) The gearbox top cover, with remote control complete, can now be taken off.

(10) Finally uncouple the propellor shaft at the rear of the gearbox. The flanges must be marked before removal, as they must go back in the same position.

(11) Remove all controls, petrol pipes and manifolds as already detailed in instructions for removing the cylinder head, also the speedometer and revolution counter cables from the engine.

(12) Place a jack under the gearbox, taking just sufficient weight to enable the four main engine bolts (gearbox to rubber mounting) to be removed.

(13) After the nuts have been removed from the engine front mounting bolts, together with the rubber blocks and retaining washers, the bolts can be unscrewed from the rubber mountings and the engine lifted away from the car.

TO INSTALL

To install, reverse the removal operations, Leave the bottom securing nuts on the radiator loose so that the position can be adjusted to suit the bonnet.

TO ADJUST FRONT ENGINE MOUNTING

The front engine mounting should be assembled as follows:

(1) The bolt is threaded through the engine plate into the rubber mounting block and tightened in the normal way, after which the small rubber block is threaded on to the bolt with its small diameter inserted in the hole in the frame bracket.

(2) This is followed by a steel washer and a sleeve nut which is screwed up through the rubber block so that a slight tension is exerted on the rubber.

(3) While the sleeve nut is held in this position the locknut is fitted and properly tightened.

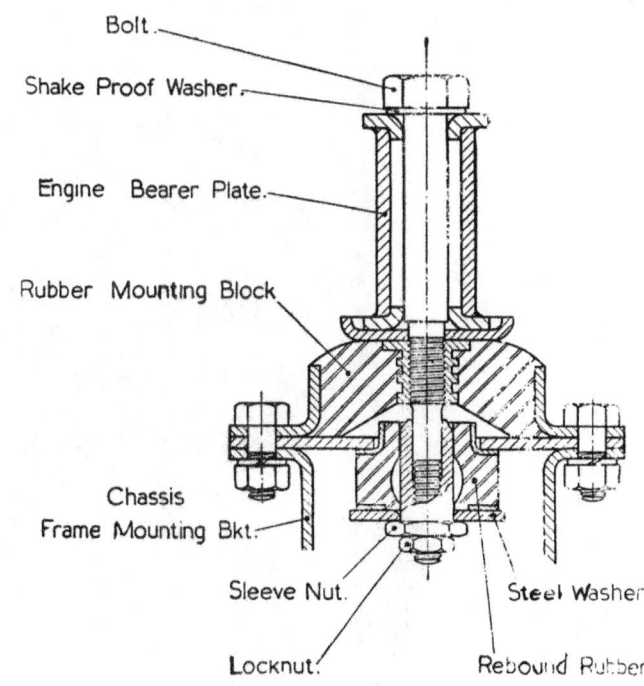

Front Engine Mounting.

NOTE: If the stabilising rubber under the front engine mounting is compressed too much, engine vibration is likely to be felt through the chassis.

4. CAMSHAFT

татто REMOVE

(1) Before the camshaft can be removed, the tappets will have to be withdrawn from their guides in the cylinder block, otherwise fouling between the cams and tappets is likely to cause damage to the running surfaces. After the push rods have been removed (also the tappet cover-plate) the tappets are free to be removed from the cylinder block.

(2) The distributor and oil pump are removed next. The distributor is released when the locking screw is removed, and the pump when the bright bolts securing the body to the cylinder block are removed.

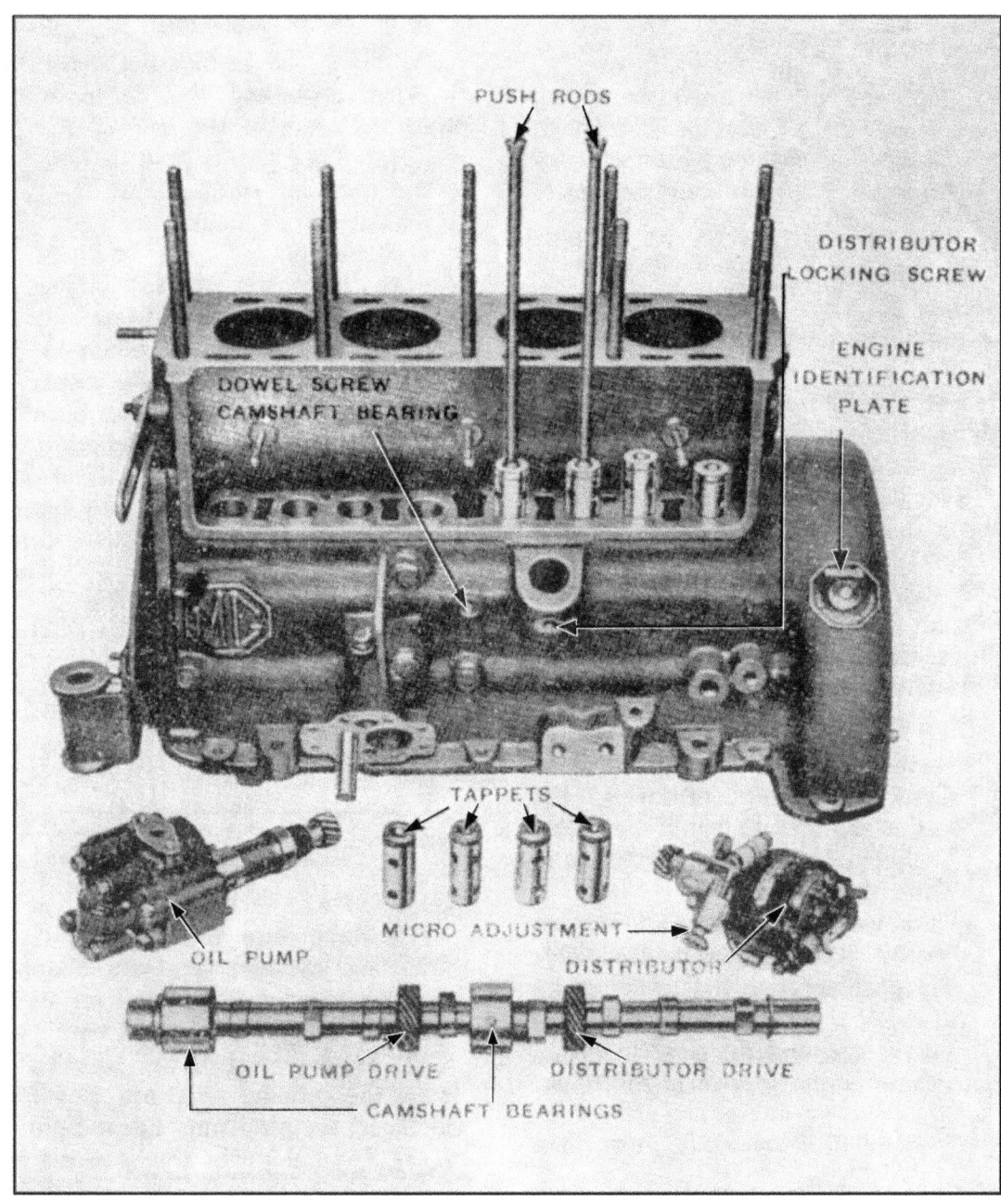

Details of Camshaft and Valve Operating Gear.

(3) The timing chain and sprockets must now be removed, and before this can be done it will be necessary to remove the sump, the crankshaft fan pulley and the timing case; a special tool, part No T93, has been designed to remove the pulley and sprockets.

(4) The camshaft is now almost clear and can be drawn forward from its rear bearing through the front bearing, carrying the centre bearing with it.

(5) The dowel screw between the oil pump and distributor aperture, which secures the centre bearing to the cylinder block, must be taken out, and when the camshaft has been drawn sufficiently to bring the centre bearing free from its housing it must be removed from the camshaft, when the withdrawal of the camshaft may be completed.

TO INSTALL

(1) The front and rear camshaft bushes being in place and the tappets being clear, the camshaft may be slid in from the front, until it is time to insert the middle bearing.

(2) With the camshaft in place the bearing may be moved about until its locating hole is opposite the locking screw hole, using a tool such as a blunt-ended scriber, to feel that the locking screw will enter properly.

(3) The locking screw should now be inserted and wired.

Timing Chain and Sprockets Showing Valve Timing Marks.

TO CHECK CAMSHAFT TIMING

The two timing sprockets are secured to the crankshaft and camshaft respectively by single keys; there is, therefore, only one position in which each can be fitted to its shaft.

It will be noticed that the timing chain has two bright links, and each of the sprockets has a tooth marked T. Between the bright links are thirteen black ones on one side of the chain and fifteen black ones on the other. The camshaft is correctly timed when each of the T-marked teeth is in a bright link with the shorter black portion of the chain uppermost. The thirteen black and two bright links are clearly shown.

The engine must be turned thirty times before the links and marked teeth come back to this position again.

TO CHECK IGNITION TIMING

When the distributor has been removed for any reason, it must be re-timed on replacement.

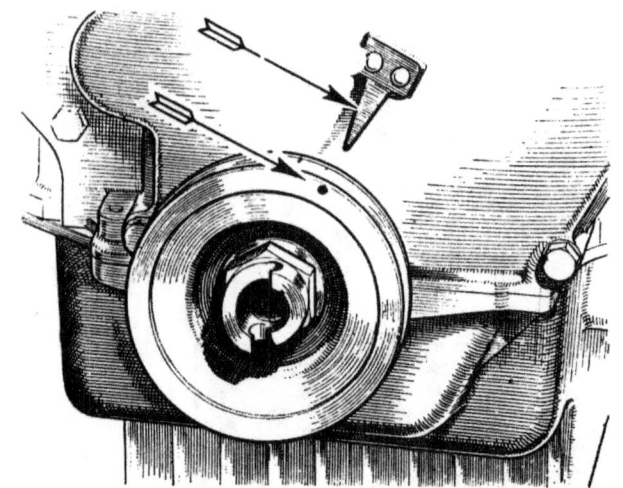

Crankshaft Pulley Mark and Pointer for tdc.

(1) First set the engine with Nos 1 and 4 cylinders on top dead centre.

(2) Then examine the valves to see which of the previously mentioned cylinders is starting its firing stroke, turn the distributor until the rotor is facing the appropriate segment (i.e., the segment connected to the high-tension cable leading to the same cylinder) and insert the distributor in its housing, feeling it in so that the nearest tooth is engaged. Turn the body about until the locking screw will enter, and lock it.

(3) Next (having verified that the point gap is correct) set the micrometer adjustment in the centre position, slack off the pinch bolt, and turn the head until the points are just breaking.

(4) The correct starting point is, points just breaking at tdc. This, of course, may be varied, but probably not more than 1° either way, to suit the grade of fuel used. One division on the micrometer scale equals 4° (crankshaft), and each division is again divided into a definite number of clicks which are easily felt.

NOTE: Before setting the timing, make sure that the automatic advance and retard mechanism is working properly and is in its fully retarded position while the timing is being set.

ENGINE TD—TF—TF 1500 SERIES

1. LUBRICATION SYSTEM

The main oil supply is carried in a removable aluminium sump. When full, it contains approximately 9 pints of oil on engines up to No 14947, and 10½ pints from engine No. 14948. It is replenished through the filler cap in the front end of the valve cover. The sump drain plug is towards the rear on the left-hand side. Three pints of oil must be added before any reading shows on the dipstick.

The gear-type oil pump draws oil from the sump through a gauze strainer which picks up the oil just above the bottom of the sump. Any sludge formed in the oil is thus allowed every opportunity to settle to the bottom.

An oil pressure relief valve, of the spring-loaded ball type, controls a passage formed in the oil pump bottom cover casting between the suction and delivery sides of the pump gears. The spring is non-adjustable, and is set to allow the valves to by-pass at 50 to 70 psi.

This provides a normal working pressure of from 40 to 45 psi, but so long as a reasonable pressure is indicated it may be taken that the circulating system is working satisfactorily.

The oil from the pump is delivered to the full-flow oil filter and then to the oil gallery, whence it is distributed through the engine. There are two possible ways from the pump. First, the normal one, through the filter cleaning element. Second, an emergency path through another spring-loaded relief valve housed in the cylinder block behind the pump body, straight into the oil gallery. The spring of the by-pass valve is such that, provided the filter is attended to periodically (fit new oil filter after the first 3,000 miles and subsequently every 6,000 miles on engines prior to No 14224, and new filter elements on engines from No 14224 onwards), the valve remains permanently closed. Should the filter become clogged, however, the by-pass valve will open and allow unfiltered oil to reach the engine.

From the oil filter outlet the oil is delivered into the internal oil gallery in the side of the cylinder block. Three drilled passages from this gallery pipe lead the oil to the camshaft and crankshaft bearings.

Taking these passages in order, counting from the front, No 1 feeds the front main bearing and the camshaft front bearing. The front main bearing feeds No 1 big end bearing through a groove cut in the white metal and a passage drilled in the crank web, which, in turn, feeds No 1 cylinder wall through the spray hole drilled in the right-hand side of the big end and by splash from the surplus oil exuding from the bearing. A feed is also taken from the front main bearing to the automatic chain tensioner.

The camshaft front bearing has a forward leak passage to the camshaft chain wheel thrust face, and from there passes through three diagonal holes in the gear wheel boss to the inside of the wheel rim, where centrifugal action forces it through radial holes on to the chain links. The three diagonal holes in the sprocket are covered by a baffle plate. This plate ensures that the oil is deflected to the radial holes at low engine speeds.

Passage No 2 feeds the camshaft centre bearing and the centre main bearing. The centre main bearing feeds Nos 2 and 3 big end bearings by diagonal drillings in the crankshaft and also lubricates the cylinder walls as already described.

Passage No 3 feeds the rear main bearing and the rear camshaft bearing. The rear main bearing also feeds No 4 big end bearing and the cylinder walls through diagonal drillings.

A vertical pipe at the rear end of the oil gallery feeds oil to the rocker shaft through passages drilled in the cylinder head to register with a hole drilled in the rear rocker shaft support, which communicates with the inside of the hollow rocker shaft. The rocker shaft is drilled at each rocker position to feed oil to the bearings, and oil which passes the bushes finds its way down the push rod tunnels and drain passages to the sump.

NOTE: When the engine is first started up and the oil is cold, higher oil pressure than normal will be indicated by the gauge. It is mainly for this reason that a gauge covering a large range of pressure readings is provided, and the risk of damage to the instrument is thus reduced to a minimum.

In the event of the oil gauge being damaged, or ceasing to function correctly, it must be renewed as soon as possible.

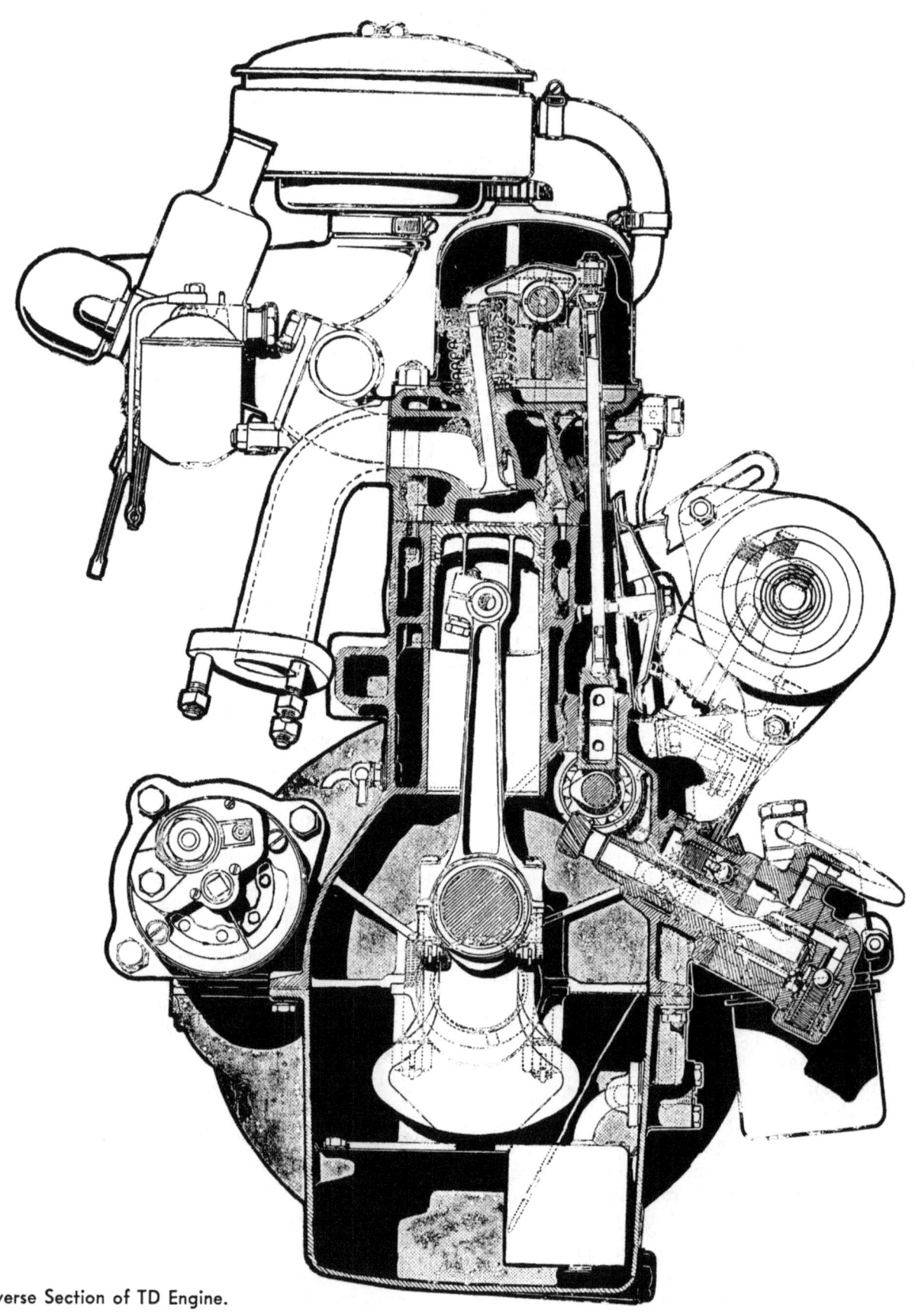

Transverse Section of TD Engine.

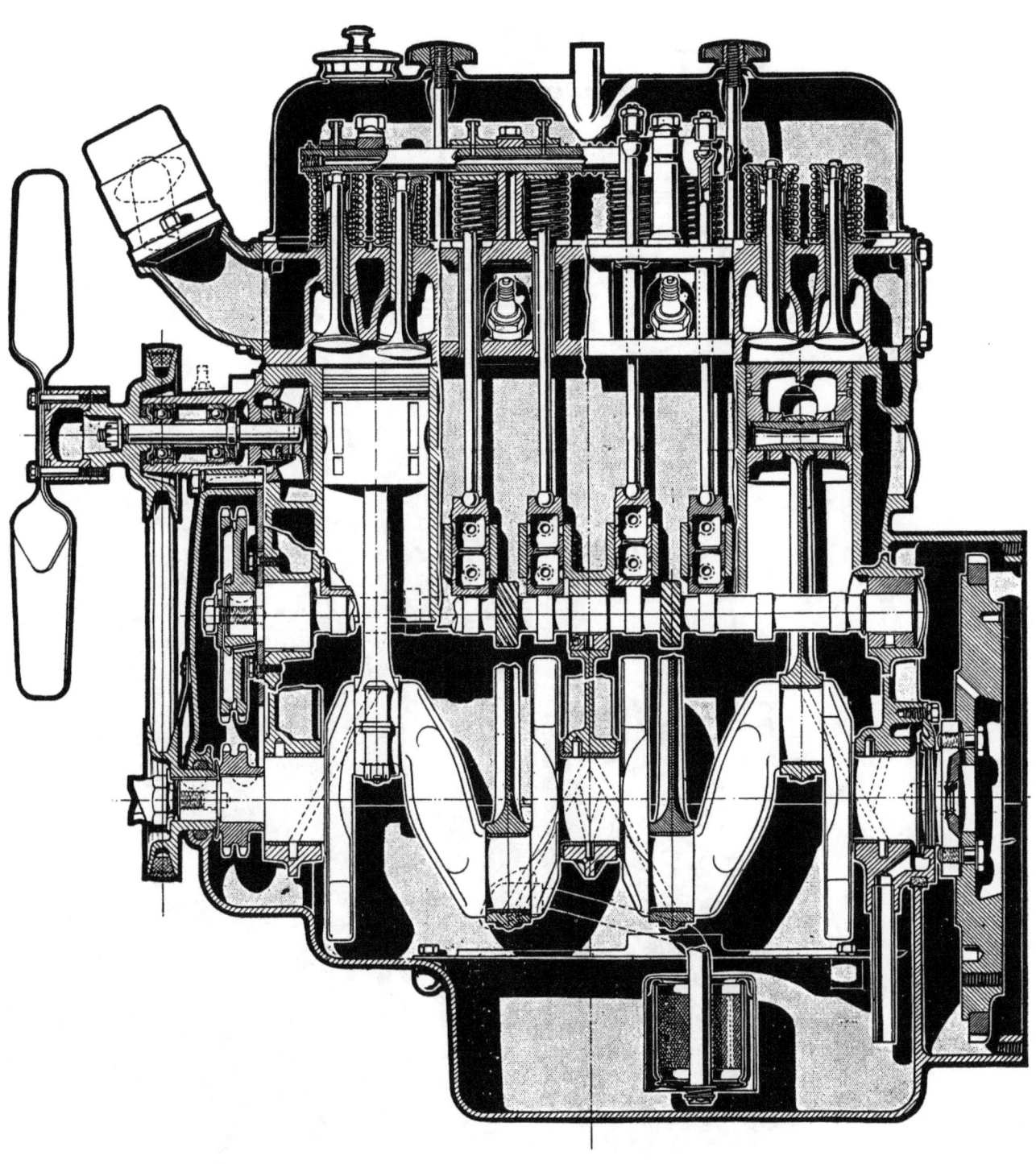

Longitudinal Section of TD Engine.

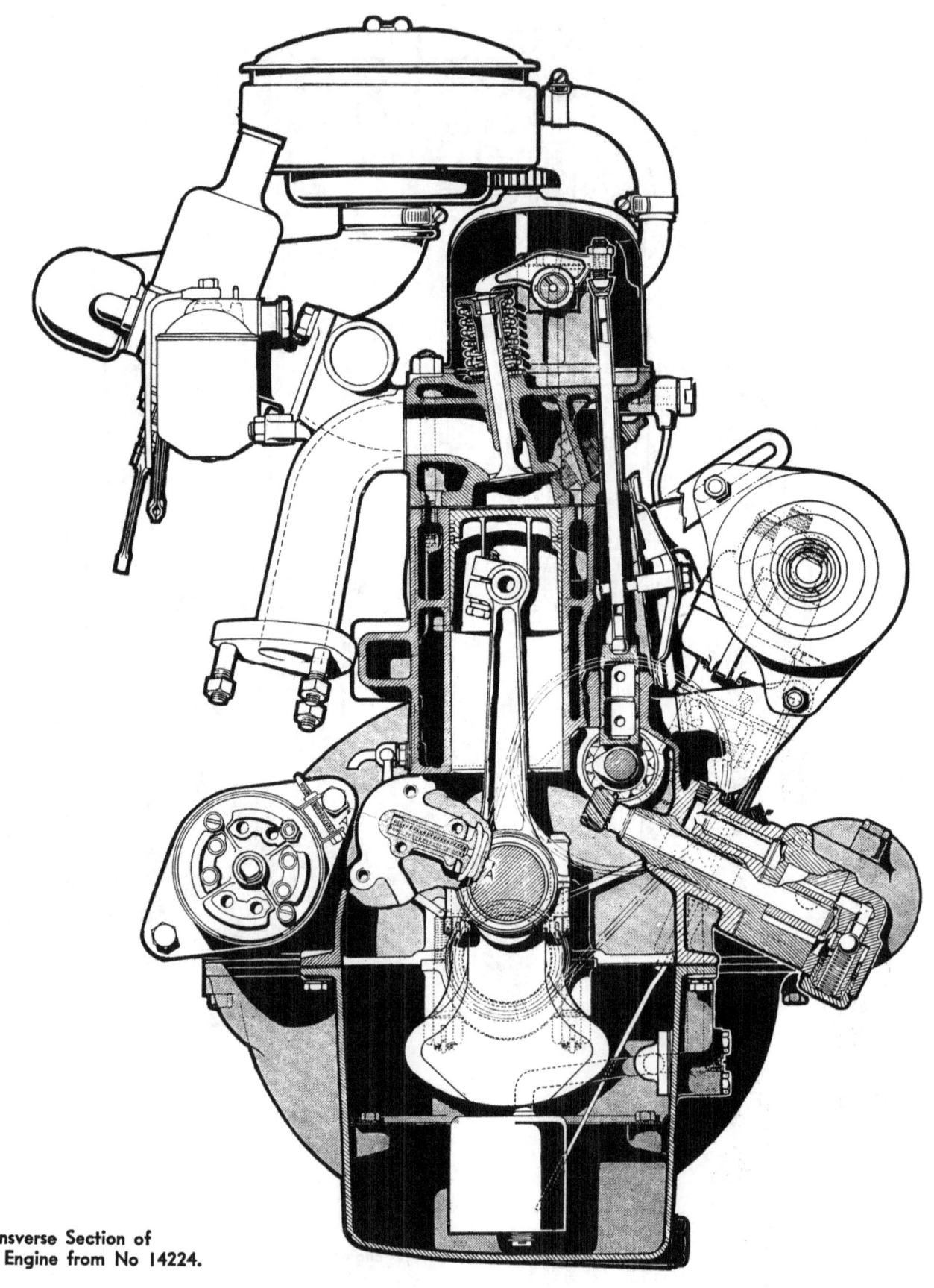

Transverse Section of TD Engine from No 14224.

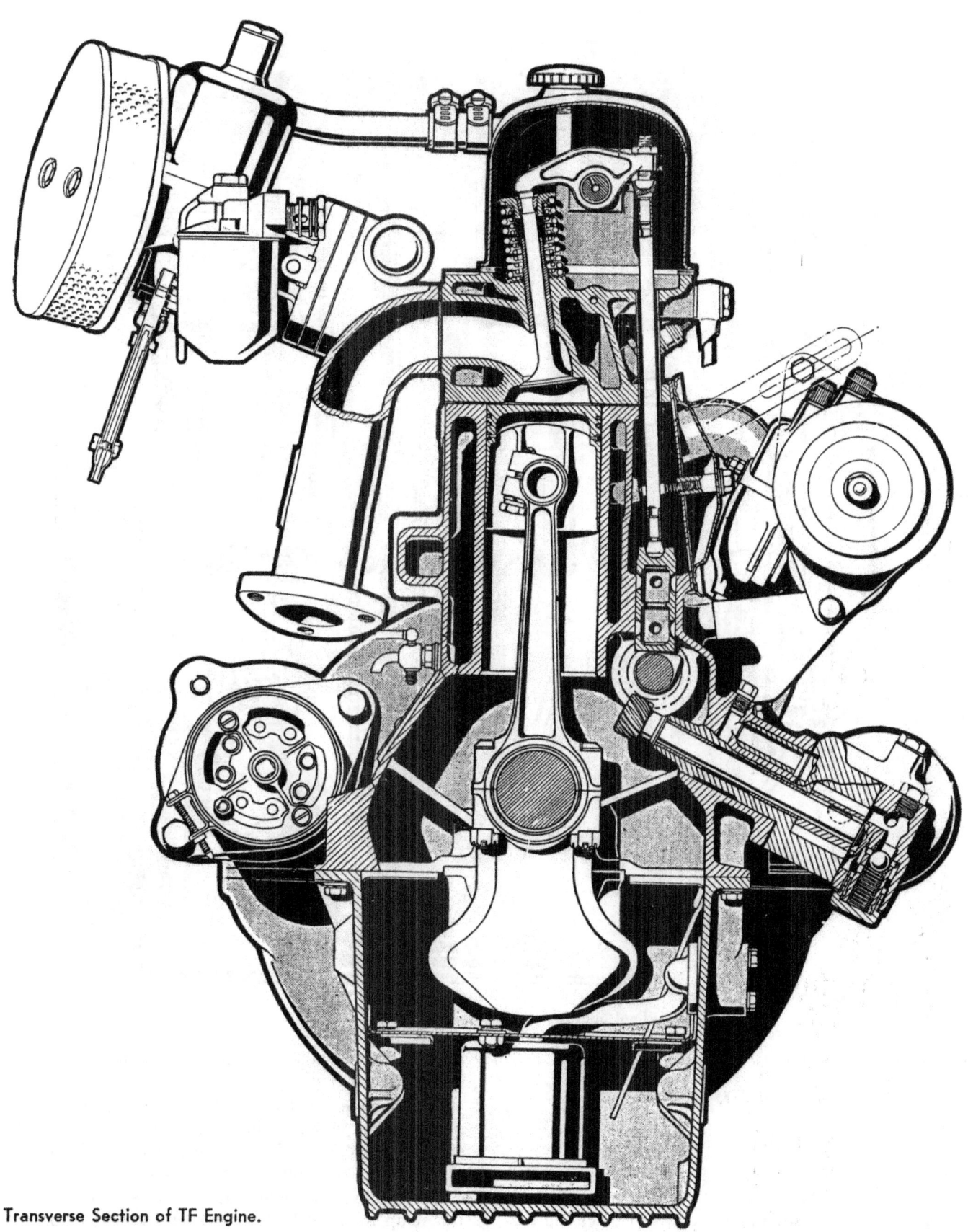

Transverse Section of TF Engine.

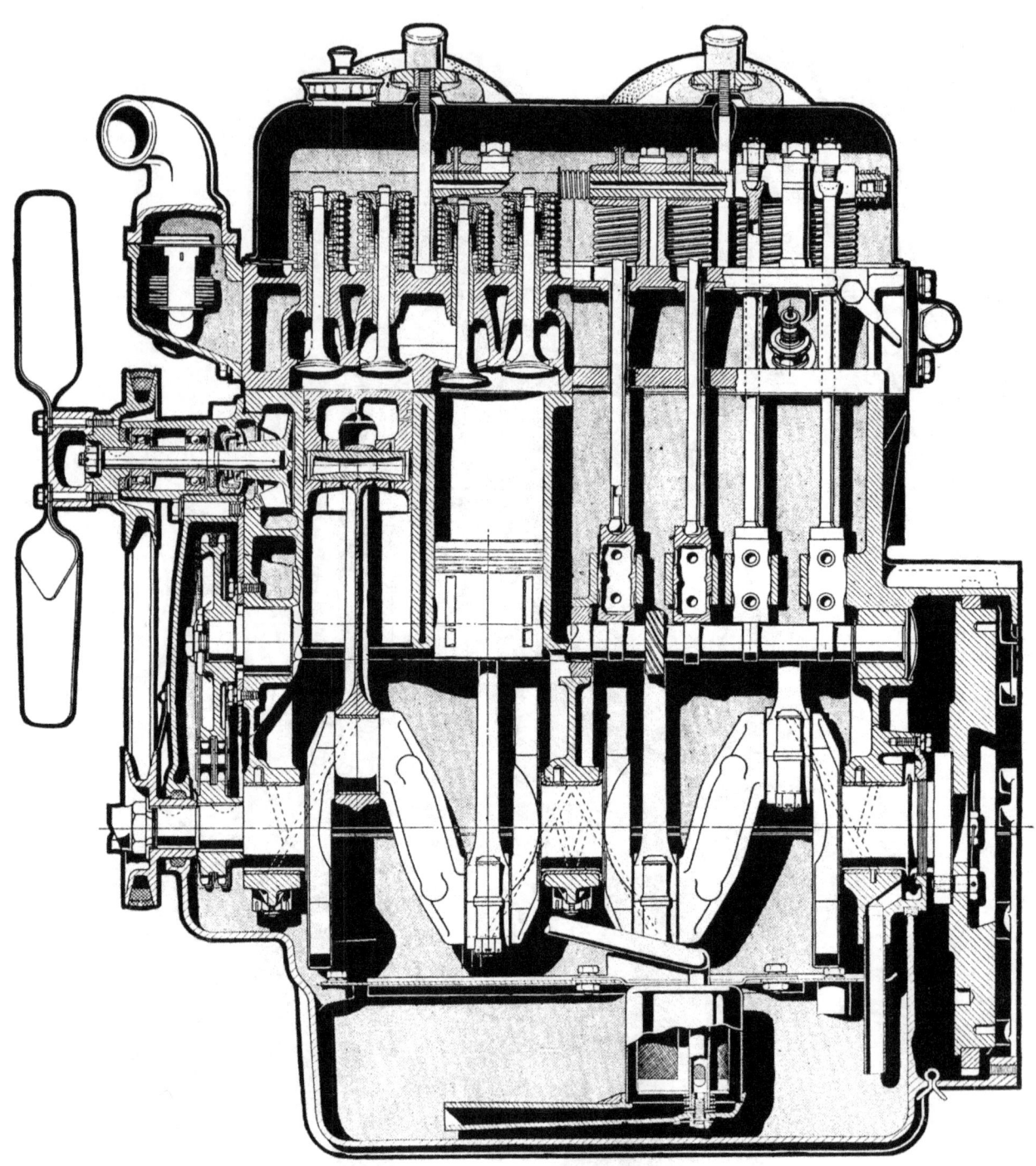

Longitudinal Section of TF Engine.

TO REMOVE SUMP

(1) Remove the exhaust system and drain the oil from the sump.

(2) Remove the dipstick.

(3) Release the clutch pedal pull-off spring from the return bracket.

(4) Remove the split pin and clevis pin securing the intermediate clutch operating lever to the clutch operating rod.

(5) Remove the two set bolts and spring washers securing the clutch cable abutment bracket to the sump, remove the split pin and washer and slide off the intermediate clutch operating lever.

(6) Remove the bolts and spring washers securing the sump to the cylinder block and flywheel housing,

16

and lower the sump to the ground. Note that the anchorage for the engine fume pipe is located on the left-hand side of the flywheel housing, on the first set-screw below the crankcase and sump joint line.

NOTE: If it is necessary, install a new sump gasket. Take care that the portion is left which goes between the rear main bearing cap cork seal and the crankcase.

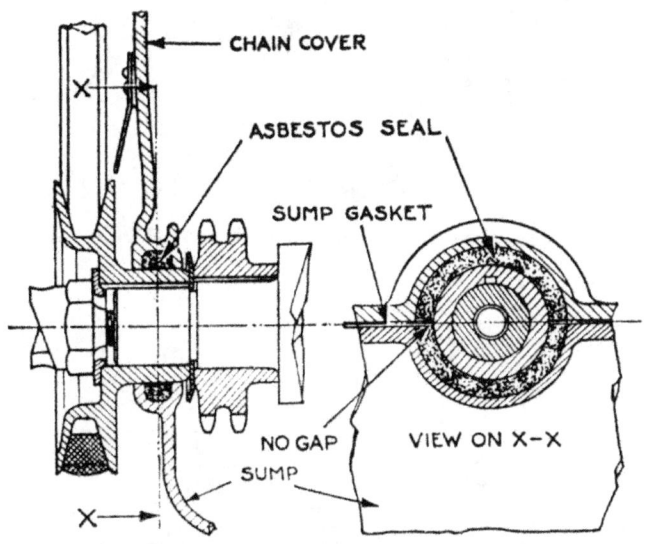

Correct Fitting of Oil Seal and Front Sump Gasket.

(7) Examine the cork composition packing ring in the groove of the rear main bearing cap, and if damaged install a new one. It is essential to install this seal correctly in conjunction with the sump gasket; pay special attention to this point to prevent oil leaks.

NOTE: It is important to ensure that the ends of the sump gasket fit snugly into the recess in the ends of the rear bearing cork seal.

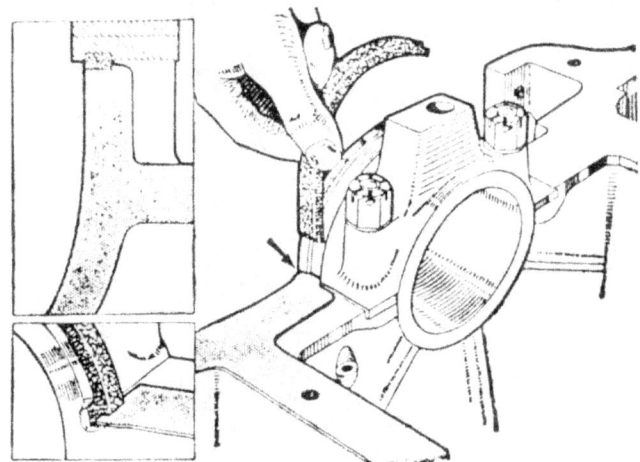

When fitting Cork Seal for Rear Main Bearing, it is Important that Stepped End be in Engagement with Sump Gasket.

(8) Examine the asbestos seal, fitted into the recess at the front of the sump. If replacement is necessary, care should be taken that the ends of the new one are flush or a little above the face of the sump. The sump gasket must go between the ends of the seals.

(9) Should the engine be turned while the sump is removed or drained, thus emptying the suction passages, the pump will have to be primed with oil by disconnecting the delivery pipe. The main feed oil gallery may also be primed through the special plug provided for this purpose in the cylinder block above the pump.

TO REMOVE OIL PUMP

(1) Drain the radiator and slacken off the top and bottom water hoses.

(2) Remove the front engine mounting bolts holding the engine bracket to the rubber block. Slightly jack up the engine at the front. This allows the pump to clear the frame member.

(3) Detach the main oil pipe from the filter to the pump.

(4) Remove the eight bolts securing the pump to the cylinder block. This will release the cover.

(5) Lift off the cover from the pump body. This will release the driven gear, which can easily be withdrawn.

(6) Remove the pump by gently tapping the side of the body and withdrawing it downwards.

TO DISMANTLE AND REASSEMBLE OIL PUMP

(1) After withdrawing the pump from the cylinder block as described, remove the circlip securing the driving gear to the oil pump and helical gear.

(2) Using a suitable drift, tap the oil pump shaft and gear partly through the driving gear. Extract the key and gear before completely removing the shaft, otherwise the key will damage the bush.

(3) Clean all parts, examine and check for wear.

The gear depth is 1.378" —.0016" to —.0024" with a diameter of 1.2678" + .001".

The housing depth is 1.378" + .0012" with a bore of 1.2795" + .001" to — .0006".

This results in a gear end float of .0016" to .0035" with the end cover fitted, and a radial clearance of .0057" to .0064". The backlash between the teeth is approximately .020" to .025". The pump housing and driven gear are fitted with renewable bushes.

The oil pump is assembled and replaced on the engine in the reverse manner to that detailed for dismantling and removal.

TO REMOVE AND INSTALL OIL PRESSURE RELIEF VALVE

The oil pump automatic relief valve, comprising ball, spring and ball guide, is incorporated in the oil pump cover. The spring should be of .056″ diameter wire, .500″ overall diameter and 1.476″ free length. Total number of coils is 13½, giving a load of 7 lb, when compressed to 1.063″.

It is not adjustable and should be dismantled only for cleaning and examination. The parts are dismantled by unscrewing the retaining plug in the bottom side of the oil pump cover which permits their withdrawal.

Throwaway filter fitted to TC and early TD models

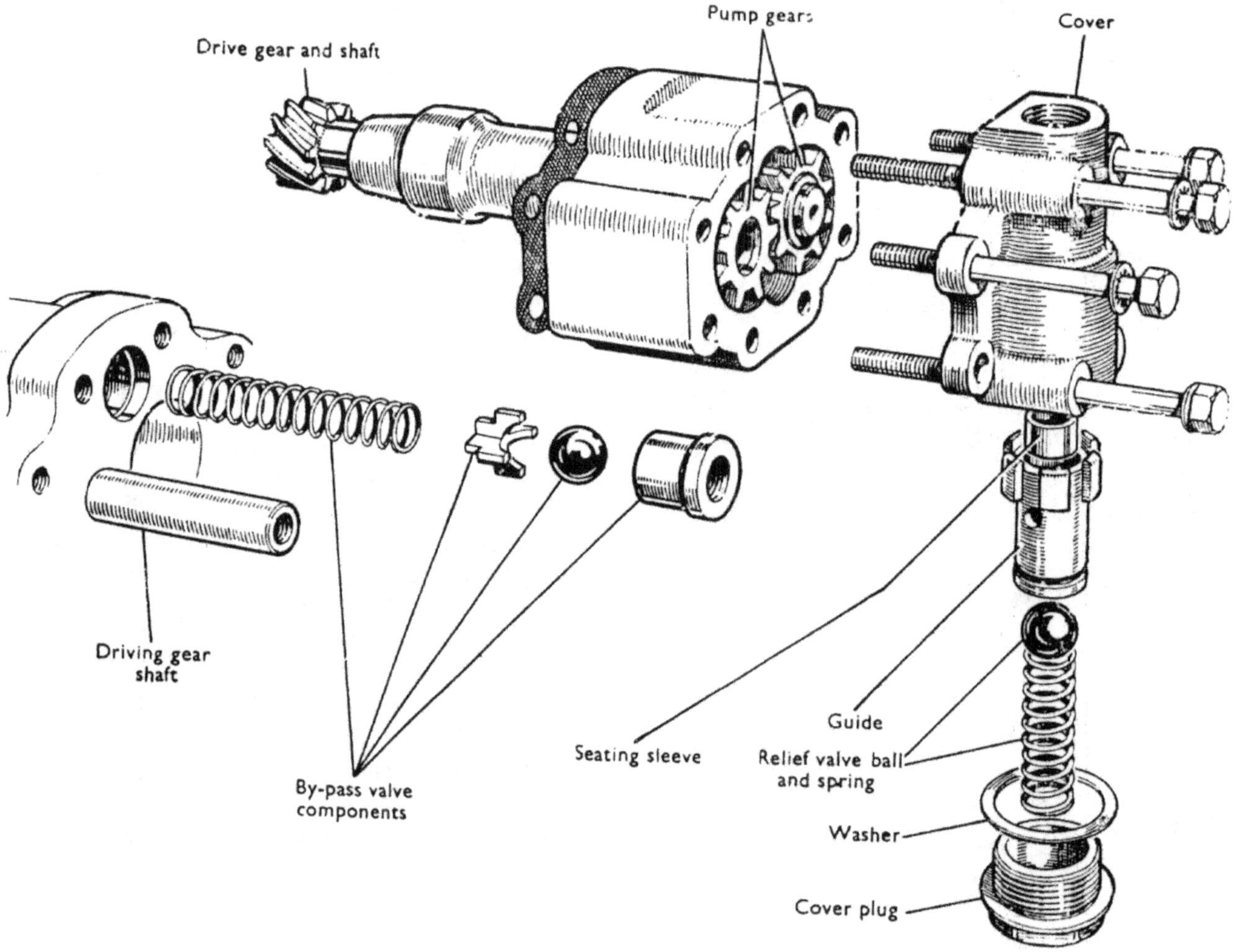

Dismantled View of Early Oil Pump.

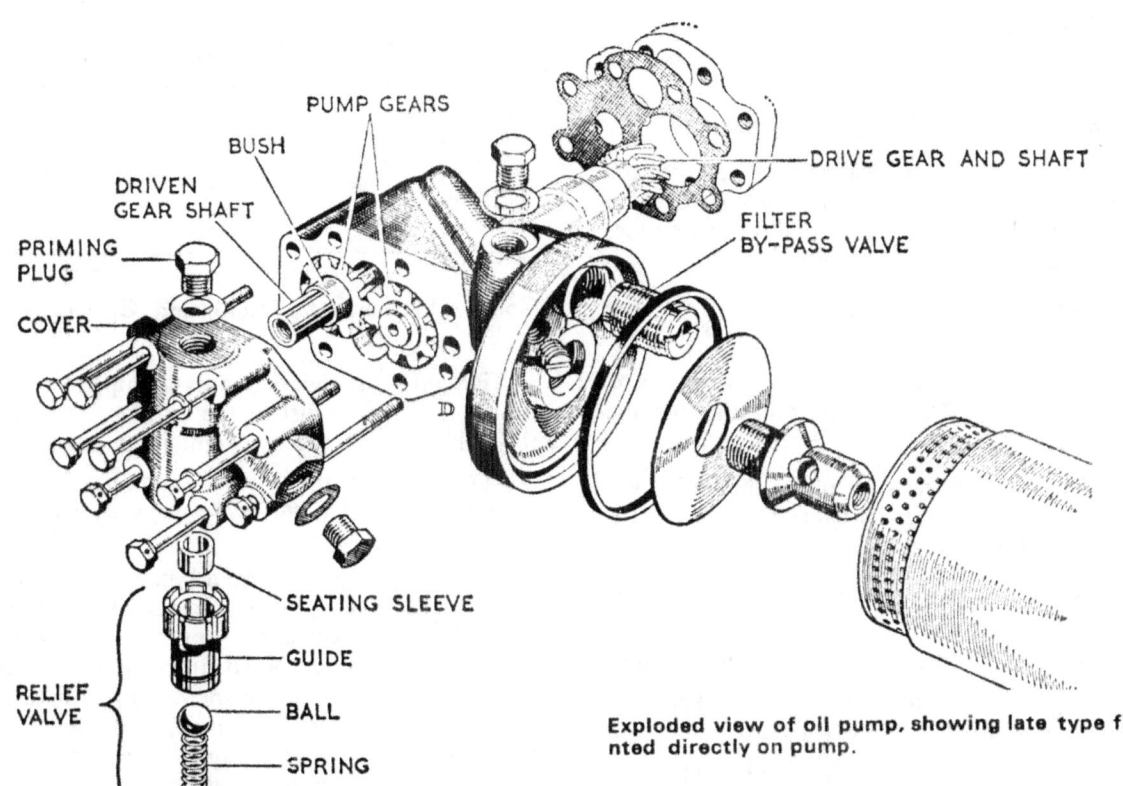

Exploded view of oil pump, showing late type filter mounted directly on pump.

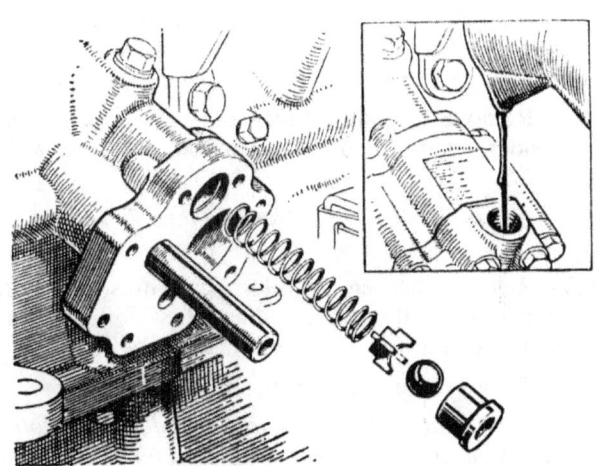

By-pass Relief Valve in Oil Pump with its Components Withdrawn and (insert) Priming Early Type Oil Pump through Delivery Opening on Pump Cover. Later Pumps, with Integral Filter, are also Primed through a Similar Plug, but a certain number of these Pumps are not fitted with a Special Priming Plug.

TO REMOVE AND CHECK RELIEF VALVE

If the filter element becomes clogged through neglect, an automatic safety device is provided. It consists of a spring-loaded ball valve which allows the oil to by-pass the filter, thus maintaining engine lubrication until a new filter is fitted. This is mounted in the cylinder block above the oil pump. It can be withdrawn by the use of a suitable 8 mm stud and distance piece.

The spring for this ball valve should be of .040" diameter wire, .5354" overall diameter, 2.224" free length. Total number of coils is 12, giving a load of 5 lb when compressed to a length of .649".

2. CYLINDER HEAD

TO REMOVE

(1) Drain the water system by opening the tap at the bottom of the radiator and the tap in the cylinder block immediately below and in front of the exhaust manifold.

(2) Remove the bonnet after taking out the two screws at the rear end of the bonnet hinge.

(3) Detach the high-tension cables from the sparking plugs.

(4) Remove the sparking plugs, being careful not to break or damage the porcelain insulators.

(5) Disconnect the throttle controls and mixture controls.

(6) Uncouple the exhaust pipe from the manifold.

(7) Disconnect the fuel pipe.

(8) Disconnect the breather pipe connection.

(9) Slacken the hose clips and remove the air cleaner, remembering that the central wing nut also serves to hold the cleaner on to the air intake pipe, and that it is full of oil.

(10) Disconnect the intake pipe steady on the manifold.

(11) Undo the four bolts holding the intake pipe and remove it complete. Remove the bolt clipping the exhaust pipe to the gearbox.

(12) Remove the four nuts securing the induction and exhaust manifold to the cylinder head and withdraw the clamps and manifold.

(13) Loosen the top clips on the thermostat by-pass pipe.

(14) Take off the top radiator hose and thermostat.

(15) Remove the oil feed pipe for the rocker gear from its attachment to the cylinder head.

It is also necessary to slacken the fume pipe and remove the side inspection cover. If the gasket of this cover is damaged, a new one must be fitted before the engine is run.

(16) Remove the valve cover and rocker gear from the cylinder head, when the push rods may be withdrawn.

NOTE: It is advisable to keep these in order of removal.

(17) Release the ten cylinder head nuts a partial turn at a time in the order indicated, see illustration, until they are free for complete removal by hand.

(18) Remove the cylinder head.

NOTE: To facilitate breaking the cylinder head joint, tap each side of the head with a hammer, using a piece of wood interposed to take the blow. When lifting the head a direct pull should be given, so that the head is pulled evenly up the studs.

TO INSTALL

(1) Make sure that the surfaces of both the cylinder block and cylinder head are clean; it is not necessary to use jointing compound for the gasket, but it may be smeared with grease to advantage.

(2) Having slipped the gasket over the studs, next lower the cylinder head into position, and fit the cylinder head securing nuts finger-tight in the correct order. It is essential that they should be tightened down gradually half a turn at a time in the order given if a good joint is to be achieved.

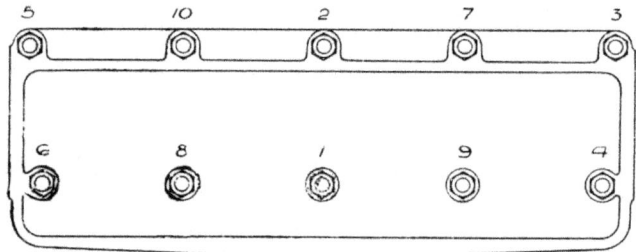

Correct Sequence for Tightening Cylinder Head Nuts.

Tightening individual nuts completely before the others is liable to distort the cylinder head and makes the achievement of a gas-tight joint impossible.

NOTE: Ensure that the gasket is fitted with the elongated hole for the waterways to the rear of the cylinder head.

(3) The push rods should be installed next, after which the rocker gear is reassembled. Whenever the head has been disturbed, or the valves have been ground in or otherwise disturbed, it is necessary to check the tappet adjustment and make sure the clearances are adequate; these, of course, will finally be adjusted after the engine has been completely assembled and run for a short period.

(4) Now install the valve cover, not forgetting the cork gasket. The gasket is not very wide, and care must be taken to see that the cover fits squarely. It is advantageous to stick the cork gasket to the cylinder head with jointing compound, but not to the valve cover.

(5) Reconnect the oil feed pipe to the cylinder head.

(6) Tighten the side inspection cover and fume pipe, making sure that the gasket is satisfactory. Should there be any doubt as to its condition, replace with a new one. Care should be taken that the oil drain holes in the gasket are at the bottom.

(7) Clean out the exhaust manifold if it is carboned up.

(8) Examine the exhaust manifold gaskets and renew if necessary.

(9) Install the induction and exhaust manifold complete with the carburettor assembly.

(10) The securing nuts holding the manifold should be tightened down evenly.

(11) Fit the mixture control, throttle controls and exhaust pipe to the manifold.

(12) Check and adjust the sparking plugs, replace, and connect the high-tension leads to the plugs.

(13) Install the thermostat body and radiator connecting hose and tighten the hose clips.

(14) Connect the fuel pipe to the fuel pump, and install the bonnet.

(15) Switch on the ignition, and check the fuel connections for leaks.

(16) The engine can now be started and allowed to run briskly until the water rises to a temperature between 70°C and 80°C, or 160°F and 175°F.

(17) The valve clearances should then be checked carefully.

TO REMOVE AND INSTALL ROCKER ASSEMBLY

(1) Remove the air cleaner. Detach the cylinder head cover by removing the two retaining hand nuts and fibre washers.

(2) Tap back the tabs of the lockwashers from the eight rocker shaft bracket fixing bolts and unscrew the bolts gradually a turn at a time, until all load has been taken off the rocker shaft, then completely unscrew the bolts.

(3) Remove the rocker assembly, complete with brackets and rockers, and withdraw the eight push rods, marking them so that they may be replaced in the same positions. To dismantle the rocker shaft assembly, remove the two retaining clips at either end of the shaft and slide the rockers, brackets and springs from the shaft. Care should be taken not to lose the shaft bracket washers and a note made of the fact that the front and rear washers are D shaped, whereas the washers fitted to the centre brackets are of the normal pattern and engage with slots in the shaft.

(4) Remove the plugs from each end of the shaft so that the oilways can be cleaned.

Reassembly and installation is a reversal of the above procedure, but care must be taken to install the rockers and springs in their correct positions on the shaft.

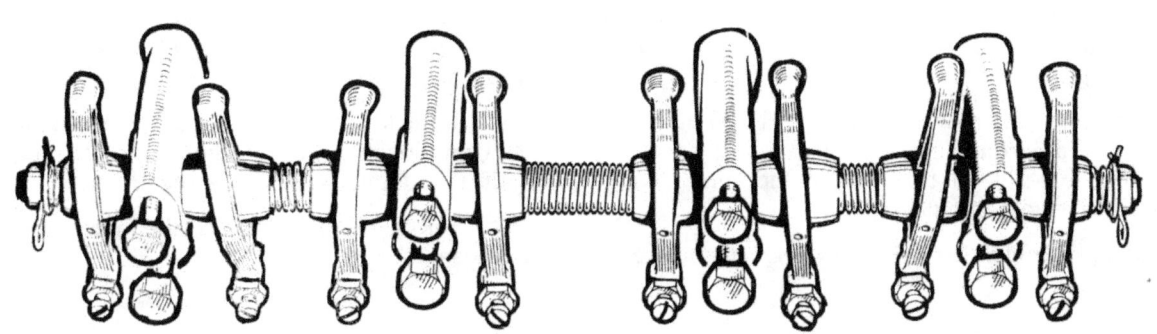

Rocker Assembly, Showing Correct Assembly of its Components. Later Assemblies have Washers between Springs and Rocker End Faces.

TO REMOVE AND INSTALL VALVES

The valve springs are secured by cups and split conical collets. In order to remove a valve the cylinder head must be removed and placed face downwards on the bench with a block of wood filling the combustion space so that the valve head is resting on it. If the spring is then depressed, the collets are exposed and may be removed, together with the valve springs. On the valve stem there is a small synthetic rubber oil seal which slips off easily.

When the valves are installed after attention, it is essential to fit new neoprene rubber sealing rings on the valve stems to avoid excessive oil consumption.

TO REMOVE AND INSTALL VALVE GUIDES

(1) Remove the cylinder head and valves.

(2) Rest the head with its machined face downwards on a clean, flat surface and drive the valve guides downwards into the combustion chamber, using a suitably sized shouldered drift. This should take the

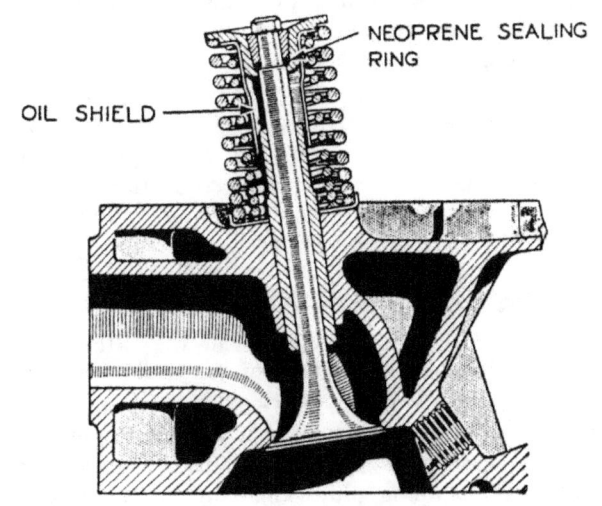

Valve Spring Should be Fitted with Closed Coils to Cylinder Head.

form of a hardened steel punch ¼" in diameter and not less than 6" in length with a locating spigot 5/16" in diameter machined on one end for a length of 1" to engage the bore of the guide.

When installing the new valve guides, press them in until .945" is protruding above the machined surface of the cylinder head.

From engine numbers XPAG/TD2/27867 and XPAG/TD3/27996, both valve guides are .964" above the cylinder head.

NOTE: The inlet valve guides are 7/32" longer than the exhaust valve guides, but all valve guides project the same distance above the valve spring seating.

(3) Recut the valve seat from the new guide, if necessary, to ensure that the valve seats correctly.

TO ADJUST TAPPETS

Set the tappet clearance to .019" (on engines prior to No XPAG/TD2/24116, and on engines from this number onwards, to .012") for both inlet and exhaust valves with the engine hot.

If the engine is cold an extra .001" should be allowed. It is important that the clearance is set when the tappet is exactly on the heel of the cam, owing to the type of cam contour employed.

To reduce the number of times the engine need be rotated, the table below will be useful when setting the tappets:

Adjust No 1 rocker with No 8 valve wide open.
„   „ 3   „   „   „ 6   „   „   „
„   „ 5   „   „   „ 4   „   „   „
„   „ 2   „   „   „ 7   „   „   „
„   „ 8   „   „   „ 1   „   „   „
„   „ 6   „   „   „ 3   „   „   „
„   „ 4   „   „   „ 5   „   „   „
„   „ 7   „   „   „ 2   „   „   „

Adjust the tappets as follows:

(1) Remove the air cleaner and rocker cover. Provision for adjusting the valve clearance is made in the rocker arm by an adjustable screw and locknut.

(2) Release the tappet adjusting screw by slackening off the hexagon locknut with a spanner, while holding the screw against rotation with a screwdriver.

(3) Set the valve clearance by rotating the screw carefully while checking the clearance with a feeler gauge at the valve stem.

(4) Relock the tappet screw by tightening the hexagon locknut, again holding the tappet screw against rotation with the screwdriver.

(5) Check the clearance again to ensure that it has not changed.

3. PISTONS AND CONNECTING RODS

TO REMOVE AND INSTALL

Follow the dismantling procedure as set out and withdraw the piston and connecting rod assembly past the crankshaft on the left-hand side of the engine.

NOTE: It is essential that pistons be fitted in the same bores as they were before removal. The gudgeon pin pinch bolt must be on the right-hand side of the engine. The same connecting rod and cap, complete with bearings, must be fitted to the journal from which they were removed.

TO DISMANTLE AND REASSEMBLE

The gudgeon pin is clamped in the little end by means of a pinch bolt which must be removed before the gudgeon pin can be pushed out.

In order to hold the assembly whilst the pinch bolt is being undone it is essential to use two special shouldered clamping plugs engaging each end of the gudgeon pin.

NOTE: Care must be taken when installing the piston on the connecting rod to observe that:

(a) The pinch bolt will screw readily into its hole.

(b) The spring washer has sufficient tension.

(c) The gudgeon pin is positioned so that the groove clears the pinch bolt when the latter is screwed into place.

(d) The assembly is fitted to the engine with the pinch bolt on the right hand side.

TO REMOVE AND INSTALL PISTON RINGS

If a special piston ring expander is not available, a piece of thin steel may be used (approximately 3" long by ¼" wide by .020" thick) as follows:

(1) Raise one end of the ring while the steel strip is slipped under the end.

(2) Next move the strip round the piston and apply a slight upward pressure to the ring until it rests on the land above the ring grooves.

(3) Then ease the ring off the piston.

Do not move the rings down over the piston skirt.

Always remove and replace them from the top of the piston.

(4) Before installing new rings clear the piston grooves of carbon, but be careful not to remove any metal from the piston during the process or excessive side clearance will result.

NOTE: New rings must be tested in the cylinder bore to make quite sure they have the correct clearance between the two ends. This clearance must be between .006" and .010".

When checking this gap make sure the ring is square to the bore by holding it on top of a piston inserted about 1" down the bore while the measurement is being taken.

4. PISTONS AND CYLINDER BORES

When fitting new pistons selective assembly is necessary, and to facilitate this the pistons are marked on their crowns, with an indication of their bore size. Note particularly that the piston markings indicate the correct size cylinder bore for which they are suitable, the correct working clearance having been allowed in the grading operation. The piston size should therefore correspond with the marking on the top face of the cylinder block on the right-hand side, which indicates the actual size of each cylinder bore.

The bores and pistons are graded in four sizes:

Bores of nominal size +.000" to +.00049", marked STD.

Bores of nominal size +.0005" to +.00099", marked +.0005".

Bores of nominal size +.0010" to +.00149", marked +.0010".

Bores of nominal size +.0015" to +.00199", marked +.0015".

The piston clearance is .0021" minimum to .0029" maximum, measured at the top of the skirt, immediately below the oil return ring, and across the thrust faces, i.e., at 90° to the gudgeon pin axis. This is important as the piston skirt is tapered and oval, and the clearance can only be measured in this one position.

To facilitate correct measurement of the bores and pistons, the actual sizes of the various gradings are given in the table below.

The markings on the top face of the cylinder block will indicate these sizes clearly.

Oversize bores on reconditioned engines supplied under the MG reconditioned engine scheme are limited to two oversizes.

+.020" graded in 4 sizes as the standard grading.
+.040" graded in 4 sizes as the standard grading.
The actual sizes of these pistons and bores are provided in the following table:

Piston Size (across thrust faces below oil ring)	Piston marking	Suitable for bore size
2.6156"	To suit	2.6181"
2.6160"	STD bore	2.6185"
2.6161"	To suit	2.6186"
2.6165"	+.0005" bore	2.6190"
2.6166"	To suit	2.6191"
2.6170"	+.001" bore	2.6195"
2.6171"	To suit	2.6196"
2.6175"	+.0015" bore	2.6200"

Standard piston sizes — Production engines with bores .002" oversize or over are made into +.010" bores and graded in the same steps as the standard bore engines.

Oversize piston sizes +.020" range:

Piston size (across thrust faces below oil ring)	Piston marking	Suitable for bore size
2.6356"	To suit	2.6381"
2.6360"	+.020" bore	2.6385"
2.6361"	To suit	2.6386"
2.6365"	+.0205" bore	2.6390"
2.6366"	To suit	2.6391"
2.6370"	+.021" bore	2.6395"
2.6371"	To suit	2.6396"
2.6375"	+.0215" bore	2.6400"

Oversize piston sizes +.040" range:

Piston size (across thrust faces below oil ring)	Piston marking	Suitable for bore size
2.6556"	To suit	2.6581"
2.6560"	+.040" bore	2.6585"
2.6561"	To suit	2.6586"
2.6565"	+.0405" bore	2.6590"
2.6566"	To suit	2.6591"
2.6570"	+.041" bore	2.6595"
2.6571"	To suit	2.6596"
2.6575"	+.0415" bore	2.6600"

5. TIMING CHAIN AND SPROCKETS

TO REMOVE TIMING CHAIN CASE

To carry out this operation with the engine in the frame it is necessary to remove the radiator.

(1) Remove the fan belt as detailed and take off the engine control link.

NOTE: Mark the position of the adjuster so that this may be refitted to the same setting.

(2) Remove the water pump.

(3) Undo the starting handle dog nut, taking care of the packing shims behind it.

(4) Take off the crankshaft fan pulley with an extractor, and remove the nine set-screws holding the timing cover to the crankcase, and withdraw the cover.

TO REMOVE TIMING CHAIN

(1) Remove the sump and take off the timing chain case.

(2) Undo the bolt securing the camshaft sprocket to the camshaft and remove the chain tensioner.

(3) Extract the crankshaft and camshaft sprockets, complete with the chain, by means of short, flat levers, or with tool No T123.

NOTE: Take care of the chain tensioner slipper and chain tensioner spring.

TO INSTALL TIMING CHAIN

The two timing sprockets are secured to their shafts by single keys.

The timing chain has two bright links, and each of the sprockets has one tooth marked T. Between the bright links are thirteen black ones on one side of the chain and fifteen black links on the other. One bright link of the chain should engage the tooth of the camshaft sprocket marked T while the tooth of the crankshaft sprocket marked T should be opposite the other bright link. See illustration.

(1) With the shorter position of the chain to the left engage the camshaft sprocket tooth marked T with the top bright link, and the crankshaft sprocket tooth marked T with the other bright link.

(2) Place the keyways of the crankshaft and camshaft in a suitable position to register with the sprocket keyways and install the sprockets complete with the chain.

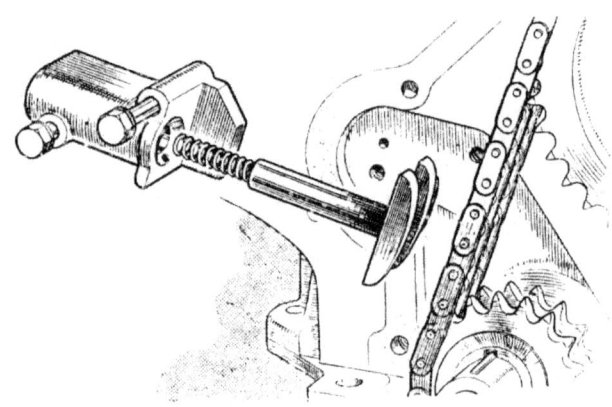

Timing Chain Tensioner.

(3) Install the chain tensioner, checking the paper gasket to make sure an oil-tight joint is achieved.

(4) Install the bolt securing the camshaft sprocket to the camshaft, and knock over the lockwasher into engagement with the hole in the sprocket and one flat of the nut.

(5) Install the timing chain case.

(6) To carry out this operation with the engine in the frame it will be necessary to remove the radiator.

NOTE: The engine must be turned twenty times before the links and marked teeth again coincide.

TIMING CHAIN TENSIONER

The chain tensioner consists of a hydraulically damped, spring-loaded plunger and combined slipper block, encased in a housing which is bolted to the cylinder block. The slipper is held against the chain by the tension of the spring and the oil pressure.

The plunger is fed with oil from the crankshaft front main bearing via an oilway drilled through the cylinder block, mating with an oilway in the tensioner housing or feed block. This oilway is then reduced in diameter to .040″ and the oil feeds through to the

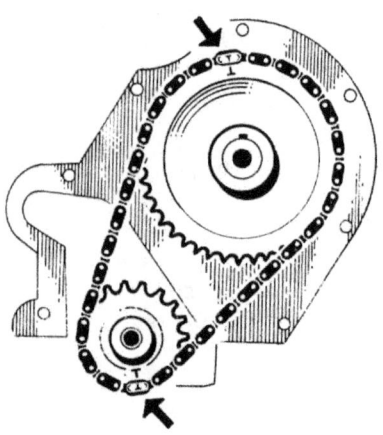

Positions of Timing Chain Bright Links in Relation to Sprocket Marks for Correct Valve Timing.

stem of the plunger, which is .430″ diameter, and then through the bleed hole in the plunger, which is 0.10″ diameter. This causes an increased pressure and produces a cushioning effect between the chain and the slipper.

TO REMOVE CHAIN TENSIONER

(1) Break the lockwire at the two setscrews securing the chain tensioner feed block to the cylinder block and unscrew them, taking care to hold the assembly against the chain to overcome the tension of the spring.

(2) Before installing, examine the bore of the feed block for wear (this should be .430″ ± .004″ and make sure that the oilway is clear. Look for any wear on the chain tensioner — the outside diameter of the stem should be .430″—.004″ to —.012″. When installing make sure to rewire the setscrews securing the feed block.

6. CAMSHAFT BEARINGS

TO REMOVE

(1) Drain the radiator and remove the bonnet.

(2) Extract the tappets and take off the sump.

(3) Disconnect the high-tension leads from the plugs and remove the distributor after taking out the location bolt from the side of the cylinder block housing.

(4) Remove the oil pump and take off the timing chain case, the timing chain and chain wheels.

(5) Remove the radiator and unscrew the dowel screws which secure the intermediate rear bearings to the cylinder block.

(6) Remove the front thrust plate and draw the camshaft forward through the front bearing, carrying the centre bearing with it. This should be removed when the camshaft has been withdrawn far enough to bring the centre bearing free from its housing.

TO INSTALL

Installation is carried out in the reverse manner to that detailed for removal, but the following points must be noted:

(1) The split centre bearing may easily be fitted incorrectly. Ensure that the dowel hole in the bearing is in line with that in the crankcase and that the oilway through the bearing is correctly aligned with the oil passage in the crankcase. When correctly installed, the two pin-spanner holes in the side should be towards the front of the engine in the lower half of the bearings.

(2) It is essential to make quite sure that the dowel hole in the bearing is exactly in register with the dowel screw hole in the crankcase.

(3) After installing and tightening the dowel locating the centre bearing make sure that the camshaft is still free to rotate, ie, that the dowel bolt does not bottom in its hole.

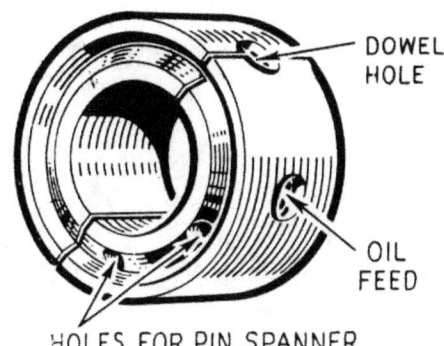

Relative Positions of Holes in Camshaft Centre Bearing.

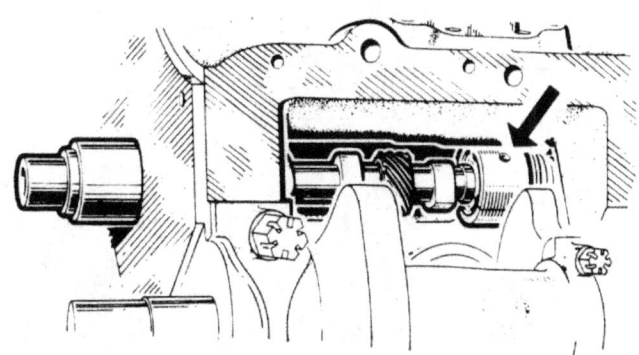

Camshaft Partly Inserted. Note Position of Centre Bearing.

TO INSTALL CAMSHAFT BEARINGS

When installing new camshaft bearings it will be found that the centre and rear bearings are strict replacements, but when the front bearing is pressed into the housing this will need reaming in line with tool No T111. The bearing must have the locking nick knocked into the crankcase slot.

The end-float of the camshaft is taken in both directions by a plate between the back of the camshaft chain wheel and the shoulder of the camshaft front journal.

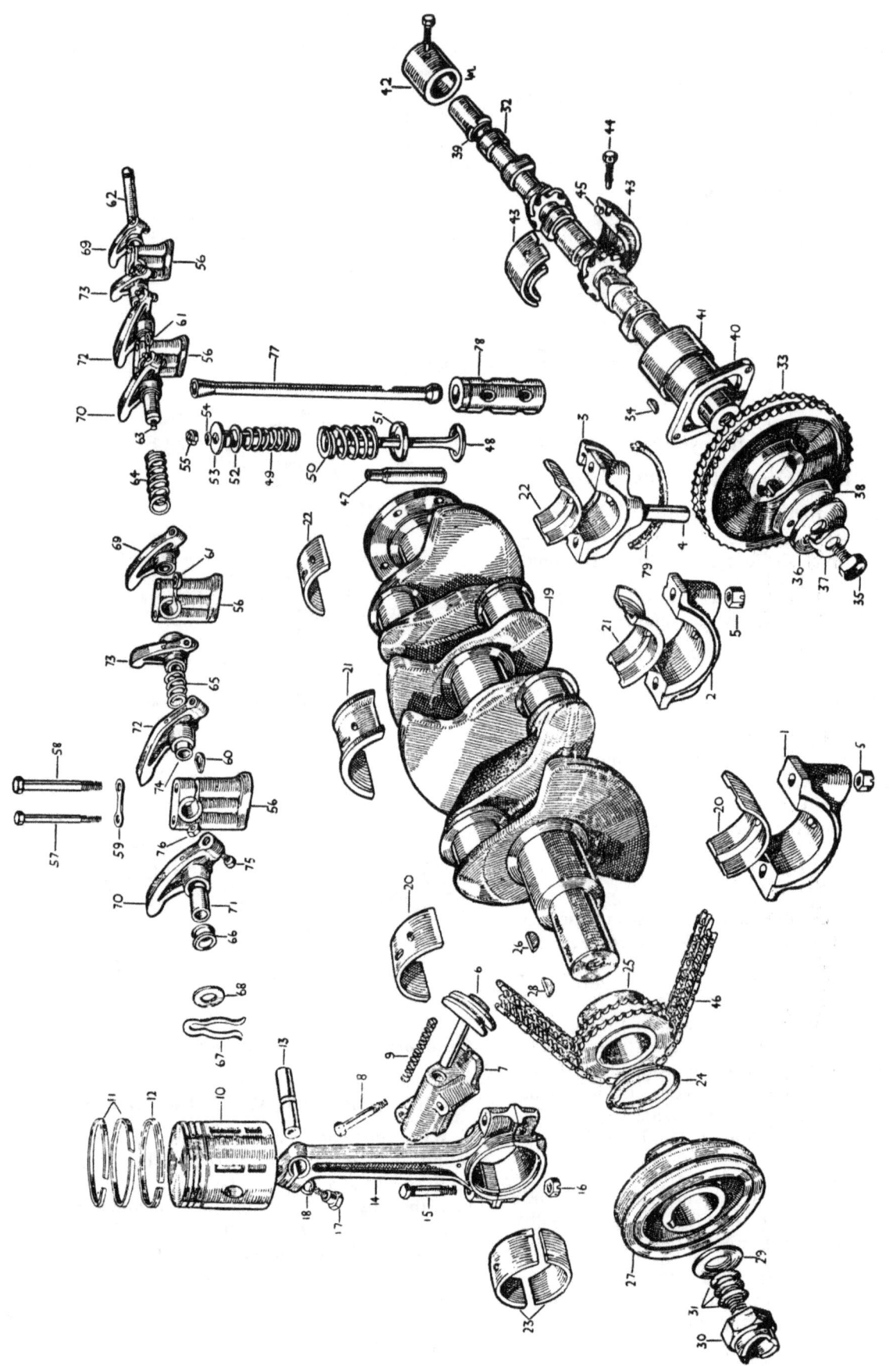

Engine Internal Components, Showing Later Rocker Shaft Assembly.

1. Main bearing cap — front
2. Main bearing cap — centre
3. Main bearing cap — rear
4. Pipe — rear cap
5. Nuts — bearing cap
6. Tensioner — chain
7. Feed block — tensioner
8. Bolt — feed block
9. Spring — tensioner
10. Piston complete (with rings and gudgeon pin)
11. Piston rings (compression)
12. Piston ring (oil control)
13. Gudgeon pin
14. Connecting rod with cap and bolts
15. Bolt — connecting rod cap
16. Nut — connecting rod cap bolt
17. Clamp screw — gudgeon pin
18. Spring washer — clamp screw
19. Crankshaft complete (with main big end bearings)
20. Bearing — front
21. Bearing — intermediate
22. Bearing — rear
23. Bearing — connecting rod
24. Oil thrower — crankshaft
25. Chain sprocket
26. Key — chain sprocket
27. Pulley — on crankshaft
28. Key — crankshaft pulley
29. Washer
30. Nut — crankshaft
31. Shims — nut
32. Camshaft
33. Chain sprocket
34. Key — chain sprocket
35. Bolt — camshaft
36. Washer — chain sprocket
37. Lockwasher — chain sprocket
38. Oil thrower — camshaft
39. Circlip — camshaft — rear
40. Thrust plate — camshaft
41. Bearing — camshaft — front
42. Bearing — camshaft — rear
43. Bearing — camshaft — intermediate
44. Screw dowel — bearing
45. Plain dowel — bearing
46. Timing chain
47. Valve guide — inlet and exhaust
48. Valve — inlet and exhaust
49. Spring — valve — inner
50. Spring — valve — outer
51. Cap — spring — bottom
52. Oil deflector — valve
53. Cap — spring — top
54. Packing ring — valve
55. Split cotters — valve spring
56. Support bracket — rocker shaft
57. Bolt — support bracket (8 mm)
58. Bolt — support bracket (10 mm)
59. Lock plate — support bracket bolts
60. Washer — Nos 1 and 5 brackets
61. Washer — Nos 2 and 3 brackets
62. Rocker shaft with plugs
63. Plug — rocker shaft
64. Spacer spring — long — centre
65. Spacer spring — medium — outer
66. Spacer spring — short — front and rear
67. Spring clip — rocker shaft
68. Washer — spring clip
69. Valve rocker with bush (Nos 4 and 8 valves)
70. Valve rocker with bush (Nos 1 and 5 valves).
71. Bush for Valve Rocker (Nos 1, 4, 5 and 8 valves).
72. Valve rocker with bush (Nos 2 and 6 valves)
73. Valve rocker with Bush (Nos 3 and 7 valves
74. Bush for valve rocker (Nos 2, 3, 6 and 7 valves)
75. Adjusting screw — rocker
76. Locknut — adjusting screw
77. Bush rod assembly
78. Valve tappet
79. Seal — rear bearing

7. ENGINE AND GEARBOX ASSEMBLY

TO REMOVE AND INSTALL

(1) Drain the cooling system and take off the bonnet and radiator.

(2) Disconnect the battery earth lead, detach the fuel line at the fuel pump and uncouple the high-tension lead from the coil. Remove the tow-tension wire from the distributor body and disconnect the mixture control inner and outer cables at the rear carburettor attachments.

(3) Disconnect the throttle ball joint at the forward end of the accelerator pedal arm, detach the accelerator control spring and release the starter cable from the starter terminal and undo the three brass nuts holding the exhaust pipe to the manifold.

(4) Then remove the clip holding the exhaust pipe to the gearbox, which will allow the front of the exhaust pipe to drop clear of the manifold.

(5) Undo the oil pressure gauge pipe at the cylinder block and detach the revolution counter drive from the rear end of the generator.

(6) Disconnect the generator leads, noting that the green wire on the generator goes to the field terminal F.

(7) Remove the two bolts holding the engine front mounting to its rubber block. Take off the outer nut on the engine steady and detach the clutch operating mechanism from the side of the sump.

(8) Remove the starter motor and take off the air cleaner and carburettors. When removing the cleaner remember that the wing nut at the top holds the unit to the intake pipe (TD).

(9) Disconnect the earthing strip between the engine breather pipe and chassis. Remove the seats and take up the carpets. Detach the toeboard on the passenger's side and remove both floorboards, the gear lever knob and the gearbox cowl.

(10) Take off the gearbox top cover complete and fit a piece of cardboard over the opening in order to prevent dirt reaching the inside.

NOTE: Care must be taken when removing or installing the gearchange lever and its housing. If the selector shaft is withdrawn past the first stop the synchromesh mechanism will slide apart and the synchro balls will drop to the bottom of the gearbox. Later boxes were fitted with an extended 1st and 3rd selector shaft with a retaining circlip at the forward end to overcome this difficulty.

(11) Unscrew the screws round the pedal draught excluder and disconnect the speedometer drive.

(12) Detach the forward end of the propeller shaft, marking the flanges so that they can be reassembled in the same position.

(13) Disconnect the engine rear mounting and place a sling round the unit, just behind the front mounting and also just forward of the flywheel housing.

(14) Remove the unit by lifting it forward and upwards, taking care to disengage the steady link from its bracket.

(15) To install, reverse the removal procedure.

8. CRANKSHAFT AND BEARINGS

TO REMOVE AND INSTALL MAIN AND BIG-END BEARINGS

The replacement of big-end bearings can be carried out after removal of the sump without taking the engine from the frame, but in order to replace the main bearings the engine must be removed. Renewable steel-backed bearings are used for both the main and the big ends. It is imperative that no adjustments be made to the bearings. Bearings which are worn should be replaced.

The big-end bearings are located in position by a small tag on one side of each half-bearing, and the bearings are fitted so that the tags come on the same side of the bearings housing. Main bearings are located in position by dowels in the bearing caps, and in the crankshaft housing.

To detach the big-end bearings, remove the connecting rod caps and extract the bearing journals. No scraping is required, as the bearings are machined to give the correct diametrical clearance of between .0005" and .002" and a side clearance of from .004" to .006"

To install the main bearings it is necessary to first remove the main bearing caps, in order to lift the crankshaft from the crankcase.

Having cleaned the oilways drilled in the crankshaft and the bearing journals, the new bearings are placed in position on their locating dowels, and the crankshaft replaced. No scraping is required as the bearings are machined to give the correct diametrical clearance of from .0008" to .003" and the side clearance of from .0014" to .0037" on the centre bearing. The end bearings have no end location.

TO REMOVE AND INSTALL CRANKSHAFT

(1) Remove the sump and take off the fan driving pulley and timing chain case. Detach the timing chain, remove the pistons and connecting rods.

(2) Remove the crankshaft and flywheel.

NOTE: It is advisable to mark each bearing cap and bearing to ensure their correct replacement.

Installation of the crankshaft is carried out in the reverse manner to that detailed for removal, but before doing so, clean the oilways.

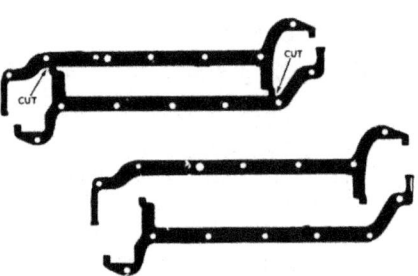

Correct Method of Cutting New Sump Gasket. It is Important that Ears are left on the Projecting Portions of Gasket.

9. IGNITION TIMING

TOP DEAD CENTRE MARK

An indicating arrow is fitted on the timing chain case and a hole is drilled or a groove cut in the outer face of the crankshaft fan pulley. Turn the engine until the hole or groove in the pulley is in line with the arrow on the cover for top dead centre on No 1 and No 4 cylinders.

TO INSTALL DISTRIBUTOR

When the distributor has been removed, it must be retimed on replacement. It should be set with points just breaking at tdc. To do this proceed as follows:

(1) Set the engine with the Nos 1 and 4 cylinders on top dead centre.

(2) Examine the valves to see which of the previously mentioned cylinders is starting its firing stroke.

(3) Turn the distributor until the rotor is facing the appropriate segment and insert the distributor in its housing, so that the nearest tooth is engaged. Turn the body about until the locking screw will enter, and lock it.

(4) Set the contact points to .012", and check that the hole in the crankshaft pulley still coincides with the arrow on the timing cover. The contact breaker

points should now be commencing to open. Should this not be the case, release the clamping bolt at the base of the distributor, turn the distributor anti-clockwise until the points are fully closed, and then turn carefully clockwise until the contact points just commence to open.

(5) Securely tighten the clamp bolt.

(6) Re-check the timing to make sure that tightening the clamp bolt has not altered the setting.

NOTE: Before setting the timing, make sure that the automatic advance and retard mechanism is working properly and is in its fully retarded position while the timing is being set.

10. ENGINE MOUNTING AND CONTROL LINK

The power unit is flexibly mounted to the chassis frame on a rubber block at the front and on two rubber blocks underneath the gearbox at the rear. As the location of these rubber mountings would permit a large rocking movement of the power unit under certain circumstances, a control link is fitted at the forward end to control the torque reaction effects.

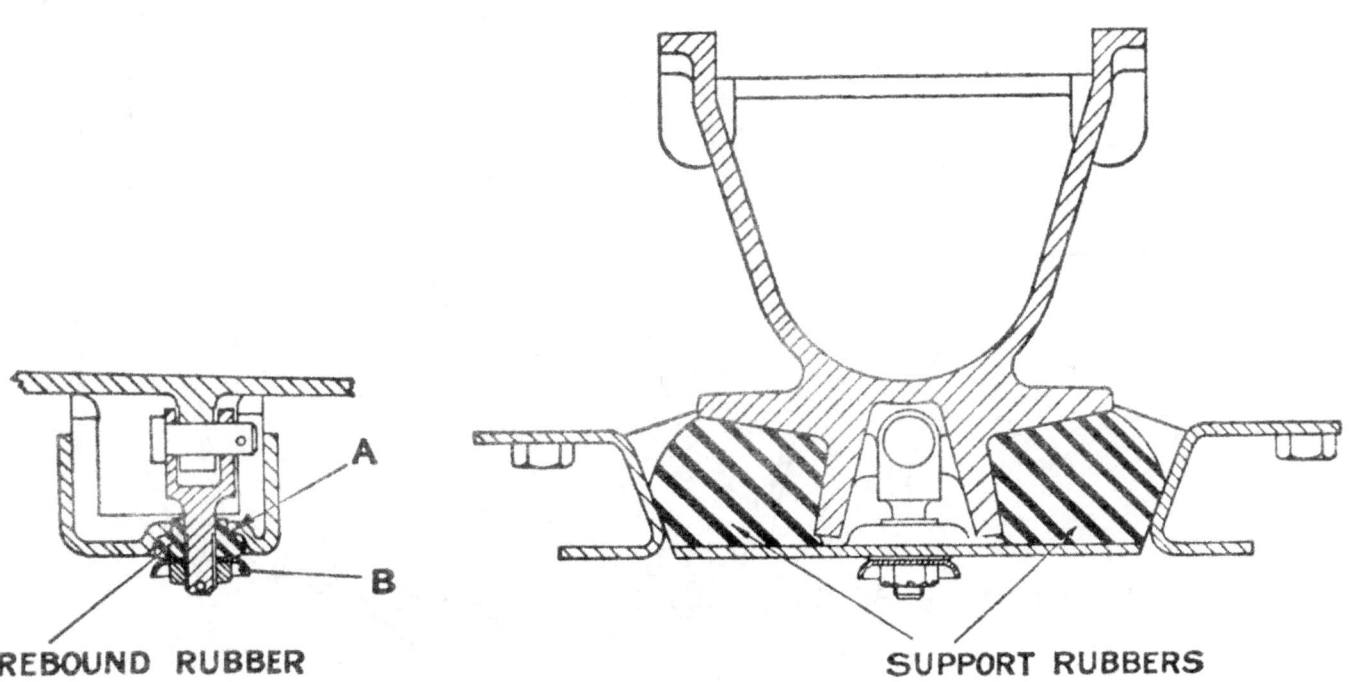

REBOUND RUBBER   SUPPORT RUBBERS

Engine Rear Mounting.

The rear mounting consists of two loose rubber blocks on which the engine rests and which are housed in a cradle on the chassis frame cross-member. A rebound rubber is also provided to limit the upward movement.

The exhaust system is rigidly attached to the exhaust manifold and the side of the gearbox, but attached to the chassis frame by a flexible mounting. This allows the exhaust system to float with the power unit.

TO REMOVE CONTROL LINK

The engine control link is removed by withdrawing the split pins from the slotted nuts at each end, unscrewing the nuts, withdrawing the flat washers, and the cups and rubbers. If the locknuts of the central adjuster are slackened back (right- and left-hand threads) the link can be shortened by screwing the adjuster in the appropriate direction, allowing the assembly to be removed complete with inner rubbers and cups, by rocking the engine.

TO INSTALL CONTROL LINK

(1) Screw the adjuster locknuts right home on the threads of the two adjusting rods and screw the rods into the adjuster barrel as far as they will go.

(2) Place the two inner cups and rubbers on the ends of the adjusting rods.

(3) Insert one end of the assembly through the bracket on the engine and, holding it with its rubber tight against the bracket, rock the engine towards the left of the car on its rubber mountings to enable the other end of the adjusting rod assembly to be entered into the frame bracket.

(4) Release the engine and, to ensure that it is in

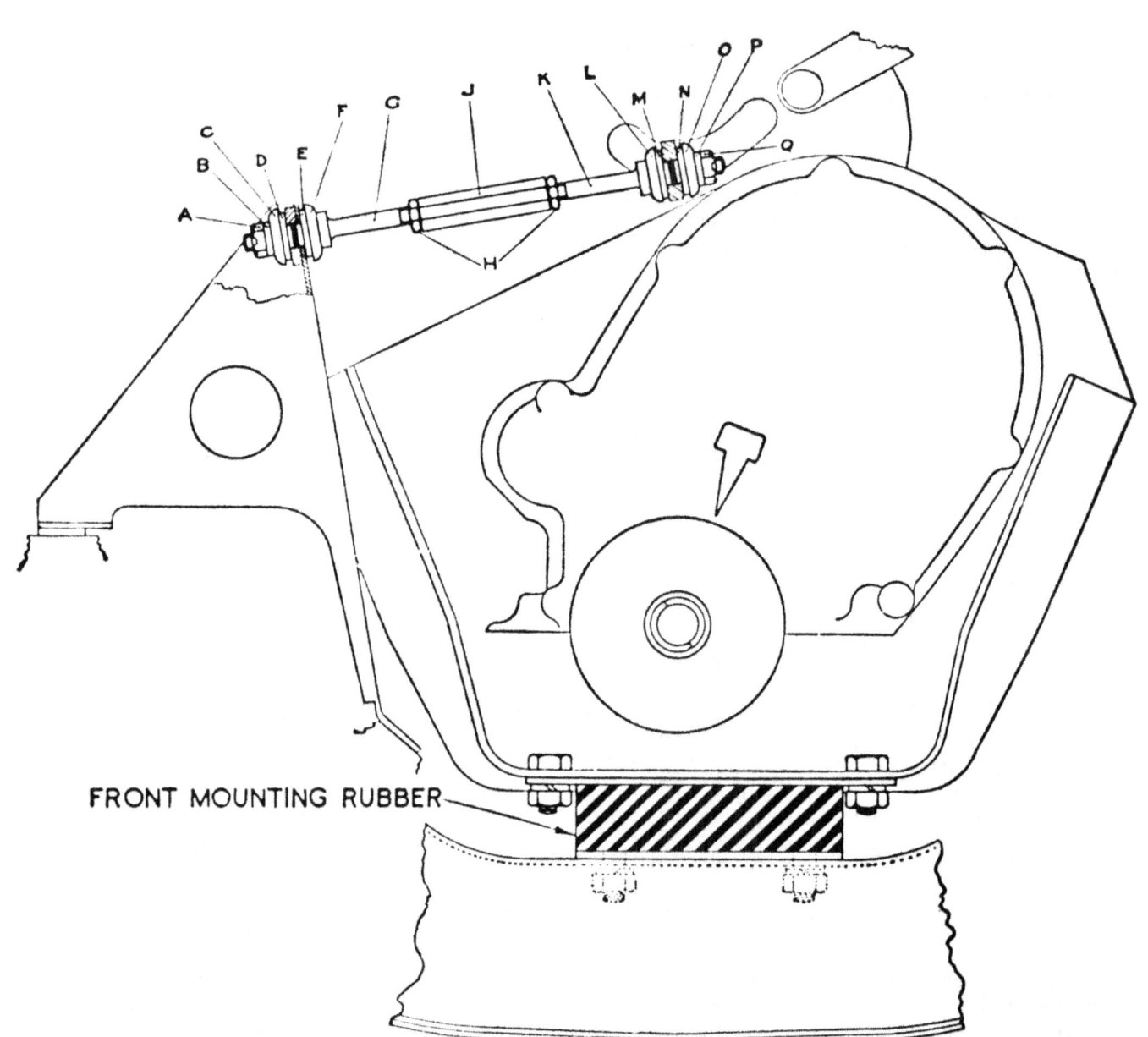

Front engine mounting and control link

A Slotted nut	B Washer	C Cup	D Rubber	E Rubber
F Cup	G Link rod	H Locknuts	J Adjuster	K Link rod
L Cup	M Rubber	N Rubber	O Cup	P Washer	Q Slotted nut

the natural position on its mountings, rock it gently from side to side a few times. As an additional precaution the exhaust pipe should be uncoupled from its attachments to the exhaust manifold and gearbox bracket while this is done.

(5) If a noise or knock is heard when the engine is rocked gently, examine the installation to make sure there is ample clearance everywhere.

(6) Couple up the exhaust system.

(7) Lengthen out the adjuster until the rubbers at each end are bearing lightly but firmly against the faces of the control link brackets, without disturbing the position of the engine. Fit the outer cups and rubbers, the flat washers, and finally the slotted nuts.

(8) Tighten up the slotted nuts only just sufficiently to nip the rubbers and insert the split pins through the nearest slot.

NOTE: The engine control link is to control engine movement and it must not be subjected to constant load through being too long or too short.

11. MODIFICATIONS

EXCESSIVE OIL CONSUMPTION

Some early cars of the TD series had a heavy oil consumption.

In some cases this has been found to be due to oil passing from the valve cover into the air cleaner and being consumed in the engine.

This can be prevented by inserting a restrictor or washer in the air cleaner engine breather pipe.

Later production engines had this modification incorporated as standard.

MODIFIED OIL PUMP

Commencing at engine No XPAG/TD2/14224, a modified oil pump, incorporating the external oil filter head, has been fitted.

This has eliminated all possibility of fracture of oil pipes and introduces the advantage of a renewable filter element.

The filter element should be removed and cleaned at intervals of 3000 miles and a new filter element should be fitted every 6000 miles. The filter element is a Tecalemit FG2381 (Part No 162451), or a Purolator element (Part No 162429).

From engine No XPAG/TD2/20972, a special priming plug has been fitted to the pump cover to permit the pump to be primed when the lubrication system has been drained completely.

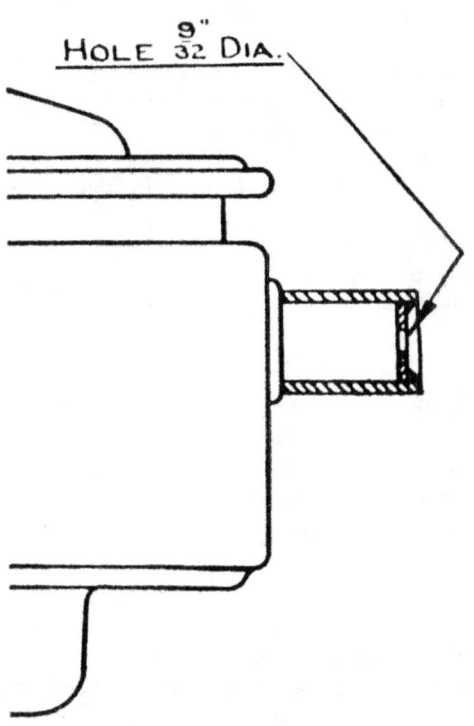

Oil restrictor modification

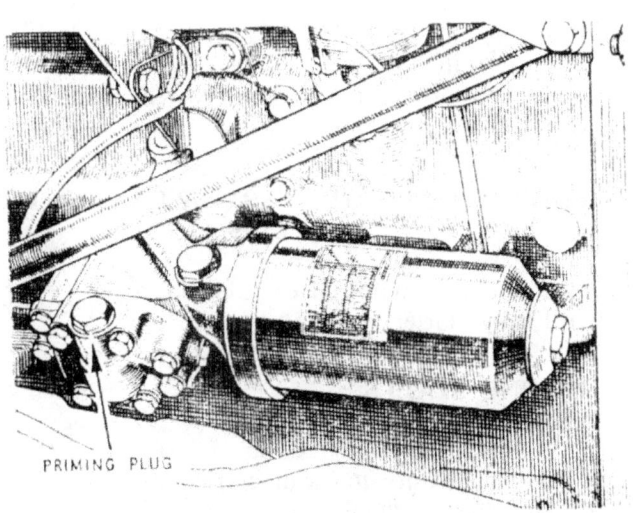

Oil pump fitted to later TD and TF models with renewable filter, showing position of priming plug

CYLINDER HEAD AND CYLINDER BLOCK MODIFICATIONS

Starting at engine No XPAG/TD/17969, a modified cylinder block (Part No SA2404/11) is fitted in conjunction with cylinder head gasket (Part No X24481). This gasket (illustrated) will also serve all engines prior to that quoted above and will be issued against all orders for replacement gaskets.

Engines from No XPAG/TD2/22735 onwards are fitted with the modified cylinder block SA2404/11 and a modified cylinder head (Part No SA2403/10). Such engines have a new gasket (Part No 168423), and only this gasket may be used on these engines. In addition, they are fitted with Champion NA8 sparking plugs instead of the Champion L10S previously used.

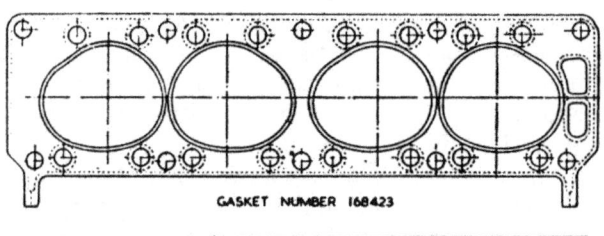
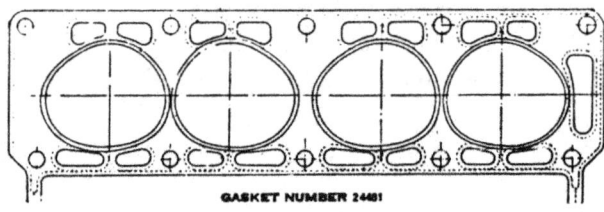

Modified Cylinder Head Gaskets. They can Readily be Identified by Difference in Shape of Water Passage Apertures.

12. ENGINE FAULT DIAGNOSIS

(1) ENGINE WILL NOT START BY NORMAL CRANKING.

Possible Cause	Remedy
(a) Dirty or corroded distributor points.	— Clean or renew and adjust points.
(b) Carburettor flooding.	— Check needle valve and float, clean out fuel system.
(c) Moisture on high tension wires and/or inside distributor cap.	— Dry out high tension wires and cap.
(d) Dirt or water in carburettor and fuel system.	— Clean out carburettor and fuel system.
(e) Incorrectly set spark plug gaps.	— Reset spark plug gaps to specification.
(f) Faulty coil or capacitor.	— Test and renew faulty component.
(g) Faulty low or high tension wires.	— Test and renew faulty wires.
(h) Fuel vapour lock.	— Check source of vapour lock and insulate against heat.
(i) Faulty fuel pump.	— Test and overhaul fuel pump.
(j) Incorrectly set ignition timing.	— Check and retime ignition.
(k) Broken or short-circuited low tension lead to distributor points.	— Test and renew lead.

(2) ENGINE WILL NOT START—WEAK OR ERRATIC CRANKING.

Possible Cause	Remedy
(a) Weak or faulty battery.	— Recharge or renew battery.
(b) Fault in starter lead or solenoid.	— Test and renew faulty component.
(c) Faulty starter.	— Test and overhaul starter.

(3) ENGINE STALLS.

Possible Cause	Remedy
(a) Idling speed set too slow.	— Readjust idling speed stop screw.
(b) Idling mixture too lean or rich.	— Readjust idling mixture screw and idling speed screw.
(c) Carburettor flooding or float level incorrectly set.	— Check needle valve or reset float level.
(d) Fault in coil or capacitor.	— Test and renew faulty component.
(e) Valve clearance or lash out of adjustment.	— Adjust valve clearance or lash.
(f) Air leak at inlet manifold or carburettor flange.	— Tighten securing bolts or renew gaskets.

(4) ENGINE MISSING AT IDLING SPEED.

Possible Cause	Remedy
(a) Dirty, defective or incorrectly set spark plugs.	— Clean or renew and set spark plugs.
(b) Burned or pitted distributor contact points.	— Clean or renew and adjust contacts.
(c) Loose or broken low or high tension wires in ignition system.	— Tighten or renew defective components.
(d) Carburettor idling mixture out of adjustment.	— Adjust idling mixture screw.
(e) Burned or cracked distributor rotor.	— Renew faulty component.
(f) Moisture on high tension wires, spark plugs or distributor cap.	— Dry out high tension system and cap.
(g) Carbon tracking or cracked distributor cap.	— Clean or renew cap.
(h) Weak or faulty battery and/or corroded terminals.	— Recharge or renew battery and/or clean or renew terminals.
(i) Carburettor flooding or incorrect float level setting.	— Check needle valve or reset float level.
(j) Faulty coil or capacitor.	— Test and renew faulty component.
(k) Excessive wear in distributor shaft and bushes or contact breaker cam.	— Renew worn components.
(l) Burned, warped or pitted valves.	— Carry out top overhaul on engine.

(5) ENGINE MISSES ON ACCELERATION.

Possible Cause	Remedy
(a) Distributor points dirty or incorrectly adjusted.	— Clean and readjust points.
(b) Spark plug/s dirty, faulty or gap set too wide.	— Clean or renew and reset faulty plug/s.
(c) Dirt or water in carburettor.	— Clean and blow out carburettor and fuel pump filte
(d) Carburettor jet partial block.	— Clean out carburettor.
(e) Coil or capacitor faulty.	— Renew defective component.
(f) Incorrect ignition timing.	— Check and reset ignition timing.
(g) Burned, warped or pitted valves.	— Carry out top overhaul on engine.

(6) ENGINE MISSES AT HIGH SPEED.

Possible Cause	Remedy
(a) Distributor points dirty or incorrectly adjusted.	— Clean and readjust points.
(b) Spark plug/s dirty, faulty or gap set too wide.	— Clean or renew and reset faulty plug/s.
(c) Dirt or water in carburettor.	— Clean out carburettor and fuel pump filter.
(d) Burned or cracked distributor rotor.	— Renew faulty component.
(e) Faulty coil or capacitor.	— Renew faulty component.
(f) Dirt in carburettor power jet.	— Clean and blow out carburettor.
(g) Incorrect ignition timing.	— Check and reset ignition timing.
(h) Excessive wear in distributor, shaft or cam.	— Renew faulty components.

(7) ENGINE LACKS POWER.

Possible Cause	Remedy
(a) Dirty or incorrectly set spark plugs.	— Clean and reset gap to specifications.
(b) Dirt or water in carburettor and fuel system.	— Drain and clean out fuel system and carburettor.
(c) Incorrect ignition timing.	— Check and reset ignition timing.
(d) Incorrect carburettor float level.	— Check and reset float level.
(e) Faulty fuel pump.	— Check and overhaul fuel pump.
(f) Incorrect valve clearance or lash adjustment.	— Check and readjust valve clearance or lash.
(g) Faulty distributor automatic advance.	— Check and rectify or renew.
(h) Restricted muffler or tail pipe.	— Check and clean as necessary.
(i) Faulty coil or capacitor.	— Renew faulty component.
(j) Burned or cracked distributor rotor.	— Renew faulty component.
(k) Excessive wear in distributor shaft or cam.	— Renew faulty components.
(l) Incorrect valve timing.	— Check and reset as necessary.
(m) Burned, warped or pitted valves.	— Carry out top overhaul on engine.
(n) Blown cylinder head gasket.	— Renew gasket.
(o) Loss of compression.	— Carry out compression test and rectify.

(8) NOISY VALVE OPERATION.

Possible Cause
(a) Incorrectly adjusted clearance or lash.
(b) Weak or broken valve springs.
(c) Worn valve guides.
(d) Worn tappets.

Remedy
— Check and adjust to specifications.
— Check and renew faulty components.
— Renew valve guides.
— Renew or fit oversize tappets.

(9) BIG END BEARING NOISE.

Possible Cause
(a) Lack of adequate oil supply.

(b) Excessive bearing clearance.

(c) Thin oil or crankcase dilution.

(d) Low oil pressure.

(e) Misaligned big end bearings.

Remedy
— Check oil level in sump, condition of oil pump and relief valve. Renew oil filter element.
— Renew bearing shells check and regrind journals if oval.
— Change to correct oil grade. Check operating conditions and cooling system thermostat.
— Check pressure relief valve and spring, oil filter by-pass valve.
— Align connecting rods and renew bearings if necessary.

(10) APPARENT MAIN BEARING NOISE.

Possible Cause
(a) Loose flywheel.
(b) Loose crankshaft pulley.
(c) Low oil pressure.

(d) Excessive crankshaft end play.
(e) Crankshaft journals out of round and excessive bearing to journal clearance.
(f) Insufficient oil supply.

Remedy
— Tighten securing bolts to specified torque.
— Renew or tighten pulley.
— Check bearing to journal clearance, check condition of oil pump and pressure relief valve. Recondition as necessary.
— Renew centre main bearing thrust washers.
— Regrind journals and fit undersize bearings.

— Replenish oil in sump to correct level.

(11) EXCESSIVE OIL CONSUMPTION.

Possible Cause
(a) Oil leaks.
(b) Damaged or worn valve stem oil seals.
(c) Excessive clearance, valve stem to valve guide.

(d) Worn or broken rings.
(e) Rings too tight or stuck in grooves.
(f) Excessive wear in cylinders, pistons and rings.
(g) Compression rings incorrectly installed, oil rings clogged or broken.

Remedy
— Check and renew gaskets as necessary.
— Renew damaged or worn components.
— Renew valve guides bushes and valves, or ream and fit oversize valves.
— Renew rings.
— Renew rings and clean out ring grooves.
— Recondition cylinders and renew pistons and rings.
— Renew rings.

(12) DROP IN OIL PRESSURE.

Possible Cause
(a) Oil level low in sump.
(b) Thin or diluted oil.

(c) Oil pump relief valve stuck or spring broken.
(d) Excessive bearing clearance.

(e) Excessive wear of oil pump components.
(f) Air leak in oiling system.

Remedy
— Check and replenish to full mark.
— Change to correct oil grade and rectify source of dilution.
— Free valve or renew broken spring.
— Renew bearing shells or recondition journals as necessary.
— Renew or recondition oil pump.
— Rectify as necessary.

FUEL SYSTEM
1. CARBURETTOR - GENERAL DESCRIPTION AND OPERATION

The main constructional features of a typical horizontal carburettor in its simplest form are shown in the illustrations.

(1) A butterfly throttle is mounted on spindle at the engine end of the main air passage, and an adjustable idling stop screw is arranged to prevent complete closure.

Towards the other end of the main passage is mounted the suction piston unit, its lower and smaller diameter forming a shutter which enlarges or diminishes the size of the main air passage over the fuel jet as the piston rises or falls under the influence of engine suction (controlled by the degree of throttle opening) on its upper and larger diameter moving axially within the suction chamber.

As the tapered fuel metering needle is fixed into the piston by setscrew, the rising or falling piston, in addition to varying the air passage, also correspondingly varies the jet discharge.

The rising and falling piston is guided by the very accurate fit of the hardened piston rod in the cast iron guide bush incorporated in the suction chamber. The upper and larger diameter of the piston does not touch the bore of the suction chamber, but is held slightly out of contact with an extremely fine clearance (see Timing of the Piston Drop), and similarly the tapered needle, although at idling speed very closely approaching the bore of the jet, should never actually touch it—this is achieved by making the complete jet unit floating in sideways location when its large clamping screw is slackened off; it can then be exactly centralised on the largest portion of the tapered needle and then locked in this final position. (Full details of this jet centering operation are given in Sticking Piston and Incorrect Jet Centering).

The piston, falling either by its own weight or assisted by a light compression spring, impacts on to the internal rectangular facing called the jet bridge, the impact being taken by a small spring-loaded pin projecting about .010" from the piston face.

The piston rises under the influence of induction depression (which is controlled by the throttle opening), this taking effect through single or twin holes in the lower face of the small diameter and exerting suction on the top of the larger diameter; the under face of this larger diameter is vented back to atmosphere by ducts not shown on the diagram.

These ducts were vented back to free air on older carburettors, but as this led, in some tropical and dusty climates, to the smoothness of the piston travel being marred by deposits of dust inside the suction chamber, in later dustproof carburettors these ducts are taken back into the air cleaner or pipe, using filtered air.

To prevent the piston rising too quickly as a result of brisk throttle opening, an oil-damped plunger unit is positioned inside the hollow piston rod, and this puts a fluid brake on too rapid a piston rise but exerts no restriction on its fall. It provides an appropriate degree of enrichment for acceleration and improves cold starting and driveability from cold.

The oil reservoir in the hollow piston rod in which the damper plunger functions should be topped up periodically, about every three or four months, with thin engine oil, SAE 20 preferably (but no thicker than SAE 30), and this topping-up level is not critical; simply unscrew and remove the damper unit and then pour sufficient oil into the reservoir to bring the oil to within about ½" of the top of the rod. Screw the plunger unit back into position.

The jet proper is housed and slides in an upper bearing and a lower bearing, and positioned in each bearing is a small cork gland sealing washer which prevents fuel leakage, a compression spring giving the necessary loading on each gland.

A large cork (or synthetic rubber) sealing ring prevents leakage between the main body and the jet locking screw. This screw clamps the complete jet unit in the necessary concentric position relative to the taper needle (see Sticking Piston and Incorrect Jet Centering).

The jet head under normal running conditions should abut hard up against the adjusting nut, the position of which determines the idling mixture strength when the engine is fully warmed up. For cold starting this jet head is lowered manually, approximately ⅜" away from the tapered needle, thus giving a larger fuel discharge area and producing a very rich mixture necessary for cold starting.

For winter conditions it is sometimes preferable, after a cold start, to bring the jet only part way back, not reaching the full weak position, so that the first mile or two of running with a near-cold engine is done with a slightly lowered jet giving a mildly richer mixture than normal—the best intermediate position of the dashboard control giving this slightly lowered jet will be readily found after a little experience, care being taken not to run needlessly rich.

The lowering of the jet is done through the jet lever, and a tension spring provides the necessary upward thrust on the jet head, ensuring that after a cold start the jet always tends to be brought back to full weak and kept there during normal running.

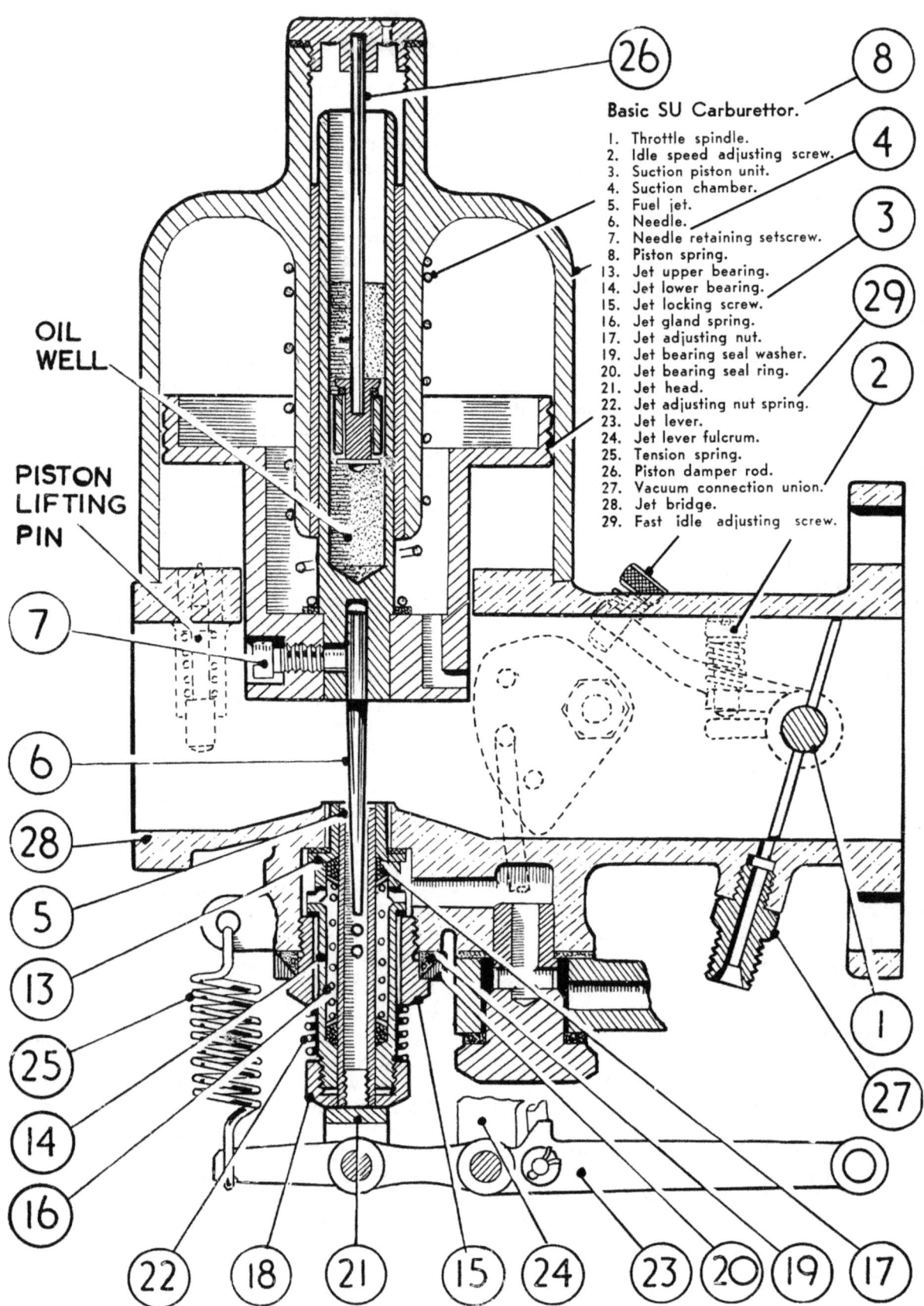

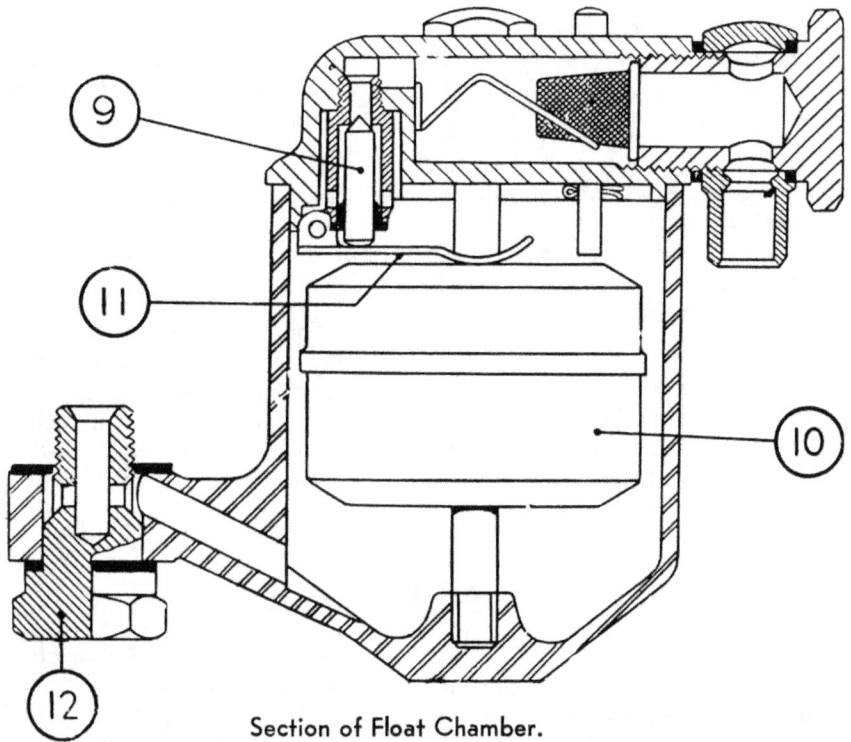

Section of Float Chamber.
9. Needle valve 10. Float 11. Float lever 12. Assembly bolt

Referring again to cold starting: It was normal on pre-war cars to have two separate controls on the carburettor, one of which enriches the mixture, and the other gave a modest degree of throttle opening. In later years, however, it has become usual to have only one hand control combining both functions, so that on the carburettor the lever controlling the lowering of the jet is also interconnected with a throttle opening mechanism.

On an earlier type of this throttle and jet interconnection the two movements, throttle opening and jet lowering, took place together, but in a later type (using a cam operation in place of a rocker) the throttle is opened in advance of the lowering of the jet and also closes after the raising of the jet. This can be an advantage in winter as it prevents the engine stalling during slow speed manoeuvring with a cold engine as it enables a generous amount of hand throttle to be used.

With this cam-type interconnection, or its preceding rocker type, the outer adjusting screw should be about $\frac{1}{64}''$ (thickness of a visiting card) away from the cam face or rocker face when the engine is warm and idling on a closed throttle, with the rocker type this figure should not be exceeded, but with the cam type a larger gap can be used if desired.

An entirely different solution of the cold starting problem is given by the thermostatic type of carburettor, where, in addition to the main instrument, a separate and auxiliary carburettor is brought into action to provide the initial very rich mixture for cold starting and also the milder degree of enrichment necessary during the warming-up period. After a matter of two or three miles, when the engine has reached full working temperature, an automatic thermostatic switch (sometimes an alternative hand switch is used) cuts off the current which brings this auxiliary carburettor into action, and the main instrument then provides all the necessary mixture.

The majority of current body castings incorporate a throttle edge union for actuation of an automatic ignition control. On certain carburettors there is an additional similar pipe and union fitting, for actuating what is termed the weakening device, providing a weakened-off mixture for part throttle cruising when the engine is pulling against a light load. This fitting cannot be supplied except as a car manufacturer's original equipment, owing to the complicated tuning problems involved.

JET AIR BLEED

On some carburettors produced between 1950 and 1954 a small air bleed was added to the chamber housing the main jet assembly. The top of this air bleed unit protrudes at an angle from the side of the carburettor body, and its function is to stabilise the jet discharge under certain conditions.

The jet bleed protrudes through the side of the jet housing to finish with a screwed union and pipe line leading either to the lid of the float chamber or to some portion of the air inlet pipe.

To inspect the orifice of this air bleed it is only necessary to detach the pipe line nut at the union close to the carburettor body, and inspect the actual bleed hole which is part of the bore of the union.

There is nothing that can go wrong with these air bleeds apart from blockage by dirt—and the average driver would not detect the slight deterioration in performance which results. If, however, the screwed union of the pipe line unit worked loose, then a drastic weakening effect on the mixture strength would immediately be noticeable.

Turning now to the float chamber (see illustration), it will be observed to be of orthodox construction, comprising a needle valve located within a separate seating screwed into the casting of the float lid, and a float, the upward movement of which in response to the rising fuel level, causes final closure of the needle upon its seating through the action of the hinged fork.

It will be seen that the float chamber is a unit separate from the main body of the carburettor, to which it is attached by means of bolt, suitable drillings in the float chamber, bolt, and body casting leading the fuel to the jet.

The fuel level in the float chamber need not be exact or to a critical dimension (unlike a fixed choke carburettor), but the standard level is $\frac{3}{8}''$ below the level of the rectangular facing known as the jet bridge and full details of this and any corrections that may be necessary are given later.

2. ADJUSTMENTS

GENERAL DESCRIPTION

On the bulk of carburettor installations, which are car manufacturer's original equipment, the type of needle (of which there are many) fitted to a specific car has been settled only after prolonged tests, and therefore it is not usual for the recommended type to need changing in practice.

If, however, unsatisfactory carburation raises a doubt about the correctness of the needle type fitted, it can be withdrawn for inspection after first detaching the suction chamber and piston unit and loosening the needle clamping screw. The needle type, identified by letters or numerals (or both), is rolled around the shank diameter or stamped upon the shank end—and owing to the smallness of the available space these markings are not too obvious; a magnifying glass may assist.

Having re-inserted the needle after checking that the identification marking indicates a suitable needle form, tuning is confined to correct idling adjustment.

When relocking the needle in place, which should be done firmly, note that the standard needle position is with the shoulder on the needle shank just flush with the bottom of the piston into which it is inserted. See To position Needle in Piston for full details of needle fitting.

Idling adjustment is carried out by movement of the idling stop screw and the jet stop nut, but before making these adjustments it is essential that the engine should have attained its normal running temperature.

It is advisable, before commencing adjustments to nut, to slacken off the choke cable clamp anchored to the end of the jet lever, otherwise a taut cable may prevent the jet head from correctly abutting the nut.

When the idling tuning has reached a satisfactory conclusion, this control should be reclamped in such a position that there is a small amount of cable slack and the taut condition avoided.

The stop screw should be carefully slackened off until the slowest idling speed is found, and then the jet position should be so adjusted, vertically, that for this given position of screw the fastest idling speed is obtained consistent with even firing.

If the firing is uneven, with a splashy, irregular type of misfire and a colorless exhaust, then the mixture is too weak and the jet position should be suitably lowered; whilst if the firing is uneven, with a rhythmical or regular misfire and a blackish exhaust, then the mixture is too rich and the jet position should be raised.

Here it may be observed that there are two methods of finalising the vertical position of the jet to give a satisfactory mixture as follows:

First method—Detach the return spring, and screw the nut up to its topmost position out of the way and leave it there while the jet proper is moved vertically into the most satisfactory position for idling mixture by careful movement of the lever, and when this position has been found screw the stop nut carefully downwards until it meets the shoulder on the jet head without disturbing the setting just obtained; the return spring can then be replaced.

It must be emphasised that with this first method the lever must be moved with great care as, disregarding possible backlash, a movement of $\frac{1}{64}''$ of the end of the lever on some engines will give an observable difference in engine beat, and a movement of $\frac{1}{16}''$ a marked alteration.

Second method—In this method, leave the spring in its normal position so that it keeps the jet head always hard up against the stop nut, then adjust the nut upwards for weakening or downwards for enriching until a satisfactory engine beat is obtained. Bear in mind that really good slow running is critical, on some engines to a sixth of a turn (one flat of the hexagon) of the stop nut.

Having adjusted the mixture strength to suit the originally set position of the stop screw, the idling speed may be found to be too fast. A slight slackening off of the stop screw can be made to lower this speed, which may also entail a small alteration to the stop nut, possibly to the extent of one flat.

If any difficulty is found in obtaining a good idling speed with the needle in the standard position, it may be necessary, very occasionaly, to vary it, as described in To position Needle in Piston.

Note that where an alteration in mixture strength is required for the main throttle range (that is, not idling speed), then a different type of needle should be fitted, but the jet will remain the same.

Before arriving at the conclusion that a change of needle is necessary in order to restore satisfactory carburation, a careful examination should be undertaken for the detection of other possible faults in the carburettor, for air leaks in flange gaskets, for faults in the sparking plugs or ignition system, or the general mechanical condition of the engine, including sticking valves or defective valve seats.

The influence of air cleaner type should be checked if a change (not usually to be recommended) is made from the standard size or type, as the carburettor may be affected—also a carburettor originally tuned with a cleaner will show a pronounced weakening off if run without it.

EFFECT OF ALTITUDE AND CLIMATIC EXTREMES ON STANDARD TUNING

The standard tuning employs a jet needle broadly suitable for temperature climates from sea level up to 3000 feet. Above that altitude it may be necessary, depending on extremes of climatic heat and humidity, to use a weaker tuning.

The factors of altitude, extreme climatic heat, and humidity each tend to demand a weaker tuning, and a combination of any of these factors would naturally emphasise this demand. This is a situation which cannot be met by a hard and fast factory recommendation owing to the wide variations in the conditions existing, and in such cases the owner will have to do a little experimenting with alternative weaker needles until one which is satisfactory is found.

If the carburettor is fitted with a spring-loaded suction piston, the necessary weakening may be effected by changing to a weaker type of spring or even discarding the spring itself and running without one.

TO TUNE TWIN CARBURETTORS

To make a thorough job of adjusting the carburettors it is first advisable to check all engine details which affect performance, such as compression, tappet clearances, plug gaps and distributor gap, with the engine manufacturer's recommendations.

The carburettors should then be checked over for dirt-free suction chambers and pistons, and also that the piston falls freely into a correctly centred jet assembly—if it does not the jet unit will need recentering.

Now slacken the clamping bolts on the universally jointed connections between the throttle spindles so that the throttles can be set independently of each other, and disconnect the mixture control linkage by removing one of the fork swivel pins. While the suction chambers are off for cleaning see that the needles are located in the same position in all the pistons, and that the jets are the same distance below the rectangular facing of the jet bridge; one method of making sure of this is to screw each adjusting nut right up to its topmost position and then unscrew each nut one full turn or six flats of the hexagon, which is a reasonable starting point.

Unscrew the throttle adjusting screws and screw these back until they will just hold a thin strip of paper between the end of the screw and the fixed stop web on the body casting when the throttle disc is fully shut; then screw them in one complete turn.

The engine may now be started and left running until thoroughly warmed up, when it may be found necessary to re-adjust the idling screws by equal amounts in either direction according to whether a higher or lower speed is required. To check for exact matching of the throttle openings, it is best to listen to the air intake hiss, after first removing the air cleaners. This is most easily done by holding one end of a piece of rubber tubing against the ear and the other end against the intake of each carburettor in turn, when the intensity of the intake hiss can be gauged. The larger the throttle opening, the more intense is the intake hiss, and with this as a guide the necessary adjustments for matching can readily be made after a little experience.

When the degree of throttle opening has been dealt with, the mixture strength given by each jet can be varied by moving all jet adjusting nuts, the same amount, either upwards for weakening or downwards for enriching, until a satisfactory engine beat has been found, which should give the fastest idling speed consistent with even firing.

When this has been found, it may be necessary to lower the idling speed by slackening off slightly the throttle adjusting screws, all an equal amount.

Note that a weak idling mixture gives a splashy irregular type of misfire, with a colorless exhaust, while a rich idling mixture gives a rhythmical or regular misfire, with a blackish exhaust.

When the mixture strength is correct on both carburettors, lifting the piston about $\frac{1}{8}$″ with a pen-knife blade (or by the special piston lifting pin on the side of the body casting) will give uneven firing from excessive weakness on that particular carburettor.

If lifting the piston of one carburettor stops the engine and lifting that of another does not, this indicates that the mixture on the first carburettor is set weaker than that on the second, and therefore the mixture strength on the first one should be enriched by unscrewing the jet adjusting nut one or two flats of the hexagon.

Make sure that the jet is hard up against the bottom face of the adjusting nut after any movement of the latter; and also check the same point when reconnecting the link rod between the jet units, as it may be necessary to lengthen or shorten this linkage so that the clevis pin can be inserted easily when the jets are in the correct hard-up position.

The throttle connection bolts may now be retightened, taking care to see that light pressure is put on the head of each throttle stop screw as the last bolt is tightened.

The lower arrow shows one of the universal joints on the throttle spindle. The top arrow and screwdriver show the two throttle stop screws for setting the engine speed

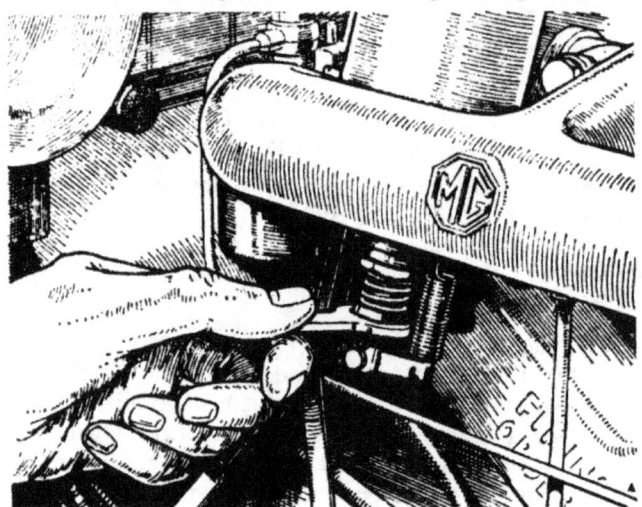
Setting the jet

Setting screw for the interconnected rich mixture and throttle control (fast idling)

Carburetter on TF Model with air cleaner removed to show air holes for piston and (arrowed) the piston lifting pin

3. TROUBLESHOOTING

In the case of unsatisfactory behavior of the engine, before proceeding to a detailed examination of the carburettor it is advisable to carry out a check of the general condition of the engine, attention being directed in particular to the following:

(1) The ignition system, including plug leads and condenser.

(2) Incorrectly adjusted contact breaker gap; pitted or dirty contact breaker points.

(3) Incorrect plug gaps or oily or dirty plugs.

(4) Sticking valves or worn inlet valve guides.

(5) Defective fuel supply.

(6) Air leaks at carburettor flange gasket or induction pipe gasket.

(7) Poor or uneven compressions.

(8) Incorrect tappet clearances.

If none of the above defects is present to a degree which would account for the unsatisfactory engine performance, the carburettor should be checked over for the faults detailed below.

STICKING PISTON AND INCORRECT JET CENTERING

It is essential that the piston should move smoothly and evenly within its limits of travel, and if any sticking does take place it is generally the fault of:

(a) Excessive dirt deposit on piston and bore of suction chamber.

(b) Rubbing high spots on large diameter of piston or bore of chamber.

(c) Jet unit incorrectly centred on needle.

(d) A bent needle.

A sticking piston can be checked on the older type of carburettor by inserting a wire nail upwards through one of the air vent holes underneath the suction chamber mounting, and then pushing the piston upwards, after which it should fall freely until it hits the jet bridge with a soft metallic click — on later carburettors not having these air vent holes, a spring-loaded lifting pin is provided in the same position and this gives a limited piston lft.

A sticking piston may give erratic running, stalling of the engine at idling speed, and a lack of power probably accompanied by a heavy fuel consumption.

The cure for (a) is easily effected and consists of detaching the suction chamber and piston and cleaning, with a rag moistened in petrol, the inside large bore of the chamber and the two piston diameters, reassembling in a dead dry and clean condition with a few spots of thin oil on the piston rod only.

To trace (b) is a little more difficult, but if metallic contact is taking place between high spots either in the large bore of the suction chamber or the corresponding large piston diameter (an uncommon fault), these rubbing surfaces should be located and carefully eased down, using a scraper in the bore of the chamber or a flat superfine file on the piston—do not use emery cloth, however, as this method is not exact enough, and serious harm may result.

The fault of the sticking piston is more commonly attributable to (c) because the jet unit is incorrectly centred on the taper needle. This may be checked by raising the piston manually, as already described, and observing whether, when released, the piston hits the jet bridge with a soft but definite click—if it only does so when the jet is fully lowered, then the whole jet unit needs recentering, and this important operation is relatively simple if the following instructions are followed carefully:

(1) Remove the pivot pin holding the jet lever to the jet head, and swing the linkage well to one side (also it may be necessary to detach the lower end of the link rod between the jet lever and throttle).

(2) Withdraw the jet and unscrew the jet adjusting nut, removing its lock spring, which should be placed on one side. Replace the adjusting nut and screw it right up to its topmost position; replace the jet and see that the slot in the jet head lies in the same angular position as when assembled on the jet lever, marking with a pencil the one face adjacent to the air inlet.

(3) Slacken off the large jet locking screw (which locks the whole jet unit in position) until the bottom half jet bearing is just free to rotate by finger pressure.

(4) It will now be evident that if the tapered needle (locked into the piston and suction chamber, already in position) is lowered into the jet bore, with the jet in its highest position, until the piston hits the inner jet bridge, then the complete jet unit will have been concentrically located around the needle. Gentle pressure with the end of a pencil on the top of the piston rod (damper or oil cap removed) will make sure that the piston is completely down on the jet bridge.

(5) Tighten the jet locking screw, observing that the jet head is still in its correct angular position.

(6) Lift the piston and check that it falls freely

and evenly, hitting the jet bridge with a soft metallic click. Then fully lower the jet and recheck to see if there is any difference in the sound of the impact, and if there is and the second test produces a sharper impact sound, the centering operation will have to be repeated until successful.

(7) In the occasional obstinate case, the jet adjusting nut (as well as its lock spring) should be temporarily removed to enable the jet to reach a higher positioning and so make the centering effect more positive, the nut and lock spring being replaced after the successful conclusion of the operation.

The correct diagnosis of a bent jet needle (d) is not always obvious as most of the symptoms are similar to those given by an incorrectly centered jet, except that with a bent needle the piston may fall freely just before hitting the jet bridge, but be inclined to stick at the top position or half-way down.

The best check is to detach the suction chamber and piston unit, and with the needle in its normal position spin the piston on its rod whilst the suction chamber is held steady in a horizontal position on a table top. Any eccentricity of the point of the needle, indicating a bent axis, can then be observed. It is practically impossible to straighten a bent needle, and replacement is the only cure.

Do not forget that after checking any of the points (a), (b), (c) and (d) the oil reservoir in the hollow piston rod will need refilling.

JET GLAND LEAKAGE

If persistent slow leakage is observed at the base of the jet unit (a mere surface dampness can genarally be disregarded) it is possible that the two small jet cork glands and the large sealing cork ring require replacement. Careful study of the illustrations should enable the replacement to be performed without difficulty. The jet lever should first be detached from the jet head, the locking screw removed and the jet unit can then be withdrawn. After refitting complete with the new glands, the whole unit must be correctly centred on the taper needle as previously described—this is most important.

Incidentally, whilst a defective bottom jet gland is apparent by a fuel leak from the base of the jet unit, a similar leak from the top gland is not so noticeable, but its effect is that of enrichment of the mixture strength, particularly at idling speeds. If the jet nut is then raised (in ignorance of the true fault) in order to correct this richness, the mixture strength for the general throttle range may be found to be on the weak side—possibly definitely so.

A similar unwanted richening effect can be given by a piece of grit or swarf under the top copper washer of the top bearing after careless assembly of the jet unit. Therefore the top gland and the top copper washer should be checked if an unduly rich idling mixture is given with the jet adjusting nut right up, and if the needle and jet are both unworn and correct in type and position.

STICKING JET

After long service the outside diameter of the jet proper tends to oxidise slightly just under the shoulder by the jet head, and this may tend to prevent the head abutting hard up against the adjusting nut. In such a case, smear a little petroleum jelly or grease around the lower part of the jet when in its fully lowered position, and then raise and lower the jet several times in order to work the lubricant well over the surfaces; a little oil should also be added to the various pivot pins and the linkage, as these are frequently neglected for long periods.

FAILURE OF FUEL SUPPLY TO FLOAT CHAMBER

If the engine is found to stop under idling or light running conditions, notwithstanding the fact that a good supply of fuel is present at the float chamber inlet union (observable by momentarily disconnecting this), it is possible that the needle has become stuck to its seating. This possibility arises in the rare cases where some gummy substance is present in the fuel system. The most probable substance of this nature is the polymerised gum which sometimes results from the protracted storage of fuel in the tank.

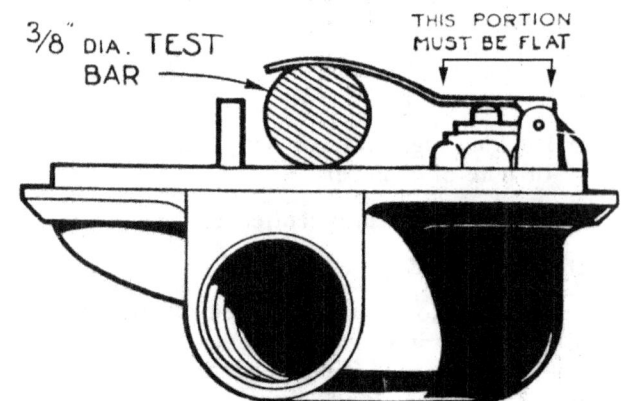

Correct Method of Setting Float Lever.

After removal of the float chamber lid and float lever the needle may be withdrawn, and its point thoroughly wiped with a rag dipped in alcohol. Similar treatment should also be applied to the needle seating, which can conveniently be cleaned by means of a matchstick and cloth dipped in alcohol.

The pre-1955 float lever and needle can easily be withdrawn for cleaning, but after that date the $\frac{3}{32}''$ hinge pin was fixed and cleaning is necessarily confined to brisk agitation of the complete lid in a bowl of clean alcohol. Persistent trouble of this nature can only be cured properly by complete mechanical cleansing of the tank and fuel system or, in the worst cases, complete renewal of these parts.

If the engine is found to suffer from a serious lack of power, which becomes evident at higher speeds and loads, this is probably due to an inadequately sustained fuel system; the fuel pump output should be checked and any filters in the system inspected and cleaned.

FLOODING FROM FLOAT CHAMBER OR JET

This can be caused by:

(a) A fuel level which has been set too high, giving intermittent flooding.

(b) Dirt or grit on the needle seating.

(c) Worn needle seating.

(d) Defective float.

Regarding (a), the position of the fuel level need not be exact and to a critical dimension, but the standard level is $\frac{1}{8}''$ below the level of the rectangular facing known as the jet bridge. If it is higher and only just short of the jet bridge, then leaving the car idling on a fairly steep drive may cause slow flooding, and in this circumstance resetting to a lower level is desirable.

Even with the piston unit removed and the jet fully lowered it is not easy to observe the top surface of the bead of fuel in the jet well, so an alternative mechanical cut-off position of the hinged lever is given, this being much simpler to observe.

This cut-off position is checked by sliding a rod of a given diameter between the lid and the inside curve of the forked end of the needle actuating lever as shown (see illustration). The diameter of the rod is: For the smallest T 1 type float chamber, $\frac{7}{16}''$; for the largest T 4 type float chamber, $\frac{5}{8}''$. The diameters of the float chambers are: T 1, $1\frac{7}{8}''$; T 2, $2\frac{1}{4}''$; and T 4, $3''$.

If the hinged lever fails to conform to within $\frac{1}{32}''$ of these check figures it must be carefully bent at the start of the fork section, downwards to lower the level and upwards to raise it in the necessary direction for correction.

When bending, see that both fork prongs are approximately level in a horizontal plane.

The cure for (b) is the simple and obvious one of cleaning—agitating the complete float lid in a bowl of clean fuel is one method, after first detaching the hinge pin, fork and stainless steel needle, if that can easily be done, as in the pre-1955 type.

(c) Can be checked by observing whether slow flooding gradually takes place at idling speeds, when the leak past a defective seating may exceed the flow required by the idling engine. A few very light taps on the end of the stainless steel needle may provide a cure, but generally a new seating and needle will require fitting (note that a hexagon box spanner .338" across the flats is required to tighten the seating).

(d) A defective float is sometimes due to porosity or leakage around one of the soldered seams—shaking such a float gives a swishing liquid sound, not to be confused with the rattle of bits of loose solder. Immersion in boiling water will indicate the exact position of the leak by bubbles, and when all the fuel has been evaporated out, a temporary repair can be made with a blob of solder until a replacement float can be obtained.

WATER OR DIRT IN FLOAT CHAMBER

Very occasionally it happens that a deposit of water condensate or grit may accumulate in the bottom of the float chamber and cause erratic running. To remove, detach the complete float chamber at the central holding-up bolt and thoroughly clean out the inside of the chamber, the angular feed hole in the arm, and also the hollow holding-up bolt after first removing the float lid and float.

POOR COLD STARTING

The carburettor is very seldom the cause of this fault, although it is frequently blamed for it, and the only two likely mal-adjustments concerned on an SU are insufficient jet drop or lack of oil in the piston damper. It should be remembered that poor cold starting is more likely to be the result of bad valve seats, incorrectly adjusted plug gaps or distributor points, or other engine or ignition faults.

When fully lowered the jet head should drop away from the adjusting nut by at least $\frac{5}{16}''$, and preferably $\frac{3}{8}''$ if severe winter conditions are involved or the engine concerned is known to be poor at cold starting.

If this dimension is not being achieved it is probably because the setting of the jet adjusting nut is four or five full turns down from its topmost position, and this therefore cuts into the total travel available for the jet.

The normal position of the jet adjusting nut can be raised by repositioning the needle about $\frac{1}{16}''$ farther into the piston, which will allow the adjusting nut to be raised by an equal amount, this in turn giving a more generous jet travel. (A normal position of the jet adjusting nut can be anywhere between three flats or half a turn down from the topmost position to three full turns down.)

It should be noted that with the jet adjusting nut

screwed up to its topmost position, the full available jet travel should be at least $\frac{13}{32}''$ and at most $\frac{15}{32}''$. If the minimum figure is not being attained, a judicious filing of the small stop lug on the jet lever, where it contacts the link, may be indicated—do not overdo this filing and exceed the maximum drop figure of $\frac{15}{32}''$.

The second possible fault of lack of oil in the damper should be investigated, as although the chief gain result from this fitment is improved acceleration, nevertheless on some particular engines it gives a marked improvement in cold starting.

4. CARBURETTOR SERVICE AND ADJUSTMENTS

TO ASSEMBLE THE JET UNIT—STANDARD TYPE

The correct sequence of assembly of the various parts in the unit is as follows (see illustration):

(1) Assemble the bottom half jet bearing, its mating copper washer, the jet screw, the jet adjusting nut and its locking spring, which should be screwed up as far as it will go by hand or very light spanner pressure.

(2) Then insert the jet upwards into the bottom half

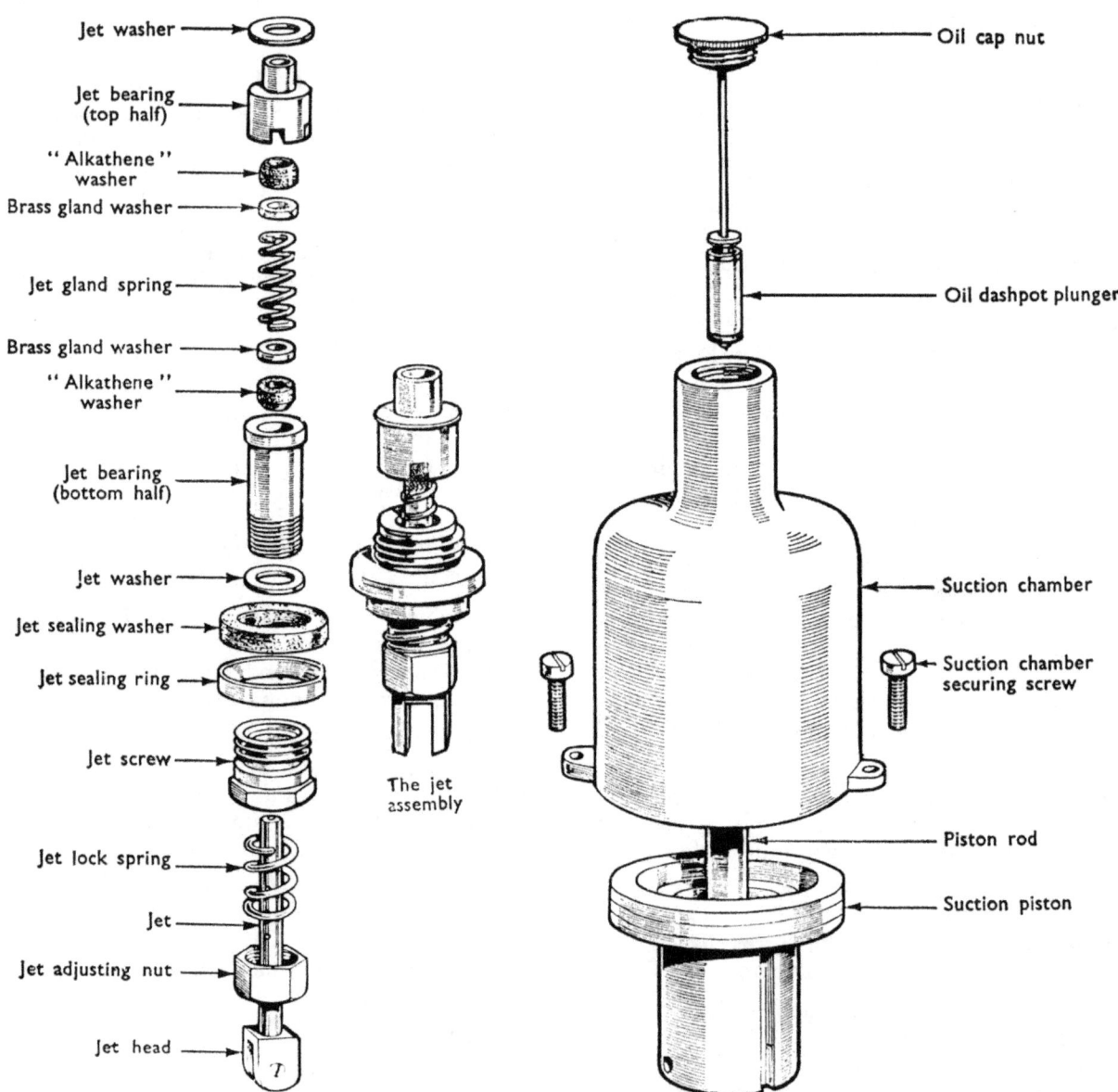

Components of Standard Jet and Suction Chamber.

bearing, and next slide one of the small cork glands with its mating brass gland (dish facing downwards) into the bottom of the jet bearing, using the gland spring to push them there.

(3) Then drop the large coned metal sealing ring over the jet screw, cone upwards, and add the large cork sealing ring. (This ring is sometimes supplied in synthetic rubber).

(4) Next slide over the top of the jet the second small brass gland (dish uppermost) and the second small cork jet gland, then the top half bearing, and finally the top copper washer.

(5) The complete unit can then be screwed into the body casting, but only finger tight, as it will need correct centering on the piston and needle assembly, as described in Sticking Piston and Incorrect Jet Centering, before it is finally tightened.

Jets of the two smaller sizes are marked with a numeral 9, identifying a .090" size jet, or 1 for the larger .100" size.

There are three larger sizes of .125", .1875" and .250", which are used chiefly on racing and special high-performance cars, and the last two sizes are always of the fixed racing type, having no adjustment at all, whilst the .125" size can either be of this fixed racing type or, alternatively, of the fully slidable and adjustable variety, as the standard jet.

If a jet has worn oversize and thereby gives an unduly rich mixture, this wear is almost invariably caused by the needle rubbing slightly on the inside bore of the jet because the jet unit has not been centered correctly. In this circumstance a polished streak down the side of the needle, where the rubbing has taken place, is much more definite evidence of jet wear than checking the jet bore with a plug gauge, which cannot give evidence of local wear only, such as produced by a rubbing needle.

If the wear has been sufficient to give an increase in fuel consumption a new jet and needle should be fitted, and this must be carefully centered as described in Sticking Piston and Incorrect Jet Centering.

TO CLEAN SUCTION CHAMBER AND PISTON PERIODICALLY

This unit can only be supplied in its complete form and individual pistons or suction chambers are not issued separately owing to the very fine measurements involved in the pairing up. The two parts can, of course, be separated for inspection and cleaning, which should be done about every 12 months.

The cleaning should be carried out on the two outside discs of the piston, and the large bore of the suction chamber, with a clean rag moistened in fuel.

After this the parts should be reassembled in a dry and clean condition, with a few spots of thin oil on the steel piston rod only.

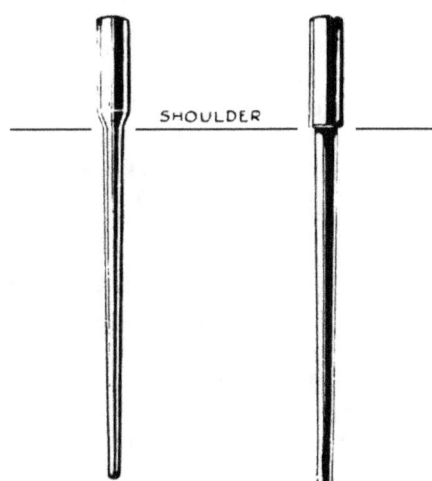

Carburettor Needles have Two Different Types of Shoulders. See Text for Correct Assembly of Different Types.

If oil finds its way on to the outside diameter of the piston or large bore of the suction chamber, harm will result until it is cleaned off. When cleaning the piston take care that the needle is not bent in the general handling (this can be checked by rotating the piston in the suction chamber): also put a screwdriver on the clamp screw holding the needle and check that it is tight.

TO POSITION THE NEEDLE IN PISTON

The recommended position is with the shoulder on the needle shank just flush with the end face of the piston. In older needles (made by a now superseded method) the shoulder was rounded and rather vague in definition so that its correct positioning was not so easily carried out. However, the illustration clearly shows the two types of needle and their shoulder positions in relation to the end face of the piston.

If, with this recommended position of the needle, the idling mixture is unduly rich even with the jet adjusting nut in the topmost position, this is probably due to a worn needle and jet which must be replaced and correctly centred. Alternatively, the rich mixture may be the result of a defective top jet gland or top copper washer (see Jet Gland Leakage).

Also, when finding by trial and error a suitable needle for a special job having no recommended needle tuning, it is sometimes necessary to locate the needle about $\frac{1}{32}$" farther into the piston to avoid a too low position of the jet adjusting nut. The nut should not be lower than three full turns from the topmost position, and any excess over this figure would cut down cold starting capability in extreme winter conditions.

From the two preceding paragraphs it will be seen that, although not advisable in normal circumstances, it may sometimes be necessary to vary the position of the needle in the piston as a form of rough tuning, making the final fine adjustment on the jet adjusting nut. On those carburettors, few in number, fitted with the large fixed racing jets, adjustment of the position of the needle in the piston is the only method of mixture variation.

A cautionary word may be necessary about the practice of lightly tapping the small end of the needle with the wooden handle of a screwdriver when positioning it, and if this is done to the odd needle which is a tightish fit in the piston, difficulty may be experienced when trying to extract it. If this should happen and the needle be jammed, grip the last ⅛" only in a good pair of pliers or a small vice and gently ease the needle out, using a steady twisting and pulling motion, but avoiding side thrust or the needle will be bent and will have to be scrapped.

TYPES OF SUCTION PISTON AND PISTON SPRING

(a) Zinc die-cast pistons were used up to 1939 in the majority of carburettors, but this metal sometimes had the defect of slowly distorting or growing with age, leading to loosened piston rods (originally a tight press fit). This can be checked by holding the piston firmly in one hand (not a vice) whilst the second hand grasps the rod and checks for shake—if this is detected there is nothing that can be done as a remedy and the complete piston and suction chamber will have to be renewed.

(b) The brass piston replaced the zinc type and ran in general production up to 1950; there was, of course, no trouble with instability of this metal.

(c) The current thin-walled aluminium piston used with a weak compression spring in turn displaced both the previous types, and can also be used as a service replacement for either, providing a suitable strength of spring is selected.

To select a correct spring, weigh the old brass or zinc piston complete with rod, and then similarly weigh the new aluminium piston and rod, and the difference in weight, in ounces, should be taken as the required spring rating, varying if anything on the weaker side; e.g., old piston unit weighs 10½ oz, new unit 5 oz, giving a difference of 5½ oz, so use a 4½ oz spring.

The springs available are.

2½ oz. colored	Light Blue	on end coil
4½ „ „	Red	„ „ „
8 „ „	Yellow	„ „ „
12 „ „	Green	„ „ „

(d) The old pre-war thick-walled aluminium piston used without a spring, dropping by its own gravity weight, was used generally on twin- and triple-carburettor layouts and is now practically out of production. It can be replaced by the current thin-walled type plus a piston spring, the rating of which can be found as already explained in the previous paragraph.

PISTON SPRINGS AND SKID WASHERS

The four piston springs in common use, colored Blue, Red, Yellow and Green, and giving loads of 2½ oz, 4½ oz, 8 oz and 12 oz, in their original pattern incorporated a reduced end coil which was diminished to fit over the ¼" diameter piston rod, and under this smaller end coil was positioned a thin flat skid washer made from stainless steel or hard rolled brass.

The function of this washer was to prevent accidental winding up of the compression spring, which if it occurred would put a continual twisting force on the piston against its guide key, thereby altering the rise and fall characteristic of the piston and upsetting mixture strength.

After 1955, however, it was decided to eliminate this smaller end coil in order to gain a little extra piston fit, and for the same reason the flat skid washer was eliminated and replaced on the larger carburettors by a pressed cup performing the same function, but on the smaller carburettors any such fitting was dispensed with.

DUSTPROOFING OF SUCTION CHAMBERS AND PISTONS

There are two degrees of dustproofing on the suction piston assembly: the milder type achieves a very substantial degree of imperviousness to dust, whilst the second type gives complete protection at some slight cost of simplicity. This latter type is identified by a small $\frac{3}{32}$" diameter transverse hole in the neck of the suction chamber, drilled from just below the inner thread for the damper cap into the main chamber and at an angle.

Note that the piston damper used on this chamber having the transverse hole must be of the type having no vent hole in the top brass cap; whereas the damper having a vent hole in the cap is always fitted to the first-mentioned suction chamber with no transverse hole.

Briefly, the rule is if there is a hole in the suction chamber neck there is no hole in the damper cap; and vice versa.

TIMING OF PISTON DROP

The large outside diameter of the piston should not touch the bore of the suction chamber; there should be a clearance of between .002" and .003".

If high spots or bruises have grown either on this

piston diameter or on the corresponding bore of the suction chamber (causing piston sticking or uneven travel), then these high spots should be carefully eased down with a superfine file on the piston, or a scraper in the bore of the chamber.

Although a new and accurate piston will revolve easily or fall easily (when detached from the carburettor) in any position of the suction chamber, in actual working conditions it is only called upon to operate in one position. Old pistons, where some slight metal distortion due to age has taken place, should be checked for free falling at least in their functioning position in relation to the suction chamber. If a piston sticks or jams elsewhere it is only a mild defect and not detrimental to essential working.

The fixed clearance between the piston outside diameter and the bore of the suction chamber is important as it governs the rate of piston rise, and therefore of choke area.

This clearance is checked, not mechanically, but by counting in seconds the time taken by a given quantity of air to leak through it—obviously if the clearance or gap is larger, the time taken will be shorter, and vice versa.

Or translated into practice, if the suction piston assembly is held upside down, with the smaller piston diameter uppermost, the index finger of the holding hand blocking off and sealing the small suction hole, the other hand can then steady the suction chamber in its topmost position — then if this hand is withdrawn the chamber will slowly, as the air is drawn inwards through the circumferential gap, fall downwards and away from the piston; in a typical case of a $1\frac{1}{4}''$ throttle horizontal carburettor this time will be between three and five seconds for the piston to reach the bottom of its travel.

If the suction chamber is of the fully dustproofed type having a $\frac{3}{32}''$ transverse hole, before making the above check screw the damper into position, even although it is obvious that no oil can be introduced into the inverted piston rod.

The time in seconds for this piston drop varies from three to five seconds for the smaller carburettors, up to five to seven seconds for the larger $1\frac{1}{2}''$ and $1\frac{3}{4}''$ throttle carburettors.

A fast piston timing, if it is markedly so, will have a richening effect on the standard tuning, and a slow piston timing a weakening effect, sometimes even taking the general mixture strength outside the range normally given by the standard needle.

OIL DAMPER UNIT IN PISTON

If a piston damper is replaced, see that the replacement resembles the original fitting either by having a small $\frac{1}{16}''$ diameter vent hole in the top brass cap, or by not having this vent hole. The two types are not interchangeable, and if wrongly used in an attempt to make them so, serious trouble will result.

At a pinch, of course, one type can be made into the other by plugging the hole in the one case, or drilling the extra hole in the second, but this should only be done in the case of supply difficulty.

Prior to 1955, the identification of these two types was much more obvious as the type with the vent hole had a circular knurled top brass cap, whereas the type without the vent hole had a hexagon brass cap; since 1955 both caps have been hexagonal owing to a tendency for the knurled one failing to remain tight on particular engines inclined to vibrate.

An earlier type of damper used between 1938 and 1948 had a rather slender centre spoke which could be bent by rough handling, and if this happened the resulting side drag of the brass plunger on the inside bore of the piston rod could have a bad effect on the smoothness and uniformity of the piston lift.

In such a case straightening and truing of this centre spoke is necessary, followed by a check to see that the piston falls smoothly and evenly after assembly, when lifted by hand.

TYPES OF NEEDLES AND SEATS IN FLOAT LIDS

There are two sizes of needle seatings in common use, both made from .338" A/C flat hexagon stock, and looking very similar on the outside, except that close to the six small radial holes, either one groove or two grooves are turned on the outside.

The one groove identifies the smallest type T1 seat, having a feed hole of .086" diameter, and is used on the size T1 float chamber when this is fed by a low-pressure petrol pump (eg, the SU L type pump); but it is also used by a high-pressure pump (eg, the SU high-pressure pump).

The seating with two grooves identifies the T2 seat having a .100" feed hole, and this is used on the T2 size float chamber when fed by a low-pressure pump.

It may be noticed that the stainless steel needle used with these seatings has been issued in the past with two differing types of pointed end. The original type, used up to 1954, had a straight coned point, whereas since that date a curved spearpoint has been used, as it has a slight mechanical advantage in operation.

Regarding the largest size float chamber, type T 4, of 3" outside diameter, this is only encountered rarely, chiefly on racing cars, and it uses two sizes of needle seating (both respectively $\frac{5}{32}''$ and $\frac{3}{16}''$ diameter feed holes, according to whether a high- or medium-pressure fuel feed is used).

A cautionary word is necessary about the practice of tapping the end of the stainless steel needle into the seating, using a light hammer or spanner end to improve the cutting-off effect and cure occasional or slow flooding. If this is done, the blows must be very light indeed, or the original finely machined seating will crumble slightly under the impacts and will be worsened, not improved.

If a suspected seating does not respond to this very mild impact treatment, and it has been checked that the flooding is not due to other parts or circumstances, then replacement seats and needles will be necessary.

Service replacement seatings and needles are supplied already matched together, pressure tested and sealed in small envelopes.

TYPES OF FLOAT CHAMBER HOLDING-UP BOLTS AND THEIR WASHERS

Early types of holding-up bolts used for attaching the float chamber to the main body casting employ a sunk cork ring for a seal, and as this is enclosed on three sides in the head of the bolt, it will last almost indefinitely providing no attempt is made to dig it out, when replacement is almost inevitable.

The cork ring type was followed by a different bolt using a simple flat seating made on to a solid flat aluminium washer, or its later successor, a rolled bronze washer.

These two washers were in turn displaced (but using the same bolt) by a set of three washers, twin fibre ones in the outer positions with a brass centre washer sandwiched between them.

GENERAL NOTES ON FLOAT CHAMBER DETAILS

The float chamber on fully-downdraught carburettors can be confused rather easily with the standard float chamber for the horizontal carburettor, but in fact it gives a $\frac{5}{16}''$ higher petrol level as the attachment arm is positioned much lower compared with the needle and seat mechanism in the lid. If this downdraught float chamber were used on a horizontal carburettor, fairly severe flooding would take place.

Regarding the hinged fork lever attached to the float lid, the mechanical fit of this, either axially or radially, is not important and a rather definite degree of play or slackness can be disregarded—it must not on any part suffer from even the slightest friction or tightness. The hinge pin itself, until 1955, was generally a loose sliding fit in the lugs on the lid, but since that date it has been made a light press fit—the later press fit is quite suitable for the old float lid.

The smaller T 1 and T 2 needle seats can be screwed into position with a hexagon box spanner .338″ across the flats, and there is no separate sealing washer between the seat and the lid. It is a metal to metal seal; but do not, on this account, put too much pressure on the box spanner or the seating may be distorted or the thread stripped.

The tickler pin has, since 1955, been generally discarded owing to the necessity on many layouts for making the top of the float chamber air-tight; and in the majority of cases service replacement lids will not have ticklers, even although the original fitting had.

When reconditioning a float chamber lid it is advisable to renew the twin fibre washers on the main fuel feed banjo bolt as old washers in this position can give a small but annoying leak.

1. PUMP SERVICE AND ADJUSTMENTS
TC—TD—TF—TF 1500 SERIES

Should it be found necessary to overhaul an SU fuel pump, particular attention should be paid to the condition of the diaphragm, valves, and contact breaker parts.

To examine these parts it is necessary to dismantle the pump completely (see illustration).

When reassembling, first see that all parts are clean. The valves should be fitted with the smooth side downwards. Care should be taken that the valve retaining clip in the delivery valve cage is correctly located in its groove. A thin hard red fibre washer should be fitted under and a medium one above the valve cage and also above the filter plug. The washer on the inlet union is a thick hard red fibre one.

The brass body of the old-type L pump has been replaced and entirely superseded by one of aluminium. The only difference besides that of material is the method of manufacture, which results in a minor alteration to the assembly.

In place of the original hot brass stamping with the back plate soldered in position, the aluminium body is an assembly of two pressure die castings held together by the screws, which secure it to the cast iron coil housing, a fabric gasket being used as a seal. These screws are longer than those used with the brass type, and are not interchangeable.

16—Fuel System

The contact breaker should be assembled on to the pedestal in such a way that the rockers are a free fit on it, but without side play. Excessive side play on the outer rocker permits the points to get out of line. Excessive thickness makes the contact breaker sluggish. It may be necessary to square up the outer rocker after assembly with a pair of thin-nosed pliers.

Soft wire must not be used for a hinge pin; the standard hinge pin is case-hardened.

The contact blade should be fitted next to the bakelite pedestal, that is, underneath the tag. It should rest against the ledge on the pedestal when the points are apart, and it must not be so stiff as to prevent the outer rocker from coming right forward when the points are in contact. The points should just make contact when the rocker is in its mid-way position. The simplest way to check this is to hold the blade in contact with the pedestal, being careful not to press on the overhanging portion, and then to test the gap between the white rollers and the cast iron body of the pump; it should be .030″. If necessary, the tip of the blade may be set in order to correct the gap.

The spring washer on the 2 BA screw to which the earthing connection is taken should be fitted below the tag, that is, next to the pedestal. The reason for this is that the spring washer cannot be relied on as a conductor, and the brass tag should therefore be next to the head of the screw.

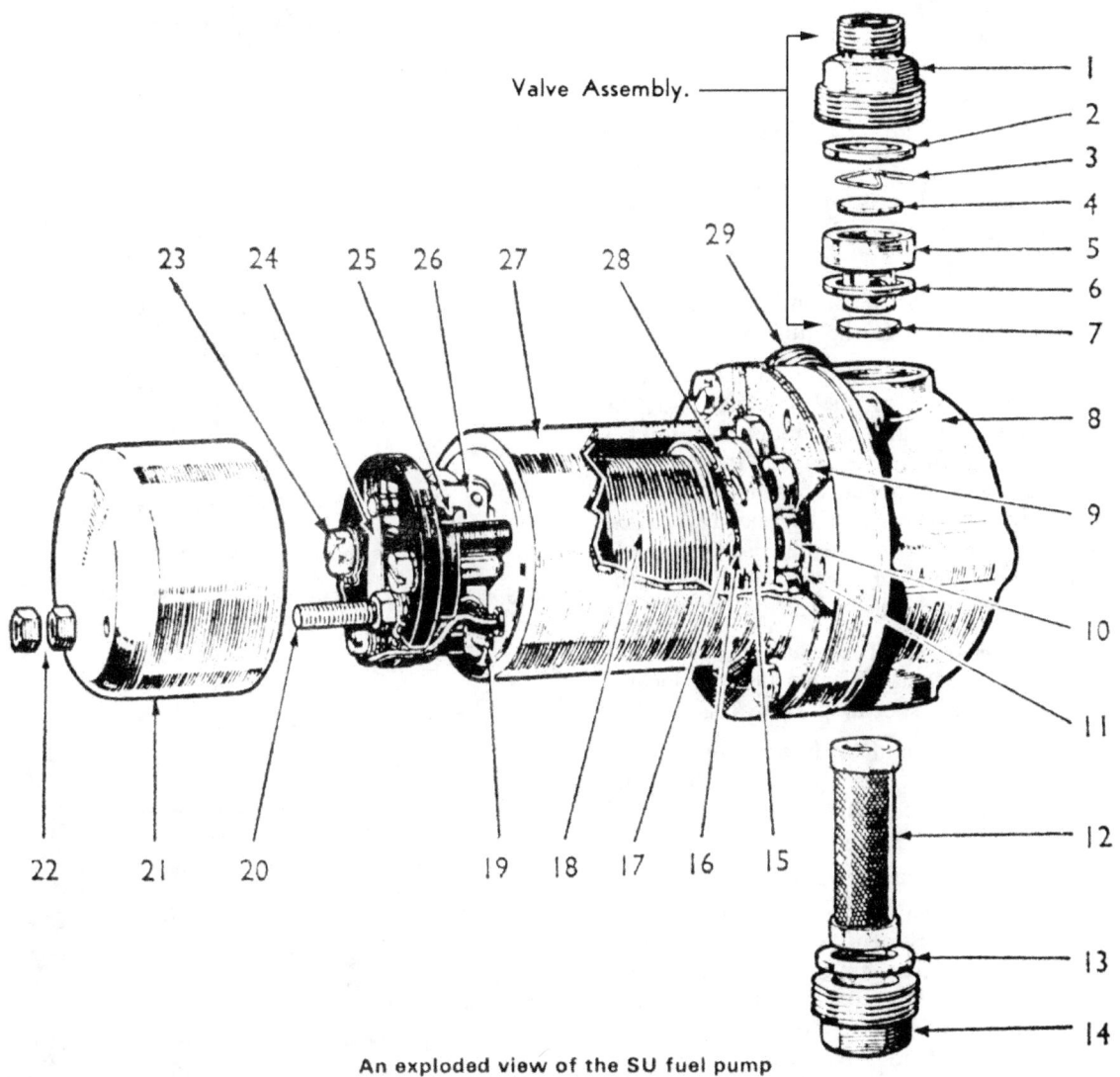

An exploded view of the SU fuel pump

1 Outlet union   2 Fibre washer (thick orange)   3 Spring clip   4 Delivery valve disc   5 Valve cage   6 Fibre washer
7 Suction valve disc   8 Pump body   9 Diaphragm assembly   10 Armature guide rollers   11 Retaining plate   12 Filter
13 Fibre washer (thick orange)   14 Filter plug   15 Steel armature   16 Push-rod   17 Magnet iron core   18 Magnet coil
19 Rocker hinge pin   20 Terminal screw   21 Cover   22 Cover and terminal nuts   23 Earth terminal screw
24 Spring blade   25 Inner rocker   26 Outer rocker   27 Magnet housing   28 Volute spring   29 Inlet union

 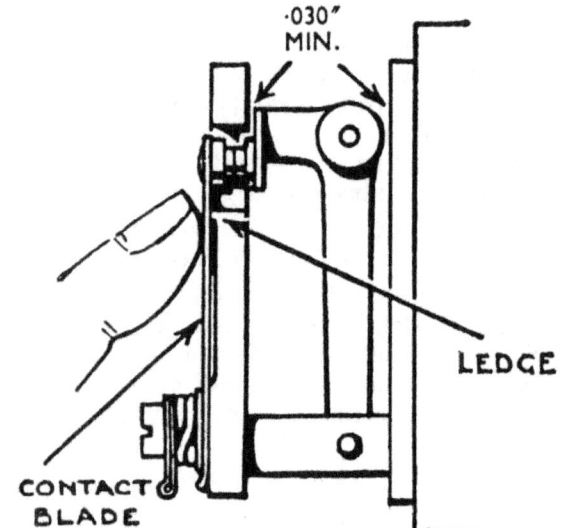

Measuring Correct Gap for Pump Points.

All four connections, that is, the two ends of the earthing tag and the two ends of the coil, should be soldered.

The coil end going to the terminal should be soldered to its tag and not to the nut.

The correct order for the assembly on the terminal, is the spring washer next to the bakelite pedestal, then the tag, lead washer, and a countersunk nut. A lead washer has been found necessary at this point as some cases of bad connection have been found. This assembly must never be shortened by leaving out the spring washer or by any other means, as this would probably result in breakage of the pedestal when the nut holding the cover in position was tightened.

Under no circumstances should any attempt be made to move the core of the magnet. This can only be located in position correctly with special press tools.

The armature spring should be fitted with its large diameter in the mouth of the pot and the small diameter resting against the armature. Do not stretch the spring.

The armature should be adjusted as follows:

(1) The contact blade on the pump must be swung to one side while the adjustment is being made. Care should be taken to see that an impact washer (see illustration) is fitted in the recess in the armature, and the latter should then be screwed in and the rollers put in position. There are eleven of these. Do not use jointing compound on the diaphragm.

(2) The magnet assembly should then be held in the left hand in an approximately horizontal position and the armature pushed in with the thumb of the right hand, pressing firmly but steadily.

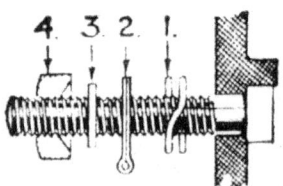

Terminal Assembly.

Fuel pump terminal screw, attachment to **pedestal**.

1 Spring washer 2 Coil end tag 3 Lead washer 4 Recessed nut

Checking the fuel pump armature setting

(3) If the contact breaker throws over, the armature should be screwed in farther until it does not. It should then be unscrewed one-sixth of a turn at a time until a point is found at which the contact breaker just throws over, care being taken that the armature is not jerked in but pressed in with a steady pressure.

(4) The armature should then be unscrewed a further two-thirds of a turn, that is, four holes, and the setting is correct. Do not forget that this is to be done with the points out of contact. When a new diaphragm is fitted, it is possible that considerable pressure will be required to push it right home. If there is any doubt about the point at which the contact breaker throws over, come back one-sixth of a turn.

(5) The cast iron magnet body should then be placed in position on the main body, the drain hole in the former being in line with the filter plug on the main body, that is, at the bottom.

(6) Care should be taken to see that the magnet body sits down on the main body before the screws which hold them together are inserted. If one of the rollers has fallen out of position, it will get trapped between the two parts and will cut a hole in the diaphragm.

(7) Five screws and the earthing terminal should then be fitted to hold the two parts together. (Later models have six screws and a separate earthing screw in a boss on the magnet casting). These should not be screwed right home at first. Before tightening them down it is absolutely necessary to stretch the diaphragm to its outermost position. This is most easily effected by using a special forked wedge, which can be made from ordinary mild steel to the dimensions given (see illustration).

This is inserted between the white rollers on the outer rocker and pressed in under the tips of the inner rocker until it lifts the trunnion in the centre of the inner rocker as far as it will go. If this is not available the diaphragm may be stretched by holding the points in contact by inserting a matchstick under one of the white fibre rollers and passing a current through the pump. While the diaphragm is held in this position the six screws (one an earthing terminal on early models) should be tightened down fully.

Three important points are frequently overlooked:

(1) Keep the blade out of contact while setting the diaphragm.

(2) Press steadily and firmly on the armature—do not bump—while setting.

(3) Stretch the diaphragm to the end of its stroke while tightening the screws.

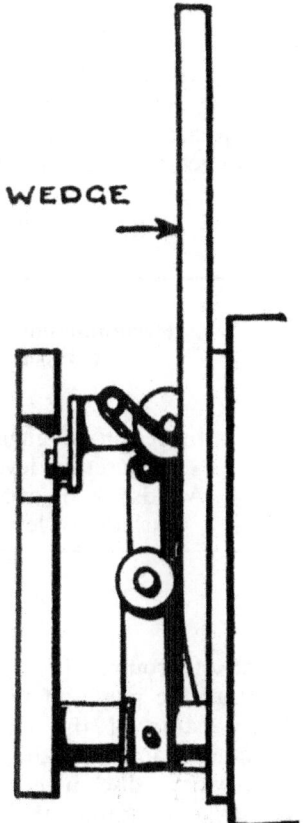

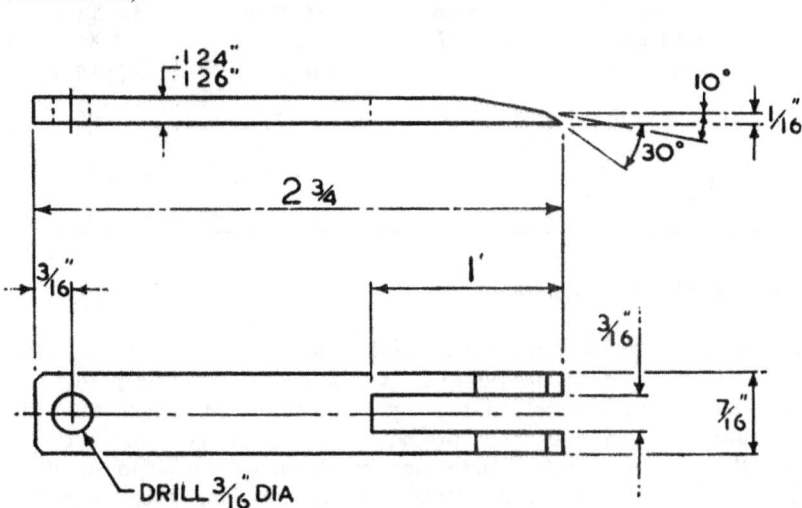

Diaphragm Stretching Wedge Dimensions

Using a forked wedge to position the fuel pump armature

2. TEST RIG

A special testing device is used by the makers and their agents and when testing a pump on one of these it is best to use a cut-away cover while testing the pump, as this prevents the hinge pin from falling out and at the same time make it possible to observe the action of the contact breaker.

When the pump is switched on it should prime promptly, and the kerosene, which is normally used for testing, should rise in the glass tube until it flows over the top of the pipe having a $\frac{5}{32}''$ hole drilled in it. If the output of the pump is not up to normal, the $\frac{5}{32}''$ hole will be able to carry all the kerosene pumped and the liquid will not flow over the top.

If by any chance there is an air leak in the pump or in its connections, bubbles will be seen coming out of the pipe projecting downwards into the flowmeter. Bubbles will certainly come through here for a short while after starting up, but they should cease after the pump has been running for a minute or so. The tap should then be turned right off and the pump should stand without repeating for at least 15 seconds. If it repeats, the foot valve is not seating correctly.

The tap should then be turned on slightly to see if the pump idles satisfactorily, and that the outer rocker comes forward till it makes contact with the pedestal, and while it is in this position the tip of the blade should be pressed inwards gradually to reduce the stroke of the pump. However much this stroke is reduced, the pump should go on pumping normally until it fails altogether owing to there being no gap left. If instead of pumping it buzzes, it usually indicates excessive flexibility in the diaphragm. This, of course, is not likely to be experienced with a new diaphragm. The tap should then be turned on again and the pump tested on 8 volts, and it should work satisfactorily under these conditions, although probably with a reduced output.

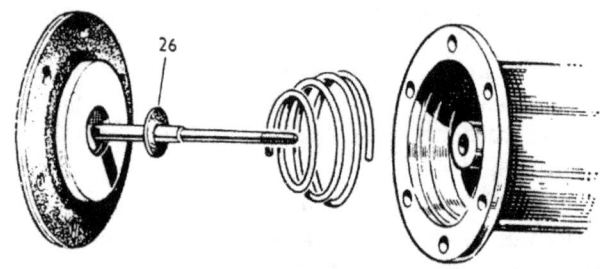

Diaphragm Spindle Impact Washer (26)

It is as well to let the pump run for ten minutes or so before carrying out these various tests. The cover, which is black for 12-volt, should then be fitted and held in place with an ordinary brass nut and an insulated dome nut fitted on the end of the terminal. The voltage of the pump can always be identified by the color of the sleeving on the coil ends, this being red, black or brown for 12-volt.

NOTE: A special attachment is required for testing type HP pumps. This attachment is easily fitted and can be obtained through the usual channels.

3. PUMP LOCATION

Type	Recommended Mounting Position	Fuel Pipe Outside Diameter	Maximum Output Gal/Hr	Maximum Suction Lift (approx)	Maximum Output Lift (approx)
L	In region of engine, at approx carburettor level	$\frac{5}{16}''$ single $\frac{3}{8}''$ dual	8	48''	24''
HP	Amidships or over rear tank, at carburettor level or just below	$\frac{5}{16}''$ single $\frac{3}{8}''$ dual	10	33''	48''

4. TROUBLESHOOTING

In the event of trouble, first disconnect the fuel delivery pipe from the pump. If the latter then works, the most likely cause of the trouble is a sticking needle in the float chamber of the carburettor. Should the pump not work, disconnect the lead from the terminal and strike it against the body of the pump to see if it sparks and therefore if any current is available in the wire. If the current is there, remove the bakelite cover and touch the terminal with the lead. If the pump does not operate and the points are in contact and a spark cannot be struck off the terminal, it is probable that there is some dirt on the points. These may be cleaned by inserting a piece of thin card between them, pinching them together and sliding the card backwards and forwards. If, when the wire is connected to the terminal and the tickler of the carburettor is depressed, the points fail to break, it is possible that there is either an obstruction in the suction pipe, which should be cleaned by blowing down it with a tyre pump, or something in the pump itself which is preventing a correct movement. This may be due either to the diaphragm having stiffened or to foreign matter in the roller assembly which supports the diaghragm.

The diaphragm should therefore be removed, and the whole assembly cleaned and reassembled in accordance with the instructions given in Assembling and Testing.

If the pump becomes noisy, look for an air leak on the suction side. The simplest way to check up on this is to disconnect the fuel pipe from the carburettor and allow the pump to pump fuel into a pint can. If the end of the pipe is then submerged in the fuel and bubbles come through, there must be an air leak, and it must be found and cured. Noise can also be caused by fuel boiling before it gets to the pump. This occurs most particularly on cars on which the fuel pipe runs near the exhaust pipe, and this is usually noticed in hot weather when slowing down after having been driving hard. This trouble can often be overcome by using a different brand of fuel.

If the pump keeps on beating without delivering any fuel, it is possible that a piece of dirt is lodged under one of the valves. This can be remedied by removing the top lid and unscrewing the valve cage in order to examine both valves.

A choked filter or an obstruction on the suction side will make the pump get very hot and eventually cause a failure. Make sure also that the six flange screws clamping the diaphragm are tight.

5. FUEL SYSTEM FAULT DIAGNOSIS

(1) ENGINE WILL NOT START

Possible cause — *Remedy*

(a) Lack of fuel in bowl. — Check fuel pump delivery, sticking or clogged needle valve.

(b) Engine flooded with fuel when cold, by excessive use of choke or accelerator. — Hold accelerator flat until engine starts and revise starting procedure.

(c) Engine flooded when hot, as in (b) above. — Hold accelerator pedal flat until engine starts.

(2) ENGINE STALLS AT IDLE SPEED

Possible cause — *Remedy*

(a) Incorrect adjustment of idling speed and/or jet adjustment nut. — Check and adjust.

(b) Carburettor float bowl flooding. — Check float level and for sticking needle valve or punctured float. Clean and blow out carburettor.

(c) Carburettor starving for fuel. — Check fuel delivery at needle valve. Clean and blow out carburettor. Check fuel pump.

(d) Carburettor to manifold attachment bolts loose. — Check and tighten bolts.

(e) Leaking carburettor flange or intake manifold gaskets. — Check and renew faulty gaskets.

(3) FLAT SPOT ON ACCELERATION

Possible cause — *Remedy*

(a) Sticky piston on carburettor. — Clean out piston assembly and oil piston rod lightly.

(b) Jet needle not concentric with jet tube. — Adjust for concentricity.

(4) ENGINE MISFIRES OR CUTS OUT AT HIGH SPEED

Possible cause — *Remedy*

(a) Obstruction in jet tube. — Clean and blow out jet tube.

(b) Low fuel level in float chamber or float chamber starving for fuel. — Check float level setting, check pump and supply lines.

(c) Failure of fuel pump to deliver fuel. — Overhaul fuel pump.

(d) Blockage in fuel tank pipe. — Remove blockage and clean pipe.

(e) Restriction in fuel pump filter. — Clean or renew filter.

(f) Air leak between fuel pump or tank. — Rectify air leak.

(g) Water in carburettor. — Drain and clean fuel system.

(5) EXCESSIVE FUEL CONSUMPTION

Possible cause — *Remedy*

(a) Float level too high. — Check and readjust float level.

(b) Air cleaner element dirty or requires renewal. — Clean element or renew.

(c) Jet tube adjustment giving rich mixtures. — Raise jet tube for correct range of mixtures.

(d) Jet needle of incorrect size. — Check and replace needle as necessary.

(e) Fuel pump delivery pressure too high. — Check and fit correct diaphragm spring.

(f) Faulty fuel pump diaphragm. — Overhaul fuel pump and renew as necessary.

(g) Leaks between fuel pump and fuel tank, or fuel pump and carburettor. — Check and rectify leaks.

(h) Choke not being fully returned to 'off' position. — Check free movement of choke control linkage.

(i) Jerky use of accelerator pedal. — Revise driving habits.

COOLING SYSTEM   TC—TD—TF—TF 1500 SERIES

1. RADIATOR

TO REMOVE (TC, TD CARS)

(1) Take off the bonnet by undoing the rear hinge bracket and withdrawing the bonnet rearwards from the front hinge.

(2) Detach the forward ends of the radiator stays, and disconnect the by-pass hose at the thermostat, the hose on the elbow at the pump and the main hose at the top of the thermostat.

(3) Take out the two large, shouldered bolts holding the radiator to the headlamp brackets.

(4) Remove the fixing nuts and locknuts from the mounting brackets. Note the position of the rubber buffers, retaining rings and washers.

(5) The shell and radiator block will then come away together.

Radiator drain tap

TO REMOVE (TF CARS)

(1) Take off the bonnet by undoing the rear hinge bracket and withdrawing the bonnet rearwards from the front hinge.

(2) Detach the forward ends of the radiator stays.

(3) Remove the bolt at each side bracket securing the radiator to the valances at the top.

(4) Remove the two set bolts screwing into captive nuts in the radiator grille at each side, accessible below the wings.

(5) Disconnect the by-pass hose at the thermostat, the hose on the elbow at the pump, the lower hose at the radiator and the main hose at the top of the thermostat.

(6) Unscrew and remove the nuts below the radiator securing it to the front cross-member.

(7) The shell and radiator block will then come away together.

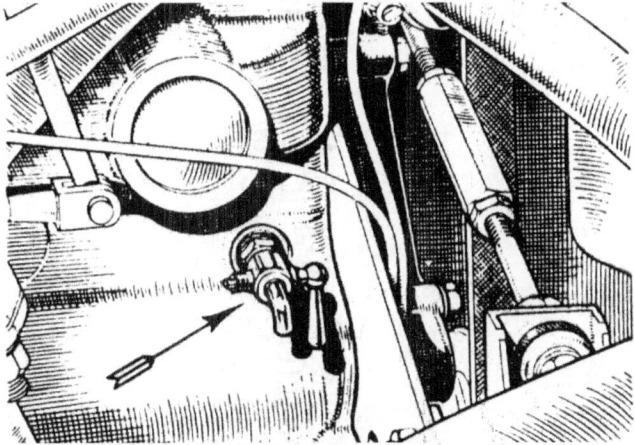

Drain tap on cylinder block

2. WATER PUMP

TO REMOVE AND INSTALL

(1) Drain the cooling system through the radiator and cylinder block drain taps, and release the generator on its mountings so that the driving belt may be withdrawn.

(2) Remove the valance tie-bar.

(3) Detach the rubber hose at the pump body and remove the fan blades by withdrawing the four attachment set screws complete with spring washers.

Model TF filler cap showing retaining cam on filler neck and safety lobes

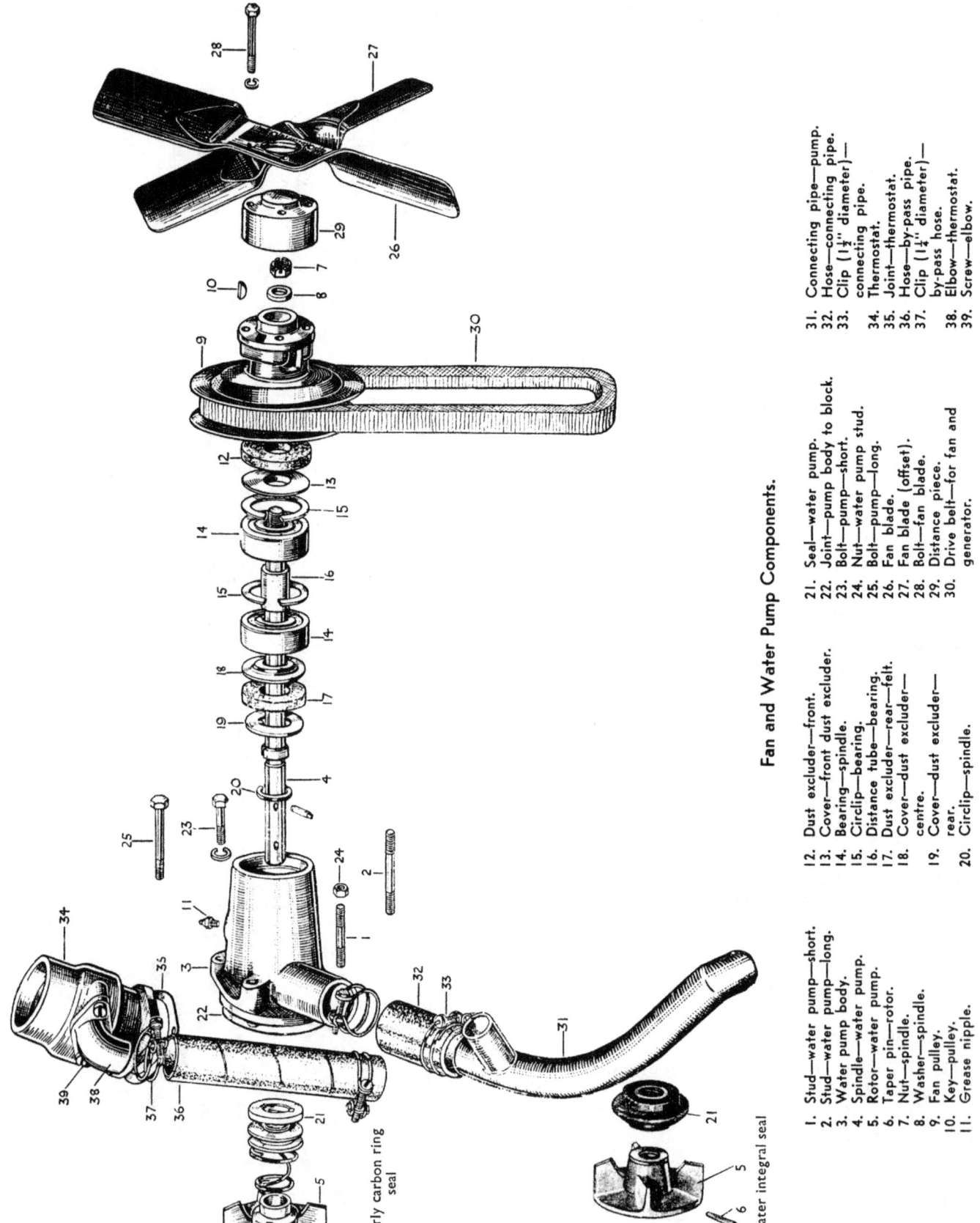

Fan and Water Pump Components.

1. Stud—water pump—short.
2. Stud—water pump—long.
3. Water pump body.
4. Spindle—water pump.
5. Rotor—water pump.
6. Taper pin—rotor.
7. Nut—spindle.
8. Washer—spindle.
9. Fan pulley.
10. Key—pulley.
11. Grease nipple.
12. Dust excluder—front.
13. Cover—front dust excluder.
14. Bearing—spindle.
15. Circlip—bearing.
16. Distance tube—bearing.
17. Dust excluder—rear—felt.
18. Cover—dust excluder—centre.
19. Cover—dust excluder—rear.
20. Circlip—spindle.
21. Seal—water pump.
22. Joint—pump body to block.
23. Bolt—pump—short.
24. Nut—water pump stud.
25. Bolt—pump—long.
26. Fan blade.
27. Fan blade (offset).
28. Bolt—fan blade.
29. Distance piece.
30. Drive belt—for fan and generator.
31. Connecting pipe—pump.
32. Hose—connecting pipe.
33. Clip (1½" diameter)—connecting pipe.
34. Thermostat.
35. Joint—thermostat.
36. Hose—by-pass pipe.
37. Clip (1¼" diameter)—by-pass hose.
38. Elbow—thermostat.
39. Screw—elbow.

(4) Undo the four bolts with spring washers attaching the pump body to the cylinder block, noting that they are of different lengths, and withdraw the pump unit.

(5) To install, reverse the removal procedure making sure the flange washer is in good order and that the pump bolts are replaced in their correct positions.

TO DISMANTLE AND REASSEMBLE

The water pump is fitted to the front face of the cylinder block, and is driven by a belt from the crankshaft. This belt also drives the generator. The pump is fitted with a special carbon gland ring which provides a water seal and needs no lubrication or adjustment. In the early life of the car a slight leak may occur, but this will automatically cease as the carbon ring beds itself down. Should it be necessary to dismantle the unit, proceed as follows:

(1) Take off the fan blades and remove the fan belt.

(2) Remove the pump unit by breaking the joint between the impeller housing flange and the cylinder block, moving the inner control link bracket outwards to clear.

(3) Dismantle the pump by removing the impeller from the shaft, tapping out the taper pin attaching it to the shaft and taking care to see that it is knocked out in the right direction.

(4) Withdraw the pressure spring and washer which gives access to the carbon seal and gland washer assembly. Care should be taken not to damage the carbon ring, which is relatively brittle, the working face of the rubber seal, and not to lose the driving pin for the carbon gland, which is a loose fit in the shaft.

(5) The pump spindle is carried on two ball races, which should give no trouble unless they have been neglected. Access to the races is obtained by releasing the impeller and gland as described above, removing the drive pin for the gland, removing the attachment nut in the centre of the drive pulley, withdrawing the pulley, pulley key, felt sealing ring and retainer.

(6) Remove the outer bearing circlip, with a pair of long-nosed pliers.

(7) Pour a little kerosene into the impeller body around the outer bearing and tap the inner end of the spindle on a piece of wood until the outer bearing can be withdrawn. This will release the distance piece between the bearings, which can be withdrawn, giving access to the inner race.

(8) Remove the inner circlip by contracting the ring and inserting a screwdriver behind it to ease it out of its groove. After removal of the circlip the retaining bearing and the impeller spindle can be withdrawn.

(9) If the felt oil sealing rings are badly worn or the bearings unduly slack, they should be renewed. Carefully examine the carbon sealing ring for cracks or undue wear and renew if necessary. The face of the brass sealing washer should be examined for flatness and all edges should be freed from burrs as this may damage the synthetic rubber seal. Fit a new seal if damaged.

(10) To reassemble, reverse the removal procedure, taking care that the flange jointing washer is in good condition.

(11) Partially fill the space between the two races with grease and liberally soak the felt washers in engine oil or grease before replacement.

(12) Do not over tighten the slotted nut retaining the pulley; as long as it is just firm it will be satisfactory.

TO ADJUST FAN BELT

(1) The adjustment of the generator and fan belt tension is effected by slackening slightly the two bolts on which the generator pivots, releasing the bolt securing it to the slotted link, and the nut securing the slotted link to the engine.

(2) Raise the generator bodily until the belt tension is correct.

(3) Tighten up the bolts with the generator in this position.

NOTE: A gentle hand pull only must be exerted on the generator, or the belt tension will be excessive and undue strain thrown on the generator bearings.

(4) To check the tension for correctness rotate the fan blades. If the generator pulley slips inside the fan belt, the tension is insufficient. When the tension is correct, it should be possible to move the belt from side to side to the extent of 1" at the centre of the longest belt run.

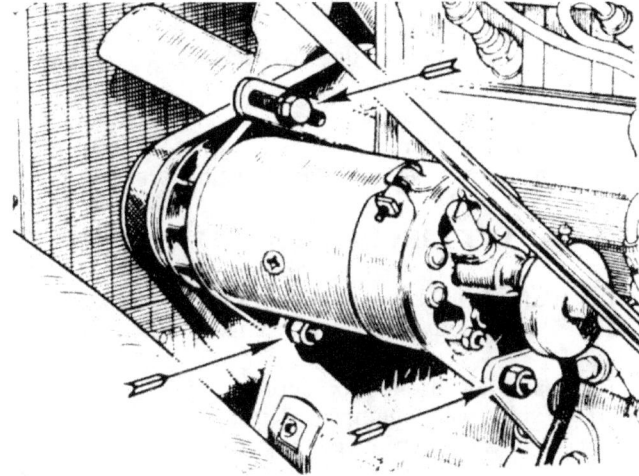

Bolts which must be Slackened for Fan Belt Adjustment.

3. COOLING SYSTEM FAULT DIAGNOSIS

(1) COOLANT LEAK—EXTERNAL

Possible cause — *Remedy*

(a) Loose hose clips or faulty hoses. — Tighten hose clips or renew faulty components.
(b) Leaking radiator core or tanks. — Repair or renew radiator.
(c) Worn or damaged water pump seal assembly. — Renew seal assembly.
(d) Worn or damaged water pump bearing assembly. — Renew water pump bearing and shaft assembly.
(e) Loose or rusted expansion plugs. — Renew faulty components.
(f) External crack in cylinder block or head. — Renew faulty components.
(g) Faulty cylinder head gasket or loose holding down bolts. — Renew gasket and correctly tighten cylinder head bolts.
(h) Leaks at thermostat cover and/or water pump joint gaskets. — Rectify leaks.

(2) COOLANT LEAKAGE—INTERNAL

Possible cause — *Remedy*

(a) Crack in cylinder bore wall. — Renew cylinder block.
(b) Crack in cylinder head, combustion chambers or valve ports. — Renew cylinder head.
(c) Cylinder head cracked and leaking into valve rocker compartment. — Renew cylinder head.
(d) Cracked cylinder block water jacket, leaking into engine tappet compartment. — Renew cylinder block.
(e) Cylinder head gasket leak due to warped head. — Reface cylinder head and renew gasket.

(3) COOLANT LOSS BY OVERFLOW

Possible cause — *Remedy*

(a) Over-full system. — Drain and refill to ½″ below filler neck.
(b) Faulty pressurised radiator cap. — Renew faulty cap.
(c) Blocked radiator core tubes. — Clean or renew radiator core.
(d) Coolant foaming due to poor quality anti-freeze or corrosion inhibitor. — Drain system and renew coolant and additive.

(4) ENGINE OVERHEATING

Possible cause — *Remedy*

(a) Obstructed air passage through radiator core from front to rear. — Blow out obstruction from rear to front of radiator core with compressed air or water pressure.
(b) Incorrect ignition timing. — Check and reset ignition timing.
(c) Incorrect valve timing. — Check and reset valve timing.
(d) Low engine oil level. — Stop engine immediately and replenish oil in sump.
(e) Engine tight after overhaul. — Check and if satisfactory, stop engine and allow to cool out.
(f) Poor circulation. — Check and rectify as under item (5).
(g) Loss of coolant due to overflow. — Check and rectify as under item (3).
(h) Faulty thermostat. — Renew thermostat.
(i) Restricted muffler or tail pipe, accompanied by loss of power. — Remove restrictions or renew component/s.
(j) Incorrectly adjusted or dragging brakes. — Check and rectify by adjustment or renewal of components.

(5) COOLANT CIRCULATION FAULTY

Possible cause — *Remedy*

(a) Partial blockage of radiator core tubes. — Clean out or renew radiator core.
(b) Water sludge deposits in engine water jacket. — Clean and flush engine water jacket and add rust inhibitor to coolant.
(c) Fan belt broken or slipping. — Renew or adjust fan belt.
(d) Faulty water pump or thermostat. — Overhaul or renew water pump, renew thermostat.
(e) Collapsing lower radiator hose. — Check and renew lower radiator hose and check radiator core tubes.
(f) Insufficient coolant in system. — Replenish coolant.

CLUTCH TC—TD—TF—TF 1500 SERIES

1. GENERAL DESCRIPTION

Operation of the Borg and Beck clutch as fitted to the TC, TD, TF and TF 1500 is by means of rod and cable with a later modification to rod only.

DRIVEN PLATE ASSEMBLY

This has a flexible centre in which the splined hub is indirectly attached to the clutch plate and transmits the power and over-run through a number of coil springs held in position by retaining wires. Two friction facings are riveted to the clutch plate, one on each side.

COVER ASSEMBLY

The cover assembly (see illustration) consists of a pressed-steel cover and a cast iron pressure plate loaded by six thrust springs. Mounted on the pressure plate are three release levers which pivot on floating pins retained by eyebolts. Adjusting nuts are screwed on to the eyebolts and secured by lock pins or staking. Struts are interposed between lugs on the pressure plate and the outer ends of the release levers. Anti-rattle springs load the release levers, and retainer springs connect the levers to the release lever plate.

RELEASE BEARING

The release bearing consists of a graphite bearing shrunk into a bearing cup, the cup being located by the operating arms and release bearing retainer springs.

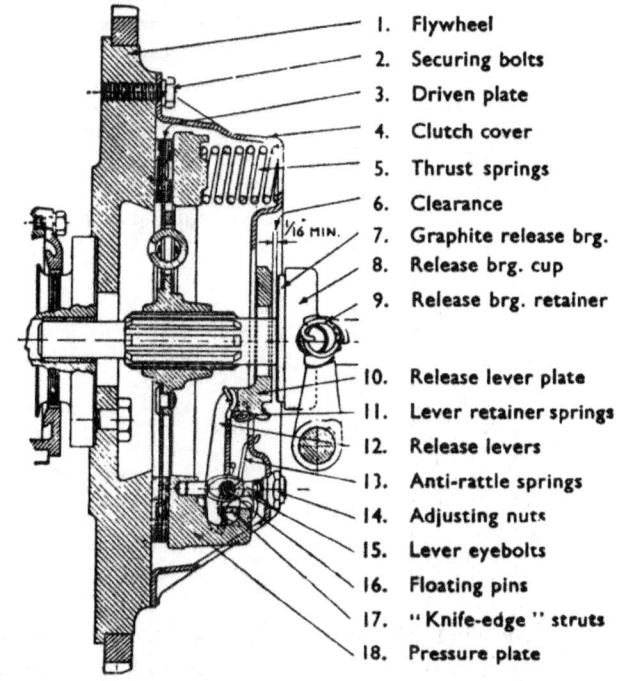

1. Flywheel
2. Securing bolts
3. Driven plate
4. Clutch cover
5. Thrust springs
6. Clearance
7. Graphite release brg.
8. Release brg. cup
9. Release brg. retainer
10. Release lever plate
11. Lever retainer springs
12. Release levers
13. Anti-rattle springs
14. Adjusting nuts
15. Lever eyebolts
16. Floating pins
17. "Knife-edge" struts
18. Pressure plate

Clutch in Section, Showing Disposition of Components (TC, TD, TF and TF-1500)

NOTE: The adjustment nuts are correctly set and locked when the clutch is assembled and should not be altered unless the clutch has been dismantled and new parts fitted. Interference with this adjustment will throw the pressure plate out of position and cause the clutch to judder.

2. ADJUSTMENTS

TO ADJUST PEDAL FREE MOVEMENT

The only adjustment necessary throughout the life of the driven plate facings is to restore periodically the free movement of the clutch pedal (ie, movement of the pedal before the release bearing comes into contact with the release lever plate and commences to withdraw the clutch). As the driven plate facings wear, the free movement of the pedal will gradually decrease, eventually preventing the clutch fully engaging and permitting too great a movement on withdrawal.

The minimum clearance **F** between the withdrawal lever plate and the face of the thrust bearing is $\frac{1}{16}''$, which gives a free pedal movement of $\frac{3}{4}''$ at the clutch pedal which should always be maintained.

When the clutch pedal free movement becomes less than this, it is essential to make use of the adjustment provided. This consists of an adjusting nut and locknut **A+B** at the forward end of the clutch operating cable. Care should be taken to tighten up the locknut after adjustment.

In addition, care must be taken to see that the pedal travel is not excessive, as this will apply an excessive load on the carbon thrust block, leading to its early failure. There should be approximately $1\frac{1}{8}''$ clearance between the stop nut and the abutment bracket when the pedal is slightly held with the carbon block in contact with the thrust ring by pushing lightly on the clutch pedal by hand. To obtain adjustment, grip the nut and slacken off the locknut; grip the adjuster shaft hexagon and adjust the stop nut to the required position. Retighten the locknut after adjustment. Need for this adjustment will be indicated when there is a tendency for the clutch not to free when the pedal is fully depressed.

The adjuster **E** is only for the initial adjusting of the outer cable length to give the correct flexibility between the pedal box and floating engine, and should require no subsequent setting.

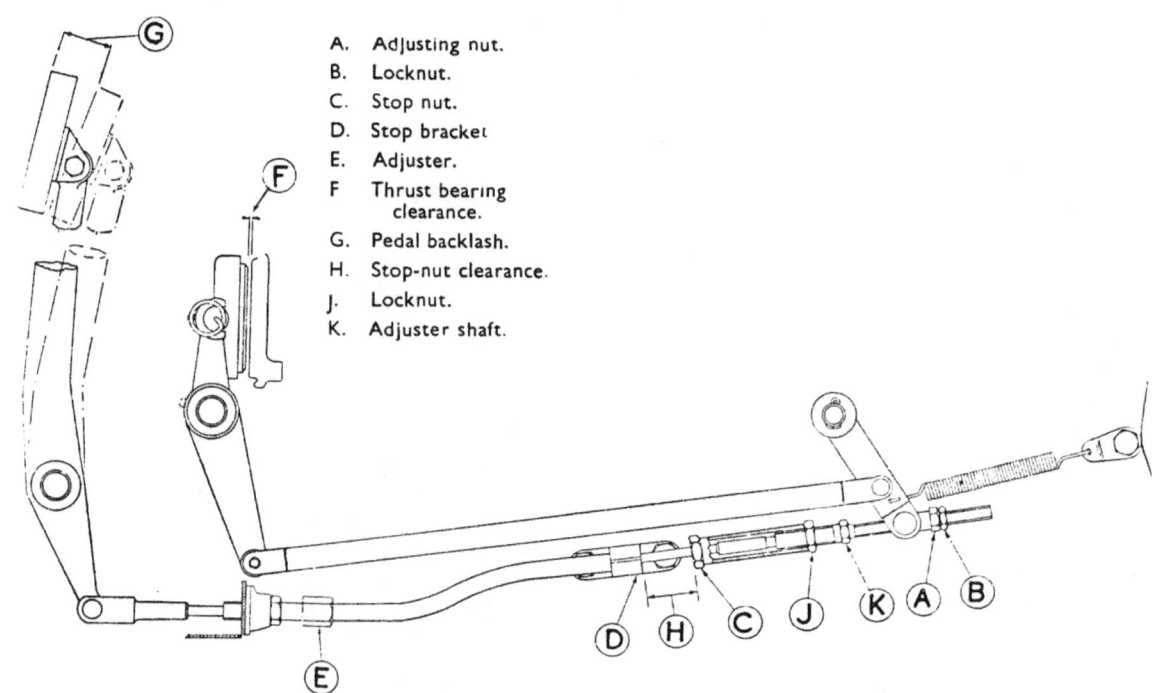

A. Adjusting nut.
B. Locknut.
C. Stop nut.
D. Stop bracket
E. Adjuster.
F. Thrust bearing clearance.
G. Pedal backlash.
H. Stop-nut clearance.
J. Locknut.
K. Adjuster shaft.

Clutch Operating Mechanism, Showing Pedal Adjustment (TC and early TD). On later TD, TF and TF-1500 the Operating Cable is Replaced by a Rod.

3. CLUTCH - SERVICE AND ADJUSTMENTS

TO REMOVE

(1) Remove the gearbox. The gearbox should be supported during this operation to prevent strain on the shaft and distortion of the driven plate assembly.

(2) Slacken the securing bolts a turn at a time by diagonal selection until the spring pressure is completely relieved.

(3) Remove the securing bolts and lift the complete clutch pressure plate and cover assembly away from the flywheel.

(4) Remove the driven plate assembly.

TO DISMANTLE

(1) Suitably mark the following parts in such a manner that they can be reassembled in the same relative positions to each other in order to preserve the balance and adjustment: cover, pressure plate lugs and release levers.

(2) Detach the release lever plate from the retainer springs and place the cover assembly under a press with the pressure plate resting on blocks of such a size that the cover is free to move downwards when pressure is applied.

(3) Place the block of wood across the top of the cover, resting on the spring bosses.

(4) Compress the cover, by means of the spindle of the press, and, while holding it under compression, remove the adjusting nuts and slowly release the pressure to prevent the thrust springs from flying out.

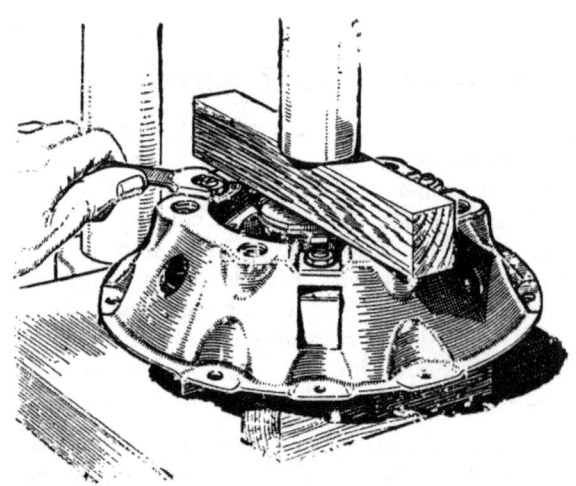

Correct Procedure to Adopt when Dismantling Clutch Cover Assembly. Note Two Wood Blocks Supporting Pressure Plate on Bed of Press. These must not Project Beyond the Pressure Plate to Ensure that they do not Foul the Cover Plate when this is Depressed by the Press.

KEY TO FLYWHEEL AND CLUTCH COMPONENTS.

1 Clutch pedal and bush 2 Pad—rubber—clutch pedal 3 Pad—brake pedal 4 Bolt—pad—brake pedal 5 Nut—pad bolt 6 Shaft—clutch 7 Seager circlip
8 Spacing washer—between pedals 9 Bush—brake pedal 10 Clutch cable assembly 11 Nut—clutch adjuster 12 Pin—clutch adjuster 13 Connecting rod—clutch
14 Yoke pin 15 Spring—clutch return 16 Pin—clutch lever 17 Dowel—clutch housing 18 Flywheel (with starter ring and dowels). 19 Dowel—clutch cover
20 Dowel—crankshaft 21 Bracket—clutch return spring 22 Bolt—bracket 23 Spring washer—bolt 24 Lever—cable and connecting rod 25 Bush—lever 26 Fulcrum pin—lever
27 Nut—fulcrum pin 28 Washer—fulcrum pin 29 Fulcrum pin—outer 30 Abutment bracket—clutch cable 31 Bolt—bracket 32 Cover—clutch 33 Release lever—clutch
34 Eyebolt and nut 35 Fulcrum pin—release lever 36 Strut—release lever 37 Spring—anti-rattle—release lever 38 Spring—retaining—release lever 39 Plate—release lever
40 Spring—pressure plate 41 Pressure plate—clutch 42 Clutch release bearing 43 Retainer—clutch release bearing 44 Clutch driven plate assembly
45 Rivet—clutch driven plate 46 Facing 47 Bolt—clutch cover 48 Clutch withdrawal shaft 49 Circlip—withdrawal shaft 50 Fork—clutch 51 Key—clutch fork
52 Taper pin—clutch fork 53 Clutch operating lever 54 Key—clutch lever 55 Taper pin—clutch lever 56 Clutch housing (with bushes) 57 Bush—clutch housing
58 Bolt—securing clutch housing 59 Clutch inspection cover 60 Screw—inspection cover 61 Bolt—flywheel securing

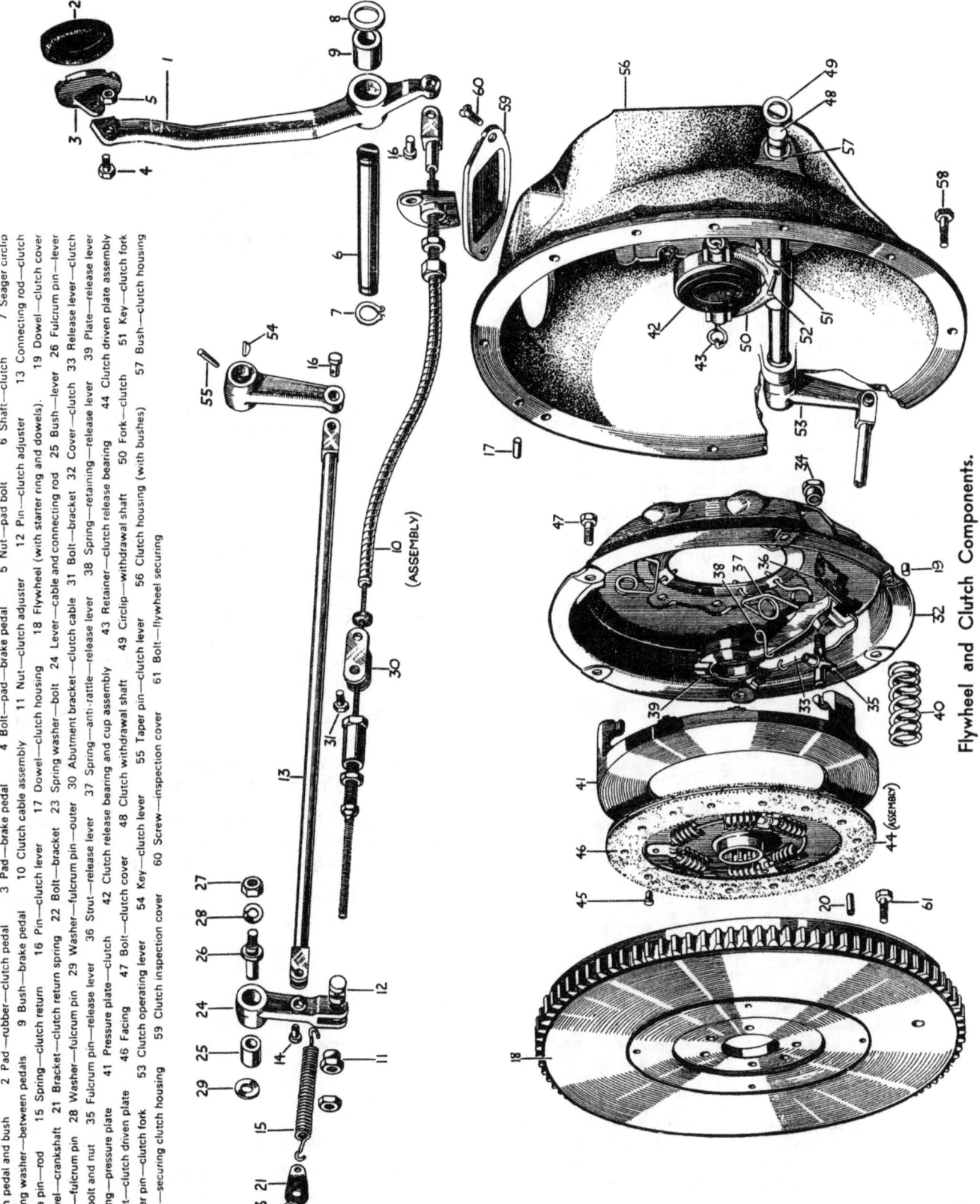

Flywheel and Clutch Components.

(5) Lift off the cover to expose all parts for inspection.

(6) Remove each release lever by grasping the lever and eyebolt between the finger and thumb so that the inner end of the lever and the threaded end of the eyebolt are as near together as possible, keeping the eyebolt pin in position in the lever.

(7) Lift the strut over the ridge on the lever and remove the eyebolt from the pressure plate.

TO ASSEMBLE

Before assembly, thoroughly clean all parts and renew those which show appreciable wear.

(1) Place the pressure plate on the blocks under the press and place the thrust springs in a vertical position on the plate, seating them on the bosses provided.

(2) Assemble the release levers, eyebolts and eyebolt pins, holding the threaded end of the eyebolt and inner end of the lever as close together as possible. With the other hand insert the strut in the slots on the pressure plate lug sufficiently to allow the plain end of the eyebolt to be inserted in the hole in the pressure plate. Move the strut upwards into the slot in the pressure plate lug and over the ridge on the short end of the lever, and drop it into the groove formed in the lever. Fit the remaining lever in a similar manner, taking care that they are being refitted into their original positions.

(3) Lay the cover over the assembled parts, ensur-

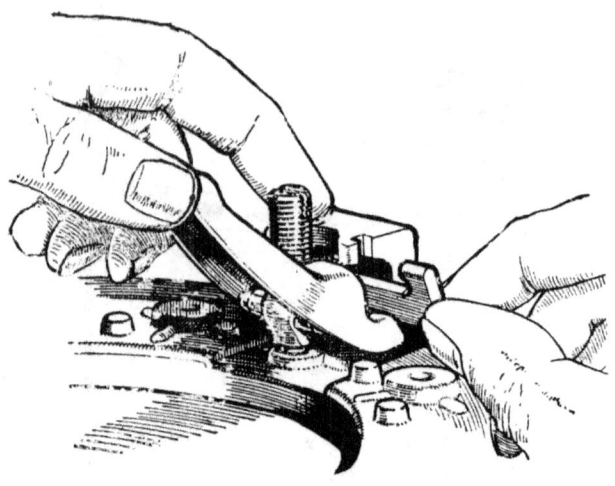

To Assemble Levers hold Threaded End of the Eyebolt and Lever close together as shown and with the other hand insert the strut in the slot of the Pressure Plate Lug sufficiently to permit the Plain End of the Eyebolt to be Inserted in the Hole in the Pressure Plate.

ing that the anti-rattle springs are in position and that the tops of the clutch springs are directly under the seats in the cover, also that the machined portions of the pressure plate lugs are directly under the slots in the cover through which they have to pass. Also ensure that the parts marked before dismantling are in their correct relative positions to maintain correct balance.

(4) Place the block of wood across the cover, and compress the clutch springs by means of the press spindle, guiding the eyebolts and pressure plate lugs through the holes in the cover.

(5) Screw the adjusting nuts on the eyebolts and secure by staking or split pins in accordance with the system originally used by the makers.

(6) Remove the clutch from the press, and assemble the lever plate on the tips of the levers and retainer springs.

NOTE: If new parts have been fitted, which may affect the adjustment, the levers should be set, using a gauge plate.

TO INSTALL

To install the clutch proceed as follows:

(1) Assemble the driven plate assembly in the flywheel, taking care to place the larger chamfered spline end of the driven plate hub towards the gearbox or the rear of the vehicle.

When Reassembling Clutch the Pressure Plate should be Supported on Wood Blocks used for Dismantling and Levers Assembled on their Shoulder Studs. The Thrust Springs should be placed in position on their Seatings, making sure that they remain correctly located when the Clutch Cover is placed in position. Make sure also that the Lever Anti-rattle Springs are properly located.

(2) Centralise the driven plate by means of the special clutch alignment bar T 124, which fits the splined bore of the driven plate hub and the pilot bearing in the flywheel. As an alternative a spare gearbox driving gear and shaft can be used.

Clutch plate aligning tool No. 18G.279 for Series TD clutch

(3) Fit the cover assembly to the flywheel by means of the securing bolts, tightening them a turn at a time by diagonal selection. Do not remove the clutch alignment bar until all the bolts are securely tightened.

(4) Remove the clutch alignment bar and instal the withdrawal bearing and the gearbox. The weight of the gearbox must be supported during installation in order to avoid strain on the shaft and distortion or displacement of the driven plate assembly.

4. MODIFICATIONS

INTRODUCTION OF THE 8" DIAMETER CLUTCH

Commencing at engine No 9408, an 8" diameter clutch was introduced. This was done to alleviate the synchro noise condition and to improve the torque carrying capacity.

The engine type description has been altered from XPAG/TD to XPAG/TD/2. This has been done for the reason that while the power unit with gearbox complete is interchangeable, neither the engine unit nor the gearbox unit separately is interchangeable with previous engines, because the clutch thrust race is in a different position relative to the engine bell housing, and the clutch shaft and thrust face position is also different in the gearbox bell housing.

The XPAG/TD gearbox can be identified by the clutch fork shaft, which has a diameter of ⅝" and the part No SA 1906/9, whereas the XPAG/TD/2 has a clutch with a fork shaft having a diameter of ¾" and the part No SA 1906/10.

INTRODUCTION OF A CLUTCH CONTROL ROD

Commencing at the chassis No TD22251, a clutch control rod was fitted in place of a clutch cable. On such cars the free pedal movement must also be maintained at ¾".

CLUTCH WITHDRAWAL LEVER PIVOT BOLT

On later types a modified clutch withdrawal lever pivot bolt (part No 11G3196) is fitted. The bolt is increased in diameter and has a shoulder to provide an abutment for the self-locking nut (part No LNZ 206) which supersedes the nut and spring washer previously fitted.

A larger bearing bush for the withdrawal lever is needed and so a modified lever (part No 11G3193) complete with bush is fitted. The bosses on the front cover (part No 11G3197) are modified to take the larger diameter bolt.

The modified parts as a whole can be fitted to earlier vehicles.

5. CLUTCH FAULT DIAGNOSIS

(1) CLUTCH SLIPPING

Possible cause	Remedy
(a) Throw-out lever free play adjustment (rod and/or cable operated clutches).	— Check throw out lever free play and adjust to specifications.
(b) Worn driven plate.	— Check and renew driven plate.
(c) Worn or scored flywheel face.	— Renew flywheel and ring gear.

(2) CLUTCH SHUDDER

Possible cause	Remedy
(a) Oil on (gummy) driven plate facings.	— Check and renew driven plate.
(b) Scored pressure plate or flywheel face.	— Renew pressure plate and cover assembly or flywheel and ring gear.
(c) Loose or damaged engine mountings.	— Check and renew mountings as necessary.
(d) Loose or damaged driven plate hub.	— Check and renew driven plate.
(e) Loose driven plate facings.	— Renew driven plate.
(f) Cracked pressure plate face.	— Renew pressure plate and cover assembly.

(3) CLUTCH GRAB

Possible cause	Remedy
(a) Gummy driven plate facings.	— Renew driven plate.
(b) Cracked pressure plate face.	— Renew pressure plate and cover assembly.
(c) Loose or broken engine mountings.	— Check and renew engine mountings as necessary.

(4) THROW OUT BEARING NOISE

Possible cause	Remedy
(a) Dry or seized bearing.	— Check and renew bearing.
(b) Incorrect throw-out lever free travel adjustment.	— Check and readjust to specifications.
(c) Faulty or broken pressure plate springs.	— Check and renew pressure plate and spring assembly.

TC SERIES
1. GEARBOX DISASSEMBLY

TO REMOVE

Having removed the ramp plate proceed as follows:

(1) Drain the gearbox, remove the gearbox lid and propeller shaft tunnel.

(2) Remove the starter motor, uncouple the clutch operating link at its forward end and let it hang on the clutch pedal.

(3) Then uncouple the propeller shaft at the front end.

(4) The steering box complete with bracket must be unbolted from the frame and the exhaust pipe between the exhaust manifold and the silencer removed.

(5) The clutch operating lever will then have to be removed from the clutch withdrawal shaft, after first drawing out the taper pin.

(6) The bolts securing the clutch housing to the flywheel housing can then be removed, when the gearbox complete can be withdrawn.

TO DISMANTLE

The dismantling of the gearbox is a comparatively simple operation.

(1) Remove the gearbox top—care must be taken that the selector ball springs are not lost. Their positions can be seen at the rear of the gearbox casing (see illustration).

(2) Remove the propeller shaft flange. Before doing so, however, it is necessary to mark both the flange and the shaft so that it can be replaced in exactly the same position. The rear cover can then be removed, also the rear engine support plate, the rearmost ball bearing, distance tube and speedometer driving gear.

(3) The clutch housing must then be removed from the gearbox casing.

(4) Remove the layshaft locking screw, which is found underneath the gearbox casing and withdraw the layshaft, allowing the gear unit to fall into the bottom of the box.

(5) Remove the selector operating gear, taking care not to lose the two interlocking balls found between the selector shafts at the rear end.

(6) Engage second gear; it must be fully engaged to give the necessary clearance for removing the mainshaft.

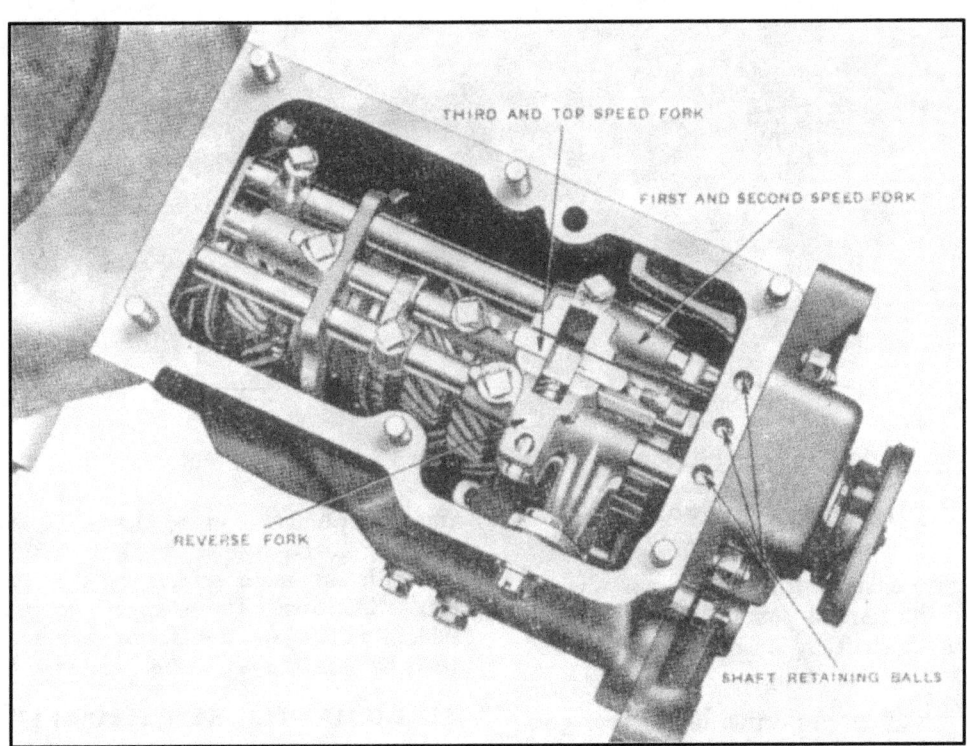

Gearbox with Top Removed Showing Selector Mechanism.

(7) The first motion shaft can then be removed complete with ball race.

(8) The mainshaft rear ball race must now be removed.

(9) The mainshaft can then be withdrawn from the gearbox casing.

(10) The reverse gear and its operating mechanism are now the only parts left in the casing, and it remains only to remove the locking screw securing the reverse gear shaft from the side of the box, also the bolt securing the actuating lever, for the whole of this mechanism to be removed.

The layshaft bearings and spacer tube are retained inside the layshaft gears by steel dowels which fit the internal bore, over which are pressed steel washers which make surfaces for the bronze thrust washers. As they are of different sizes, they cannot very well be confused.

TO REMOVE THIRD SPEED CONSTANT MESH GEAR

This gear is retained on the mainshaft by a splined ring locked in position by a spring and plunger. It will be noted that the ring has two slots cut in the outer face to enable the plunger to be depressed. The locking ring can then be rotated until its male splines match with the female splines of the mainshaft and withdrawn.

The plunger can then be removed, which will in turn allow the gear wheel and its rollers to be removed.

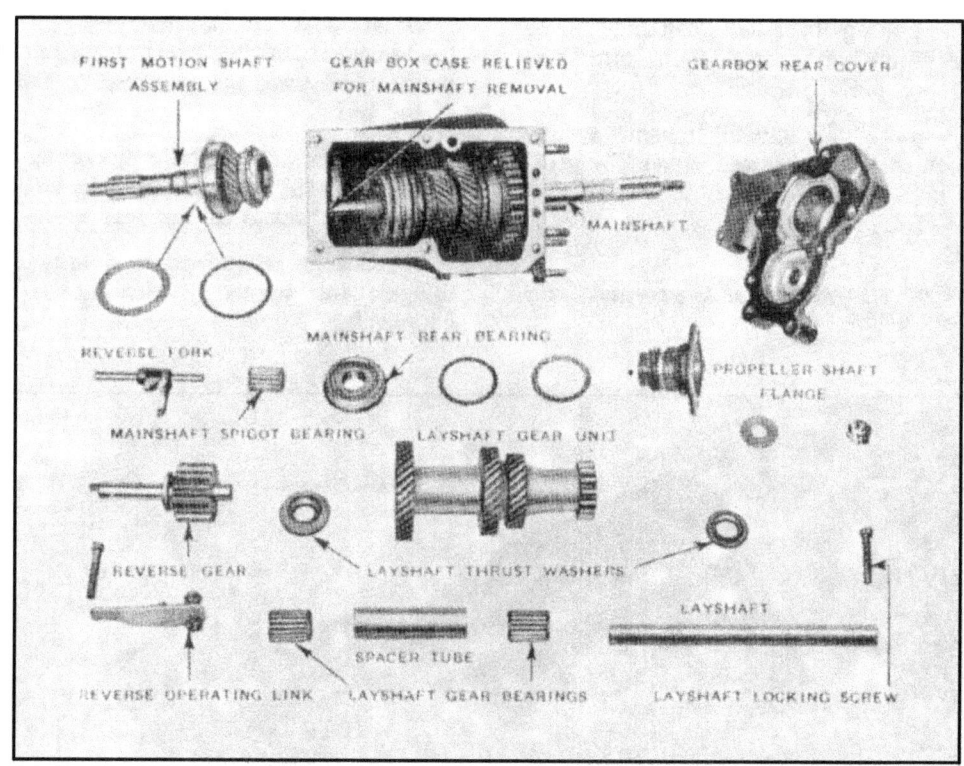

Exploded View of Gearbox Components.

TO RENEW SECOND SPEED CONSTANT MESH GEAR

The retaining arrangement for this gear is slightly different from the third speed gear. This gear is also retained on the main shaft by a splined ring locked in position by a spring and plunger.

The two holes in the coned portion of the gear give access to the plunger. By inserting a split pin through the hole in the gear and the hole in the splined ring the plunger can be depressed, which will allow the ring to be rotated until its female splines match up with the male splines of the mainshaft and the ring withdrawn. The plunger can then be removed, which will allow the needle roller retaining washer (two halves), the gear wheel and rollers to be removed.

TO DISMANTLE SYNCHROMESH MECHANISM

The striking dogs for top and third and second gears are retained on sliding hubs by balls and springs which are housed in their sliding hub. Therefore each sliding hub can be pushed out from its striking dog when sufficient effort is applied to overcome the springs.

2. GEARBOX REASSEMBLY

TO REASSEMBLE SYNCHROMESH MECHANISM

The six balls and springs must be fitted in the sliding hub and compressed by a special tool (part No T83).

The sliding hub can now be pushed into the striking dog and the tool withdrawn, when the balls will spring into an indentation ground in the centre of the teeth.

TO REASSEMBLE GEARBOX

To reassemble the gearbox reverse the dismantling operations. There are several points, however, that need special mention, which are as follows:

(1) Before putting the layshaft gears into the bottom of the box, do not forget to insert both roller bearings and the spacer tube, also the steel and bronze thrust washer assemblies. It must be remembered that the layshaft should not be replaced until the main shaft and first motion shaft have been fitted.

(2) When assembling the third speed constant mesh gear to the main shaft it is essential that the roller bearings are perfectly clean. The locking plunger and spring must be placed in the shaft, followed by the splined locking ring (see illustration). It is important to note that on the outer face of the locking ring two slots are cut. These must line up with the plunger when in the locked position. They are intended to give access to the locking plunger, to enable it to be depressed so that the locking ring may be turned to release the gears. When sliding on this locking ring, the plunger can be depressed through a hole drilled between the constant mesh gear and the striking dog mating gear.

(3) When reassembling the second speed constant mesh gear on the mainshaft the procedure is slightly different (see illustration). There are twenty-four rollers, which can be held in position with a little grease. The locking plunger spring must first be placed in position, when the second speed constant mesh gear can be slid into place. The two steel half washers should next be inserted inside the gear next to the rollers so that their protrusions line up between two splines. The splined locking ring can then be placed in position (with the slots cut on its inner face in line with the protrusions on the two half washers), having first depressed the plunger through the hole indicated. This allows the locking ring to be turned until the plunger springs up into spline and locks it.

(4) Before entering the mainshaft into the gearbox complete with its gears, do not forget to engage second gear, giving sufficient clearance to allow the spigot on the front end of the mainshaft to clear the gearbox casing.

(5) The mainshaft rear ball race can then be fitted.

The oil thrower washer, however, must be placed between the ball race and the second gear synchromesh hub with its outer edge clear of the ball race. Next to this ball race must be fitted two large steel

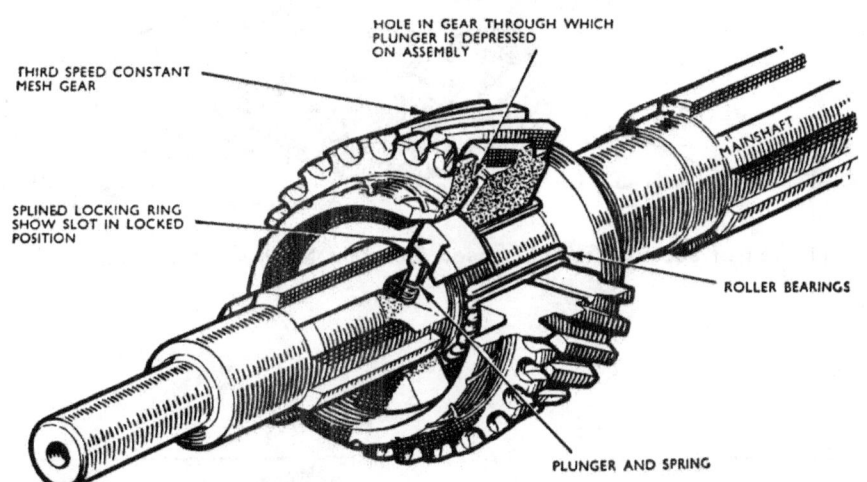

Method of Securing Third Speed Constant Mesh Gear to Mainshaft.

washers, the wide one next to the ball race and the thin one following it. The thin steel washer is of the belleville type and is designed to eliminate any slight variation between the ball race and its recess in the cover. It is important, therefore, that it is fitted the right way round, i.e., its inner diameter towards the large flat steel washer. After this the speedometer driving gear and gearbox rear cover are fitted.

(6) When installing the first motion shaft do not forget to insert the mainshaft roller race.

(7) The selector mechanism can then be installed, not forgetting the two interlocking balls between the selector shafts.

(8) After installing the layshaft do not forget to lock it with the locking screw from underneath the gearbox.

(9) When installing the clutch housing do not forget to replace the two steel washers, the wider one going next to the ball race, the thinner one following it. The same remarks apply to these washers as to those fitted to the mainshaft rear bearing. See step 5.

(10) Before installing the gearbox top do not forget to insert the three locating balls and springs.

(11) After the gearbox has been installed do not forget to refill it with the recommended lubricant.

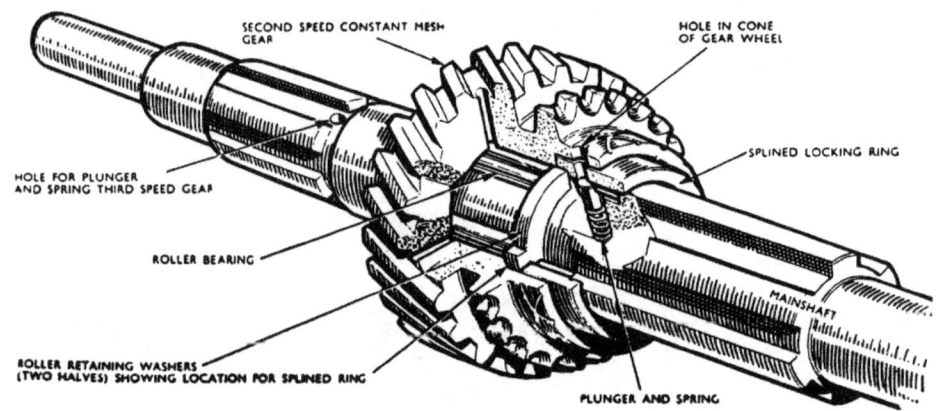

Method of Securing Second Speed Constant Mesh Gear to Mainshaft.

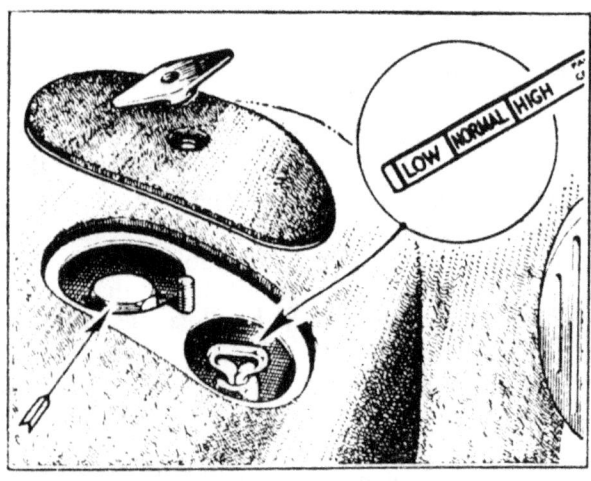

Gearbox filler and dipstick

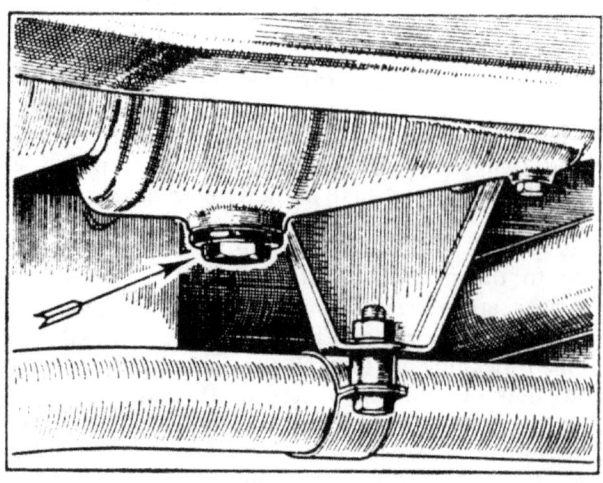

Gearbox drain plug

TD—TF—TF 1500 SERIES
1. GEARBOX DISASSEMBLY

TO REMOVE

(1) Remove the floor mats and take up the floorboards. Take off the gearbox cowl.

(2) Disconnect the propeller shaft at its forward end, marking the flanges so that they can be replaced in the same relative position on reassembly.

(3) Jack up the engine unit under the rear of the sump, using a large piece of wood between the jack and the sump to spread the load, and disconnect the speedometer drive at the gearbox end.

(4) Disconnect the clutch operating lever from its connecting rod and release the rear engine unit mounting by removing the two nuts and bolts of the rubber mounting.

(5) Undo all the retaining screws holding the bell housing to the crankcase and lift out the gearbox, taking care not to place any load on the drive gear shaft and clutch centre.

TO DISMANTLE GEARBOX

(1) Support the gearbox in a vice by means of a piece of steel bar approximately 1½" square by 15.0" long, this being suitably machined and threaded at one end to enable it to be screwed into the gearbox drain plug hole.

(2) Remove the dipstick from the gearbox and drain off the oil.

(3) Release the clutch housing by removing the fixing bolts and spring washers. Extract the split pin from the nut retaining the drive flange at the rear of the gearbox sliding shaft and remove the nut and plain washer.

(4) Remove the six nuts securing the top cover assembly to the gearbox and the four bolts and spring washers securing the remote control cover assembly to the gearbox extension. Pick out the three selector springs.

(5) Using the extractor, tool No T108, withdraw the propeller shaft driving flange. It is advisable to use an extractor of this type to avoid distortion of the flange face. Before doing so, it is advisable to mark both the flange and the shaft so that it can be replaced in exactly the same position.

(6) Detach the speedometer drive housing from the gearbox. Care should be exercised not to damage the paper gasket on the joint face of the housing.

(7) Extract the lock-wire from the eight square-headed screws locking the gear shifters and stops to the selector shafts and remove the screws.

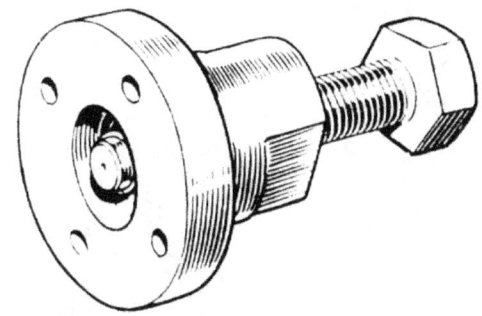

Extractor No. 18G 371 for universal joint flanges

(8) Slacken the nuts and set bolts securing the gearbox rear casing to the gearbox and withdraw sufficiently to allow the gear shifters to be removed from the ends of the selector shafts. Remove the nuts and set bolts completely and withdraw the gearbox rear casing from the gearbox.

(9) On early type gearboxes withdraw the selector shafts one at a time, taking care not to lose the selector lock balls in the process. Later models have the 3rd and top selector shaft extended at its front end and fitted with a circlip to prevent its accidental withdrawal and the loss of the synchromesh balls. In this case the circlip must, of course, be removed before the shaft can be withdrawn. This also makes it imperative to remove the gearbox from the engine before dismantling. Now lift out the selector forks. Observe the correct position of the gear shifters and stops on the selector spindles.

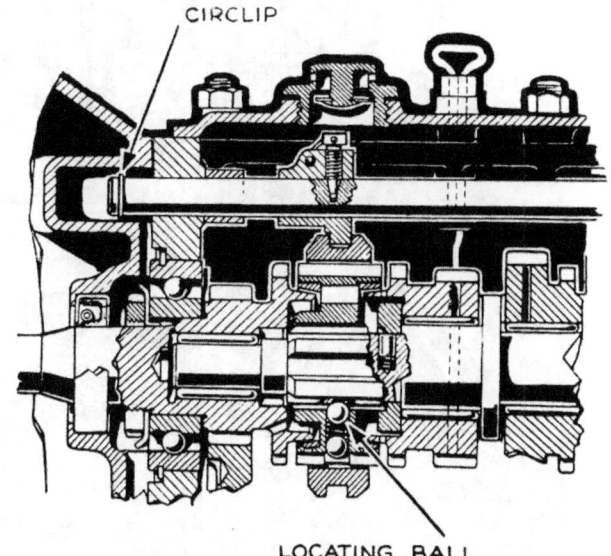

Part Section of Gearbox showing Lengthened Third Speed Shifter Shaft with Retaining Circlip and Location of Additional Detent Ball in the Synchromesh Hub.

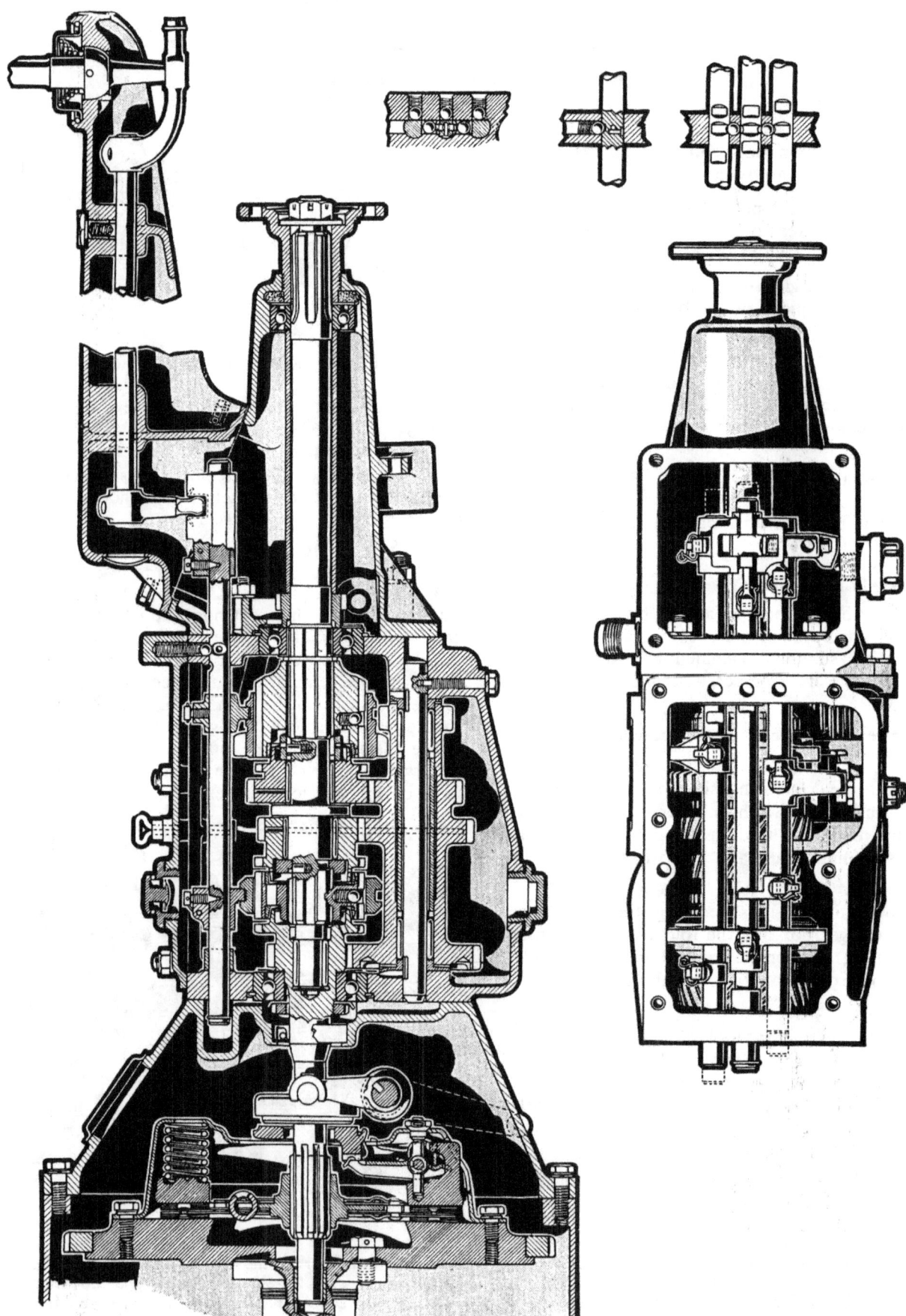

Section and Plan Views of Gearbox.

(10) Remove the layshaft spindle locating screw from the rear of the gearbox.

(11) Extract the layshaft spindle by tapping it at the forward end with a suitable copper or brass drift.

(12) Remove the drive gear with its journal bearing by tapping the mainshaft towards the front of the gearbox.

(13) Before the mainshaft can be removed it is necessary to extract the journal bearing from its housing. The mainshaft assembly can then be withdrawn from the gearbox.

(14) Extract the layshaft gear unit, observing that the tabs on the thrust pads line up with the slots cut in the boss at the front rear walls of the gearbox.

TO DISMANTLE MAINSHAFT

(1) Withdraw the top and third gear synchromesh hub from the forward end of the shaft, observing that the plain side of the hub goes to the rear of the gearbox.

(2) Remove the third speed gear collar by pressing down the spring-loaded locking plunger and rotating the collar until the female splines register with the male splines on the mainshaft. The third gear can now be withdrawn.

(3) Care must be exercised to prevent the loss of the plunger and spring or the thirty-two needle bearings on which the third gear is mounted.

(4) Extract the circlip from the rear end of the mainshaft and remove the first and second gear synchromesh hub; the conical lining end of the hub faces to the front of the gearbox.

(5) The withdrawal of the second gear from the mainshaft is executed in a similar manner to that for the third gear, namely, by pressing down the locking plunger through the hole provided and rotating the collar until the two sets of splines coincide. Again, care must be exercised not to lose the spring and plunger or the twenty-eight needle bearings. It must be noted that next to the second gear collar is a thrust washer, which is in two halves, having tongues which engage with slots in the forward face of the collar. It is important that this washer is correctly replaced on reassembly to centralise the collar.

TO DISMANTLE SYNCHROMESH MECHANISM

The striking dogs for top, third and second gears are retained on sliding hubs by balls and springs which are housed within the sliding hubs and register with a central groove in the internally cut teeth of the striking dogs. Each sliding hub, therefore, can be pushed out from its striking dog when sufficient effort is applied to overcome the springs.

The ball housing openings are peened over to retain the balls in position.

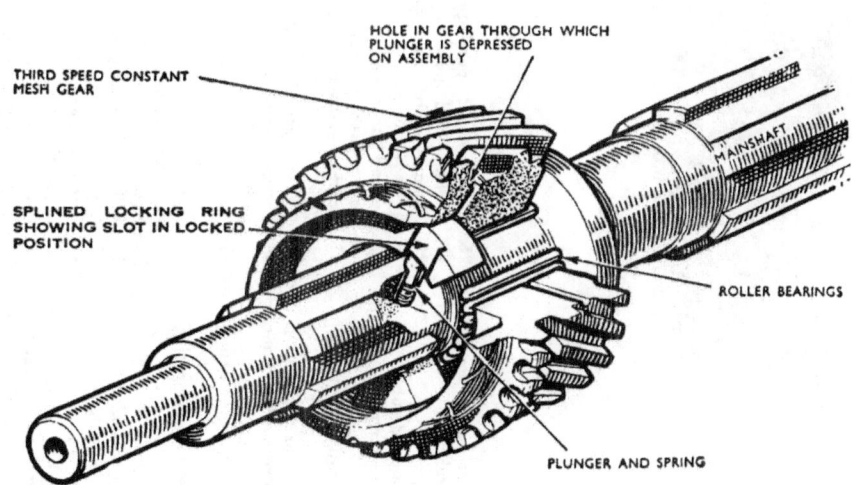

Method of Securing Third Speed Constant Mesh Gear to Mainshaft.

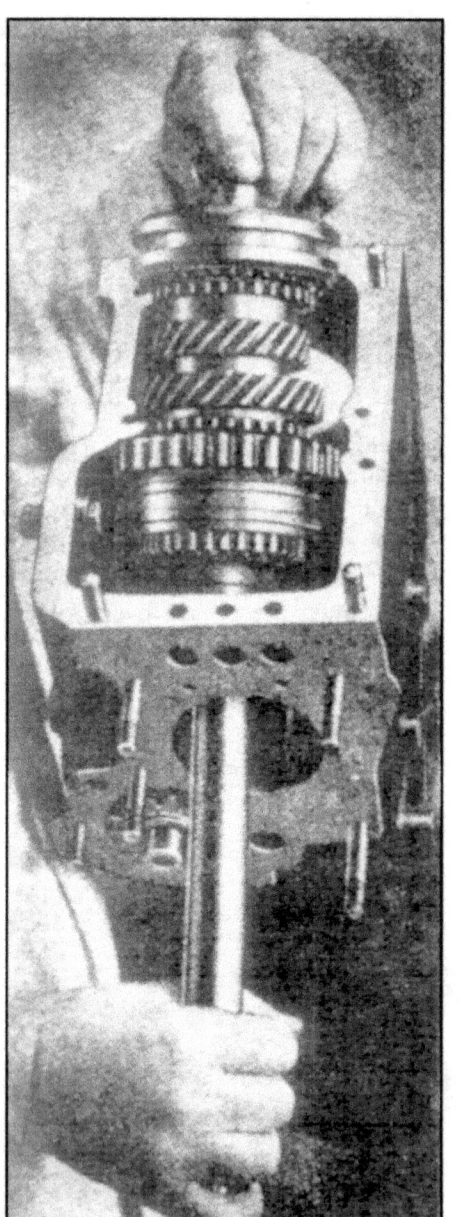

Withdrawing or refitting mainshaft assembly (TD)

KEY TO GEARBOX COMPONENTS.

1. Engine rear bearer bracket.
2. Support rubber.
3. Fork end.
4. Engine rebound rubber.
5. Clevis pin—fork end.
6. Washer.
7. Gearbox casing (with studs).
8. Stud—gearbox top cover.
9. Stud—speedometer casing (medium).
10. Stud—speedometer casing (long).
11. Stud—speedometer casing (short).
12. Plug—oil drain.
13. Washer—drain plug.
14. Oil lever indicator.
15. Mainshaft.
16. Mainshaft bearings.
17. Circlip—mainshaft bearing.
18. Guard—bearing—first motion shaft.
19. Plate—guard.
20. Spring plate—guard.
21. Striking dog.
22. Sliding hub assembly (top and third).
23. Spring—sliding hub.
24. Ball—sliding hub.
25. Third speed gear.
26. Rollers—third speed gear.
27. Collar—third speed gear.
28. Plunger—third speed gear.
29. Spring—plunger.
30. Second speed gear.
31. Rollers—second speed gear.
32. Washer—second speed gear.
33. Collar—second speed gear.
34. Plunger—second speed gear.
35. Spring—plunger.
36. Sliding hub—(first and second.)
37. First speed gear.
38. Spring—first speed gear.
39. Ball—first speed gear.
40. Circlip.
41. Distance piece.
42. Layshaft.
43. Gear unit—layshaft.
44. Rollers—layshaft gear unit.
45. Spacer—layshaft gear unit.
46. Washer—layshaft.
47. Thrust washer—front.
48. Thrust washer—rear.
49. Bearing plate—front.
50. Bearing plate—rear.
51. Screw—layshaft.
52. First motion shaft.
53. Bearing—first motion shaft.
54. Circlip—first motion shaft.
55. Guard—bearing (first motion shaft).
56. Nut—first motion shaft bearing.
57. Lockwasher—bearing.
58. Spigot bearing rollers.
59. Oil seal—first motion shaft.
60. Reverse gear (with bush).
61. Shaft—reverse gear.
62. Plug—reverse shaft.
63. Screw—reverse shaft.
64. Top and third gear selector.
65. Locating screw—selector.
66. Top and third gear shifter.
67. Locating screw—shifter.
68. Distance tube—top and third.
69. Shaft—top and third shifter.
70. First and second gear shifter.
71. Locating screw.
72. First and second gear selector.
73. Locating screw.
74. Shaft—first and second shifter.
75. Stop—shaft.
76. Locating screw—stop.
77. Reverse gear selector.
78. Plunger—reverse gear selector.
79. Spring—plunger.
80. Ball—reverse plunger.
81. Spring—ball.
82. Locating screw.
83. Shaft—reverse selector.
84. Steady—reverse selector shaft.
85. Locating screw—steady.
86. Gear shifter—reverse selector shaft.
87. Gear shifter—reverse gear.
88. Shaft—reverse gear shifter.
89. Reverse link assembly.
90. Fulcrum pin—link.
91. Nut—fulcrum pin.
92. Washer—fulcrum pin.
93. Ball—shaft.
94. Spring—shifter shaft.
95. Gearbox cover.
96. Gasket—cover.
97. Nut—cover.
98. Filler plug—gearbox.
99. Washer for plug.
100. Nut—rear casing.
101. Rear casing.
102. Ball bearing.
103. Guard.
104. Oil retaining washer.
105. Plug—reverse light.
107. Speedometer gear.
108. Speedometer pinion and shaft.
109. Bearing—pinion.
110. Screw—pinion bearing.
111. Flange—universal joint.
112. Washer—flange nut.
113. Nut—flange to mainshaft.
114. Remote control cover.
115. Gasket—cover.
116. Cover bolt—to rear casing.
117. Housing cover plunger.
118. Plug—operating shaft.
119. Spring—operating shaft.
120. Remote control shaft.
121. Selector lever (front).
122. Selector lever (rear).
123. Ball—lever.
124. Key—actuating shaft and selector levers.
125. Bolt—actuating shaft and selector levers.
126. Change speed lever.
127. Knob—change speed lever.
128. Cover—lever.
129. Spring—anti-rattle change speed lever.
130. Circlip—cover.
131. Circlip—shaft—third and top.

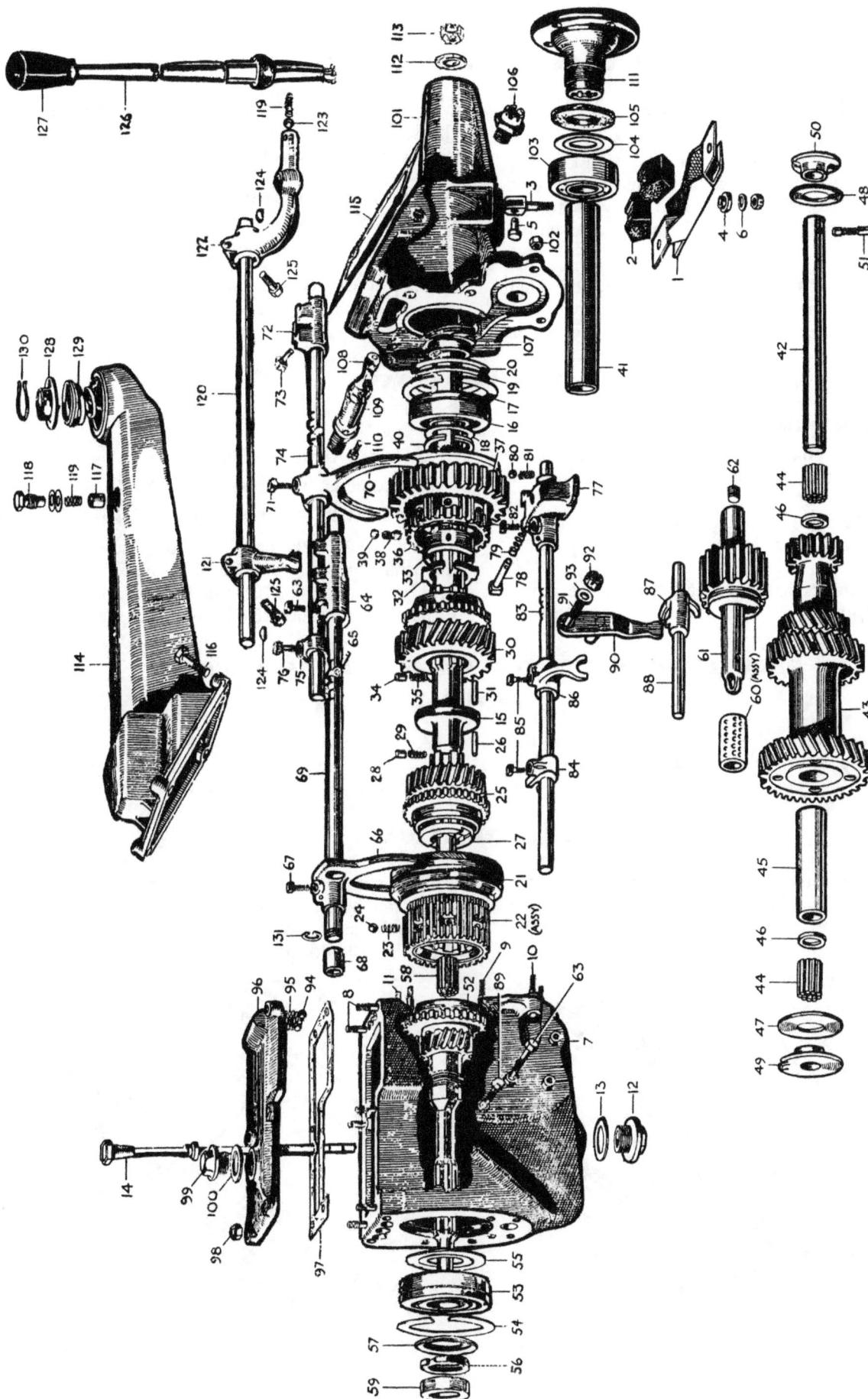

Exploded View of the Gearbox Components.

73

2. GEARBOX REASSEMBLY

TO REASSEMBLE SYNCHROMESH MECHANISM

The striking dog is placed against the end of the sliding hub and pushed through into engagement with it, when the balls will spring into an indentation ground in the centre of the teeth and the assembly is completed.

The reassembly of the gearbox, mainshaft, and other items, is carried out in the reverse manner to that detailed for dismantling, but care must be taken when fitting the layshaft to see that the tags on the thrust washers at each end fit into the grooves in the bosses in the gearbox.

NOTE: For easy assembly of the layshaft with its bearings, it is recommended that a dummy shaft $\frac{9}{16}''$ diameter by $6\frac{11}{32}''$ long be used.

Care must also be taken in the case of the later boxes to replace the circlip on the forward end of the third and top selector shaft.

3. MODIFICATIONS

SPEEDOMETER DRIVE

Starting at gearbox No TW396, the speedometer gear is keyed to the gearbox mainshaft to provide a more positive drive.

Care must therefore be taken when dismantling not to lose the key and to make sure that it is in position on reassembly.

New part numbers have been allotted to the modified parts as follows:

Mainshaft (part No 168209).

Speedometer gear (part No 168210).

Speedometer gear key (part No X20139).

Part No 168209 can be used to service the earlier mainshafts to part No X24467, and the speedometer gear (part No 168210) can be used to service gears to part No MG900/231 by omitting the key

PROPELLER SHAFT TC—TD—TF—TF 1500 SERIES

1. GENERAL

The propeller shaft and universal joints are of the Hardy Spicer type with needle roller bearings.

A single shaft connects the rear axle and the gearbox. To accommodate fore and aft movement of the axle a sliding joint is provided at the gearbox end.

2. LUBRICATION

A lubricator is fitted to each front and rear spider and also the sliding yoke at the front end of the propeller shaft. They should be charged fully at overhaul periods and subsequently given three or four strokes with the grease gun every 1,000 miles with a recommended grease.

If a large amount of grease exudes from the seal the joint should be dismantled and new seals fitted.

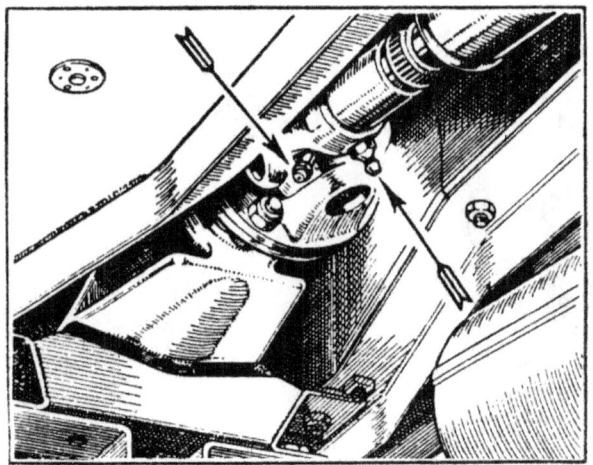 

Lubrication of front universal joint and propeller shaft sliding joint — Lubrication of rear universal joint

3. PROPELLER SHAFT ASSEMBLY

TO TEST FOR WEAR

Wear on the thrust faces is ascertained by testing the lift in the joint, either by hand or with the aid of a length of wood suitably pivoted.

Any circumferential movement of the shaft relative to the flange yokes indicates wear in the needle roller bearings, or in the splined shaft in the case of the forward joint.

TO REMOVE

NOTE: Before removing the bolts and nuts securing the propeller shaft joint flange to the rear axle flange, carefully mark the flanges to assist in refitting them in their original positions.

Remove the nuts, washers, and bolts securing the flanges and lower the propeller shaft.

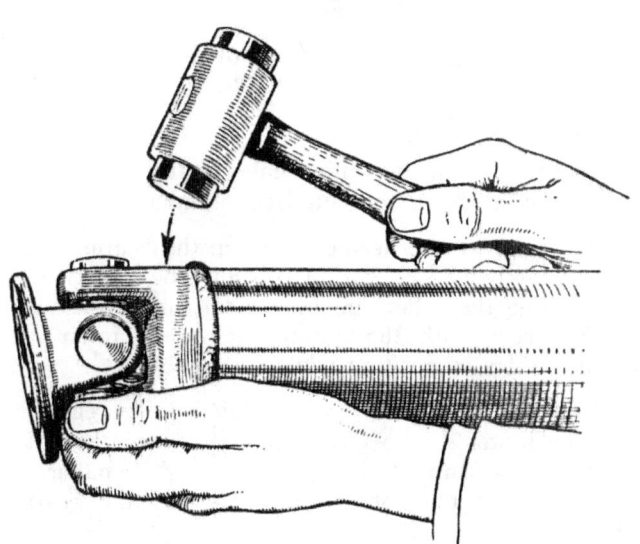

Where to Apply Light Blows to Yoke after Removing Circlip.

TO DISMANTLE

Unscrew the dust cover and pull the sliding joint from the splined shaft. Remove the steel washer and the cork washer.

(1) Remove the enamel and dirt from the end rings and bearing races. Remove all the snap rings by pinching their ears together with a pair of thin-nosed pliers and prising them out with a screwdriver.

(2) If a ring does not slide out of its groove readily, tap the end of the bearing race slightly to relieve the pressure against the ring. Remove the lubricator from the journal and, holding the joint in one hand, tap the radius of the yoke lightly with a copper hammer. The bearing should begin to emerge; turn the joint over and finally remove with the fingers. If necessary, tap the bearing race from inside with a small diameter bar, taking care not to damage the bearing face, or grip the needle bearing race in a vice and tap the flange yoke clear.

(3) Be sure to hold the bearing in a vertical position, and when free remove the race from the bottom side to avoid dropping the needle rollers.

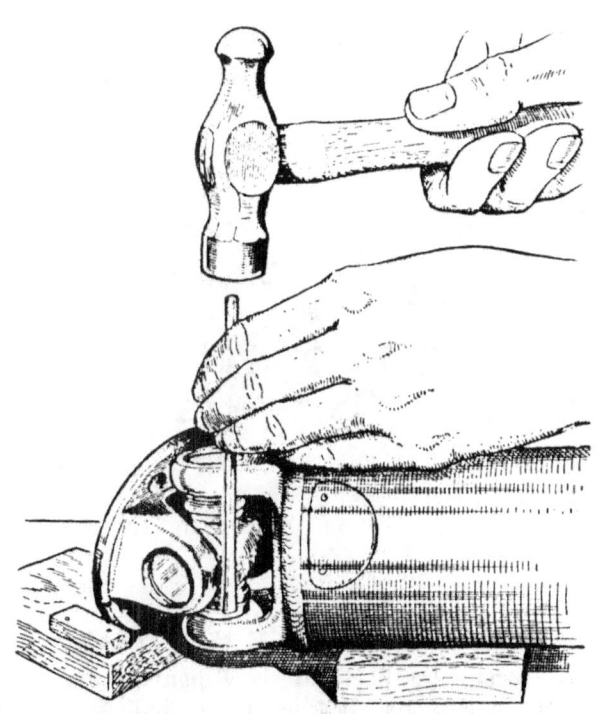

When Dismantling a Universal Joint, Bearings may be Tapped Out with a Small Diameter Rod from inside as shown. Take care not to damage Roller Races.

(4) Repeat this operation for the opposite bearing.

(5) Rest the two exposed trunnions on wood or lead blocks to protect their ground surfaces, and tap the top lug of the flange yoke to remove the bearing race.

(6) Turn the yoke over and repeat the operation.

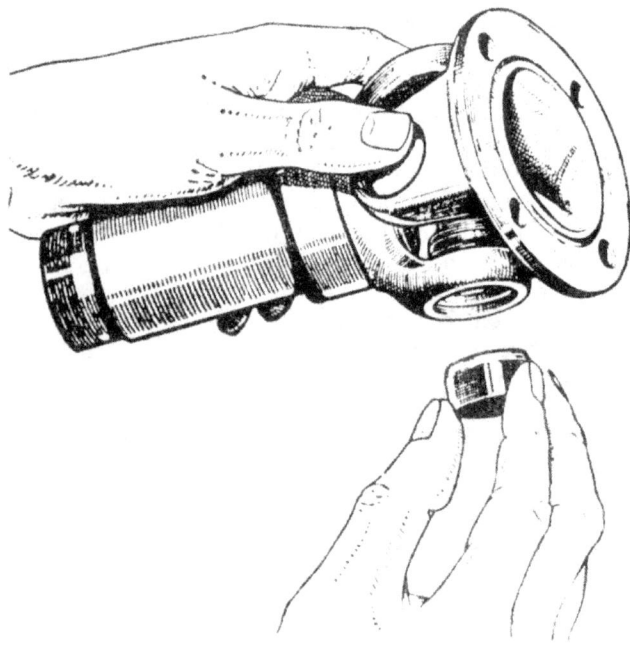

Withdrawing universal joint bearing

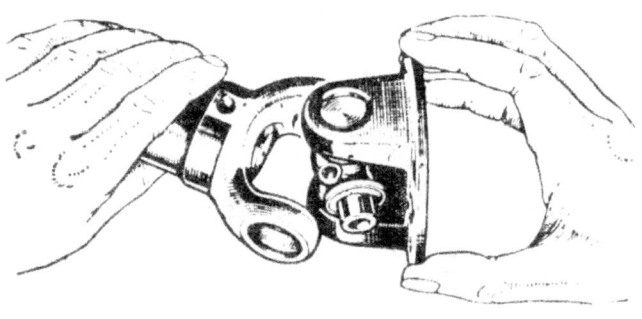

Separating the universal joint

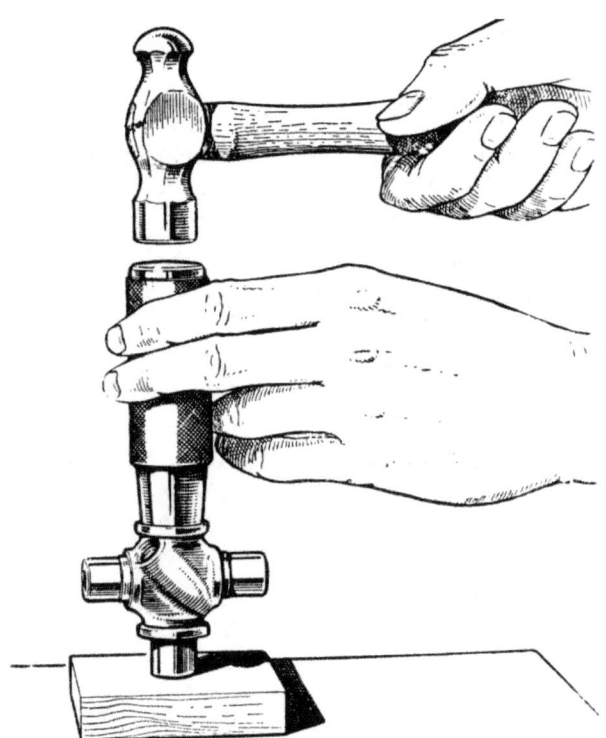

When Replacing a Seal Retainer, use a Hollow Drift to tap it into place.

TO REASSEMBLE

(1) See that all the drilled holes in the journals are thoroughly cleaned out and free of grease.

(2) Assemble the needle rollers in the bearing races and fill with grease. Should difficulty be experienced in retaining the rollers under control, smear the walls of the races with the correct grease to retain the needle rollers in position while reassembling.

(3) Insert the spider in the flange yoke, ensuring that the lubricator boss is fitted away from the yoke. Using a soft-nosed drift, about $\frac{1}{32}''$ smaller in diameter than the hole in the yoke, tap the bearing into position.

(4) Repeat this operation for the other three bearings.

(5) Replace the circlips and be sure that these are firmly located in their grooves. If the joint appears to bind, tap lightly with a wooden mallet; this will relieve any pressure of the bearings on the end of the journals.

It is always advisable to replace the cork gasket and the gasket retainers on the spider journals by means of the tubular drift (see illustration). The spider journal shoulders should be shellacked prior to fitting the retainers, to ensure a good oil seal.

In addition place the dust cap, steel washer, and a new cork gasket over the splined portion of the shaft.

TO EXAMINE AND CHECK FOR WEAR

The parts most likely to show sign of wear after long usage are the bearing races and the spider journals. Should looseness, load markings, or distortion be observed, the affected part must be renewed complete, no oversized journals or races are provided.

It is essential that the bearing races are a light drive fit in the yoke trunnions. In the event of wear taking place in the yoke cross-holes, rendering them oval, the yokes must be renewed. In case of wear in the cross-holes in the fixed yoke, which is part of the tubular shaft assembly, it should be replaced by a complete tubular shaft assembly.

In addition check the splines on the sleeve and shaft for indentation.

TO INSTALL

(1) Wipe the faces of the flanges clean, and place the propeller shaft in position on the car.

(2) Ensure that the flange registers engage correctly, that the components are replaced in exactly the same relation as before removal, and that the joint faces bed down evenly all round.

(3) Insert the bolts and tighten the self-locking nuts.

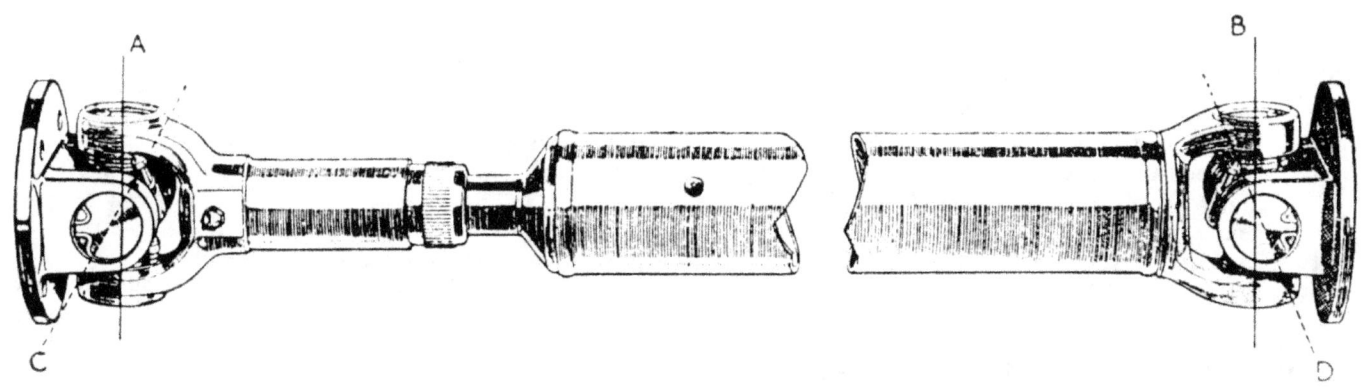

Correct method of assembling propeller shaft. A must be in line with B and C with D

4. TRANSMISSION FAULT DIAGNOSIS
GEARBOX

(1) DIFFICULT GEAR CHANGE

Possible cause
(a) Maladjustment of selector mechanism or cables.
(b) Faulty gear synchroniser mechanism.
(c) Faulty clutch or clutch release mechanism.

Remedy
— Check and adjust selector mechanism or cables.
— Overhaul gearbox.
— Check and overhaul clutch and/or adjust release mechanism.

(2) GEAR CLASH ON CHANGING DOWN

Possible cause
(a) Faulty clutch or clutch release mechanism.
(b) Faulty synchro rings and cones.
(c) Broken or incorrect positioning of synchro bar retaining springs.
(d) Gearbox lubricating oil too heavy.

Remedy
— Overhaul clutch and/or adjust release mechanism.
— Check and overhaul gearbox, renew components as required.
— Check and overhaul gearbox, renew components as required.
— Drain gear case and refill with correct quantity and grade of oil.

(3) SLIPPING OUT OF GEAR (1st and 2nd)

Possible cause
(a) Weak or broken selector shaft detent spring.
(b) Worn mainshaft sliding gear or laygear.
(c) Excessive end-float of laygear.
(d) Worn main drive gear, or mainshaft ball bearings.
(e) Incorrectly adjusted gear change mechanism.

Remedy
— Renew faulty components.
— Check and renew faulty components.
— Check and renew faulty thrust washers.
— Check and renew worn components.
— Check and re-adjust as necessary.

(4) SLIPPING OUT OF GEAR (3rd and top)

Possible cause	Remedy
(a) Weak or broken selector shaft detent spring.	— Check and renew faulty components.
(b) Worn synchro teeth on third or top speeds.	— Check and renew worn components.
(c) Excessive end-float of laygear.	— Check and renew worn thrust washers.
(d) Worn ball bearings on main drive gear or mainshaft.	— Check and renew worn bearings.
(e) Incorrectly adjusted gear change mechanism.	— Check and re-adjust as necessary.

(5) GEARBOX NOISE (in neutral)

Possible cause	Remedy
(a) Worn main drive ball bearing.	— Overhaul and renew bearing.
(b) Chipped or pitted constant mesh gears (laygear, main drive or 2nd and 3rd speed mainshaft gear).	— Overhaul and renew components as necessary.
(c) Excessive laygear end-float.	— Check and renew laygear thrust washers.
(d) Lack of sufficient lubricant.	— Drain and refill gear case with correct quantity and grade of oil.

(6) GEAR BOX NOISE (forward gears engaged)

Possible cause	Remedy
(a) Worn main drive or mainshaft ball bearing.	— Overhaul and renew bearing.
(b) Chipped or pitted constant mesh gears (laygear, main drive gear or 2nd speed or 3rd mainshaft gear).	— Overhaul and renew components as necessary.
(c) Excessive laygear end-float.	— Check and renew laygear thrust washers.
(d) Chipped or pitted reverse idler gear.	— Check and renew components as necessary.
(e) Lack of sufficient lubricant.	— Drain and refill gear case with correct quantity and grade of oil.

PROPELLER SHAFT

(1) SHAFT VIBRATION

Possible cause	Remedy
(a) Bent propeller shaft.	— Renew shaft.
(b) Excessive wear in universal joint trunnion and bearings.	— Renew complete universal joint (trunnion and bearings).
(c) Propeller shaft out of balance.	— Renew complete propeller shaft.
(d) Excessive wear of front joint sleeve in rear extension bush bearing.	— Renew extension housing bush assembly.
(e) Rear universal joint to pinion flange bolts loose.	— Renew and tighten loose bolts.

(2) EXCESSIVE BACKLASH

Possible cause	Remedy
(a) Worn universal joint trunnion and bearings.	— Renew joint trunnion and bearings as assembly.
(b) Worn mainshaft and universal joint sleeve splines.	— Renew worn components.

TC SERIES
1. REAR AXLE ASSEMBLY

TO REMOVE

(1) After removing the seats and seat squab, uncouple the propeller shaft rear flange. Uncouple the handbrake cables from the brake cross shaft and unbolt the cable supports.

(2) Disconnect the copper pipes on either side of the T piece secured to the axle casing and remove the clip securing the offside pipe to the axle casing.

(3) Unbolt the T piece from the axle casing and allow the brake fluid to drain into a receptacle.

(4) Drain the rear axle oil by removing the plug under the differential housing.

(5) As the rear axle is above the chassis frame it must be withdrawn through the wheel arch, necessitating the removal of the brake back plate on one side. Assuming this to be the off-side, proceed as follows:

(6) After the wheels have been removed, unbolt and draw off the brake drums, then replace the wheel nuts on the hubs and drive out the axle half-shafts, with hubs complete, by hitting the nut ears with a copper hammer.

(7) Having removed the half-shafts, tap back the tab washer locking the bearing securing nut on the off-side only, and remove this nut and withdraw the bearing housing complete with bearing.

(8) Remove the brake shoes and the brake back plate with the handbrake cable and Lockheed pipe attached.

(9) Remove the axle check straps. The nuts securing the differential housing to the axle casing can now be removed, and the differential, complete, can be withdrawn.

(10) Disconnect the axle from the rear springs. The remainder of the rear axle can then be withdrawn through the body, through the near-side wheel arch.

Exploded View of Rear Axle and Differential Assembly.

2. DIFFERENTIAL UNIT

TO DISMANTLE AND REASSEMBLE

(1) Remove the four nuts securing the pinion bearing housing assembly to the differential carrier, after which the assembly can be withdrawn.

(2) The shims should then be taken off the studs.

(3) After the propeller shaft flange and the countersunk screws securing the cap are removed, the pinion can be withdrawn from its housing complete with the ball race and the inner portion of the roller race.

(4) The outer track of the roller race can now be taken away from the housing after the retaining circlip has been removed.

(5) The crownwheel and differential unit should then be removed from its carrier; it is held in place by the two caps. It is necessary to remove only the eight bolts which secure the crownwheel to the differential housing for this unit to be dismantled completely.

(6) To reassemble the differential unit, reverse the operation described above, watching the following points:

(a) That the shims for adjusting the bevel pinion are clean and undamaged.

(b) That the eight bolts securing the crownwheel and pinion to the differential assembly are tight and split pinned (do not over-tighten).

(c) That the differential ball bearings are against the shoulders in the differential carrier caps.

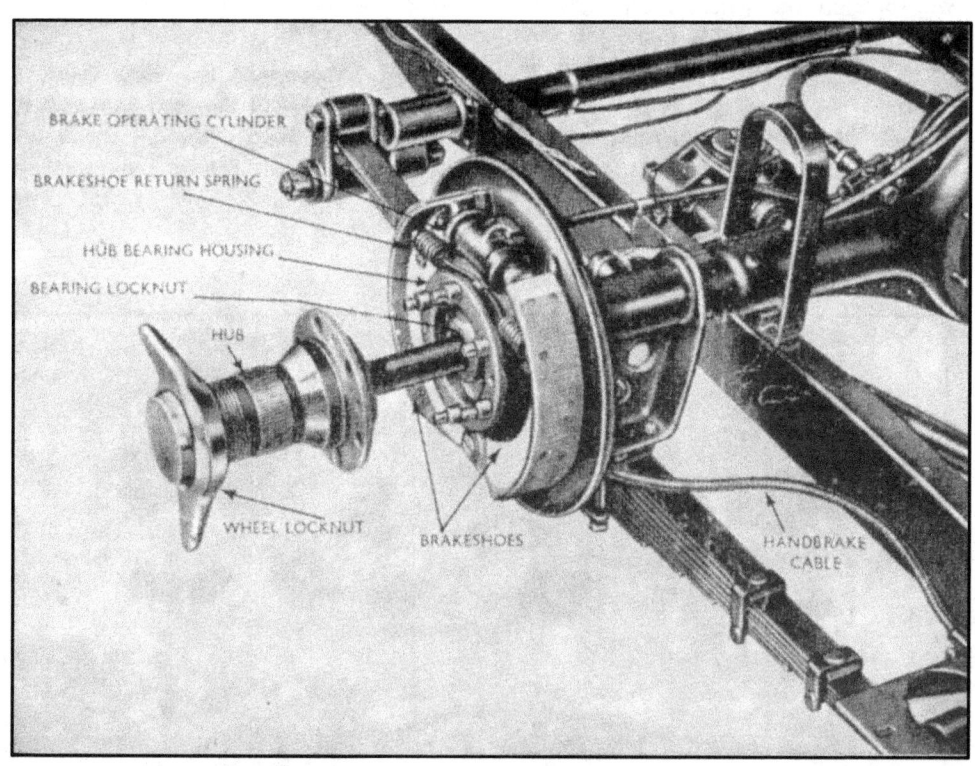

Axle Shaft and Wheel Bearing Mechanism.

3. CROWNWHEEL AND PINION

TO ADJUST

Two adjustments are provided:

(a) Of the bevel pinion to or from the crownwheel, by means of the shims between the pinion housing and the differential carrier.

(b) Of the crownwheel, across the car, by means of the two nuts on the outside of the differential ball bearings.

As it is very essential that the ball race outer tracks are against the shoulders machined in the differential housing caps, tap each ball race outer track against the shoulder before tightening the bolts securing the caps.

After tightening the cap bolts, adjust the ball race nuts so that they just pinch the ball race inner track, at the same time bringing the nut locking screw in line with one of the serrations in the locking washer. After this the off-side adjusting nut must be tightened one further serration to obtain a slight pre-load, which is necessary to prevent any slackness in the races when the axle is under load.

The best method of obtaining this position is as follows:

(1) As a starting point, insert a .017" thickness of shims behind the pinion housing.

(2) Adjust the differential assembly to give .007" to .010" clearance between the teeth of the crownwheel and pinion, not forgetting to adjust the differential thrust races as previously described.

(3) Cover the teeth of the crownwheel with a mixture of red lead and oil, mixed into a fairly stiff paste. A short bristle brush will ensure even distribution.

(4) The differential must then be revolved in both directions. A handle will be required for this, which can easily be made up.

When the gears have been revolved in both directions the tooth mating markings can be seen on the crownwheel. These markings must be identical on both sides of the teeth and in the centre of each tooth. It must be noted, however, that the tooth markings should only extend for half the length of the tooth, but under load will extend for the full length.

Too much backlash between the gears is indicated by a very narrow tooth marking, and insufficient backlash is indicated by the tooth rooting or bottoming.

If further adjustment is necessary when the car is on test, shims can be removed from behind the pinion housing, not exceeding .004", or alternatively additional shims inserted, also not exceeding .004".

Where adjustment as described is not satisfactory, before the gears are condemned, all bearings should be carefully inspected for slackness, particularly the pinion rear roller race, which must be renewed if a feeler of .0015" thickness can be inserted between the rollers and the outer track.

4. REAR WHEEL BEARINGS

TO CHECK

(1) Naturally, it is necessary first to jack up the rear of the car and remove the wheel attached to the hub which is to be examined.

(2) Undo the ring of bolts securing the brake drum to the hub and remove the brake drum (first be sure the handbrake is off).

(3) Now replace the wheel locknut and withdraw the half-shaft by tapping the back of the locknut ears with a copper hammer.

(4) Having removed the half-shaft, tap back the tab washer locking the bearing securing nut, undo the nut and withdraw the bearing housing complete with the bearing; the assistance of a suitable puller will in all probability be required.

(5) When reassembling, smear the ball race with grease.

While the wheel bearing is removed, it is advisable to examine the oil retaining seal behind the bearing.

TD—TF—TF 1500 SERIES
1. REAR AXLE ASSEMBLY

The rear axle is of the semi-floating type. It is of unit construction, and no repairs or adjustments apart from those connected with the half-shafts and rear wheel bearings, brake drums and shoe mechanism can be carried out without removing the complete axle unit from the car.

The rear wheel bearing outer races are carried in an extension of the rear axle casing and the inner races bear directly on the axle half-shafts. The wheel hubs are attached to the axle shafts by splines and a tapered split collar.

Contrary to previous MG practice, the axle half-shafts can only be withdrawn after removing the wheel, wheel hub and brake drum, brake back plate assembly and the wheel bearing housing.

The brake drums are of cast iron integral with the hub or permanently attached to the wheel hub flanges by countersunk-headed screws, which must not be disturbed.

Hypoid-type final reduction gears are used and the axle housing is divided close to its centre for assembly purposes, the pinion assembly being mounted in the right-hand half or axle casing.

The bearings of the differential and crownwheel assembly are carried in recesses machined in the axle casing and cover, which are bolted together and, since no inspection apertures are provided, all adjustments have to be carried out by pre-measurement in conjunction with special gauges.

Adjustment of the position of both the crownwheel and the pinion in the axle is effected by distance pieces, which are selected on initial assembly, and there is no other provision for adjustment. The crownwheels and pinions are only supplied in pairs.

The use of hypoid gears enables a much larger pinion to be used, providing more silent running and a greatly increased life.

The rear brake gear is of the normal two-shoe type, operated hydraulically from the brake pedal and also mechanically by hand-operated mechanism actuating the same shoes. The operating cylinder for the shoes is mounted vertically on the brake plates and acts directly on the brake shoes.

Adjustment is by means of a serrated snail cam with screwdriver operation through holes in the brake drum disc.

Suspension is by means of semi-elliptic leaf springs with rubber interleaving and rubber mounting. The shackles and the spring anchorage are both fitted with flexing rubber bushes needing no lubrication.

TO REMOVE AND INSTALL

(1) Raise the rear of the car by means of a suitable sling and block up under the chassis just forward of the spring front mountings.

(2) Remove both the road wheels and release the handbrake. Disconnect the brake flexible pipe at its junction to the bracket on the chassis.

(3) Disconnect the brake cable casings from their anchorage to the spring brackets by removing the retaining nuts and spring washers.

(4) Disconnect the brake cables by removing the clevis pin attaching the forked yoke to the brake shoe actuating levers on the brake plates.

(5) Disconnect the shock absorber arms at their lower ends.

(6) Mark the propeller shaft coupling flanges so that they are replaced in the same relative positions. Now uncouple the propeller shaft at the rear flange by unscrewing the four coupling nuts and bolts. Support the tail end of the propeller shaft.

(7) Undo all the spring U bolt nuts so that the axle rests on the rebound straps. Take the weight of the axle by means of jacks or a suitable axle stand.

(8) Remove the rebound straps, lower the exhaust pipe and the axle can now be withdrawn sideways.

(9) To install reverse the removal procedure, but do not forget to bleed the hydraulic brake system after coupling up the flexible hose.

2. HUB AND BRAKE DRUM

TO REMOVE AND INSTALL

The brake drums are permanently attached to the wheel hubs by countersunk-headed screws, the inner ends of which are riveted over. These screws should not be disturbed, and if it is necessary to fit a new drum or hub a complete assembly should be used as the hubs and brake drums are machined after assembly. On some models the hub and drum are made in one piece.

(1) Jack up the axle so that the wheel to be operated on is clear of the ground and place chocks on either side of the wheels remaining on the ground. Release the handbrake fully.

(2) Remove the hub cover and take off the wheel.

(3) Remove the split pin and the axle nut and unscrew the nut. The axle half-shafts are threaded right-handed on both sides of the car and are interchangeable.

(4) Free the hub from the taper. The wheel hub is locked to the axle half-shaft by means of a tapered split collar in addition to the driving splines. It is therefore to be expected that some resistance will be evident when the extractor is used to free the hub from the taper.

(5) When installing the rear hub it is essential to

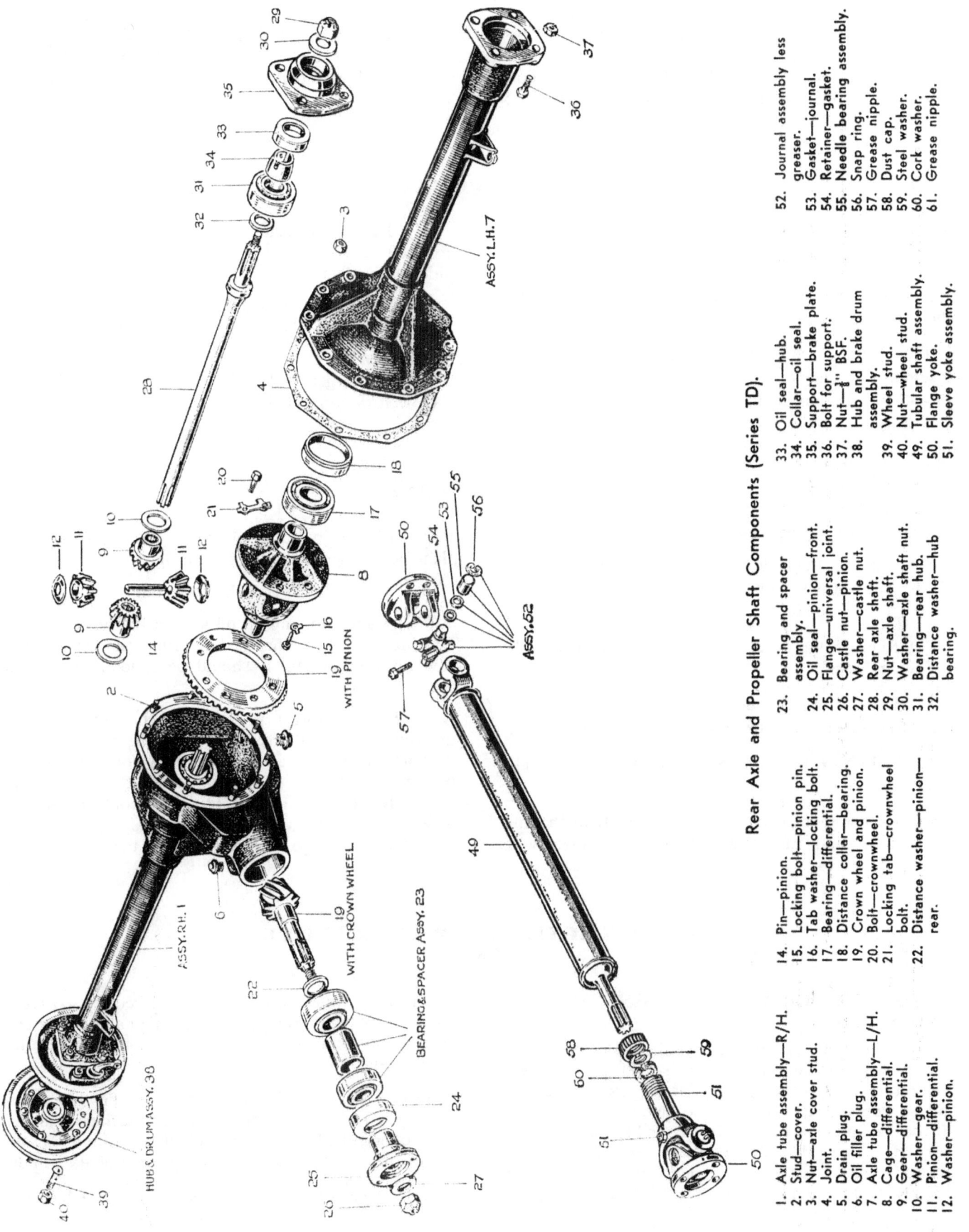

Rear Axle and Propeller Shaft Components (Series TD).

1. Axle tube assembly—R/H.
2. Stud—cover.
3. Nut—axle cover stud.
4. Joint.
5. Drain plug.
6. Oil filler plug.
7. Axle tube assembly—L/H.
8. Cage—differential.
9. Gear—differential.
10. Washer—gear.
11. Pinion—differential.
12. Washer—pinion.
14. Pin—pinion.
15. Locking bolt—pinion pin.
16. Tab washer—locking bolt.
17. Bearing—differential.
18. Distance collar—bearing.
19. Crown wheel and pinion.
20. Bolt—crownwheel.
21. Locking tab—crownwheel bolt.
22. Distance washer—pinion rear.
23. Bearing and spacer assembly.
24. Oil seal—pinion—front.
25. Flange—universal joint.
26. Castle nut—pinion.
27. Washer—castle nut.
28. Nut—axle shaft.
29. Washer—axle shaft nut.
30. Bearing—rear hub.
31. Distance washer—hub bearing.
33. Oil seal—hub.
34. Collar—oil seal.
35. Support—brake plate.
36. Bolt for support.
37. Nut—⅜" BSF.
38. Hub and brake drum assembly.
39. Wheel stud.
40. Nut—wheel stud.
49. Tubular shaft assembly.
50. Flange yoke.
51. Sleeve yoke assembly.
52. Journal assembly less greaser.
53. Gasket—journal.
54. Retainer—gasket.
55. Needle bearing assembly.
56. Snap ring.
57. Grease nipple.
58. Dust cap.
59. Steel washer.
60. Cork washer.
61. Grease nipple.

make quite sure that the tapered split collar is right home against the inner race of the wheel bearing before any attempt is made to offer up the hub. It is, in fact, advisable to tap the collar lightly into position with a hide hammer, taking the utmost care not to damage it in any way. It is also essential to see that the parallel portion of the collar engaging the oil seal is absolutely free from blemishes before it is replaced and that the oil seal is not damaged in any way.

3. BRAKE PLATE ASSEMBLY

TO REMOVE AND INSTALL

(1) Jack up the axle and remove the wheel.

(2) See that the handbrake is fully released and then remove the hub.

(3) If it is required to remove the brake plate assembly to the bench for attention, the oil pipe should be disconnected.

(4) The brake plate assembly is attached to the axle by four bolts with the nuts fitted on the inner side of the flange.

(5) To install, reverse the removal procedure and make sure that the retaining nuts are screwed up tight.

Do not forget to bleed the brakes if the pipeline has been disconnected.

4. AXLE SHAFT

TO REMOVE AND INSTALL

(1) Jack up the axle as outlined or raise the rear of the car with a sling attached to the bumper supports.

(2) Remove the wheel and see that the handbrake is fully released.

(3) Remove the hub and brake drum assembly and the brake plate and shoe assembly.

(4) Withdraw the split collar from the axle half-shaft.

(5) Fit the special tool (part No 68823) to the end of the axle shaft and release the shaft complete with bearings, housing and oil seal. The half-shaft can then be pressed out of the bearing.

(6) To install, reverse the foregoing.

(7) When installing an oil seal in the wheel bearing housing, see that the sealing edge of the bore is towards the bearing. It should be a good press fit in the axle end cap.

(8) Do not forget to see that the split collar is perfectly clean and free from blemish, particularly on its parallel portion, and pushed well home against the bearing inner race before replacing the wheel hub. It is advisable to tap it lightly into contact with the axle bearing with a hide hammer, taking the utmost care not to damage it in any way in the process.

5. DIFFERENTIAL AND FINAL DRIVE ASSEMBLY

IMPORTANT POINTS CONCERNING AXLE ATTENTION

No adjustment is provided in the accepted sense. The crownwheel and pinion are set in their correct relation to each other by means of distance pieces and spacers selected to provide the correct location of the components on initial assembly. Should the components be dismantled, their relative positions should be carefully observed and each part marked suitably so that it can be reassembled correctly.

Various components can be replaced by correctly combining the markings on the original components against those on the new parts in the manner detailed in subsequent sections.

Spacers between the outer races of the differential bearings and faces of the recesses machined in the axle casing and cover control the position of the crownwheel in relation to the centre line of the pinion.

Adjustment of the pinion position is made by varying the thickness of the pinion washer, and that of the crownwheel by the varying thickness of the differential bearing spacers.

The following operations are possible without the use of special tools:

(a) To replace a crownwheel and pinion with a pair carrying markings which are identical to the originals.

(b) To replace a crownwheel bearing alone, since these are of the controlled width type, provided genuine MG replacements are used.

(c) To replace an axle cover which carries markings identical to the original.

The following replacements are possible by calculations alone:

(d) To replace the differential cage by one carrying a different marking from the original.

(e) To replace an axle cover carrying different markings from the original.

The following replacements can be carried out by calculations and the use of special tools:

(f) To replace the axle case carrying different markings from the original.

(g) To replace a crownwheel and pinion carrying different markings from the originals.

(h) To replace bearings on the pinion shaft.

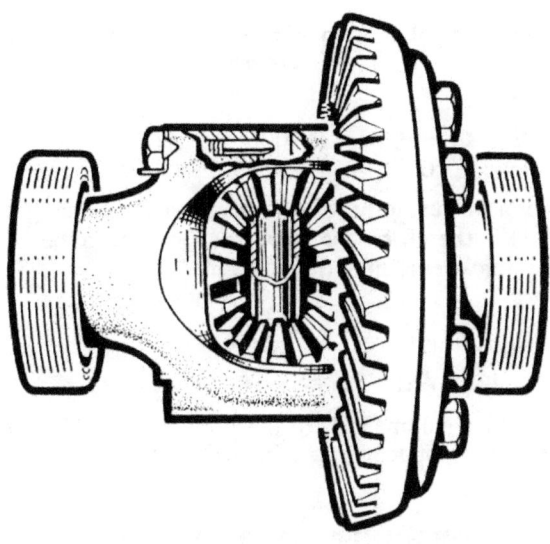

Differential and Crownwheel Assembly with Ball Races in Position on Differential Cage. The Bolt Locking the Shaft for the Differential Pinions is clearly seen in the upper left hand corner of the Cage.

Operations (a), (b) and (c) merely call for the fitting of the new parts in the positions occupied by the old. The remaining operations entail special precautions and are detailed subsequently.

The axle or half-shafts, rear hub bearings, brake drums and shoe mechanism can all be removed and installed with the axle in position on the car.

TO DISMANTLE AXLE AND REMOVE DIFFERENTIAL ASSEMBLY

(1) Remove the axle from the car.

(2) To dismantle the axle, first remove the hub and brake drum assemblies and the brake back plates.

(3) Take out the axle half-shaft.

(4) Remove the series of bolts joining the axle casing and cover together and carefully part them, taking care to see that both halves of the axle are suitably supported to avoid damage to the differential assembly. The withdrawal of the axle cover from the casing releases the differential and crownwheel assembly, which can now be taken out.

NOTE: Spacers are fitted between the differential bearings and the bearing housings and they are important because they control the position of the differential assembly in the axle.

It is important that they be replaced in their original locations on assembly, so make a note of the positions from which they are removed.

All original spacers are marked o/s and n/s.

It must also be noted that the axle casing and cover are marked on the surface of one of the outside webs or tubes with one of the following figures: Zero, 1, 2, 3, 4, 5, 6, all being positive.

TO DISMANTLE DIFFERENTIAL AND CROWNWHEEL ASSEMBLY

(1) When the differential assembly has been removed from the axle casing, it is dismantled by bending back the tab of the locking plate of the bolt locating the differential pinion shaft, withdrawing the bolt and removing the shaft (see illustration).

(2) The differential pinions can now be removed from the differential cage by swinging them round with their dished thrust plates until they register with the openings in the differential cage, through which they can be removed.

(3) The differential cage gears can then be withdrawn from inside the differential through the openings together with their thrust washers.

(4) The crownwheel is attached to the differential cage by bolts locked by lock plates. Bending back the

tabs of the lock plates and removing the bolts releases the crownwheel from the differential cage.

NOTE: The crownwheels are marked on their back faces with one of the following figures: + 2, + 1, Zero (or no marking), −1, −2.

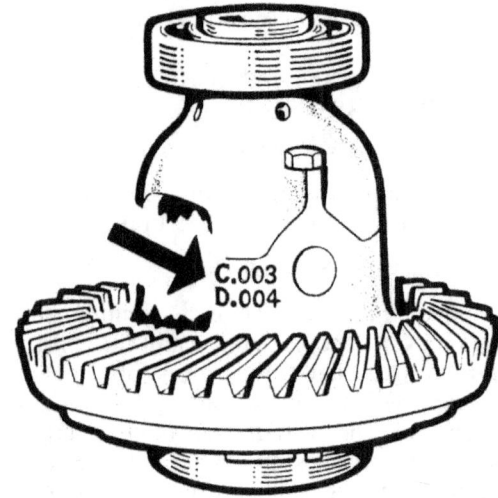

Markings on Differential Cage to indicate Assembly Dimensions. C dimension is .003" and D dimension is .004".

TO INSTALL DIFFERENTIAL CAGE

Selecting an axle casing spacer: All differential cages are stamped with two letters (C and D) together with a figure (see illustration). The prefix C indicates the dimension over the differential bearings and the dimensional range is from .000" to .012". D indicates the dimension from the crownwheel back face to the outside face of the right-hand bearing outer race and the range is from .000" to + .006".

Differential cages can be interchanged by applying the following procedure:

Balance the D dimensions of the two cages and from the result select differential bearing spacers which will produce the same final location of the crownwheel on assembly.

Example (1):

If the D dimension of the old cage was .005" and the D dimension on the new cage is .002" giving a difference of + .003", then this difference must be added to the old spacer thickness.

That is to say, if the old spacer is marked .503" the new spacer must be .506" thick.

Example (2):

If the D dimension of the old cage was .001" and the D dimension of the new cage is .005", giving a difference of −.004", then this difference must be subtracted from the original spacer thickness.

That is to say, if the old spacer was .509" thick, then the new spacer must be .505" thick.

TO SELECT AXLE COVER SPACER

In this case subtract the D dimension from the C dimension on both the old and the new differential cages.

If the resultant of the dimensions on the new cage is greater than that on the old cage, the new spacer for the axle cover is less than the old one by the difference and vice versa.

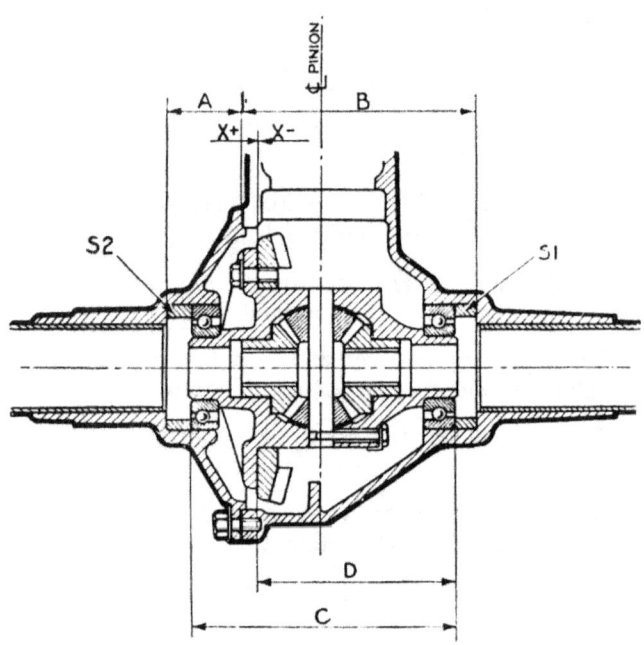

Diagram Indicating Significance of A, B, C and D dimensions.

Example (1):
   Old: C .006" − D .005" = .001"
   New: C .007" − D .002" = .005"

The new resultant of the new cage is the greater by .004", therefore the new spacer should be .004" less in thickness than the old one.

Example (2):
   Old: C .002" − D .001" = −.001"
   New: C .001" − D .005" = −.004"

The old resultant is here the greater by .005", therefore the new spacer must be .005" thicker than the old one.

TO ASSEMBLE DIFFERENTIAL AND CROWNWHEEL

(1) The differential is assembled by first inserting the differential gears inside the differential cage with their thrust washers in position.

NOTE: When new washers are fitted it is necessary to see that they are properly bedded in or it may be difficult to insert the pinions.

(2) The differential pinions are next inserted through the opening of the cage with their distance pieces and thrust washers.

(3) The pinions are then rotated in the cage until they register with the holes in the cage for the shaft.

(4) The pinion spindle, which should be a light push fit in the cage, is then inserted, taking care to line up the locking bolt holes.

NOTE: The slot in the shaft can be used as a guide.

(5) Install the locking bolt and turn up the tab of its locking washer.

(6) Install the crownwheel to the differential cage after making sure that the mating surfaces are perfectly clean and the edges free from burrs.

(7) Check the crownwheel for truth by spinning the assembly on a roller fixture with a dial gauge registering against the outer edge of the crownwheel. The maximum permissible error of alignment is .001″ and if the figure registered is in excess of this the crownwheel should be removed from the differential cage and the flange of the cage checked for truth. If necessary, instal a replacement cage.

(8) Provided the flange is true within the permissible error, clean all parts carefully and reassemble the crownwheel to the cage in a different position from that in which it was first assembled and checked, then re-check. This process should be repeated several times before finally deciding to discard the crownwheel and pinion.

(9) The differential ball races can now be pressed on.

(10) If a new crownwheel or differential cage has been installed it is essential to measure the C dimensions over the outer ball races, and D dimensions from the crownwheel back face to the right-hand bearing outer race outside face.

TO INSTALL PINION

(a) The old pinion in a new axle casing.

(b) New pinion and new matched set of bearings and distance piece in an old casing.

(c) New pinion and old bearings and distance piece in an old casing.

(d) Old pinion and new matched set of bearings and distance piece in an old casing.

In all cases the pinion must be set accurately in the axle casing, remembering that the roller races and their distance pieces are supplied in sets giving the correct amount of pre-load on assembly. They can, therefore, only be replaced as sets and not individually.

The pinions may be marked on their heads with one of the following figures:

A ringed figure +2, +1, Zero (or no marking), −1, −2, and possibly an unringed figure −2 or −1.

The pinion washer controls the position of the pinion in relation to the axis of the crownwheel, and it is fitted between the head of the pinion and its rear bearing.

Adjustment of the pinion position is made by varying the thickness of the pinion washer. These are available in a range of thickness varying by .001″, and are marked on spares replacements only.

The pinion is fitted to the axle in the following way:

(1) Install the pinion bearing outer races in the pinion housing, then assemble the rear pinion bearing inner race to the special dummy pinion spindle (part No 68829) and place in position in the spindle housing, inserting it through the cover opening in the axle casing.

(2) Fit the front bearing inner race.

NOTE: The bearing spacer is omitted because the correct pre-load can only be obtained with the bearing in position when the universal joint flange is locked up tight. This is due to the calculated compression of the bearing spacer under this locking load.

(3) Fit the spindle nut and tighten it up to give the correct pre-load of 6 to 8 in/lb to the bearings. This can be checked by applying the special tool, part No 68839.

(4) Rotate the spindle eight or ten times to seat the bearings.

(5) Fit the checking fixture (part No 68829) in the axle cover opening and make sure that the locating arm makes firm contact with the side of the dummy spindle head.

This leaves a gap between the dummy pinion head and the checking anvil of the fixture, and this is the actual thickness of the pinion washer required for a standard pinion or one that has no marking.

(6) Select a washer which will just slide between these faces and install it behind the pinion head when reassembling.

To assist manufacturing conditions it is occasionally necessary that a pinion be assembled away from the

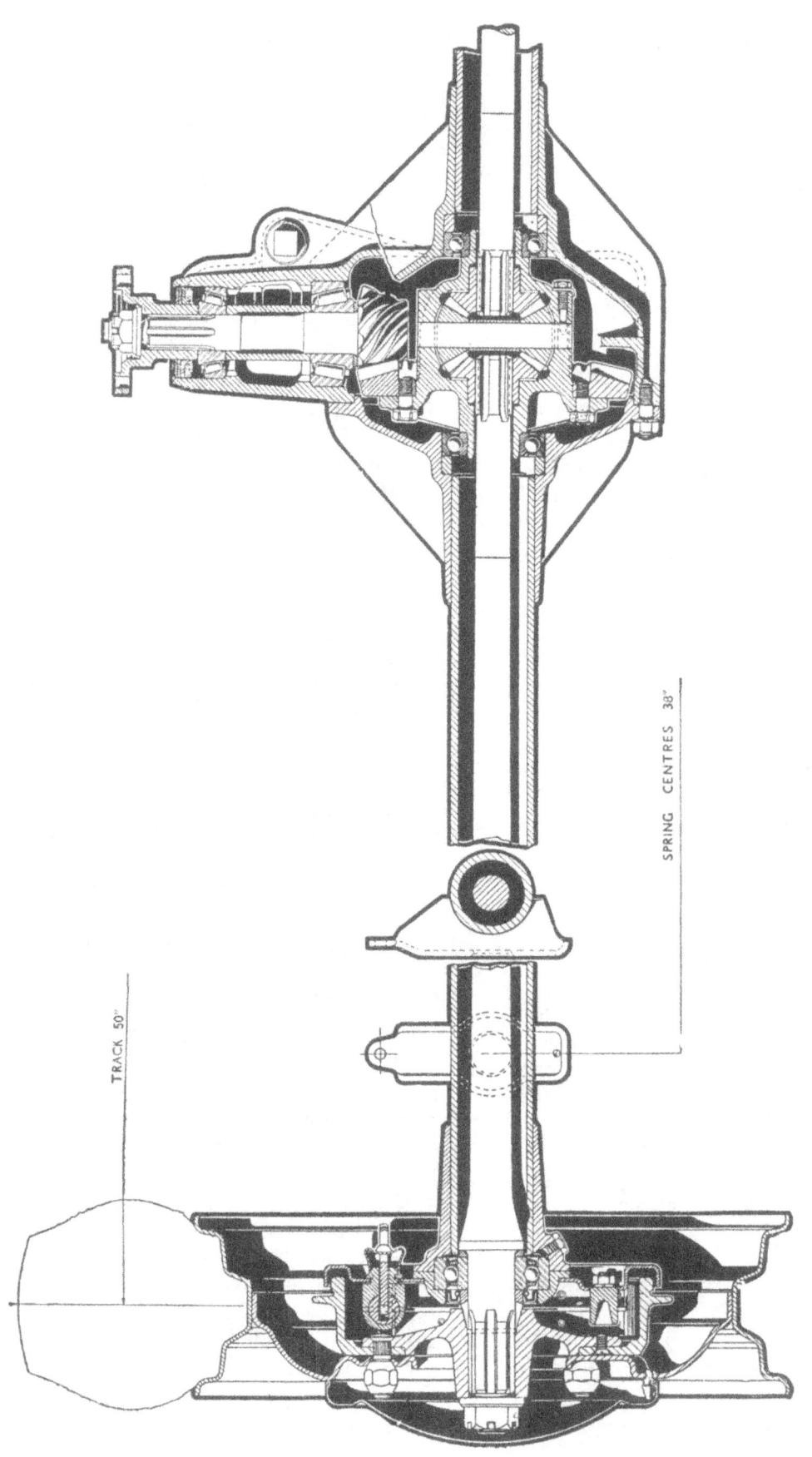

A Sectional View of Rear Axle.

standard position. If this is so the variation is marked on the pinion head in a ring such as (+2), the sign + meaning that the centres are increased by .002". Correction has to be made for this, and when the figure is + (plus) the amount must be taken from the washer thickness, and if the figure is — (minus) then the amount has to be added to the washer thickness.

Example (a):

A washer fitting the gap of the dummy pinion with a marking of .127" must be replaced by a washer having the marking .129" when refitting a pinion with the marking —2 or —.002".

Example (b):

A washer fitting the gap of the dummy pinion bearing the marking .127" must be replaced by a washer marked .125" when the pinion is marked + 2 or + .002" on its head.

A plain or unringed figure may be marked on the pinion head in addition to a ringed figure, but this is only an indication of the variation of the pinion head thickness from standard and is always minus. It has no bearing on the pinion setting.

(7) When the correct spacing washer has been decided upon the actual pinion installation can take place, but the importance of making the measurements correctly must be appreciated, since it is impossible to check the adjustment when the axle is assembled.

(8) The actual pinion installation is carried out by threading the special pinion washer just selected on the pinion shaft, bevelled side against the pinion, and pressing on the rear roller bearing inner race with its projecting side against the washer. This subassembly is then inserted into the casing through the axle cover opening and located in position in the pinion housing of the axle casing.

(9) The distance piece and forward roller bearing inner race are next passed on to the pinion shaft, with the projecting side of the inner race facing forward. These components are followed by the pinion flange with its retaining washer and nut. Tighten up the nut firmly.

(10) Rotate the pinion, using special tool, part No 68839, to ascertain that the correct degree of pre-load is present. The pinion should present the same resistance to rotation as was evident when using the special dummy spindle, namely 6 to 8 in/lb.

(11) If the pre-load is correct, undo the nut and remove the washer and flange, install the oil seal (sharp edge of the bore towards bearing), install the pinion flange, retaining washer and nut.

If the pre-load is not correct the distance piece and bearing assembly will have to be installed by the selection process until the correct pre-load is obtained.

(12) Finally tighten up the nut and fit the split pin.

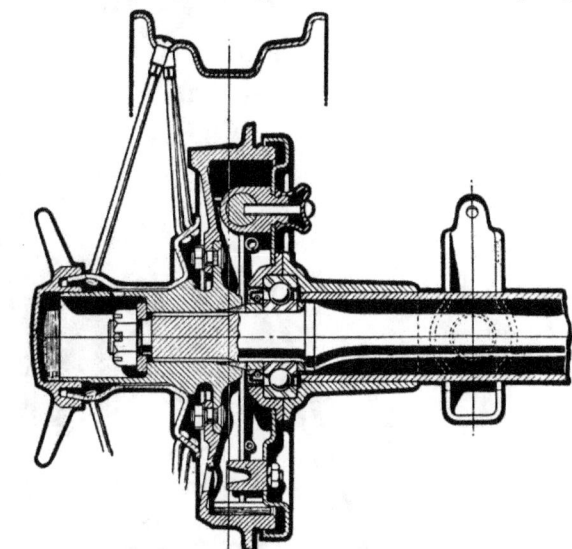

Arrangement of Rear Hub and Brake Drum on TF cars Fitted with Wire Wheels.

TO FIT NEW AXLE CASING

When a new axle case is being fitted it is necessary to refit the pinion and select a new distance collar for the differential bearing in the following manner.

Compensation for variations in the depth of the differential bearing bores is made by taking note of the markings on the old and new axle casings.

For example:

If the old casing is + .002" and the new one + .004", the positive difference .002" is added to the existing differential bearing distance collar. That is to say, if the old distance collar is marked .505", then the required new distance collar is .507".

Similarly, if the old casing is + .005", and the new one + .001", the resulting difference is negative, —.004", and must be subtracted from the bearing distance collar, i.e., if the old distance collar is .509", the required new distance collar is .505".

The distance collars are manufactured in steps of .001" and measurements should therefore be made to the nearest thousandth of an inch.

TO FIT NEW AXLE HOUSING COVER

When a new axle cover is being fitted it is not necessary to make any adjustment to the pinion.

Compensation must, however, be made for variations in the depth of the differential bearing housing in the same manner as that outlined for the axle

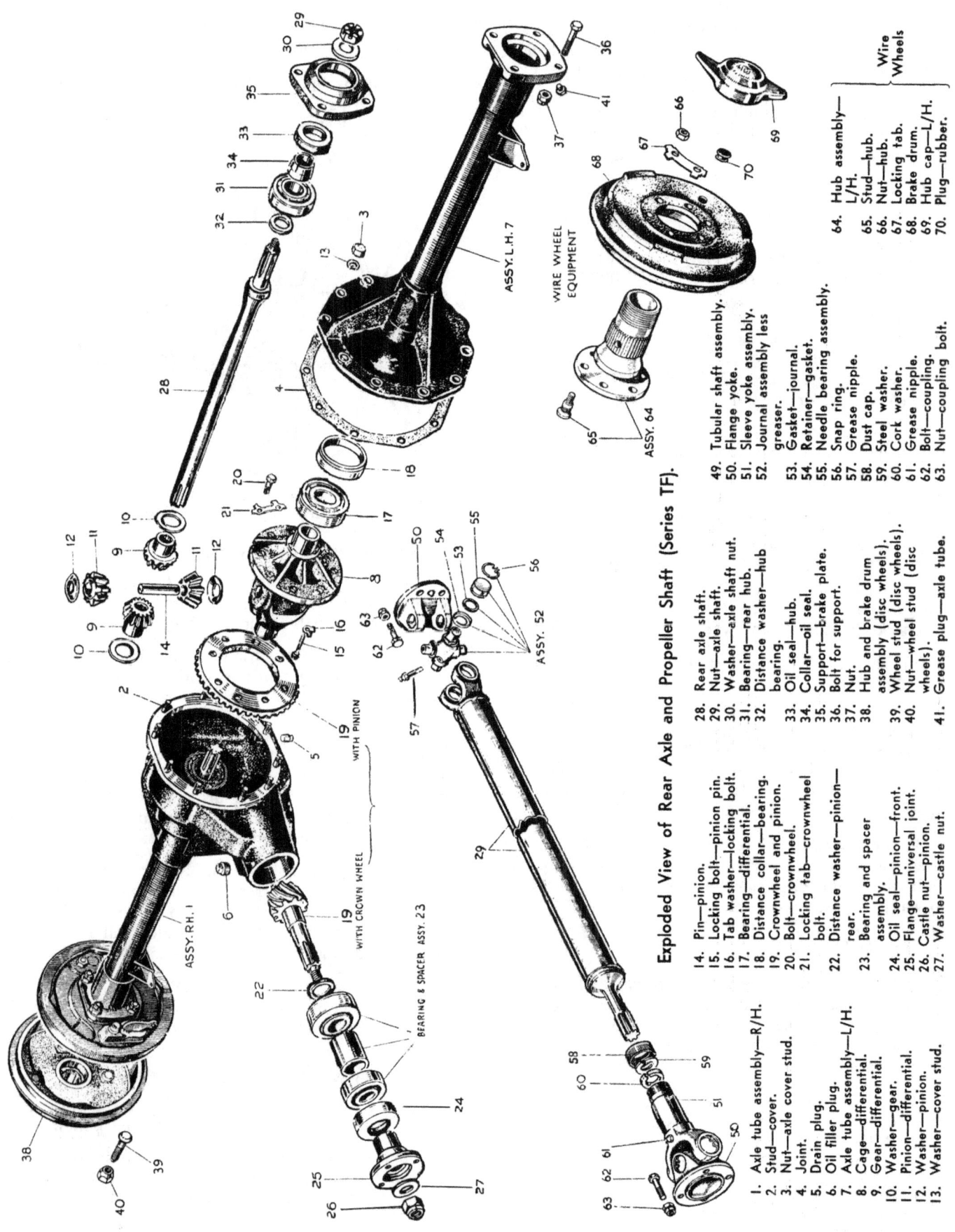

Exploded View of Rear Axle and Propeller Shaft (Series TF).

1. Axle tube assembly—R/H.
2. Stud—cover.
3. Nut—axle cover stud.
4. Drain plug.
5. Oil filler plug.
6. Axle tube assembly—L/H.
7. Cage—differential.
8. Gear—differential.
9. Washer—gear.
10. Pinion—differential.
11. Washer—pinion.
12. Washer—cover stud.
13. Pin—pinion.
14. Locking bolt—pinion pin.
15. Tab washer—locking bolt.
16. Bearing—differential.
17. Distance collar—bearing.
18. Crownwheel and pinion.
19. Bolt—crownwheel.
20. Locking tab—crownwheel bolt.
21. Distance washer—crownwheel bolt.
22. Distance washer—pinion—rear.
23. Bearing and spacer assembly.
24. Oil seal—pinion—front.
25. Flange—universal joint.
26. Castle nut—pinion.
27. Washer—castle nut.
28. Rear axle shaft.
29. Nut—axle shaft.
30. Washer—axle shaft nut.
31. Bearing—rear hub.
32. Distance washer—hub bearing.
33. Oil seal—hub.
34. Collar—oil seal.
35. Support—brake plate.
36. Bolt for support.
37. Nut.
38. Hub and brake drum assembly (disc wheels).
39. Wheel stud (disc wheels).
40. Nut—wheel stud (disc wheels).
41. Grease plug—axle tube.
49. Tubular shaft assembly.
50. Flange yoke.
51. Sleeve yoke assembly.
52. Journal assembly less greaser.
53. Gasket—journal.
54. Retainer—gasket.
55. Needle bearing assembly.
56. Snap ring.
57. Grease nipple.
58. Dust cap.
59. Steel washer.
60. Cork washer.
61. Grease nipple.
62. Bolt—coupling.
63. Nut—coupling bolt.
64. Hub assembly—L/H. } Wire Wheels
65. Stud—hub.
66. Nut—hub.
67. Locking tab.
68. Brake drum.
69. Hub cap—L/H.
70. Plug—rubber.

casing and the same calculations for the selection of the required new distance collar for the differential bearings involved.

TO INSTALL CROWNWHEEL AND PINION HAVING MARKINGS DIFFERENT FROM ORIGINAL

NOTE: The crownwheels and pinions are manufactured in matched pairs and are not replaceable individually. The necessity for replacing either a pinion or crownwheel therefore necessitates the fitting of a new pair of components and the operations of fitting a new pinion and a new crownwheel are involved.

The crownwheels are marked on their back faces with one of the following markings: +2, +1, Zero (or no marking), —1 and —2.

Read off the markings from the back face of the old crownwheel and note the difference between this and the marking on the new crownwheel.

For example: If the old one is marked —1 (—.001″) and the new one +2 (+.002″), the dimensional difference is + .003″. To reassemble correctly it is thus necessary to fit a new distance collar in the axle casing which is .003″ thicker than the old one, and a new one .003″ thinner than the old one in the axle cover.

Note that the combined thickness of these distance collars must remain the same.

The setting of the pinion is carried out as described.

TO REASSEMBLE AXLE

Provided that no replacement parts are installed, the assembly of the axle is quite straightforward if proper note is taken of the positions of various distance pieces, washers and spacers on dismantling and they are replaced in exactly their original locations.

The installation of the axle cover to the axle casing is carried out with a gasket between their joint surfaces. The calculations made for adjustment provide for the thickness of the gasket, but it is important that a genuine MG replacement is used. (Thickness of gasket .005″ when compressed.)

(1) The differential assembly should be assembled in the axle casing, making sure that its bearing in the axle casing is right home in its housing and that a gasket is in position on the joint surface.

(2) The axle cover is then placed in position over the axle casing and carefully pushed home till the joint faces are in contact.

(3) The ten nuts fastening the halves of the axle housing together are then screwed lightly in position and finally tightened up a quarter of a turn at a time in a diagonal sequence to ensure even tightening and absence of distortion.

(4) The brake back plates, the axle half-shafts, and the hub and brake drum assemblies should then be installed in the manner already described.

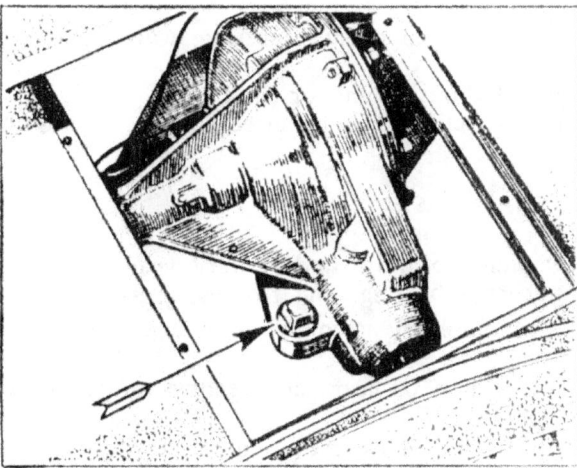

Rear axle filler plug TD, TF

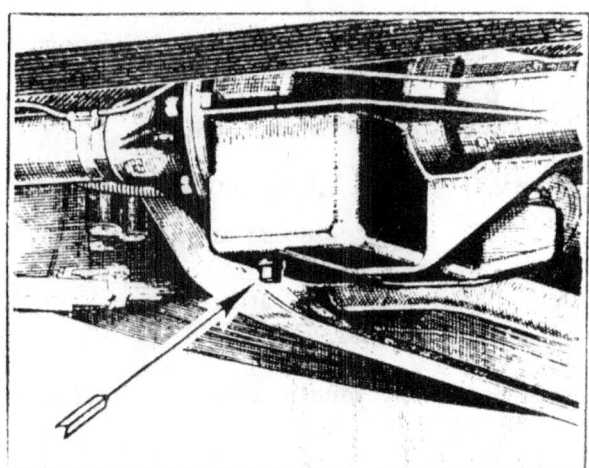

Rear axle drain plug TD, TF

6. MODIFICATIONS

A production modification on the hypoid rear axles as fitted to **TD** and **TF** models affects the interchangeability of all threaded parts such as nuts, bolts and studs. Originally, BSF threads were used, but on later axles either ANF or Unified threads will be found. It should be noted that while for all practical purposes ANF and Unified are interchangeable with one another, neither is interchangeable with BSF. All components with the Unified threads, which are now being standardized on all BMC cars, are marked in the following manner:
Nuts: A circular groove in the end face of the nut or connected circles stamped on one flat of the hexagon. Bolts and set screws: A circular depression turned on the head or connected circles stamped on one flat of the hexagon. Wheel stud nuts have a notch cut in all corners of the hexagon.

Note: Certain axles were fitted with parts having the ANF thread. There is no identification mark for ANF threads, but these axles have been fitted with wheel stud nuts with the notches as on Unified and it is by this means only that they can be identified.

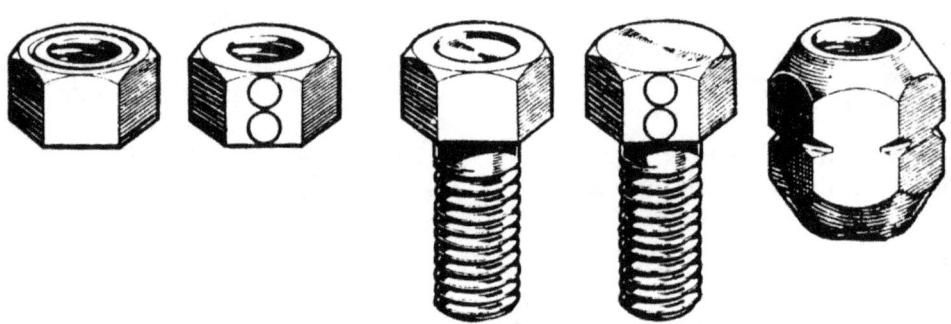

7. REAR AXLE FAULT DIAGNOSIS

(1) REAR WHEEL NOISE

Possible cause	*Remedy*
(a) Wheel loose on axle flange.	— Check condition of axle and tighten or renew components.
(b) Defective brake components (shoes or wheel cylinder).	— Renew faulty components.
(c) Worn or defective axle shaft bearing, lack of lubrication.	— Renew faulty components, lubricate with recommended fluid.
(d) Bent axle tube or shaft.	— Renew axle housing and/or shaft.
(e) Wheel out of balance or bent.	— Check and rectify wheel balance or renew or true up.

(2) FINAL DRIVE GEAR NOISE

Possible cause	*Remedy*
(a) Faulty pinion bearings.	— Renew pinion bearings and readjust gears.
(b) Faulty differential carrier bearings.	— Renew carrier bearings and readjust gears.
(c) Lack of lubrication.	— Check condition of assembly, flush and renew lubricant.
(d) Incorrectly adjusted crownwheel and pinion.	— Check condition of gears and readjust or renew as mated pair.
(e) Incorrectly adjusted bearing preload (pinion or carrier bearings).	— Check condition of assembly, adjust bearing preload or renew faulty components.
(f) Excessive noise or grind under load.	— Overhaul assembly and renew faulty components.
(g) Excessive noise or grind on overdrive.	— Overhaul assembly and renew faulty components.
(h) Excessive noise on coast.	— Faulty final drive gears and adjustment. Renew and readjust.
(i) Bent axle housing.	— Renew housing and faulty components.

(3) EXCESSIVE BACKLASH IN DIFFERENTIAL

Possible cause
Remedy

(a) Looseness between axle shaft and differential side gear splines. — Check and renew axle shafts and/or side gears.

(b) Worn differential side gear thrust washers. — Check and renew differential side gear thrust washers.

(c) Worn differential pinion thrust washers. — Check and renew differential pinion thrust washers.

(d) Excessive backlash between differential side gears and pinions. — Check condition of gear and pinion teeth and renew, or renew gear and/or pinion thrust washers.

(e) Excessive wear between differential shaft and pinions and/or shaft bore in carrier housing. — Check and renew faulty components.

(4) PINION SHAFT ROTATES BUT WILL NOT DRIVE VEHICLE (NO NOISE)

Possible cause
Remedy

(a) Broken axle shaft. — Check and renew axle shaft.

(5) REPEATED AXLE SHAFT BREAKAGE

Possible cause
Remedy

(a) Bent axle housing. — Check and renew housing.

(b) Repeated over loading. — Revise load capacity.

(c) Abnormal clutch operation. — Revise driving habits or check condition of clutch.

(6) LOSS OF REAR AXLE LUBRICANT

Possible cause
Remedy

(a) Faulty final drive pinion or axle shaft oil seals. — Check and renew oil seal/s.

(b) Clogged axle housing breather. — Remove and wash out breather in cleaning fluid.

(c) Leaking gasket between differential carrier and axle housing. — Renew faulty gasket.

(d) Incorrect type of lubricant causing excessive foaming. — Drain, flush and refill axle housing to correct level with recommended lubricant.

STEERING TC SERIES
1. STEERING BALL JOINTS

These will need periodical inspection and cleaning. If they are dismantled, be extremely careful to reassemble all parts in the same order. When adjusting, the slotted end plug should be screwed up tightly and then released half a turn and the split pin replaced. After reassembling, lubricate all parts.

In case the order of the springs and ball seats in the drag-link is lost when dismantling, the following details will give the necessary information for correct reassembly: ball seat, ball, ball seat, spring, plug and split pin at the axle arm end; spring, cup, ball, end plug and split pin at the steering drop arm end.

2. STEERING GEARBOX

The operation of the cam steering gear is quite straightforward. A cam, in which a spiral groove is cut, is mounted on the shaft carrying the steering wheel. Into this groove is inserted a follower which makes contact with the cam track.

The cam is mounted between special ball bearings expressly designed for the duty they have to perform.

The whole mechanism is contained in an oil-tight casing and replenishment at intervals is the only attention required.

It will be observed that the cam and mainshaft are mounted on ball bearings, which take the thrust from the rocker shaft, and shims of various thickness are introduced under the end cover so that the cam can be adjusted for float.

It should never be necessary to alter the adjustment which is carefully set before the car leaves the works; but if the gear is dismantled for cleaning or inspection a careful note of the number of shims should be made. On reassembly this shaft should spin with the fingers, but there should be absolutely no end play.

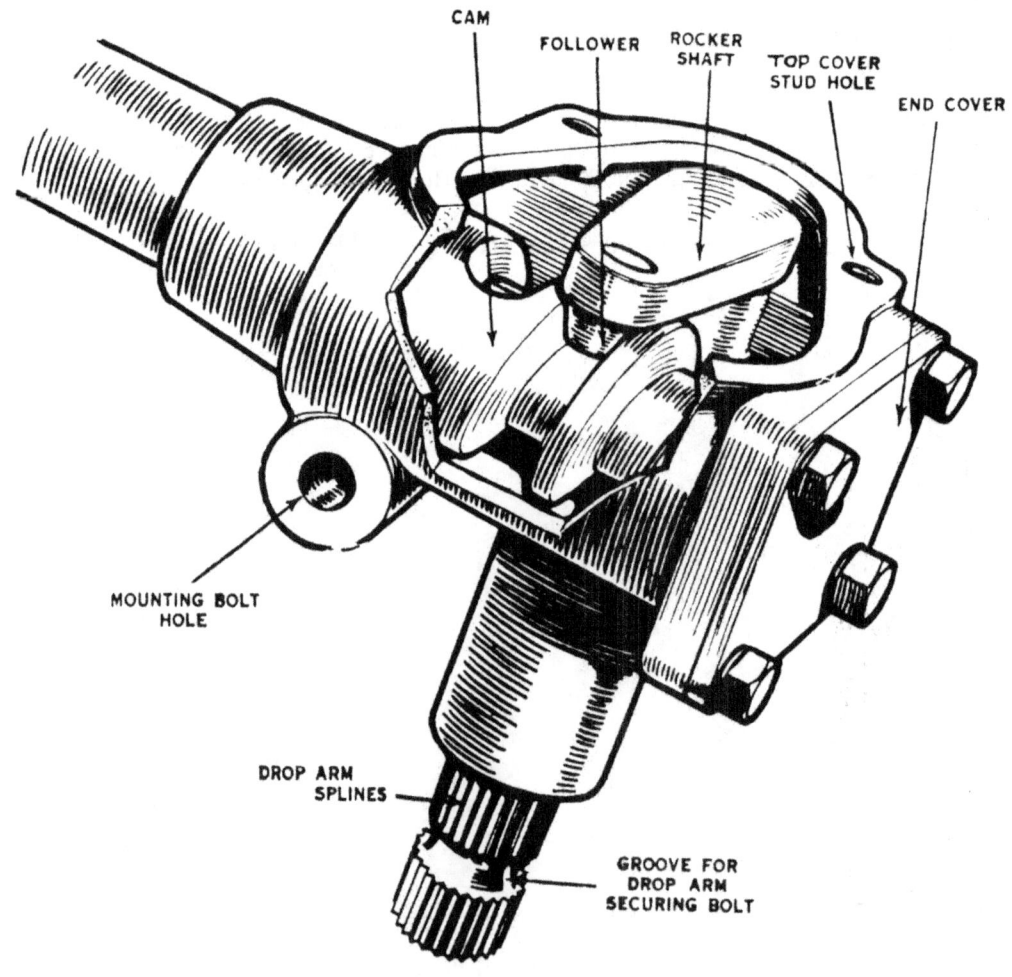

Bishop cam steering box

TO ADJUST ROCKER SHAFT

The only adjustment ever likely to be needed is the removal of one or more shims from underneath the side cover plate (see illustration) covering the lever inside the steering gearbox.

The motion of the steering wheel is transmitted to the road wheels through the cam and the follower fitted into the lever, and in time a small amount of wear (as shown by lost motion) between the steering wheel and the drop arm when the road wheels are in the straight ahead position may possibly become apparent; but the whole of this can be removed and the gear restored to its original perfection by the removal of one or more of the shims mentioned.

As these shims vary in thickness, a very fine adjustment can be obtained. If too many shims are removed the gear will become a little stiff in the centre of its travel, and this must not be permitted.

All adjustments to the steering gear should be carried out with the drag link disconnected.

TO ASSEMBLE

The cam track is slightly relieved from the centre towards each end, so that whereas in the central position there is practically metal-to-metal contact, provision is made to give a little clearance at full lock in both directions. The gear should be adjusted so that there is no play whatever when the road wheels are straight ahead.

Care should be taken to see that the flat face of the rocker shaft makes a good bearing against the hardened side cover plate, and that the felt washer is properly in place between the top face of the drop arm and the top face of the steering gearbox.

All adjustments to the gear should be made before the unit is filled with oil.

3. DROP ARM

TO REMOVE

The drop arm is attached to the rocker shaft on a splined parallel shaft and secured by a bolt and nut which passes through a groove in the splined shaft.

TO INSTALL

Should it be necessary to remove the drop arm from the rocker shaft at any time, it is recommended that the marks on the end of the rocker shaft and the boss of the drop arm be noted so that they can be fitted together again in the same relative position.

In case this marking has been obliterated the correct method of fitting, which is of some importance, is given below. Should this operation not be properly carried out, the available lock will be limited in one direction or the other, and damage may result to the internal mechanism of the gearbox.

(1) The steering column, complete with steering box, but without the drop arm attached, should (if it has been removed) first be fitted in place in the car, taking care to tighten up all the fixings holding the unit to the car, including that on the dashboard. The steering wheel should be placed in its final position.

(2) Next, the lower end of the drop arm carrying the ball pin should be fixed correctly to the drag-link, but the top end should not yet be connected to the rocker shaft of the steering box.

(3) Now jack up the front wheels and place them in the straight-ahead position.

(4) If the steering wheel is rotated gently it will be found that its movement is limited by internal stops in the steering box at each end of the travel of the internal mechanism of the gear. The number of turns of the steering wheel required to bring the gear from one end of its travel to the other should be counted. Then, commencing from one of these stops, take the wheel back half the complete number of turns available, which will bring the steering mechanism into its central position. The drop arm can then be fitted to the rocker shaft.

(5) Before tightening up, however, the following check should always be carried out.

(6) The front wheels still being jacked up, with the steering wheel pull the steering right over to lock, either right or left. With the steering wheel and front wheels in this position drop the drag-link off the drop arm and see whether you can move the steering wheel any further in the same direction. If you can, and the same procedure can be followed on the other lock, everything is in order.

Should further movement of the steering wheel be unobtainable it means that the front axle stops are not operating, and some adjustment must be made as follows:

(a) If there is movement of the steering wheel available on one lock, but not on the other, the drop arm should be put on the next serration on the rocker shaft, which may put matters right.

(b) If no serration will give free movement of the steering wheel at both locks, then the front axle stops must be altered so that there is.

(c) The amount of free movement available after dropping the drag-link off the drop arm should be the same at both locks, and this is the condition at which to aim.

TO REMOVE STEERING COLUMN

Removing the steering column from the car is quite a simple operation. It will, of course, be necessary to remove the foot ramp, steering wheel, disconnect the steering column support bracket under the scuttle, which also means removing the baffle board; remove the bolts which secure the steering column bracket to the frame, when the column complete with this bracket can be withdrawn.

STEERING TD—TF—TF 1500 SERIES
1. STEERING WHEEL AND COLUMN

TO REMOVE STEERING WHEEL AND TELESCOPIC EXTENSION

(1) Remove the clamping nut from the telescopic adjustment clamp and extract the clamping bolt; this will permit the wheel to be withdrawn to its full extent and enable the plated helical sleeve to be contracted towards the wheel to reveal the key at the upper end of the column which engages the long keyway in the splined adjustable shaft.

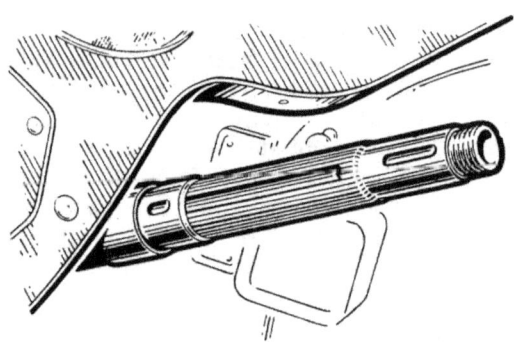

Splined Upper End of Steering Column, Showing Keyways.

(2) Remove the key from the column, this will release the steering wheel and telescopic column assembly which can then be removed to a bench for further dismantling.

(3) Take off the MG medallion at the wheel boss. There is a countersunk locating screw which enters from the side.

(4) Undo the large nut holding the wheel to the shaft.

(5) Support the hub of the wheel and with a shouldered copper drift carefully drive the splined shaft out of the wheel, taking care of the flat key locating the wheel to the splined shaft. Alternatively an extractor can be used to part the two components.

TO REMOVE STEERING COLUMN

(1) Remove the steering wheel, and take out the bolt and nut from the support clip under the dash. Then take out the bolt and nut holding the steering column to the body steady bracket (this is on the engine side of the bulkhead).

(2) Remove the split pins, take off the nuts and unscrew the three bolts at the universal joint. Do not lose the rubber inserts.

(3) This will free the inner and outer columns, which may be pulled out towards the front in the space between the radiator and the wing.

(4) When reassembling note that the screws on the universal joint should be tightened fully against their shoulders.

2. STEERING GEARBOX

TO REMOVE AND INSTALL

(1) Raise the car at the front and block up under the chassis. Remove the wheels and disconnect the two track rods at their outer ends.

(2) Detach all electric cables which, it will be found, are secured to the unit by means of clips.

(3) Remove the outer ball joint on the same side as the steering column, taking care not to lose its position for reassembly.

(4) Undo the engine steady rod and remove its mounting bracket from the chassis.

(5) Remove the three screws and nuts at the universal joint on the steering column and then detach the steering gearbox from the frame (four bolts and nuts).

(6) By sliding the complete unit to one side it will be possible to pull the track rod, from which the ball end has been removed, through the large hole in the chassis and then the whole unit may be lifted away to the front.

(7) Installation is a reversal of this process.

TO DISMANTLE AND REASSEMBLE

(1) Undo the clips and remove the rubber dust excluders.

(2) Unscrew the rack damper pad cap and the damper spring. The pressure pad can then be lifted away. A number of shims will be found under the cap.

(3) Remove the pinion shaft cap bolts and cap, then remove the coupling nut and slide off the coupling.

(4) Take off the circlip against which the coupling locates.

(5) Withdraw the pinion shaft holding the gear with the pinion upwards and leaving the thrust washer. This thrust washer is trapped behind the rack teeth.

(6) Hold the rack bar in suitable clamps in a vice, knock back the lockwashers and undo the ball joint caps with the special spanner, tool No T114. The ball seat and shims should now drop out.

(7) Screw out the ball seat housing with a special claw spanner, tool No T113.

NOTE: Should the ball joint caps come away complete with the ball seat housing it will be necessary to dismantle them with the use of tool No T122.

(8) Remove the rack damper and shims and withdraw the rack bar from the housing.

Fractures in the teeth, hollows or any roughness on the surfaces of the teeth will render the parts unserviceable.

(9) Check the rack bar and pinion shaft in the housing for wear or scoring.

(10) The diameter of the rack bar is 1.121" to 1.120" and the bore of the housing is 1.136" to 1.130" at the pinion end and 1.124" to 1.126" at the other end.

(11) The pinion shaft is .748" to .7485" diameter at the top and .624" to .6235" at the bottom. The bore of the housing is .7505" to .750" and the bore of the cap .6255" to .626". If a new cap is fitted this will be found to be supplied with an undersize bore and will need reaming in line with the housing with a special reamer, tool No T112. Make sure that the oil groove is fitted to the top when reaming.

(12) Check the felt washer and the rubber bellows and replace if necessary.

(13) Examine the steering rod balls and caps for wear and replace as necessary or re-adjust as detailed.

(14) Reassembly is a reversal of the dismantling process, with attention to the following:

NOTE: When replacing the pinion shaft see that the thrust washers have their chamfered sides towards the pinion. End-float should be .002" to .005" and is set by the shims.

(a) The oilway in the cap should be at the top and the damper pad must be adjusted as detailed.

(b) With the rack in the central position engage the pinion with the arrow uupermost.

(c) Install the coupling with a coupling bolt in line with the arrow on the shaft. This will ensure that the steering wheel spokes are in the correct position in the car.

TO ADJUST INNER STEERING BALL JOINT

(1) Install the lock plate and shims and screw home the ball seat housing into the rack bar.

(2) Insert the ball seat, and screw the ball cap home against its shoulder after inserting the ball-ended tie-rod. The ball should have no play, but must be a free rolling fit.

(3) Alter the adjustment by varying the shims, which are supplied in .003" and .005" sizes.

TO ADJUST RACK DAMPER

This is provided to ensure the required amount of damping in the steering tie-rods, and to maintain the minimum of backlash in the gear teeth.

It should be adjusted in the following manner:

(1) Check the damper spring, which should have a free length of approximately 1.024" and should give a load of 80 lb when compressed to .750".

(2) When the steering gearbox is completely assembled, fit the cap, spring and plunger but omit the shims.

(3) Screw down the cap until the plunger bottoms. While screwing down the plunger rotate the pinion shaft. When it is felt to just lock the rack bar in the housing the plunger has bottomed.

(4) With feeler gauges take a measurement of the gap left and add to this measurement .051".

(5) Select shims to this total amount and insert under the cap. This gives the correct standard pre-load. If, when checked on the road, this is found to be too slack or too tight, it is permissible to decrease the added measurement of .051" to .030" or increase to .070".

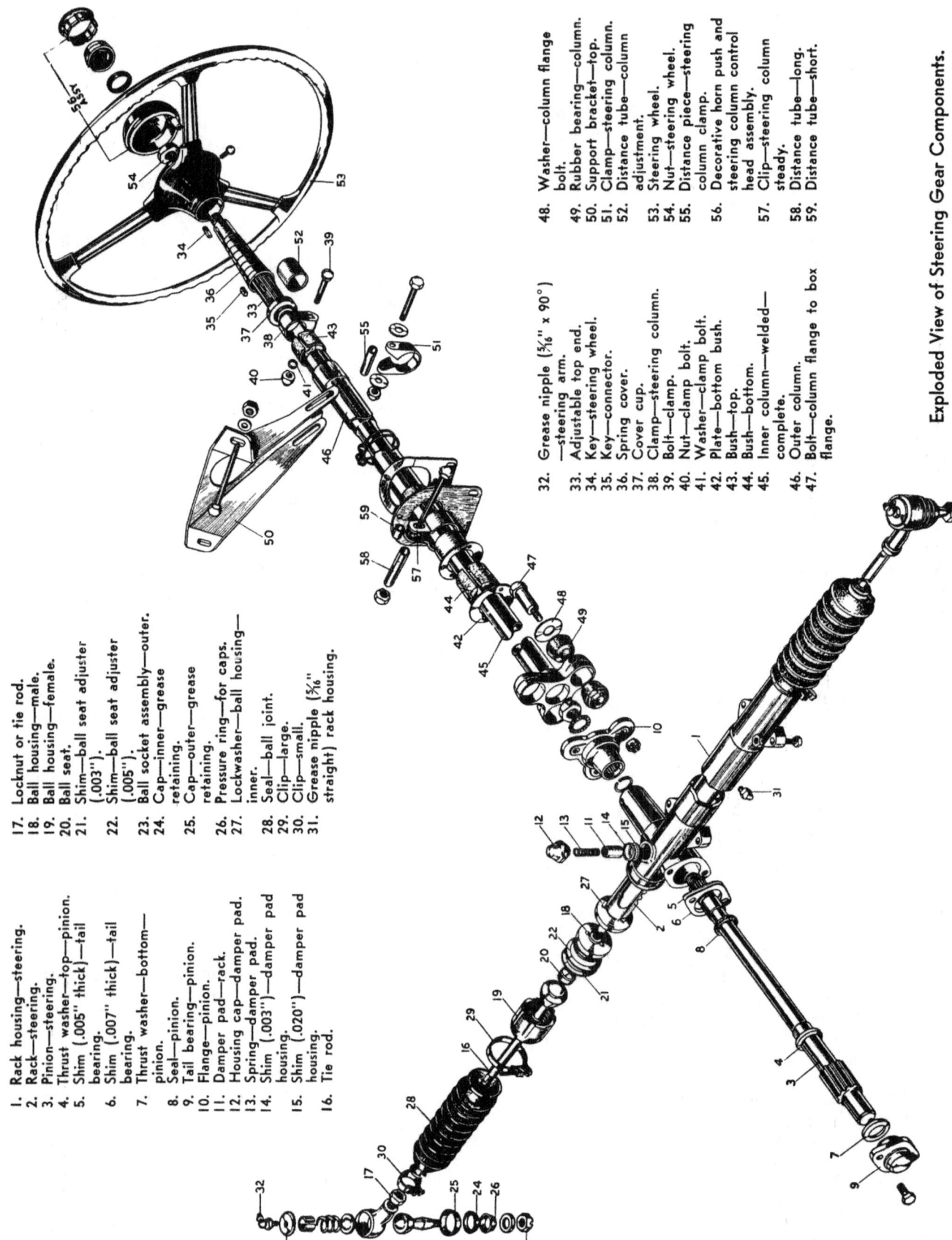

Exploded View of Steering Gear Components.

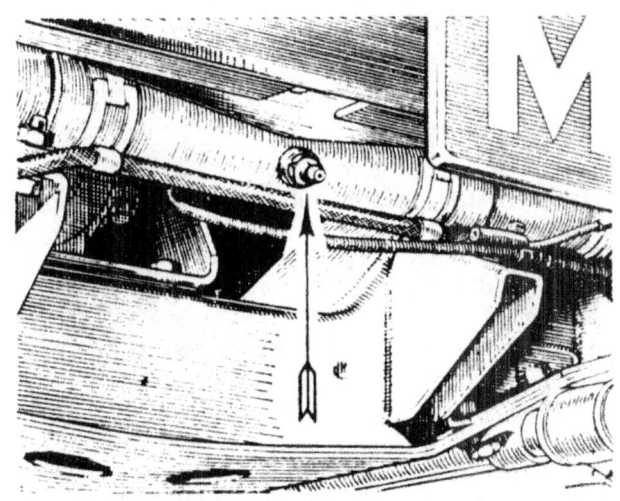

Oil nipple, rack and pinion steering

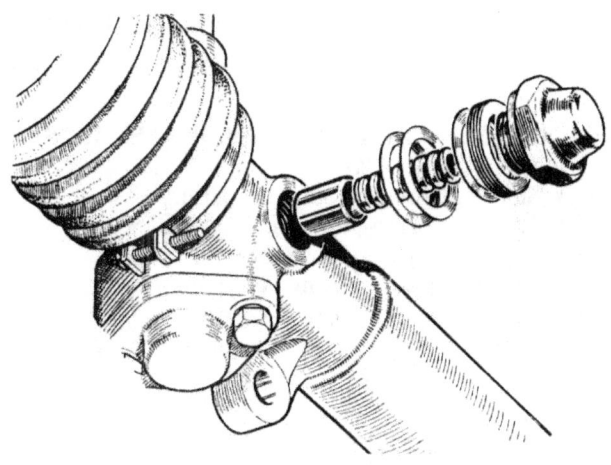

Steering Rack Damper Assembly Components.

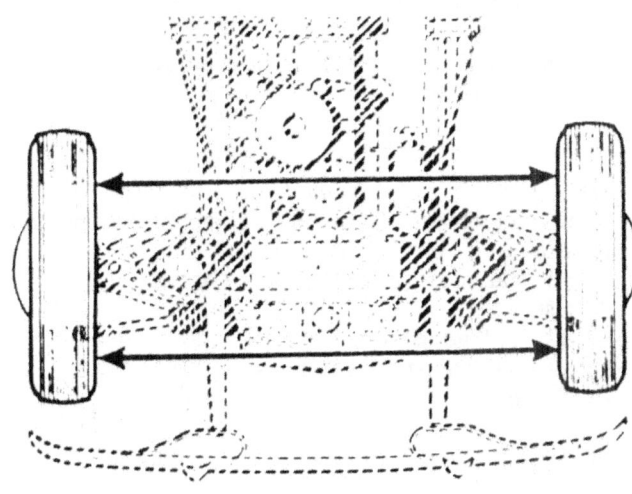

Checking front wheel alignment

Subtract the front measurement from the rear measurement to obtain the amount of toe-in. This should be:
Model TC . . . . $\frac{3}{16}$ to $\frac{1}{4}$ inch.
Models TD, TF . . . . . Nil (i.e., front wheels parallel).

STEERING ARM BALL JOINTS

If it is found necessary, through slackness, to replace the ball joints on the outer ends of the tie-rods, the complete assembly must be changed, as no adjustment is provided. If necessary the dirt excluders may be replaced separately.

3. MODIFICATIONS

STEERING BALL SOCKET ASSEMBLY THREADS

Chassis numbers TF4760 onwards are fitted with modified steering ball-end assemblies which incorporate Unified threads for the ball-pin nut and for the grease nipple. The threaded bore for the steering tie-rod remains a BSF thread.

4. STEERING FAULT DIAGNOSIS
TC SERIES

(1) EXCESSIVE PLAY OR LOOSENESS IN STEERING GEAR

Possible cause	Remedy
(a) Steering linkage loose or worn.	— Overhaul steering gear and renew worn components.
(b) Bearings, king-pins and bushings worn.	— Renew worn parts.
(c) Wheel bearings loose or worn.	— Tighten or renew.
(d) Steering gear housing loose on frame.	— Check and tighten bolts.
(e) Steering wheel loose on post.	— Tighten.
(f) Steering gear adjustment incorrect or excessive wear.	— Adjust or replace worn parts as necessary.

(2) HEAVY STEERING

Possible cause	Remedy
(a) Low or uneven tyre pressure.	— Check tyres and inflate to recommended pressures.
(b) Steering gear incorrectly adjusted.	— Check and readjust steering gear.
(c) Lack of lubrication in steering linkage joints.	— Check and lubricate as applicable.
(d) Incorrect caster, camber, toe-in or king pin inclination.	— Check, adjust or replace to obtain correct values.
(e) Steering gear and column mountings misaligned.	— Check and re-align.
(f) Springs weak or sagging.	— Replace springs.
(g) Frame bent or fractured.	— Check, repair or replace as necessary.
(h) Steering shaft or tubing bent.	— Replace bent units.

(3) STEERING PULLS TO ONE SIDE

Possible cause	Remedy
(a) Uneven tyre wear or pressure.	— Check condition of tyres and inflate to recommended pressures.
(b) Rear wheels not tracking with front wheels.	— Check rear wheel alignment and correct.
(c) Over-tight wheel bearings.	— Adjust.
(d) Incorrect front wheel alignment.	— Check and adjust.
(e) Dragging brakes.	— Check and adjust brake shoes.
(f) Distorted frame.	— Check and rectify.

(4) FRONT WHEEL WOBBLE OR SHIMMY

Possible cause	Remedy
(a) Loose spring U bolts.	— Tighten.
(b) Tyres bulged or wheels out of balance.	— Replace tyres and balance wheels.
(c) Front wheel alignment incorrect.	— Rectify as necessary.
(d) Faulty shock absorbers.	— Check and renew as a pair.
(e) Loose or worn tie rod ends.	— Check and renew faulty components.
(f) Worn or badly adjusted front wheel bearings.	— Check condition and adjust.
(g) Front end of frame damaged or distorted.	— Check and rectify front end damage and alignment.

(5) STEERING ERRATIC OR WANDERING

Possible cause	Remedy
(a) Bent steering knuckle and/or king pin.	— Replace bent parts.
(b) Incorrect or uneven camber or caster setting.	— Check and renew components as necessary.
(c) Smooth front tyres.	— Renew tyres.
(d) Excessive play in steering gear or linkage.	— Check and renew faulty components, readjust.
(e) Excessively high or low tyre pressures.	— Check and inflate to recommended pressures.
(f) Loose or incorrectly adjusted front wheel bearings.	— Check and adjust.
(g) Rear-axle housing shifted.	— Align and repair.

TD—TF—TF 1500 SERIES

(1) EXCESSIVE PLAY OR LOOSENESS IN STEERING GEAR
Possible cause — *Remedy*
- (a) Steering rack and pinion worn. — Overhaul steering gear and renew worn components.
- (b) Steerage linkage ball joints worn or loose. — Tighten or renew faulty components.
- (c) Rack housing assembly to sub frame mounting bolts loose. — Check and tighten mounting bolts.
- (d) Wear in steering column universal joint. — Renew faulty components.

(2) HEAVY STEERING
Possible cause — *Remedy*
- (a) Low or uneven tyre pressure. — Check tyres and inflate to recommended pressures.
- (b) Steering gear incorrectly adjusted. — Check and re-adjust steering gear.
- (c) Lack of lubrication in steering linkage joints. — Check and lubricate steering linkage where applicable.
- (d) Front suspension worn or out of alignment. — Check front end for wear, renew worn components and re-align front end.
- (e) Mis-alignment between steering gear and column mountings. — Check and align steering gear and column mountings.
- (f) Soft or sagging front coil springs. — Renew coil springs and check front end alignment.

(3) STEERING PULLS TO ONE SIDE
Possible cause — *Remedy*
- (a) Uneven tyre wear or pressure. — Check condition of tyres and inflate to recommended pressures.
- (b) Incorrect front end adjustment. — Check front end alignment.
- (c) Dragging brakes. — Check and adjust brake shoes.
- (d) Broken or sagging rear spring/s. — Renew faulty springs.
- (e) Broken rear spring centre bolt. — Renew faulty components.
- (f) Damaged front suspension or front sub-frame members. — Check and renew damaged components.
- (g) Faulty or damaged front crossmember. — Check and renew front crossmember.

(4) FRONT WHEEL WOBBLE OR SHIMMY
Possible cause — *Remedy*
- (a) Looseness in steering gear. — Rectify and adjust.
- (b) Uneven tyre wear or incorrect tyre pressures. — Check condition of tyres and inflate to recommended pressures.
- (c) Tyre and/or wheel unbalance. — Check and balance as necessary.
- (d) Front end damaged or out of alignment. — Check and rectify front end damage and alignment.
- (e) Worn or badly adjusted front wheel bearing. — Check condition and adjust wheel bearings.
- (f) Front wheel alignment incorrectly adjusted. — Check and adjust front wheel toe-in (alignment).
- (g) Loose or worn tie-rod ends. — Check and renew faulty components.
- (h) Faulty shock absorbers. — Check and renew as a pair.

(5) STEERING ERRATIC OR WANDERING
Possible cause — *Remedy*
- (a) Incorrect or uneven camber and/or caster setting. — Check and renew components to rectify.
- (b) Smooth front tyres. — Check and renew tyres as necessary.
- (c) Excessive play in steering gear and/or linkage. — Check and renew faulty components, readjust.
- (d) Excessively high or low tyre pressures. — Check and inflate to recommended pressures.
- (e) Loose or incorrectly adjusted front wheel bearings. — Check and adjust front wheel bearings.

TC SERIES

1. FRONT AXLE

TO REMOVE

(1) First block up the car under the chassis; the correct height is with the tyres just touching the ground when the car is resting on its blocks.

(2) Undo the spring shackles at the front and rear ends, after disconnecting the Lockheed brake pipes where the flexible hose is connected to the copper pipe on the chassis.

(3) Disconnect the drag-link at the axle end. The axle complete with springs can then be drawn clear from the car.

TO REMOVE AND INSTALL FRONT WHEEL BEARINGS

(1) Having removed a locknut and wheel, remove the grease from inside the hub. There is a hole in the hub where it is splined, covered with a steel plug. Removal of the plug gives access to the split pin locking the castellated nut, which can be withdrawn through the hole.

(2) Remove the hub nut with a box spanner. The hub can then be withdrawn complete with the bearings with the aid of a suitable puller (hub drawer, part No T 61).

(3) The outer ball race is smaller than the inner one and can easily be withdrawn from the housing, but before the inner one can be removed from the other end of the housing, the oil seal will have to be taken out.

(4) When installing, the bearings and distance piece will go together without any difficulty, but it is well, on tightening the castellated nut, to spin the hub to make sure it rotates freely.

(5) Finally, do not forget to replace the split pin, the steel plug, the grease inside the hub, and to smear the splines on the outside of the hub with general purpose grease.

TO REMOVE KING PIN

First dismantle the hub as previously described, then take off the brake back plate complete with shoes. The king pin is held in place with a small cotter, when this has been removed the king pin can be withdrawn.

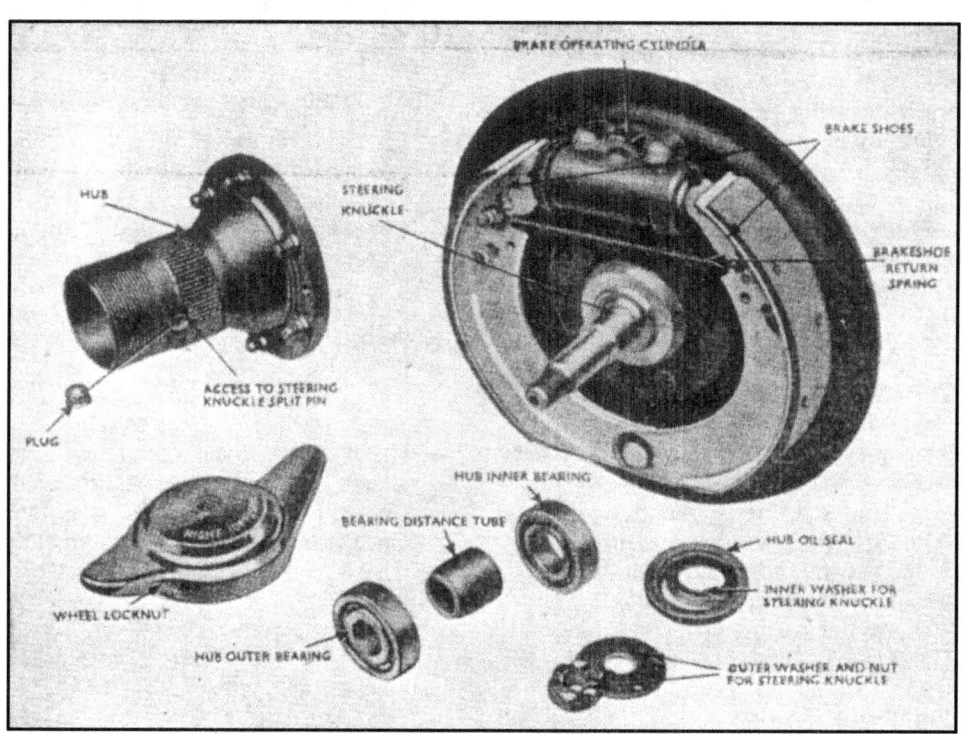

Dismantled View of Front Hub.

TO RENEW KING PIN BUSHES

When the old bushes have been pressed out from the steering knuckles and new bushes pressed in, it is necessary to ream them with a reamer of sufficient length to do the two at once, thus ensuring that they are in line with one another. Do not install a king pin too tightly, it should be just possible to press it in without the use of tools.

When installed there should be just sufficient vertical free movement to feel between the steering knuckle and the axle beam eye. If measured with a feeler, the clearance should not exceed .004" between the steel thrust washer and the flange of the brass bush.

2. FRONT ROAD SPRINGS

The forward ends of these springs are attached to the front end of the chassis by means of hardened steel suspension pins, which run directly in the spring eyes and are lubricated by way of grease gun nipples fitted into their outer ends.

If any wear takes place at these points, replacement pins will usually take care of it, but if excessive wear has also taken place in the spring eyes, new top spring leaves will be required.

At the rear end of each spring is fitted a swinging shackle. This is fitted with four special rubber bushes which are simply placed into the spring eye and frame tube from either side, and clamped up by the shackle plates. These bushes will be found to be quite a loose fit, but when clamped will expand into their housings. These bushes do not rotate on their surfaces, the angular movement being taken up by torsional deflection of the rubber.

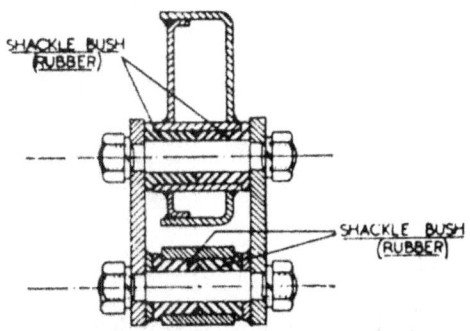

Front spring rear shackle model TC

Special attention should be taken when installing these bushes to maintain a central location, so that the expansion of each half of the bush is equal. To attain this, insert each bush so that it protrudes equally each side of the housing and tighten up the shackle plates evenly. When central, the outer flanges of the bushes should all be of equal proportions.

FRONT AXLE TD—TF—TF 1500 SERIES

1. SUSPENSION UNIT

TO REMOVE

(1) Jack up the front of the car by a suitable jack placed under the centre of the front cross-member, until the front tyres are just clear of the ground.

(2) Remove the front wheels. Block up under chassis.

(3) Place two additional jacks under the spring pans.

(4) Jack these up, taking some of the weight, until the hydraulic damper levers are just clear of the rebound rubbers.

(5) Disconnect the hydraulic brake hoses.

(6) Slacken the steering tie-rod nuts and screw the tie-rods out of the steering ball joints by means of the flats on the rods.

(7) Remove the cotters and nuts from the two outer fulcrum bolts. Draw out the bolts and take away the front hub and swivel pin units complete. (Take care of the thrust washers, rubber seals, retainers and fulcrum pins.)

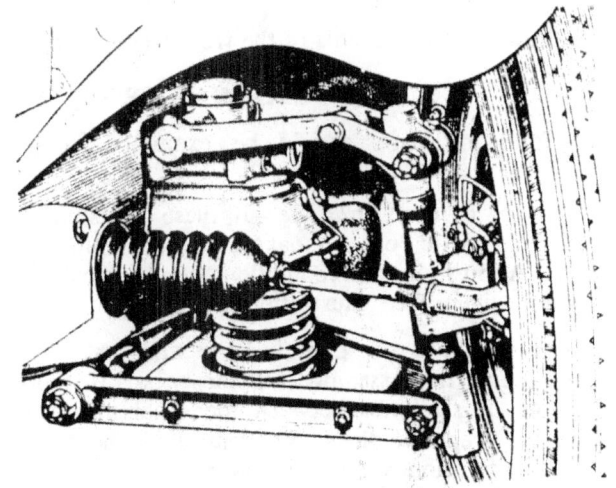

Front suspension assembly models TD and TF

(8) Release the jacks from under the spring pans.

(9) Press down the lower wishbone assemblies and remove the coil springs.

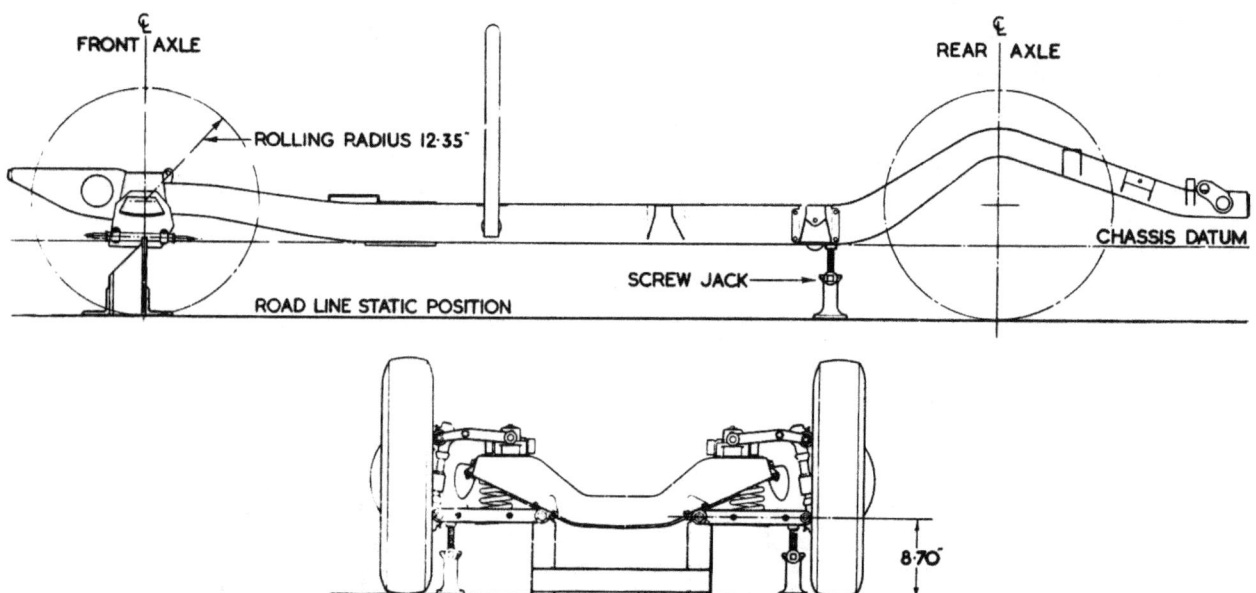

Use of Special Locating Jigs to set Chassis in its Correct Position for Checking Steering Geometry is Advised to Ensure Best Results.

(10) Remove the four bolts holding the spring pan to the levers.

(11) Remove the cotters, nuts and washers from the ends of the inner lower fulcrum pin and slide off the levers and the rubber bushes.

(12) Remove the bolts holding the lower fulcrum pins to the chassis cross-member.

(13) Remove the bolts holding the hydraulic dampers to the top of the chassis cross-member.

(14) Inside the outer ends of the front cross-member will be found the coil spring locating plates. These are each attached by one small bolt.

TO DISMANTLE SWIVEL PINS

(1) Unscrew the upper and lower links from the ends of the swivel pins. The left-hand swivel pin has a left-hand thread at each end.

(2) The stub axle is located by a collar on the swivel pin and the stem of the steering lever engages a groove in the pin. To separate the two the steering lever must be withdrawn from the stub axle, but this procedure is not advised unless absolutely necessary.

TO EXAMINE FRONT SUSPENSION PARTS FOR WEAR

The following parts should be examined before reassembly:

Bushes for bottom wishbone—If these are split or perished, eccentric or oil-soaked, they should be replaced. A bush in new condition should have the dimensions given (see illustration—*Section 4*).

Bottom wishbone — Examine the end holes for elongation and the assembly for looseness. If there is any sign of slackness between the wishbone arms and the pan, separate the components and check the bolt holes for elongation. The bolt holes are $\frac{21}{64}''$ diameter.

Coil springs — Examine for cracks and check for tension, to following details:

    Free length .... $9.59'' \pm \frac{1}{16}''$
    Loaded to 1095 lb ...... $6.44'' \pm \frac{1}{32}''$

Renew the springs if they are defective.

Swivel link assemblies—Check the swivel links. The dimension across the thrust faces should be $2.327'' \pm .0015''$. If these are appreciably worn the assembly of link and bush should be renewed. If the bush only is worn, a new one should be pressed in and reamed and burnished to $.750'' \pm .0005''$.

NOTE: When pressing in this bush see that the hole in the bush faces the threaded bore.

Also check the following:

(1) Check the threaded bores on the swivel pins. When new, these are a free turning fit without slack. An appreciable amount of slack is permissible in these threaded bearings and they do not require renewal unless they are very slack.

(2) Check the fulcrum pin distance tubes for scoring or wear. These should be $2.337'' \pm .0015''$ long by $.7485''$ to $.7480''$ diameter.

104

(3) Examine the case-hardened thrust washers for ridges; the faces should be flat and parallel within .0005".

The thickness should be .068" to .066", the bore .510" to .505", and the outside diameter 1.25".

When the swivel links, distance tubes and thrust washers are assembled, the total end clearance between the link and the thrust washers should be .008" to .013".

(4) Check that all grease nipples are clear.

(5) Examine the rubber seals, and if these are perished or split, replace them.

TO INSTALL

(1) Bolt up the coil spring top locating plates inside the front cross-member.

(2) Bolt on the hydraulic dampers. Dampers are interchangeable from side to side.

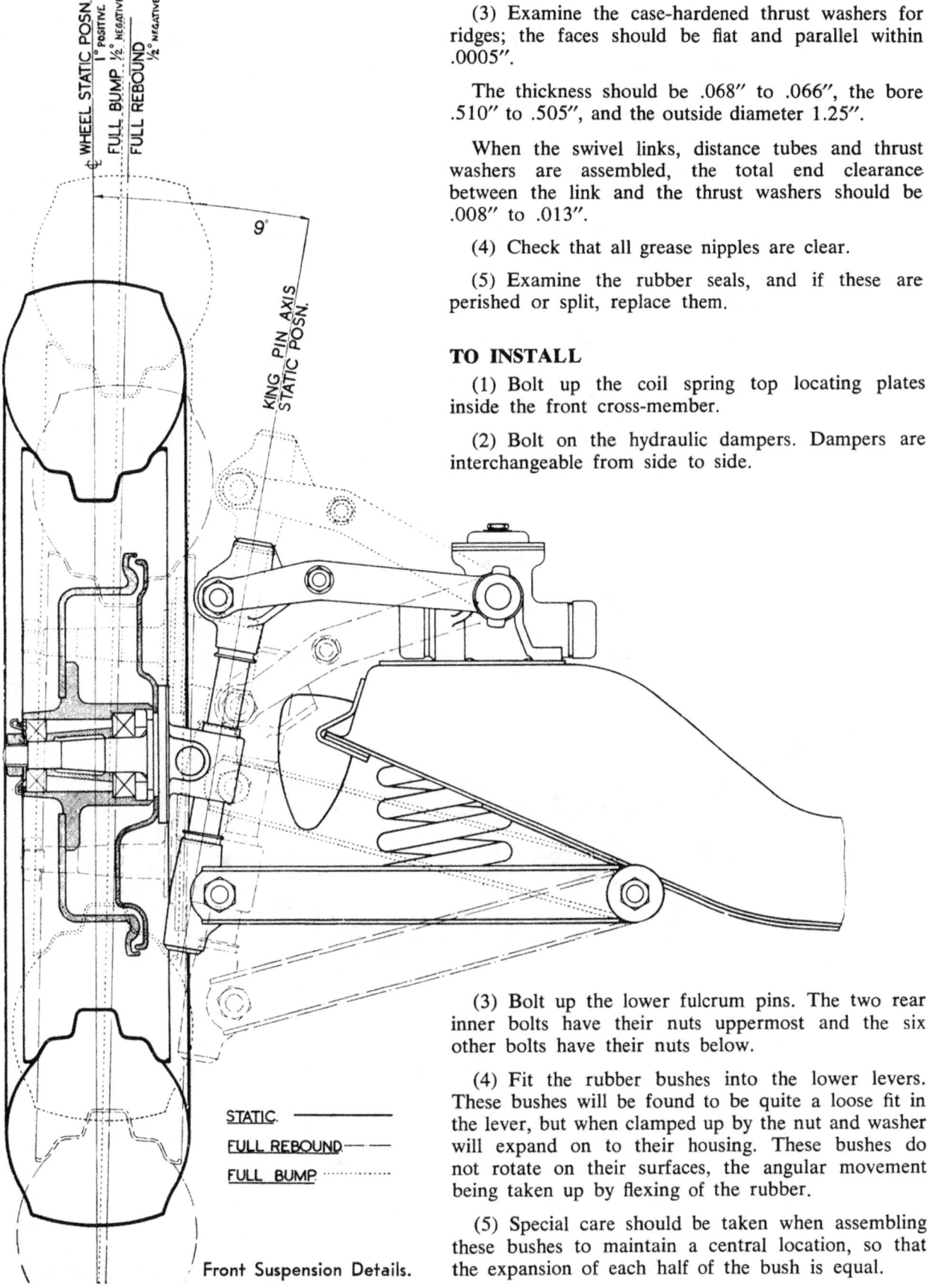

Front Suspension Details.

(3) Bolt up the lower fulcrum pins. The two rear inner bolts have their nuts uppermost and the six other bolts have their nuts below.

(4) Fit the rubber bushes into the lower levers. These bushes will be found to be quite a loose fit in the lever, but when clamped up by the nut and washer will expand on to their housing. These bushes do not rotate on their surfaces, the angular movement being taken up by flexing of the rubber.

(5) Special care should be taken when assembling these bushes to maintain a central location, so that the expansion of each half of the bush is equal.

(6) To attain this, insert each bush so that it protrudes equally each side of the housing and then clamp up with the washer and nut and fit the cotter pins. When central, the outer flanges of the bushes should all be of equal proportions.

(7) It is essential to clamp up the bushes when the lower suspension levers are set parallel with the ground to ensure even stresses on the bushes in service.

(8) Install the spring pans between the levers, but with the heads of the bolts inside the spring pan.

(9) Do not tighten up the spring pan bolts solid, but leave them half a turn slack.

(10) Press down the lower wishbone assemblies.

(11) Smear each end of the coil spring with grease to prevent any squeaking in operation.

(12) Push the coil springs up into the cross-member and over the locating plates.

(13) Jack up the lower wishbone assemblies until they are approximately parallel to the ground.

(14) Install the hub units and swivel pins.

NOTE: The stub axle and nut is right-hand thread for the right-hand side and left-hand thread for the left-hand side.

The king pin bearing threads are also right-hand thread for the right-hand side and left-hand thread for the left-hand side.

(15) Fit the front hub units to the suspension levers.

(16) Ensure that the thrust washers, rubber seals and retainers are assembled in the right order.

(17) Lubricate these parts and the fulcrum pins during assembly and again afterwards with the grease gun.

(18) Do not tighten up the top or the bottom slotted nuts solid, but leave them half a turn slack.

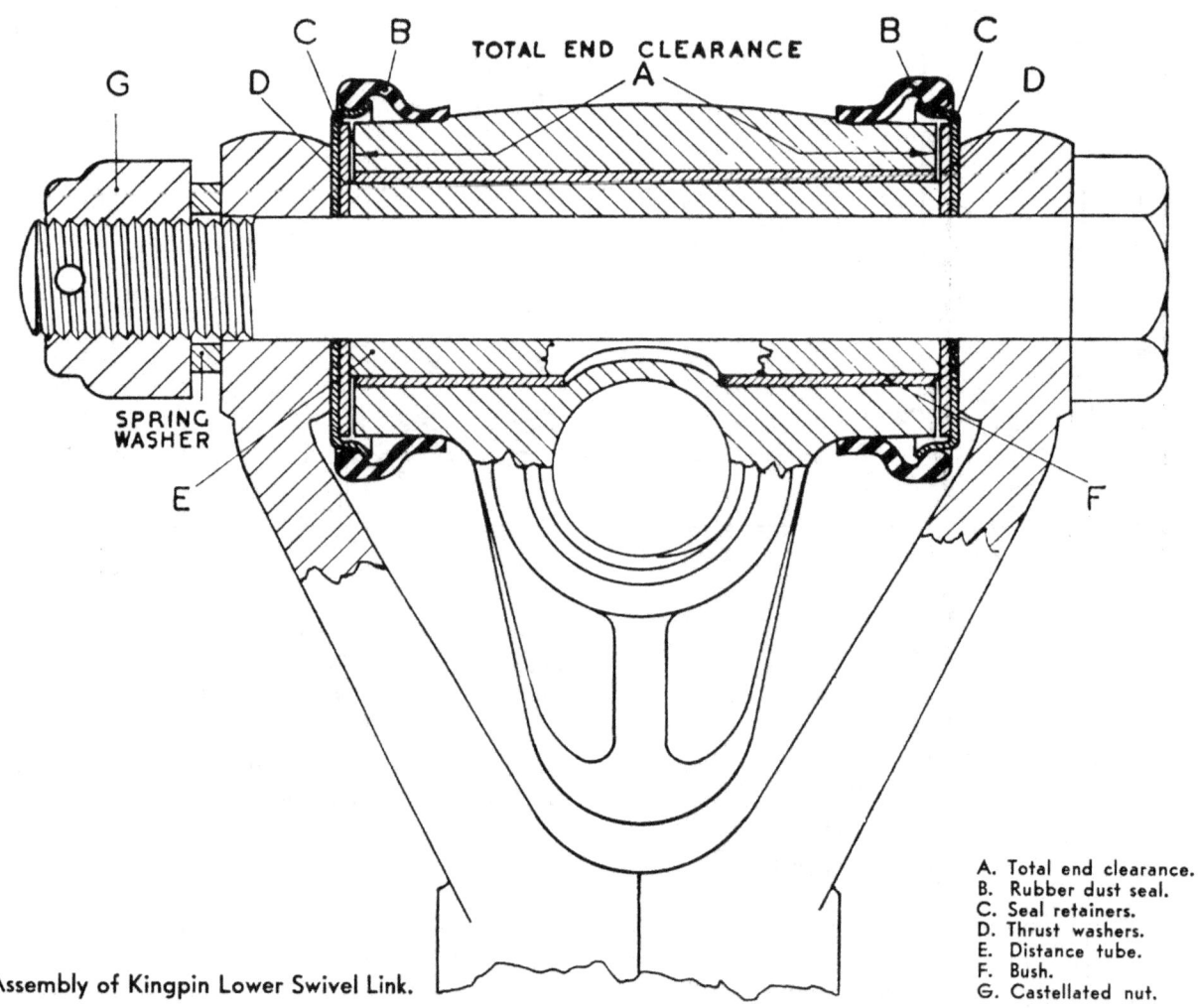

Assembly of Kingpin Lower Swivel Link.

A. Total end clearance.
B. Rubber dust seal.
C. Seal retainers.
D. Thrust washers.
E. Distance tube.
F. Bush.
G. Castellated nut.

(19) Connect up the hydraulic brake hoses.

(20) Screw the steering tie-rods into the outer steering ball joints. Screw the rods right in and then slack off five complete turns. This will give a rough wheel alignment and render subsequent accurate alignment easier.

(21) Bleed and adjust the front brakes.

(22) Install the front wheels.

(23) Bounce the front end of the car up and down a few times. This allows the suspension fulcrums to settle down.

(24) Now tighten the spring pan bolts and then tighten and cotter up the outer fulcrum bolts.

(25) Check and adjust the front wheel alignment.

TO REASSEMBLE SWIVEL PINS

The swivel pin assembly may be reassembled without difficulty by carrying out the removal instructions in the reverse order, provided the following points are given special attention.

(1) The swivel pin and links fitted to the left-hand side of the car have left-hand threads at each end and those fitted to the right-hand side of the car have right-hand threads.

(2) The swivel pin links screw on to threads on each end of the swivel pin and the threads are waisted at their centre to avoid fouling the pivot bolts passing through the links. Before the pivot bolt is replaced the link must be correctly positioned on the thread.

(3) First screw the link on to the swivel pin until the waisted portion of the pin lines up with the pivot bolt hole.

(4) Place the pivot bolt in position in the link and screw the link to the extreme of its maximum travel on the swivel pin thread; this is about three revolutions total. Screw the link back approximately one and a half turns to obtain the maximum clearance for the pivot in each direction.

(5) If the brake plate has been removed from the swivel pin assembly, the lower link must also be centralised in a similar manner before the brake plate is replaced and before the swivel pin is fitted to the suspension arm.

(6) Before the lower steering knuckle link is bolted in position ensure that both thrust washers and rubber seals are fitted correctly and make sure that the links have a total end clearance of .008" to .013" between the end faces of the link and the thrust washers.

NOTE: Make sure to locate the lower link assembly correctly because it cannot be set once the brake back plate is fitted.

2. FRONT HUB AND BRAKE DRUM

TO REMOVE

(1) Prise off the hub cover, raise the car until the wheel to be operated on is clear of the ground and unscrew the stud nuts and remove the wheel.

(2) The brake drums are attached to the wheel hubs by countersunk-headed screws, the inner ends of which are riveted over. These screws must not be disturbed and a complete brake drum and hub assembly must be used for replacement. The brake drum, complete with hub, must be removed to give access to the brake shoes. In some cases the hub and brake drum are cast in one piece.

(3) Remove the split pin from the stub axle nut and unscrew the nut, remembering that the axle on the left-hand side of the car has a left-hand thread.

(4) Remove the grease-retaining disc and felt washer.

(5) Place the hub extractor (special tool, Part No 68822) in position over the wheel studs and replace the stud nuts to retain it in position. Use the central extractor screw to withdraw the brake drum and hub assembly.

The inner ball race bearing spacer and oil seal will remain on the stub axle and must be withdrawn with the aid of the special service extractor, part No 68895. Care must be taken not to damage the oil seal at the rear of the bearing.

NOTE: When the front hub has been removed the inner bearing, oil seal and hub distance washer must be removed from the stub axle and replaced in the hub before it is refitted to the stub axle. If the hub is pressed on the shaft without first fitting the bearing and oil seal to it, the inner bearing will re-enter its housing but the oil seal will only be pushed farther from its correct position.

TO INSTALL

(1) If all grease has been cleaned from the hub and the bearings washed for examination, ensure that

they are repacked with grease before the hub is reassembled.

(2) Install the bearing spacer with the chamfered side towards the small outer bearing and then press the large bearing into position.

(3) Install the oil seal and distance washer. The metal face of the oil seal and the recessed side of the distance washer are fitted away from the bearing.

(4) Install the hub on the stub axle shaft and a new felt washer.

(5) Install the grease retainer and replace and tighten the hub nut.

3. FRONT COIL SPRING

TO REMOVE AND INSTALL

(1) Jack up the front end of the car until the wheels are clear of the ground, using a jack placed under the centre of the front cross-member.

(2) Remove the front wheel on the side affected.

(3) Place an additional jack under the lower spring pan and jack up until the hydraulic damper levers are clear of the rebound rubber.

(4) Remove the lower fulcrum bolt.

(5) Swing up the hub unit and rest it on a suitable block.

(6) Release the jack from under the spring pan, press down the lower wishbone assembly and remove the coil spring.

(7) Installation is carried out in the reverse manner to that detailed for removal.

NOTE: Take care that the thrust washers, rubber seals and retainers are assembled in the right order.

(8) Lubricate these parts and the fulcrum pins during and after installation with the grease gun.

(9) Smear each end of the coil spring with grease.

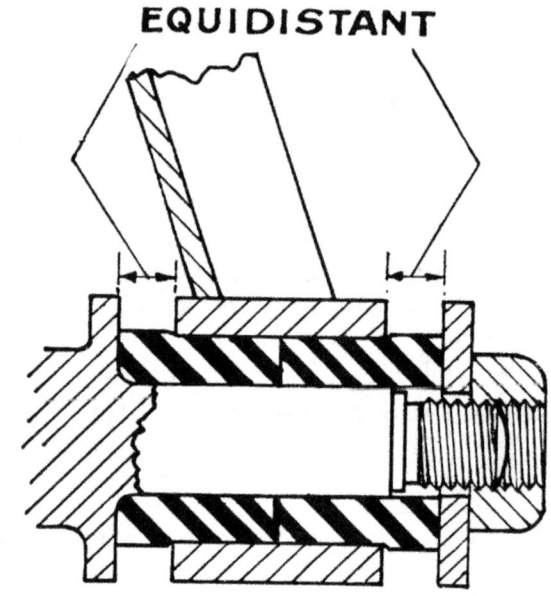

Correct Method of Fitting Lower Rubber Bushes of Suspension Arm.

4. LOWER INNER FULCRUM

TO FIT NEW RUBBER BUSHES TO LOWER WISHBONE INNER FULCRUM

(1) Remove the coil springs as detailed and take out the four bolts holding the spring pan to the levers.

(2) Remove the cotters, nuts and washers from the ends of the inner lower fulcrum pin and slide off the levers and the rubber bushes.

(3) Fit the new rubber bushes into the levers. These will be found to be quite a loose fit in the lever, but when clamped up by the nut and washer will expand into their housing. These bushes do not rotate on their surfaces, the angular movement being taken by the rubber deflecting torsionally in itself. Special care should be taken when reassembling these bushes to maintain a central location, so that the expansion of each half of the bush is equal.

(4) To attain this, insert each bush so that it protrudes equally each side of the housing, and then clamp up with the washer and nut. When central, the outer flanges of the bushes should be of equal proportions.

(5) It is essential to clamp up the bushes when the

suspension levers are set parallel with the ground to ensure even stresses on the bushes.

(6) Now install the spring pan between the levers, but with the heads of the bolts inside the spring pan.

(7) Do not tighten up the spring pan bolts solid, but leave them half a turn slack.

(8) Press down the lower wishbone assembly.

(9) Smear each end of the coil spring with grease, and push the spring up into the front cross-member and over its top locating plate.

(10) Jack up the lower wishbone assembly until it is approximately parallel to the ground. Swing down the hub unit and fit the lower fulcrum bolt.

NOTE: *Take care that the thrust washer, rubber seals and retainers are assembled in the right order.*

(11) Lubricate these and the fulcrum pin during and after installation with the grease gun.

(12) Remove the jack from under the wishbone assembly.

(13) Finally tighten up the spring pan bolts.

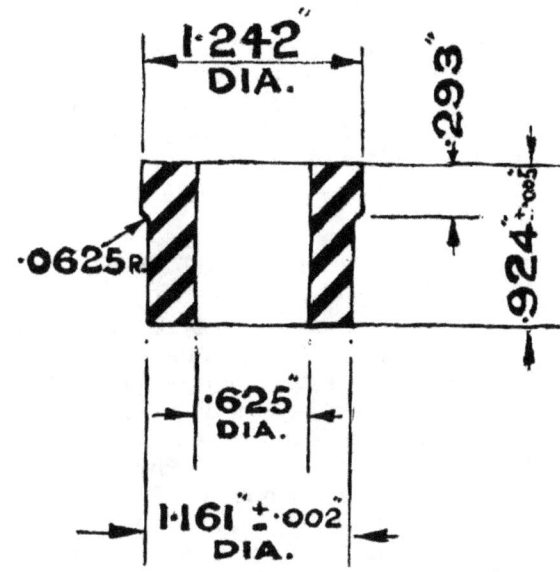

Dimensions of Lower Wishbone Bushes when in New Condition.

5. LUBRICATION

Position of grease nipples on upper and lower swivel links

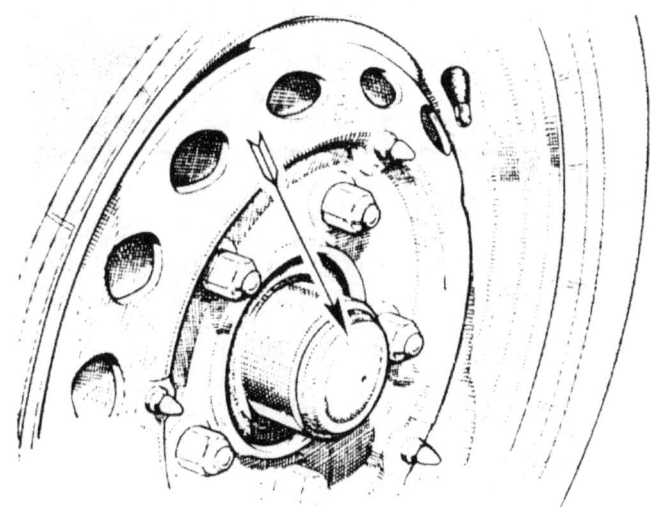

Grease cap on front hubs, later TD, TF

109

6. MODIFICATIONS

The Andrex TE1/N friction damper (illustrated) is fitted as supplementary equipment to the **TD Midget Mark II** and is in principle a development of the Hartford friction damper. The moving and fixed plates, interleaved with discs of specially impregnated wood, are under the pressure of a plate spring and are enclosed in an oil-filled casing.

The spring pressure is adjusted by means of a small set screw and locknut.

Use two spanners, one on the set screw, one on the locknut. Approximately $2\frac{1}{2}$ turns of the set screw covers the full range of adjustment, $\frac{1}{4}$ turn being equivalent to a difference of 3 lbs in loading. The dampers are pre-set by the makers at 16 lbs measured at the end of the operating arm. When fitted to the **TD Mark II** the front dampers are set to 24 lbs and the rear dampers to 22 lbs. Turn the set screw clockwise to increase the loading, anticlockwise to decrease. The casing should be filled with a heavy oil such as Esso Cantona LK 190.

Andrex friction damper

On earlier **TD** models fitted with disc wheels and a grease nipple on each front hub, grease has been found to leak past the felt sealing washer on to the outside of the hub. Later **TD** and **TF** models have a modified grease retaining cap fitted to the hub, as shown, which eliminates this trouble.

This conversion can be carried out to the front hubs of earlier cars, consisting of a grease cap with a rubber sealing gasket and held in place by a spring clip.

The parts required for this conversion are as follows:

500196	Seal	2 off
500195	Grease retainer cap	2 off
500198	Spring clip	2 off
434/F	Split pin ($\frac{1}{8}$ inch $\times$ $1\frac{1}{8}$ inch) ...	4 off
500328	Washer	2 off
500197	Distance tube	2 off
	(for one-piece hub and drum only).	

The modified hub is packed with a recommended grease every 6000 miles.

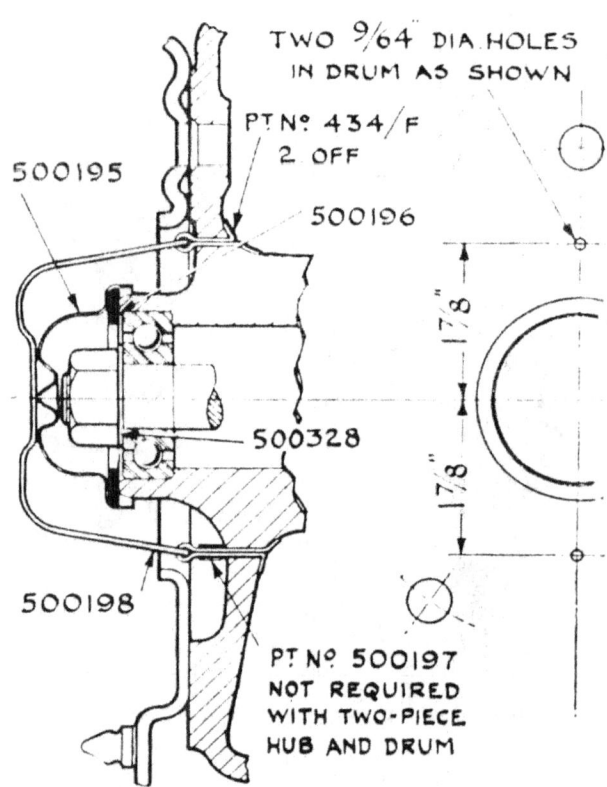

Modification to earlier type front hubs, TD

7. FRONT SUSPENSION FAULT DIAGNOSIS

(1) FRONT END NOISE

Possible cause	Remedy
(a) Loose or worn upper suspension mountings.	— Tighten nut clamping upper arm to shock absorber. Check and replace as necessary fulcrum pin and rubber bushes at swivel pin end.
(b) Loose or worn lower arm suspension mountings.	— Check rubber mountings on pivot at crossmember and replace as necessary. Check and tighten bolt at swivel pin end.

NOTE: (a) and (b) are not applicable to TC.

(c) Loose or worn suspension mountings.	— Locate points of excessive play. Tighten and replace as necessary.
(d) Noise in shock absorber.	— Renew shock absorber unit.
(e) Worn steering linkage.	— Renew defective components.
(f) Mal-adjusted front hub bearings.	— Readjust or renew hub bearings.

(2) POOR OR ERRATIC ROAD HOLDING ABILITY

Possible cause	Remedy
(a) Low or uneven tyre pressure.	— Inflate tyres to recommended pressures.
(b) Defective shock absorber operation.	— Check and renew faulty unit.
(c) Incorrect front end alignment.	— Check and re-adjust alignment as necessary.
(d) Loose or defective front crossmember.	— Check and tighten or renew member.
(e) Weak or uneven front coil springs.	— Check and renew coil springs.
(f) Broken leaf in, or weak rear spring.	— Check and renew leaf or complete rear spring.
(g) Loose or defective front hub bearings.	— Adjust or renew hub bearings.
(h) Mal-adjusted or defective steering gear or idler.	— Adjust or renew faulty components.
(i) Defective tyres or front wheel balance.	— Renew defective tyres and balance front wheels.

(3) HEAVY STEERING

Possible cause	Remedy
(a) Low or uneven tyre pressure.	— Check and inflate tyres to recommended pressures.
(b) Incorrect front end alignment.	— Check and adjust alignment.
(c) Lack of lubricant in steering gear and components.	— Check oil level in steering gear and apply grease gun to all grease nipples.
(d) Worn or damaged front suspension components.	— Check and renew worn or damaged components and adjust front end alignment.
(e) Sagging or broken coil spring/s.	— Renew coil spring/s.
(f) Incorrect adjustment of steering gear.	— Check and adjust steering gear.

(4) FRONT WHEEL WOBBLE OR SHIMMY

Possible cause	Remedy
(a) Tyre and/or wheel unbalance.	— Check and balance tyre and wheel as a unit.
(b) Rapid and uneven tyre wear.	— Check front end alignment (see Wheels and Tyres).
(c) Worn or loose hub bearings.	— Check and renew or adjust hub bearings.
(d) Worn or damaged steering linkage.	— Check, renew faulty components, and adjust.
(e) Incorrect front end alignment.	— Adjust, and/or renew suspension components to restore alignment.
(f) Mal-adjusted or worn steering gear.	— Renew and/or adjust steering gear components.
(g) Steering gear loose on frame mountings or off centre.	— Check and tighten mounting and/or centre steering gear.

(5) VEHICLE PULLS TO ONE SIDE

Possible cause	*Remedy*
(a) Low or uneven tyre pressure.	— Check and inflate tyres to recommended pressures.
(b) Incorrect or unequal front end alignment—side to side.	— Check and adjust to restore correct alignment.
(c) High road camber.	— Avoid as far as possible.
(d) Unequal coil spring length. (Not applicable to TC series)	— Check and renew sagging spring.
(e) Weak or broken rear spring.	— Renew faulty spring.
(f) Front brake dragging.	— Adjust or rectify cause.
(g) Steering gear off centre.	— Check and re-centre steering.

REAR SUSPENSION

1. TC SERIES

REAR ROAD SPRINGS AND SHACKLES

Silentbloc bushes are fitted to the front end of the rear spring. These work on the same principle as the front spring rubber bushes, but are enclosed in a metal housing, and can be pressed out of the spring eye and replaced as a unit.

The rear end of the rear spring is fitted with a rubber bushed shackle. This is identical in operation as for the front springs, and the same conditions apply, except for the lower bush, which can only be tightened from one side. Here the bushes will have to be located a little to one side, to produce an equal pinch. This is done by trial and error.

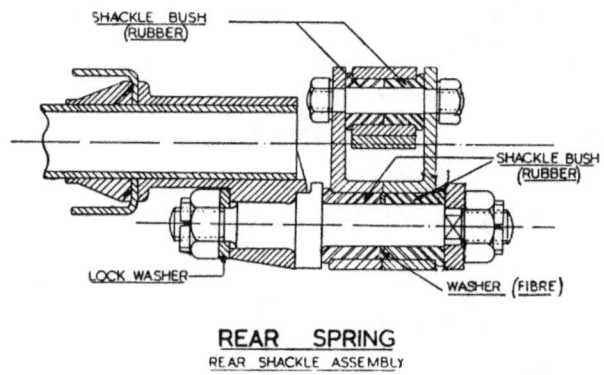

Rear spring shackle TC

2. TD—TF—TF 1500 SERIES

TO DISMANTLE SPRINGS

(1) Slacken off and remove the spring clip bolts, distance pieces and rubber packings.

(2) Release the locknut and nut from the spring centre bolt and remove the distance piece and bolt.

(3) The leaves may now be separated, releasing the twelve interleaf rubber pads.

TO INSPECT SPRINGS

Clean each leaf, and examine for cracks or breakage. Check the centre bolt for wear or distortion (this bolt forms the location for the spring on its axle pad and should be in good condition).

NOTE: When fitting new leaves it is important that they are of the correct length and thickness, and have the same curvature as the remaining leaves.

It is advisable, even when no leaves are broken, to fit replacement springs when the originals have lost their camber due to settling.

TO REASSEMBLE SPRINGS

The springs should be assembled clean, dry and free from any lubricant.

(1) Place the leaves together in their correct order, locating them with the centre bolt and positioning the interleaf rubber packings between the ends of the leaves before the bolt is tightened.

(2) The dowel head of the bolt must be on top of the spring.

(3) Install the spring clip rubber packings, clips, distance pieces and bolts.

(4) Before installing the shackle bolts, bushes and shackle plates inspect them for wear and, if necessary, replace with new components.

NOTE: Before tightening the spring bolts it is absolutely essential that the normal working load be applied to the springs so that the flexing rubber bushes are deflected to an equal extent in both directions during service. Failure to take this precaution will inevitably lead to early deterioration of the bushes.

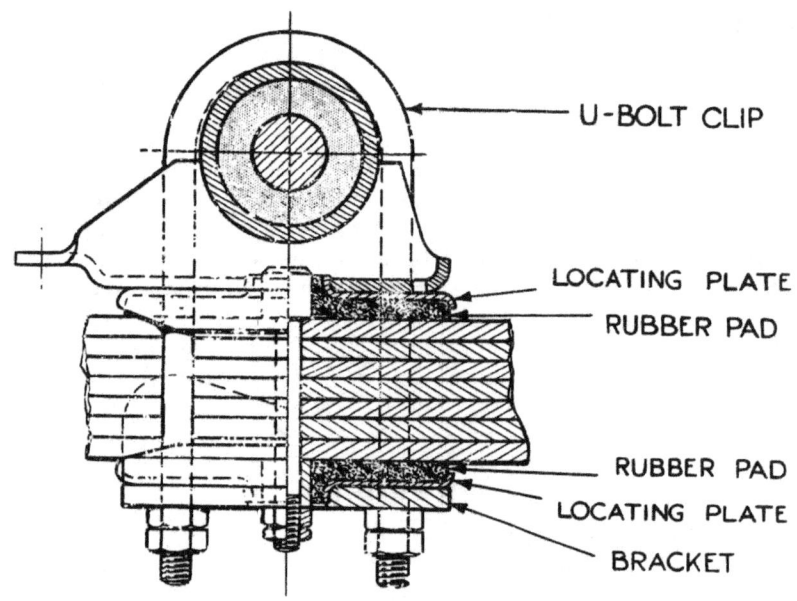

The Rubber Mounting of the Rear Springs on the Axle

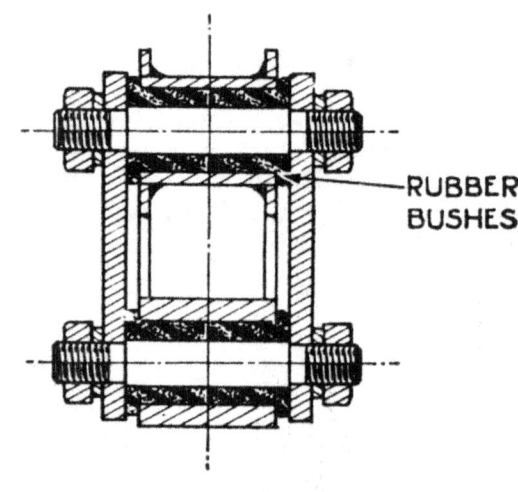

Rear spring shackle TD, TF

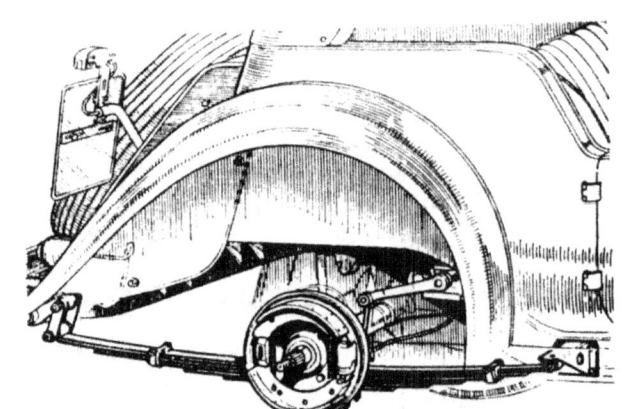

Rear suspension layout TD, TF

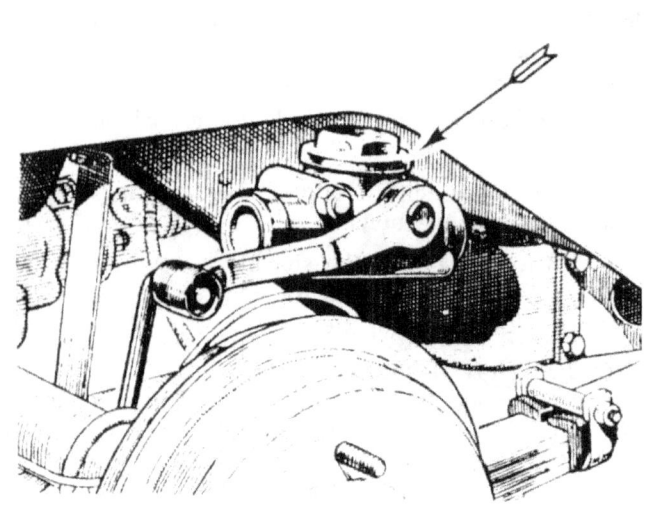

Rear damper model TD showing position of filler

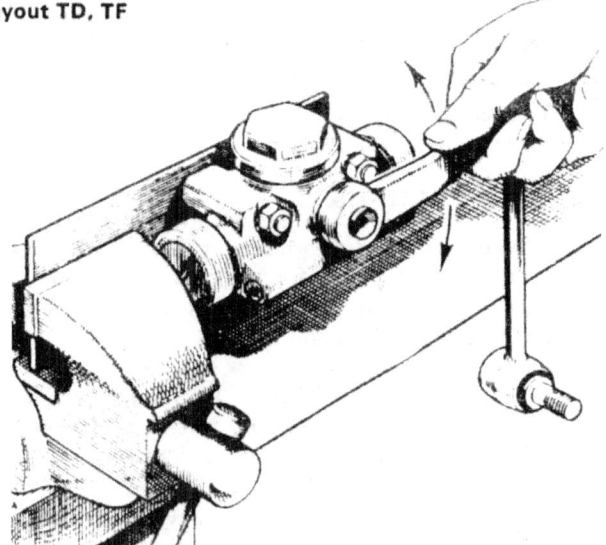

Testing hydraulic damper mounted in vice

3. REAR SUSPENSION FAULT DIAGNOSIS

(1) NOISE IN SUSPENSION

Possible cause	Remedy
(a) Defective shock absorber and/or mounting.	— Renew faulty components.
(b) Loose or worn rear shackle bolts and bushes.	— Tighten or renew loose or worn components.
(c) Loose or worn spring anchor bolt and/or bushes.	— Tighten or renew loose or worn components.
(d) Broken rear spring leaf or leaves.	— Renew broken leaves or complete spring.
(e) Sprung or bent axle tube.	— Renew axle casing.
(f) Worn or deteriorated spring leaf nylon inserts.	— Check and renew inserts.
(g) Faulty or overtight spring seat.	— Check and adjust.
(h) Loose or broken spring leaf clamps.	— Tighten or renew faulty clamps.

(2) REAR WHEELS NOT IN ALIGNMENT WITH FRONT WHEELS

Possible cause	Remedy
(a) Broken main leaf of spring, forward of spring seat.	— Renew main leaf or complete spring.
(b) Broken main leaf of spring at rear of spring seat.	— Renew main leaf or complete spring.
(c) Broken spring anchor bolt or rear shackle.	— Renew faulty components.
(d) Spring badly sagging on one side.	— Renew defective spring.
(e) Sprung or bent axle casing.	— Renew axle casing.
(f) Broken spring centre bolt.	— Renew spring centre bolt.

(3) REAR BRAKE BLOCKED ON ONE SIDE

Possible cause	Remedy
(a) Broken spring main leaf forward of spring seat.	— Renew main leaf or complete spring.
(b) Broken spring centre bolt.	— Renew spring centre bolt.
(c) Broken spring anchor bolt.	— Renew anchor bolt and bush.

BRAKES TC—TD—TF—TF 1500 SERIES

1. GENERAL DESCRIPTION

The Lockheed hydraulic brake operating equipment comprises a combined fluid supply tank and master cylinder in which the hydraulic pressure is generated, and wheel cylinders which operate the brake shoes.

Steel pipe lines, unions and flexible hoses convey the hydraulic pressure from the master cylinder to each wheel cylinder.

Each brake shoe on the front wheels has a separate wheel cylinder, thus providing two leading shoes. On the rear wheels, a single wheel cylinder, operated both hydraulically and mechanically, floats on the brake plate and operates the two shoes, giving one leading and one trailing shoe in either direction of rotation to provide adequate braking in reverse.

2. MAINTENANCE

Periodically examine the quantity of brake fluid in the master cylinder. It should never be less than half full or closer than ¼″ from the bottom of the filler neck. The necessity for frequent topping up is an indication of over-filling or a leak in the system, which should at once be traced and rectified.

Adjust the brake shoes to compensate for wear of the linings. The need for this is shown by the pedal going down almost to the floorboards before solid resistance is felt. For brake shoe adjustments refer to the relevant section.

Adjustment of the brake shoes in the manner indicated also adjusts the handbrake automatically and no separate adjustment is required or permitted.

3. HYDRAULIC SYSTEM

MASTER CYLINDER (SERIES TC)

The combination barrel type compensating master cylinder provides automatic compensation for expansion or contraction of the fluid due to temperature changes.

Within the master cylinder is a piston and a cupped washer normally held in the off position by a coiled spring. Immediately in front of the cup washer, with the piston in the off position, is a by-pass port hole connecting the cylinder interior with the supply tank. With any rise in temperature causing the fluid to expand in the system, the fluid is allowed to pass through the port into the supply tank. With any drop in temperature causing the fluid to contract, the fluid flows back through the port. Thus a constant volume of fluid is maintained in the system.

Pressure is applied to the piston by means of a push rod which is attached directly to the brake pedal.

The open end of the master cylinder is fitted with a rubber boot to prevent the ingress of dirt.

In the head of the master cylinder is a combination inlet and outlet check valve which is held in place by the return spring.

When the brakes are applied the master cylinder piston is pushed forward and fluid is forced through holes in the metal valve body, deflecting the walls of the rubber cup and so passing into the system.

When the pedal is released the master cylinder return spring forces the piston back to its off position against its stop. At the same time the pistons in the wheel cylinders, as a result of the action of the brake shoe return springs, are forcing back fluid and so lifting the whole valve assembly off its seat, until the fluid pressure balances the effort of the master cylinder return spring, and the inlet valve closes.

(SERIES TD, TF AND TF 1500)

The master cylinder is mounted on the driver's side of the car underneath the floor.

Within the cylinder is a piston, backed by a rubber cup, normally held in the off position by a piston return spring. Immediately in front of the cap, when it is in the off position, is a compensating orifice connecting the cylinder with the fluid supply.

This port allows free compensation for any expansion or contraction of the fluid, thus ensuring that the system is constantly filled; it also serves as a release for additional fluid drawn into the system during brake applications.

Pressure is applied to the piston by means of the push rod attached to the brake pedal. The push rod is adjustable and should have a slight clearance when the system is at rest to allow the piston to return fully against its stop. Without this clearance the main cup will cover the by-pass port, causing pressure to build up within the system, and produce binding of the brakes on all wheels.

The reduced skirt of the piston forms an annular space which is filled with fluid from the supply tank via the feed hole. Leakage of fluid from the open end of the cylinder is prevented by the secondary cup fitted to the flange end of the piston.

Master Cylinder on TC Series.

A. End cover.
B. Gasket.
C. Cylinder body.
D. Reservoir cap.
E. Valve seal.
F. Valve body.
G. Valve rubber.
H. Spring.
I. Spring seat.
J. Primary cup.
K. Piston.
L. Secondary cup.
M. Stop circlip.
N. Rubber boot.
O. Adjustable pushrod.

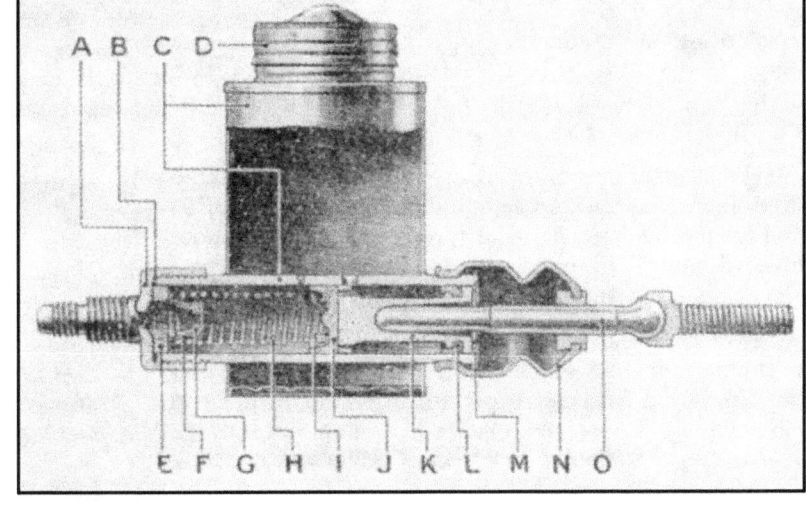

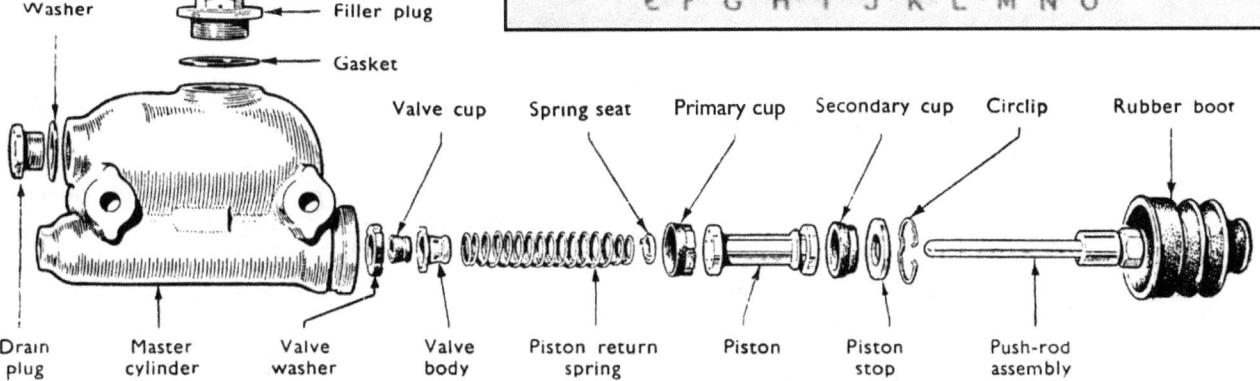

Components of Master Cylinder on TD, TF and TF-1500. Later Models have a Thin Dished Copper Washer between the Primary Cup and the end of the Piston. This Washer must be fitted with its Concave Face to the Primary Cup as shown. If the Washer is found to be missing on Dismantling, a Washer must be fitted when Reassembling.

On releasing the brake pedal, after application, the piston is returned quickly to its stop by the return spring, thus creating a vacuum in the cylinder; this vacuum causes the main cup to collapse and pass fluid through the small holes in the piston head from the annular space formed by the piston skirt.

This additional fluid finds its way back to the reserve supply under the action of the brake return springs, when the system finally comes to rest, through the outlet valve and compensating orifice. If the compensating orifice is covered by the piston cup when the system is at rest, pressure will build up as a result of the brake application.

The combination inlet and outlet check valve in the head of the cylinder is provided to allow the passage of fluid under pressure from the master piston into the pipe lines, and control its return into the cylinder, so that a small pressure of approximately 8 psi is maintained in the pipe lines to ensure that the cups of the wheel cylinder are kept expanded; it also prevents fluid pumped out from the cylinder when bleeding from returning to the cylinder, thus a fresh charge is delivered at each stroke of the pedal.

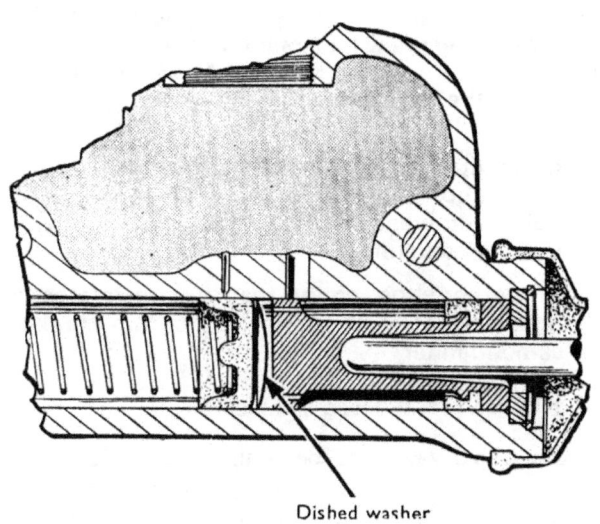

Correct Method of Fitting Thin Dished Washer between Piston Head and Primary Cup of Master Cylinder.

TO BLEED SYSTEM (TO EXPEL AIR)

Bleeding the system is not a routine maintenance job, and should only be necessary when some portion of the hydraulic equipment has been disconnected or the fluid drained off.

(1) Fill the master cylinder with Lockheed brake fluid (or, if not available, fluid to spec SAE 70R2) and keep it at least half-full throughout the operation, otherwise air will be drawn into the system, necessitating a fresh start.

(2) Attach the bleeder tube to the wheel cylinder bleeder screw and allow the free end of the tube to be submerged in a small quantity of fluid in a clean glass jar.

(3) Open the bleeder screw one full turn.

(4) Depress the brake pedal quickly, and allow it to return without assistance. Repeat this pumping action with a slight pause before each depression of the pedal.

(5) Watch the flow of fluid into the glass jar, and when air bubbles cease to appear, hold the pedal firmly against the floorboards while the bleeder screw is securely tightened.

(6) Repeat the operation on each wheel.

NOTE: Clean fluid bled from the system must be allowed to stand until it is clear of air bubbles before it is used again. Dirty fluid should be discarded.

4. BRAKE ADJUSTMENTS

TO ADJUST BRAKE PEDAL

The correct amount of free movement between the master cylinder push rod and piston is set during erection of the vehicle, and should never need alteration.

In the event of the adjustment having been disturbed, reset the effective length of the rod connecting the cylinder to the pedal until the pedal can be depressed approximately ½" before the piston begins to move. The clearance can be felt if the pedal is depressed by hand.

TO ADJUST BRAKE SHOES

As the linings wear, the pedal will travel farther before the brakes come into action. When the travel becomes excessive the brake shoes should be adjusted.

TC Series: The two adjusting nuts C will be found at the back of the brake backplate. Turn the nut in the direction of the arrow until the cam A pressing on the peg B brings the shoe into contact with the drum and locks the wheel.

Slacken the nut just sufficiently to free the wheel. Note that one complete turn of the nut is sufficient to take up all lining wear, so that only a partial turn will be needed for adjustment.

Adjust the other shoe, noting that the nut rotates in the opposite direction. Adjust the other three brakes in the same manner.

TD and TF Series, proceed as follows:

A hole sealed with a rubber plug is provided in the wheel and in the drum to allow adjustment without removal of the wheel. The hole in the drum is sealed by a neoprene tubular sleeve between the wheel and drum. When the wheel is replaced after removal for any purpose, take care to refit it with the holes in the wheel and drum in line and with both seals in position.

Front brake shoe:

(1) Jack up the front of the car and remove the wheel disc and rubber plug from the hole in the wheel.

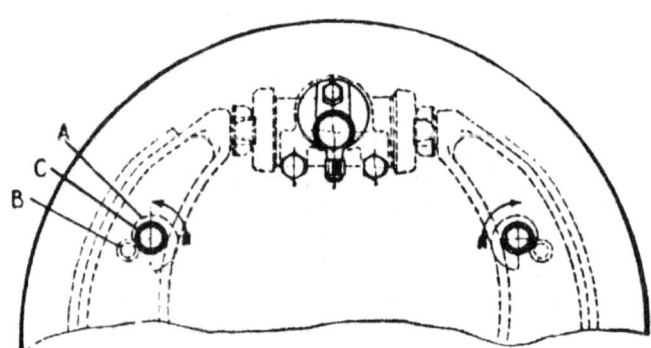

Brake shoe adjustments, model TC

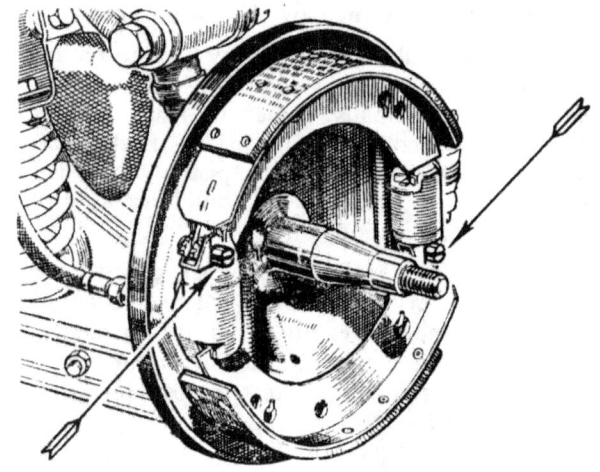

Front Brake Drum Removed to show two Micram Adjusters for Shoes. Note Position of Shoe Return Spring.

(2) Turn the wheel until one of the two adjustment screws is visible through the hole in the wheel and drum.

(3) Insert a screwdriver and turn the adjustment screw in a clockwise direction until the drum is locked and then turn it anti-clockwise one notch. Rotate the drum until the other screw is visible and repeat the adjustment.

(4) The drum should then be free to rotate without the shoes rubbing and the adjustment on that wheel is complete.

Rear brake shoe:

The procedure is similar to that detailed for the front wheels except that there is only one adjuster controlling both shoes and handbrake.

Single Micram Adjuster for Rear Brake Shoes. This adjusts the Handbrake Mechanism at the same time.

Method of brake shoe adjustment, TD, TF

5. MASTER CYLINDER

TO DISMANTLE — TC, TD, TF AND TF 1500

(1) Remove the filler cap and drain the Lockheed hydraulic brake fluid from the master cylinder.

(2) Remove the main feed pipe, union and copper washers.

(3) Push the piston down the cylinder bore and remove the retaining circlip.

(4) Remove the remaining internal parts, i.e., the piston, piston master cup, return spring, valve cup assembly and valve seating washer.

(5) To remove the secondary cup from the piston, carefully stretch it over the end flange, using the fingers only.

TO ASSEMBLE — TC, TD, TF AND TF 1500

(1) Clean all parts thoroughly, using Lockheed brake fluid for all rubber components. All traces of fuel, kerosene or trichlorethylene used for cleaning the metal parts must be removed before assembly.

(2) Examine all the rubber parts for damage or distortion. It is usually advisable to renew the rubbers when rebuilding the cylinder.

(3) Dip all the internal parts in brake fluid and assemble them wet.

(4) Stretch the secondary cup over the end flange of the piston with the lip of the cup facing towards the opposite end of the piston. When the cup is in its groove, work it round gently with the fingers to make sure it is correctly seated.

(5) Fit the valve washer, valve cup and body on to the return spring and insert the spring valve first into the cylinder. See that the spring retainer is in position.

(6) Insert the master cup, lip first, taking care not to damage or turn back the lip, and press it down on to the spring retainer. Place the dished washer in place on the end of the master cup with its concave face in contact with the cup (see illustration). It is imperative that this washer should be fitted in all cases.

(7) Insert the piston, taking care not to damage or turn back the lip of the secondary cup.

(8) Push the piston down the bore slightly, and insert the retaining circlip in the groove in the cylinder bore.

(9) Test the master cylinder by filling the tank and by pushing the piston down the bore and allowing it to return; after one or two applications fluid should flow from the outlet.

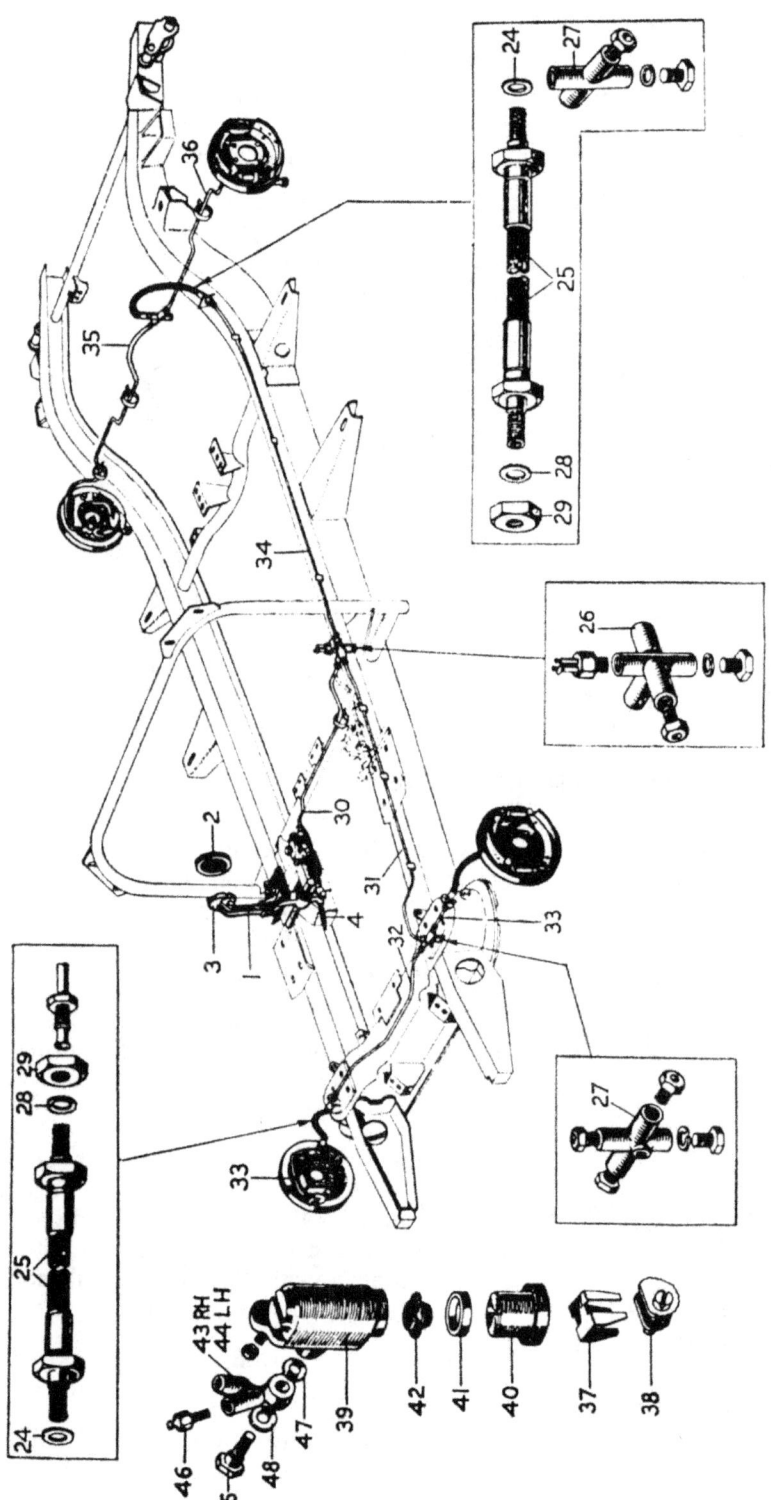

Hydraulic brake system, models TD and TF

1 Brake pedal and bush 2 Brake pedal rubber pad 3 Brake pedal pad 4 Brake pedal return spring 24 Washer (gasket)
25 Hose assembly 26 Four-way piece 27 Three-way piece 28 Lock washer 29 Hose locknut 30 Pipe (master cylinder to 4-way)
31 Pipe (4-way to 3-way) 32 Pipe (front 3-way to RH front hose pipe) 33 Pipe (front 3-way to front hose) 34 Pipe (4-way to rear hose)
35 Pipe (axle hose bracket to RH rear) 36 Pipe (axle hose bracket to LH rear) 37 Shoe adjuster mask 38 Brake-shoe adjuster
39 Body with studs and abutment 40 Piston and dust cover assembly 41 Piston cup 42 Cup filler 43 Banjo connection, forward RH
44 Banjo connection, forward LH 45 Bolt 46 Bleeder screw 47 Banjo bolt gasket, small 48 Banjo bolt gasket, large

6. WHEEL CYLINDERS

TO REMOVE FRONT WHEEL CYLINDERS

(1) Raise the front of the car and remove the hub cap and road wheel.

(2) Remove the brake drum.

(3) Draw the brake shoes apart until the assembly can be removed from the back plate.

(4) Release the flexible hose. (See To Remove Flexible Hose).

(5) Unscrew the hose from the wheel cylinder.

(6) Unscrew the unions and remove the link pipe from both cylinders.

(7) Unscrew the set bolts securing the cylinders to the back plates and remove the cylinders.

TO REMOVE REAR WHEEL CYLINDERS

(1) Raise the rear of the car and remove the wheel.

(2) Remove the brake drum.

(3) Turn and withdraw the brake shoe steady springs.

(4) Draw the brake shoes apart until they can be removed from the brake plate.

(5) Unscrew the pipe union from the cylinder, noting the positions of the copper washers.

(6) Remove the clevis pin from the handbrake cable yoke to disconnect the cable from the lever on the cylinder.

(7) Remove the rubber boot.

(8) Slide the cylinder upwards, push the lower end through the back plate and slide the cylinder downwards and away from the back plate.

TO DISMANTLE FRONT CYLINDERS

Withdraw the piston, the rubber cup, the cup filler and the spring.

TO DISMANTLE REAR CYLINDERS

Tap out the handbrake lever pivot pin and withdraw the lever. Withdraw the upper half of the piston the rubber cup, the cup filler and the spring.

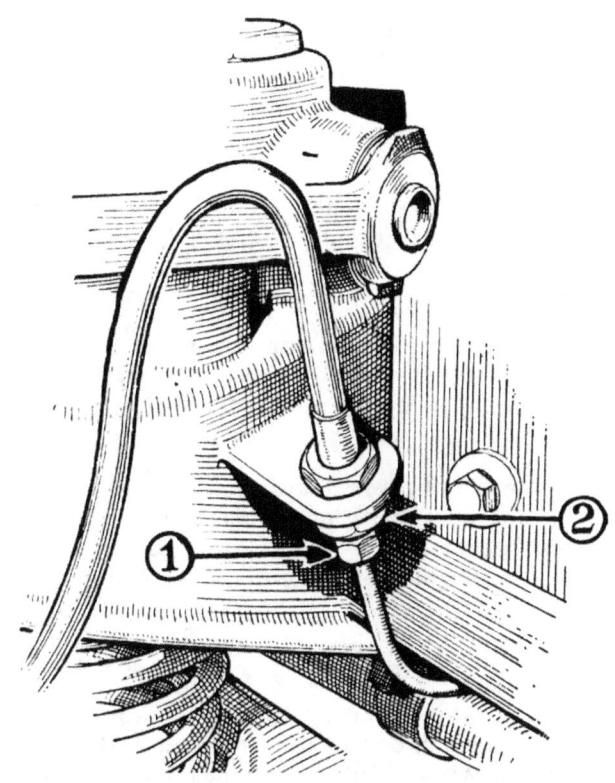

When Disconnecting Flexible Hoses, Union Nut (1) must first be Removed and then Pipe Retaining Nut (2) Disconnected. The Hexagon Shank of the Hose Must Not Be Turned.

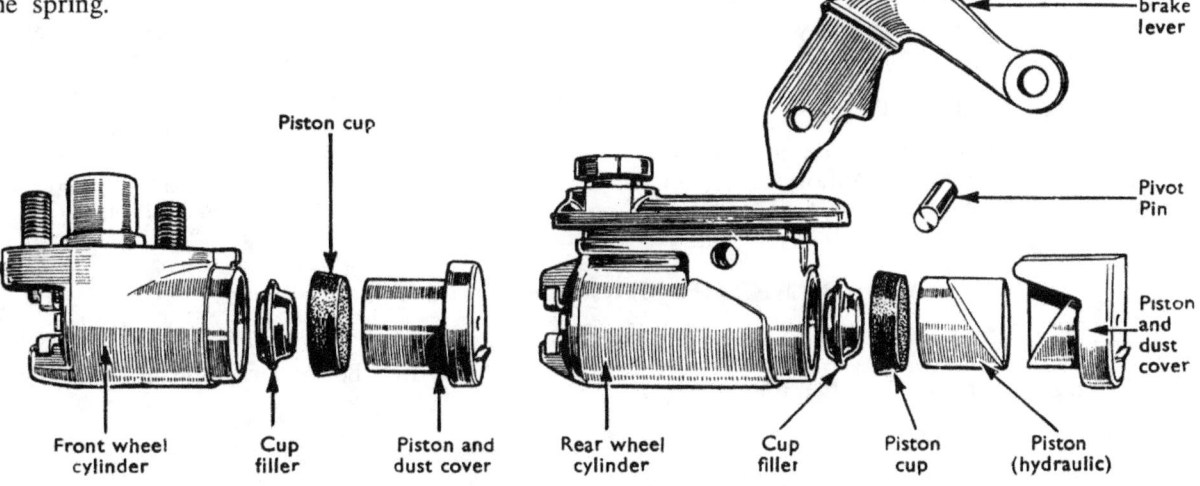

Front and Rear Wheel Cylinder Components.

TO ASSEMBLE

(1) Clean all parts thoroughly, using only Lockheed hydraulic brake fluid for the rubber components. All traces of petrol, kerosene or trichlorethylene used for cleaning the metal parts must be completely removed before assembly.

(2) Examine the rubber cups for damage, wear or distortion. Dip all parts in brake fluid and assemble wet.

(3) Insert the cup filler and spring, and the rubber cup concave side first.

(4) Install the piston, and in the case of the rear cylinders insert the handbrake lever and its pivot pin.

TO INSTALL

The procedure for installing the wheel cylinder is a reversal of the removal operations, but attention must be given to the following important points:

Front:

The front brake wheel cylinders are interchangeable but the link pipe banjo unions must be fitted to them so that the flexible hose is connected to the rear cylinder and the bleeder screw to the forward cylinder. The link pipe must pass below the centre line of the stub axle.

The brake shoes are interchangeable but the recessed ends must engage the Micram shoe adjusters.

Rear:

The wheel cylinder must be fitted on the rear side of the axle casing with the bleeder screw pointing downwards.

The brake shoes are interchangeable but the recessed end of the upper or leading shoe must engage the Micram shoe adjuster. The other shoe should also be fitted with its recessed end against the wheel cylinder.

TO REMOVE FLEXIBLE HOSE

Do not attempt to release a flexible hose by turning either end with a spanner. It should be removed as follows:

(1) Unscrew the metal pipe line union nut from its connection to the hose.

(2) Remove the locknut securing the flexible hose union to the bracket and unscrew the hose from the wheel cylinder. Note that a distance piece is fitted at the rear of the bracket securing the front hoses.

7. HANDBRAKE

On all models the handbrake is of the 'fly-off' type, the ratchet knob being depressed to hold the brake in the 'on' position, while a slight pull on the lever releases the ratchet without depressing the knob. The brake operates on the rear wheels through encased cables.

TO ADJUST—TC

On TC models the handbrake is adjusted by means of a thumb nut at the base of the lever. When adjusting, ensure that the adjustment is not too tight or the brake shoes may be in contact with the drums with the handbrake in the 'off' position.

TO ADJUST—TD, TF AND TF 1500

Details of the handbrake system on models TD and TF are shown in the illustration. Although the handbrake operates the rear brakes by means of cables, adjustment of the hydraulic brake shoes automatically adjusts the handbrake. No separate adjustment is necessary and **if the two brass nuts 36 on the lever are moved, the whole braking system will be upset.** Sufficient movement is allowed at the lever to deal with full wear at the linings. If the wheel cylinder operating cables 37 have been disconnected, they should be readjusted in the following manner:

1 Return the handbrake lever to the fully released position.

2 Remove the splitpin and clevis pin 38 retaining the brake cable to each wheel cylinder lever 21.

3 Adjust the brake shoes as described in **Section 10:2**.

4 Screw up the cable adjusting nuts 36 by equal amounts until the cable clevis pins 38 will fall into position in the cable forks without moving the wheel cylinder lever 21. Replace the split pins.

8. BRAKE SHOE ASSEMBLIES

TO REMOVE AND INSTALL

(1) Jack up the car and remove the wheel.

(2) Remove the brake drums.

(3) Turn and withdraw the steady springs (rear only).

(4) Draw the shoes apart until they can be removed from the back plate.

(5) Replacement is a reversal of the above procedure, but note the correct fitting of the shoes and springs.

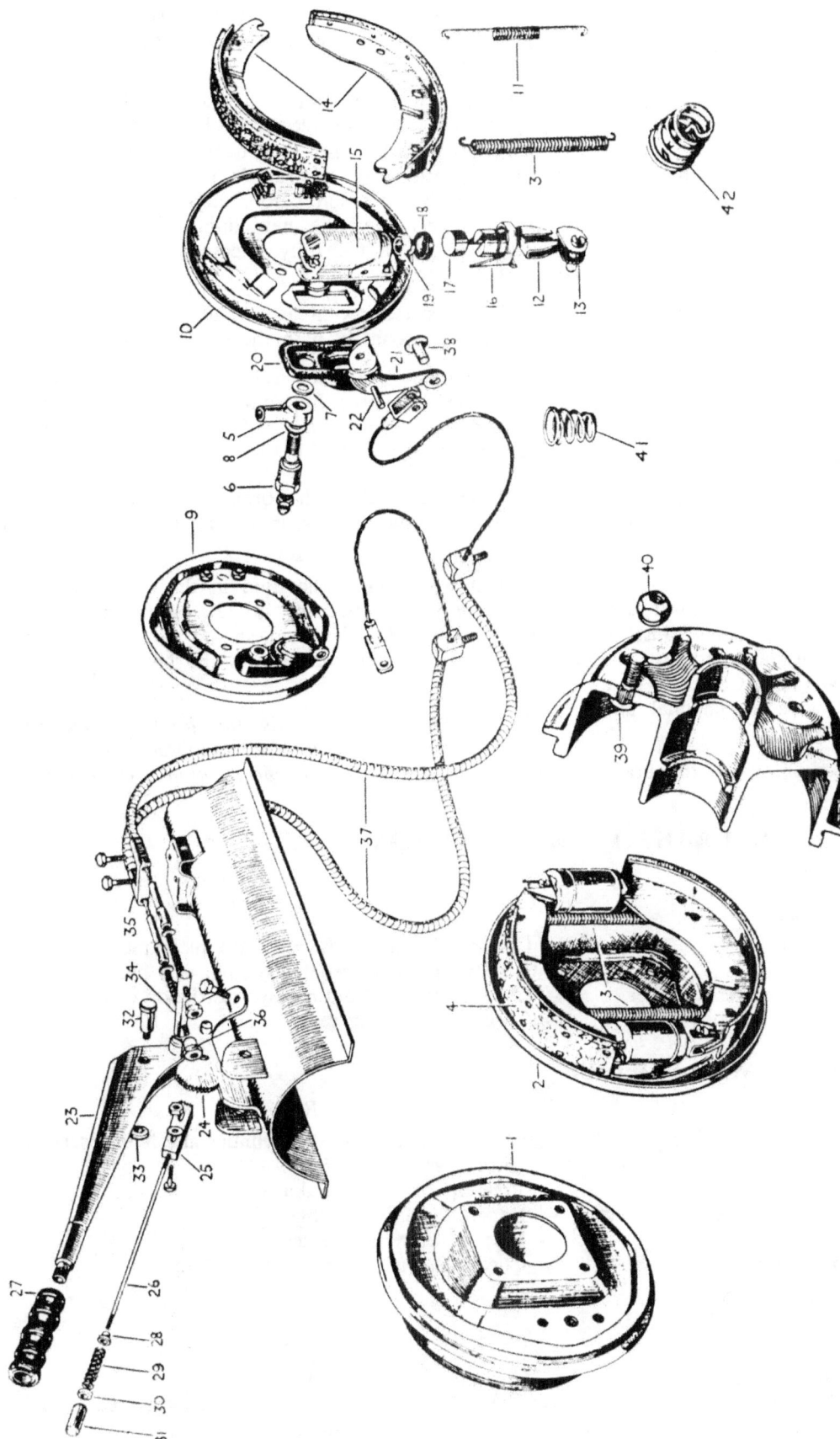

Handbrake and brakeshoe components TD, TF

1 Brake gear (front axle) back plate assembly, RH
2 Brake gear (front axle) back plate assembly, LH
3 Shoe pull-off spring
4 Front brake-shoe—lined complete
5 Banjo connections
6 Bolt
7 Banjo bolt gasket, small
8 Banjo bolt gasket, large
9 Brake gear (rear axle) back plate assembly, RH
10 Brake gear (rear axle) back plate assembly, LH
11 Shoe tension spring
12 Shoe adjuster mask
13 Brake shoe adjuster
14 Rear brake shoe—lined complete
15 Body and abutment strip
16 Piston and dust cover
17 Piston (hydraulic)
18 Piston cup
19 Cup filler
20 Wheel cylinder boot
21 Hand brake lever
22 Pivot pin, hand brake lever
23 Bush for rod
24 Ratchet assembly
25 Hand brake pawl
26 Hand brake pawl rod
27 Hand grip
28 Bush for rod
29 Spring, lever knob
30 Spring washer
31 Pawl rod knob
32 Fulcrum pin
33 Fulcrum pin washer
34 Hand brake trunnion
35 Twin cable abutment
36 Brake cable adjuster nut
37 Hand brake cable
38 Clevis pin
39 Wheel stud
40 Wheel nut
41 Spring, wheel cylinder piston
42 Spring, brake shoe steady

Front brake shoe springs:

Both springs are fitted between the shoes and the back plate.

The shoes are fitted in the recessed ends of the adjusters.

The rear spring is fitted to the rear hole in the upper shoe and the inner of the two holes in the lower shoe.

Rear brake shoe springs:

Both springs are fitted between the shoes and the back plate.

The lighter spring is fitted at the abutment end of the shoes.

Both springs are fitted to the end holes in the shoes.

TO RELINE BRAKE SHOES

Owing to the need for the brake linings to be finished so that they are perfectly concentric with the brake drums, special precautions must be taken when relining the shoes.

If renewal of the brake shoes and linings is necessary on account of excessive wear or other cause, it is most important that the material used for the lining is as specified by the MG Car Company Ltd. Any variations from this will give an unequal and unsatisfactory braking performance.

After riveting the new brake linings to the brake shoes it is essential that any high spots should be removed before replacement of the back plate assembly.

When new shoes and linings are fitted it must be appreciated that considerable adjustment has to be made on the foot brake mechanism, and it is necessary to return the Micram adjusters to their fully anti-clockwise position before attempting to refit the brake drums over the new linings. The handbrake must also be in the fully released position. Observe the following:

(1) Do not allow grease, paint, oil or brake fluid to come into contact with the brake linings.

(2) Do not clean the rubber parts with anything other than Lockheed hydraulic brake fluid. All traces of petrol, kerosene, etc, used for cleaning the metal parts must be removed before reassembly.

(3) Do not reline the brake shoes with different types of lining as this is bound to cause unequal braking.

(4) Do not allow the fluid in the master cylinder and supply tank assembly to fall below the half-full mark. When full the fluid should be ¼" below the bottom of the filler neck, with the brakes in the off position.

NOTE: Do not use any substitute for Lockheed brake fluid unless this is completely unobtainable. In such conditions use a fluid to specification SAE 70R2.

9. BRAKE FAULT DIAGNOSIS

(1) BRAKE PEDAL HARD

Possible cause	*Remedy*
(a) Incorrect shoe linings fitted.	— Check and replace linings with recommended type.
(b) Frozen pedal pivot.	— Rectify or renew pedal pivot pin and bush.
(c) Restricted brake line from master cylinder.	— Check brake line and remove restriction or renew line.
(d) Frozen wheel cylinder.	— Check, free up or renew.

(2) BRAKE DRAG DUE TO PRESSURE BUILD UP

Possible cause	*Remedy*
(a) Clogged master cylinder compensating port.	— Check and clean master cylinder and fluid reservoir.
(b) Frozen wheel cylinder.	— Check, free up or renew.
(c) Frozen handbrake linkage.	— Free up or renew linkage.
(d) Broken or stretched brake shoe return springs.	— Renew defective springs.
(e) Frozen handbrake cables.	— Free up or renew cables.
(f) Blocked vent in fluid reservoir cap.	— Check vent and remove obstruction.

(3) LOW OR SPONGY BRAKE PEDAL

Possible cause	*Remedy*
(a) Incorrectly adjusted brake shoes.	— Check and adjust brake shoes.
(b) Lack of sufficient fluid in system.	— Check for leaks, replenish fluid to specified level.
(c) Air in brake hydraulic system.	— Bleed hydraulic system.

(4) BRAKE LOCKS ON APPLICATION

Possible cause   *Remedy*

(a) Gummy linings due to oil or fluid contamination. — Clean and renew linings.
(b) Incorrect shoe adjustment. — Check and adjust shoes.
(c) Bent or eccentric brake drum/s. — Check and renew faulty drum/s.
(d) Incorrect linings fitted. — Check and renew linings in pairs with recommended type.
(e) Broken or stretched brake shoe return spring/s. — Check and renew faulty spring/s.

(5) BRAKE PEDAL PULSATES

Possible cause   *Remedy*

(a) Bent or eccentric brake drum. — Check and renew drums as required.
(b) Loose or worn front hub bearings. — Adjust or renew front hub bearings.
(c) Bent rear axle shaft. — Check and renew faulty components.

(6) BRAKE FADE AT HIGH SPEED

Possible cause   *Remedy*

(a) Incorrect shoe adjustment. — Check and adjust shoe to drum clearance.
(b) Eccentric or bent brake drum. — Check and renew faulty component.
(c) Lining/s saturated with hydraulic fluid. — Renew contaminated lining/s. Rectify fluid leakage.
(d) Incorrect linings fitted. — Check and instal recommended linings in sets.

(7) BRAKES OVERHEAT

Possible cause   *Remedy*

(a) Incorrect shoe adjustment. — Check and adjust shoe to drum clearance.
(b) Broken shoe return spring/s. — Renew faulty spring/s.
(c) Faulty handbrake cables and/or adjustment. — Check cables, renew or adjust.
(d) Frozen wheel cylinder. — Free up or renew faulty components.
(e) Obstructed or damaged hydraulic hose or line. — Remove obstruction or renew hydraulic hose or line.
(f) Obstructed master cylinder compensating port. — Clear compensating port.
(g) Blocked vent in master cylinder reservoir cap. — Check and remove obstruction in vent.
(h) Broken rear spring main leaf or centre bolt. — Check and renew faulty components.

WHEELS AND TYRES TC—TD—TF—TF 1500 SERIES
1. WHEEL AND TYRE ASSEMBLY

TO REMOVE

(1) Apply the handbrake.

(2) Remove the hub cover on the wheel concerned.

(3) Slacken the wheel nuts approximately three-quarters of a turn each.

(4) Raise the vehicle on the jack.

(5) Remove the wheel mounting nuts and take off the wheel.

TO INSTALL

Installation is a reversal of the removal procedure but note the following points:

(1) Tighten the wheel nuts in the order of 1, 3, 2, 4, in rotation and do not over-tighten.

(2) Do not exceed a torque of 62 ft/lb on the wheel nuts.

NOTE: (1) For wire wheels use a copper or wooden mallet to slacken the winged hub nut. The hub nuts on the left-hand side of the car have right-hand threads and the nuts on the right-hand side of the car have left-hand threads.

(2) Ensure that the brake adjustment hole seal is in position and line up one of the holes in the wheel with that in the drum to permit brake adjustment.

TO MAINTAIN

Proper tyre and wheel maintenance is essential for economical and safe operation.

Wire Wheel Removal and Installation.

(1) Maintain correct tyre pressures.

(2) Properly tighten wheel mounting nuts.

(3) Periodically inspect tyres for damage or abnormal wear.

(4) Periodically inspect rims for damage, especially to the flange and shoulders.

(5) Periodically rotate tyres (approximately every 3,000 miles).

(6) Maintain proper wheel balance.

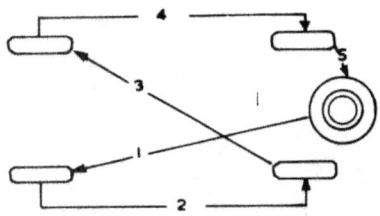

Diagram for Correct Wheel Rotation to Prolong Tyre Life and Minimise Wear.

2. TUBED TYRES

TO REMOVE

(1) Remove the wheel from the vehicle.

(2) Remove the valve cap and valve core.

(3) Separate the inside bead from the inside wheel flange and, using tyre irons with rounded edges, lever the bead of the tyre over the inside flange of the wheel.

NOTE: Use care during operation (3) to ensure that the tyre irons do not damage the inner tube against the edge of the wheel flange.

(4) Push the valve of the inner tube into the interior of the tyre and withdraw the inner tube out between the inner bead of the tyre and the wheel inner flange.

(5) Separate the outside bead of the tyre from the outside flange of the wheel and using tyre irons with rounded edges, lever the bead of the tyre over the inside flange of the wheel to separate the two components.

TO INSTALL

(1) Remove any loose or excessive scale or rust from the wheel flanges and clean with a wire brush or emery cloth.

(2) Position the inside flange of the wheel partly inside one of the tyre beads and using tyre irons in good condition, lever the remainder of the tyre bead over the wheel flange onto the wheel.

NOTE: During operation (2), ensure that the tyre bead opposite the side where the levers are applied is seated in the wellbase of the wheel rim.

(3) Position the inner tube inside the tyre and insert the valve through the hole in the wheel. Screw a valve core removing tool on the end of the valve to prevent the valve from slipping into the interior of the tyre when the other tyre bead is being positioned on the wheel.

(4) Fit the second bead of the tyre over the wheel inner flange, using the tyre irons or a rubber mallet, and ensure that the side of the bead adjacent to the valve goes over the wheel flange last.

NOTE: Align the white spot on the tyre with a similar spot on the tube to ensure correct static balance. Any further adjustment to static and dynamic balance must be obtained with wheel balancing equipment and the use of weights.

(5) Stand the wheel and tyre upright, fit the valve core, inflate the tube until the tyre beads just commence to position themselves on the wheel flanges.

(6) Bounce the tyre on the floor several times to position the tyre beads evenly over the wheel flanges, then inflate the tyre and tube to the recommended pressure.

(7) Check the valve core for leakage and install the valve cap.

3. TUBELESS TYRES

TO REMOVE

(1) Remove the wheel from the vehicle.

(2) Remove the valve cap and the valve core.

(3) Separate both the inside and outside beads from the wheel flanges so that both beads are in the base of the rim.

(4) Using tyre irons with rounded edges, lever the beads of the tyre, one at a time, off the inner flange of the wheel.

NOTE: Use a soap solution on the beads and wheel flange and see that the bead, diametrically opposite the point of leverage is seating on the bottom of the wellbase.

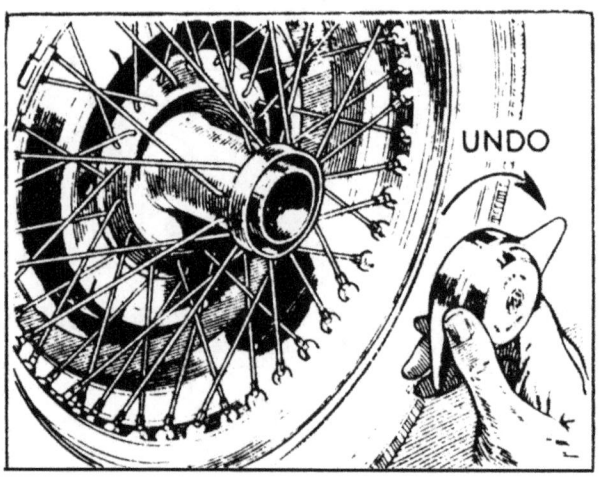

Dunlop Centre Lock Wheel. A righthand wheel is shown. Lefthand wheels undo in the opposite direction

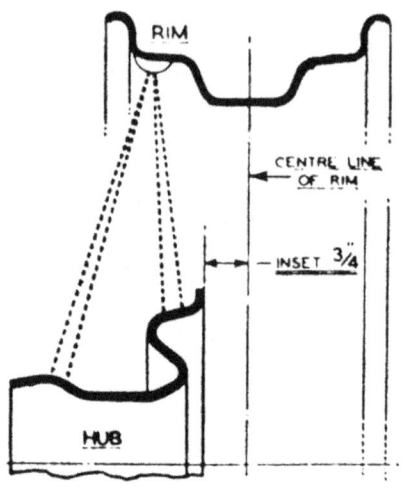

Outside dish of wire wheel TF

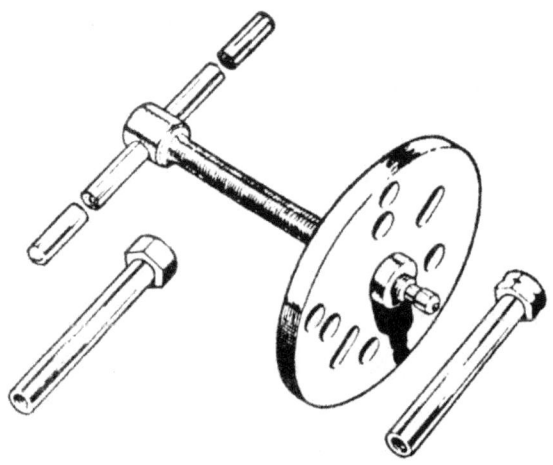

18G304 and 18G304B or 18G304A

Hub extractor for TD and TF models fitted with disc wheels

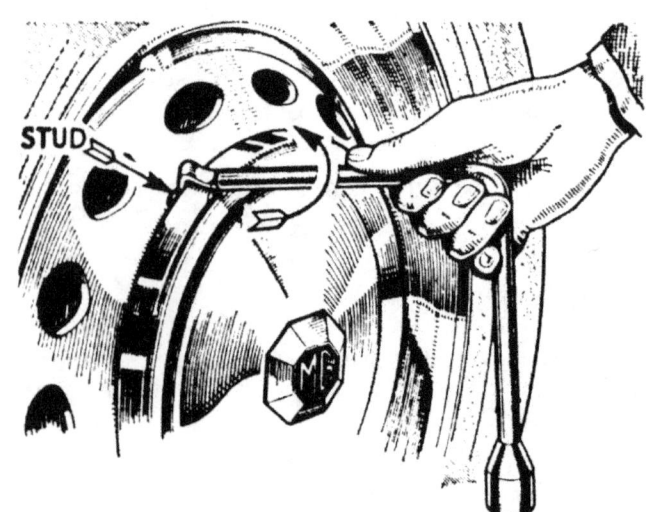

Correct method of removing hub disc TD, TF

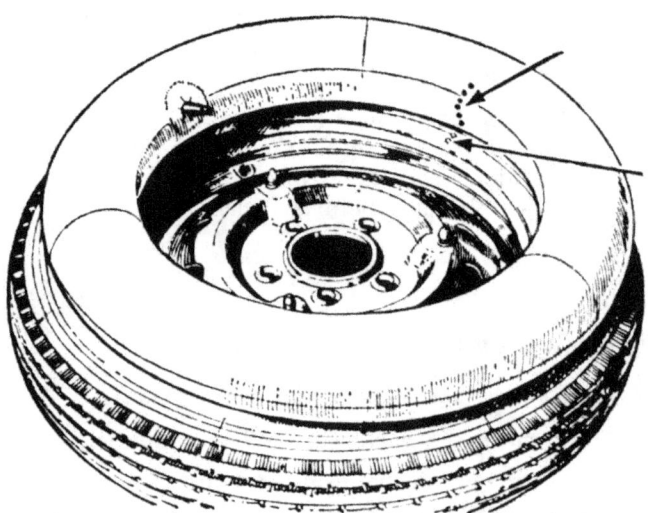

Balance marks on tyre and tube

TO RENEW A VALVE

(1) Remove the old valve from the valve hole in the wheel and clean around the hole.

(2) Wet the new valve and the valve hole with a soap solution and insert the valve in the hole from the inside of the wheel.

(3) Using Schrader tool No 553, screw the tool on the valve and pull the valve through the hole until the inner flange on the rubber base of the valve is in full contact with the inner rim surface. No attempt should be made to fit the valve with pliers.

TO INSTALL

(1) Remove loose or excessive scale or rust from the wheel, taking care not to damage the paint.

(2) Hammer out any dents in the rim flanges.

(3) Clean the rim bead seats and flanges thoroughly.

Use emery cloth, steel wool, a wire brush or a file depending on the amount of dirt, rust, rubber and surface irregularities to be removed. Smooth paint need not be removed.

(4) File or buff away any high spots at the welded joint.

(5) Wipe clean with moist rag.

NOTE: *The tyre beads and their tyre surfaces must not be damaged during fitting. Do not use a hammer or mallet.*

(6) Wipe the tyre beads with a damp cloth.

(7) Moisten tyre beads, rim surfaces and fitting levers with clean water or soap solution.

(8) Fit the tyre in the normal way, using narrow levers which are in good condition and free from sharp edges. Take small bites so as not to strain or damage the beads. Take particular care not to tear the rubber bead toes when they are lifted over the inner rim flange.

(9) Fit the second bead so that the part of the bead nearest the valve goes over the rim flange last.

NOTE: *Ensure that the marked balance spot is near the valve position.*

TO INFLATE TYRE

(1) Holding the tyre and wheel upright, bounce the tread of the tyre on the ground at several points around its circumference. This will help to snap the beads onto the tapered rim seats and provide a partial seal.

(2) Connect an air line with the valve core still removed, inflate with the wheel and tyre upright. If the first rush of air does not seal the beads, continue to bounce the tyre with the air line attached.

(3) Continue to inflate until both beads are fully home against the rim flanges.

(4) Remove the air line and fit the valve core. Then inflate to 40 psi.

(5) Test the tyre for leaks and deflate to correct running pressure.

TO INFLATE TYRE USING A TOURNIQUET

The Dunlop Tubeless Tyre Tourniquet is very suitable for assisting the inflation of tubeless tyres. Its purpose is to contract the centre of the treads so that the beads are forced outwards against the rim seats and so provide a partial seal for inflation.

(1) With the tool in the open position, buckle the strap centrally around the tread of the deflated tyre and wheel assembly. Pull the strap through the buckle as tight as possible. The strap must be threaded between the buckle bar and teeth on the clip and not between the clips and the end of the buckle.

(2) Thread the loose end of the strap through the gap between the rivet and roller on the link mechanism and compress the tread by pulling the handle through 180°.

(3) With the valve core removed attach the air line and inflate until the beads are sealed against the flanges. If they fail to seal at the first attempt, move the handle back and re-tighten the strap.

(4) When the beads are home, disconnect the air supply and fit the valve core. Then remove the tourniquet before final inflation.

(5) To remove the tourniquet, move the handle back and press the thumb on the end of the buckle, pushing the slider bar on the buckle inwards and upwards.

(6) Inflate to 40 psi and test. Deflate to correct running pressure.

NOTE: *When an air line is not available, the tourniquet enables tubeless tyres to be inflated with an efficient foot or hand pump. In necessary cases, a tourniquet may be improvised from a piece of rope and a twisting bar.*

TO TEST FOR LEAKS

A few minutes after inflation, immerse the tyre and wheel in a water tank and check for leaks.

If a water tank without submerging tool is being used, proceed as follows:

(1) Place the assembly in a tank with the valve uppermost. Submerge the valve and check.

(2) Release and allow the assembly to float, with the channel between the rim flange and the tyre filled with water. Check carefully for air bubbles above the rim flange.

(3) Turn the wheel assembly over and submerge the wheel rivets if they are not already under water. Check for leaks at the rivets.

(4) Submerge the assembly to fill the channel between the flange and tyre and then allow to float. Repeat as in (2). Check for leaks at the valve, rivets, and each flange in turn.

TO SEAL LEAKS

Leak at Top of Rim Flange:

(1) Mark on the tyre and rim the position of the leak and deflate the tyre. The leak may be caused by dirt, rust, a high weld or chipped paint.

(2) By holding the bead away from the rim seat, the cause of the leak can often be detected and removed without removal of the tyre.

(3) Make sure that the rim is clean after treatment.

Leak at Wheel Rivet:

(1) Mark the position of the leak on the rim. Deflate and remove the tyre. The leak should be sealed by peening over the rivet head with a ball peen hammer. Back up by another hammer or a solid resistance such as an anvil.

Leak at Valve Base:

(1) In the case of a metal clamp-in valve, if the valve has been fitted correctly and the valve hole is in good condition, the leak can be stopped by tightening the nut.

NOTE: After testing at 40 psi, make sure that the inflation pressure is adjusted to the correct running figure.

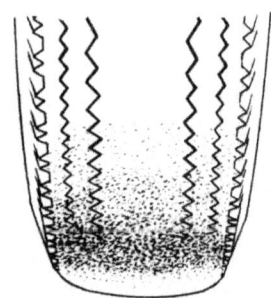

Wear in Centre of Tread due to Over Inflation

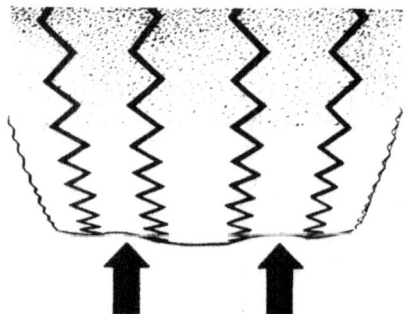

Wear Due to Under Inflation

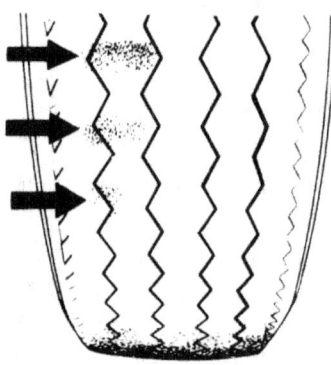

Spotty or Irregular Wear

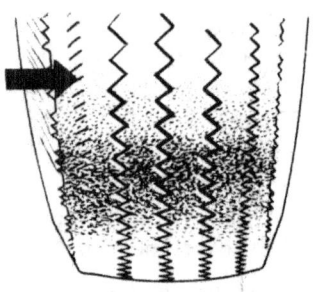

Wear Due to Incorrect Camber Angle

4. TYRE WEAR DIAGNOSIS

(1) ABNORMAL WEAR ON BOTH SIDES OF TREAD

Possible cause	*Remedy*
(a) Under inflation of tyres.	— Check and inflate to recommended pressures.
(b) Overloading.	— Reduce maximum loading.

(2) ABNORMAL WEAR IN CENTRE OF TREAD

Possible cause
(a) Over-inflation of tyres.

Remedy
— Check and reduce to recommended pressures.

(3) ABNORMAL WEAR ON INSIDE OF TREAD

Possible cause
(a) Insufficient camber angle.
(b) Sagging front coil springs.
(c) Loose or worn front hub bearings.
(d) Bent stub axle or steering knuckle support.
(e) Loose or worn suspension components.

Remedy
— Check front end alignment and rectify.
— Check and renew faulty springs.
— Check and adjust or renew hub bearings.
— Check and renew faulty components.
— Check and renew faulty components. Align front end.

(4) ABNORMAL WEAR ON OUTSIDE OF TREAD

Possible cause
(a) Excessive camber angle.
(b) Incorrect coil spring/s fitted.

Remedy
— Check front end alignment and rectify.
— Check and instal recommended replacement spring/s.

(5) SPOTTY OR IRREGULAR WEAR

Possible cause
(a) Static or dynamic unbalance of wheel and tyre assembly.
(b) Lateral run-out of wheel.
(c) Excessive play in wheel hub bearings.
(d) Excessive play in suspension mounting.

Remedy
— Check and balance wheel and tyre assembly.
— Check and true-up or renew wheel.
— Check and adjust or renew hub bearings.
— Check and renew suspension mounting.

(6) LIGHTLY WORN SPOTS AT CENTRE OF TREAD

Possible cause
(a) Static unbalance of wheel and tyre assembly.
(b) Radial run-out (eccentricity) of wheel.

Remedy
— Check and balance wheel and tyre assembly.
— Check and renew wheel.

(7) FLAT SPOTS AT CENTRE OF TREAD

Possible cause
(a) Eccentric brake drum.
(b) Repeated severe brake application.
(c) Lack of tyre rotation.

Remedy
— Check and renew brake drum.
— Revise driving habits.
— Periodically change tyres by rotation of wheel and tyre assembly.

(8) HEEL AND TOE WEAR (SAW TOOTH EFFECT)

Possible cause
(a) Over-loading.
(b) High speed driving.
(c) Excessive braking.

Remedy
— Revise maximum loading.
— Avoid as far as possible.
— Revise driving habits.

(9) FEATHERED EDGE ON ONE SIDE OF TREAD PATTERN

Possible cause
(a) Sharp inside edge-excessive toe-in.
(b) Sharp outside edge-excessive toe-out.
(c) One tyre sharp inside edge, other tyre sharp outside edge.

Remedy
— Check and adjust wheel alignment.
— Check and adjust wheel alignment.
— Check for bent steering arm and renew.

ELECTRICAL SYSTEM TC—TD—TF—TF 1500 SERIES

1. GENERAL DESCRIPTION

The 12-volt electrical equipment incorporates compensated voltage control for the charging circuit. The positive earth system of wiring is employed.

A slotted link connecting the dynamo front plate and the cylinder block enables the belt tension to be adjusted. On earlier models a rotatable mounting enables the belt tension to be adjusted.

The control box is sealed and should not normally need attention. The fuses are carried in external holders, as are the spare fuses, so that there is no need to remove the control box cover to gain access to them.

The starter motor is mounted on the flywheel housing on the right-hand side of the engine unit and operates on the flywheel through the usual sliding pinion device.

2. BATTERY

In order to keep the battery in good condition, a periodical inspection must be made, the cell specific gravity should be checked and the electrolyte should be topped up if necessary.

TO TOP UP

Remove the filler plug from each cell and examine the level of the electrolyte. Add distilled water as required to bring the level of the electrolyte in each cell just above the separators.

NOTE: Do not use tap water and do not use a naked light when examining the condition of the cells. Wipe away all dirt and moisture from the top of the battery.

TO TEST CONDITION OF BATTERY

Every 1000 miles examine the condition of the batteries by taking hydrometer readings. There is no better way of ascertaining the state of charge of a battery. The hydrometer contains a graduated float on which is indicated the specific gravity of the acid in the cell from which it is taken.

The specific gravity readings and their indications are as follows:

1.280 to 1.300	Battery fully charged.
About 1.210	Battery about half-discharged.
Below 1.150	Battery fully discharged.

These figures are given assuming an electrolyte temperature of 60 deg F (16°C). If the temperature of the electrolyte exceeds this, .002 must be added to hydrometer readings for each 5 deg F rise to give the true specific gravity. Similarly, .002 must be subtracted from hydrometer readings for every 5 deg F below 60 deg F.

The readings of all the cells should be approximately the same. If one cell gives a reading very different from the rest it may be than the electrolyte has been spilled or has leaked from the cell or there may be an internal fault. In this case it is advisable to have the battery examined by a battery specialist. Should a battery be in a low state of charge, it should be recharged by taking the car for a long daytime run or by charging from an external source of DC supply at a current rate of 5 amp until the cells are gassing freely.

After examining the battery, check the vent plugs, making sure that the air passages are clear, and screw the plugs into position. Wipe the top of the battery to remove all dirt and moisture.

TO STORE

If a battery is to be out of use for any length of time, it should first be fully charged and then given a freshening charge about every fortnight.

A battery must never be allowed to remain in a discharged condition, as this will cause the plates to become sulphated.

TO INITIALLY FILL AND CHARGE

The specific gravity of the electrolyte necessary to fill a new battery which has been supplied dry, and the specific gravity at the end of the charge are as follows:

Climate	SG of Filling Acid	SG at End of Charge [Corrected to 60°F (16°C)]
Ordinary below 80°F (27°C)	1.350	1.280 to 1.300
Between 80°F and 100°F	1.320	1.250 to 1.270
Over 100°F (38°C)	1.300	1.220 to 1.240

The electrolyte is prepared by mixing distilled water and concentrated sulphuric acid 1.835 SG. The mixing must be carried out in a lead-lined tank or a suitable glass or earthenware vessel. Steel or iron containers must not be used. The acid must be added slowly to the water, while the mixture is stirred with a glass rod. Never add the water to the acid, as the severity of the resulting chemical reaction may have dangerous consequences.

Heat is produced by the mixture of acid and water, and it should, therefore, be allowed to cool before it is poured into the battery, otherwise the plates, separators and moulded container may become damaged.

The temperature of the filling-in acid, battery and charging room should be above 32°F (0°C).

To produce electrolyte of the correct specific gravity:

To obtain Specific Gravity corrected to 60°F (16°C)	Add 1 part by volume of 1.835 SG acid to distilled water by volume as follows:
1.350	1.8 parts
1.320	2.2 parts
1.300	2.5 parts

Carefully break the seals in the filling holes and half-fill each cell in the battery with dilute sulphuric acid solution of the appropriate specific gravity (according to temperature) (see table). The quantity of electrolyte required to half-fill a two-volt cell is ¼ pint. Allow to stand for at least six hours, then complete the filling of the cells by the addition of more diluted acid of the same specific gravity as before until the level reaches the bottom of the filling holes, and allow the battery to stand for at least another two hours before commencing the first charge.

Charge at a constant current of 3.5 amp until the voltage and temperature-corrected specific gravity readings show no increase over five successive hourly readings. This period is dependent upon the length of time the battery has been stored since manufacture, and will be from forty to eighty hours, but usually not more than sixty.

Throughout the charge the acid must be kept level with the tops of the separators in each cell by the addition of acid solution of the same specific gravity as the original filling-in acid.

If, during charge, the temperature of the acid in any cell of the battery reaches the maximum permissible temperature of 120°F (49°C), the charge must be interrupted and the battery temperature allowed to fall by at least 10°F (5.5°C) before charging is resumed.

At the end of the first charge, i.e., when specific gravity and voltage measurements remain substantially constant, carefully check the specific gravity in each cell to ensure that it lies within the limits specified. If any cell requires adjustment, the electrolyte above the plates must be siphoned off and replaced either with acid of the strength used for the original filling-in, or distilled water, according to whether the specific gravity is too low or too high respectively. After such adjustment, the gassing charge should be continued for one or two hours to ensure adequate mixing of the electrolyte. Recheck, if necessary, repeating the procedure until the desired result is obtained.

3. GENERATOR

TO TEST ON VEHICLE WHEN GENERATOR IS NOT CHARGING

(1) Make sure that belt slip is not the cause of the trouble. It should be possible to deflect the belt approximately ¼″ at the centre of its longest run between two pulleys with moderate hand pressure. If the belt is too slack, tightening is effected by slackening the two generator suspension bolts and then the bolt on the slotted adjustment link. A gentle pull on the generator outwards will enable the correct tension to be applied to the belt and all three bolts should then be tightened firmly.

(2) Check that the generator and control box are connected correctly. The generator terminal D should be connected to the control box terminal D and the generator terminal F connected to control box terminal F.

(3) After switching off all lights and accessories, disconnect the cables from the generator terminals marked D and F respectively.

(4) Connect the two terminals with a short length of wire.

(5) Start the engine and set to run at normal idling speed.

(6) Clip the negative lead to a moving coil type voltmeter, calibrated 0 to 20 volts, to one generator terminal and the other lead to a good earthing point on the generator yoke.

(7) Gradually increase the engine speed, when the voltmeter reading should rise rapidly and without fluctuation. Do not allow the voltmeter reading to reach 20 volts. Do not race the engine in an attempt to increase the voltage. It is sufficient to run the generator at a speed of 1000 rpm.

If there is no reading, check the brush gear.

If the reading is low (approximately 1 volt), the field winding may be faulty.

If the reading is approximately 5 volts, the armature winding may be faulty.

(8) Remove the generator cover and examine the brushes and commutator. Hold back each of the brush springs and move the brush by pulling gently on its flexible connector. If the movement is slug-

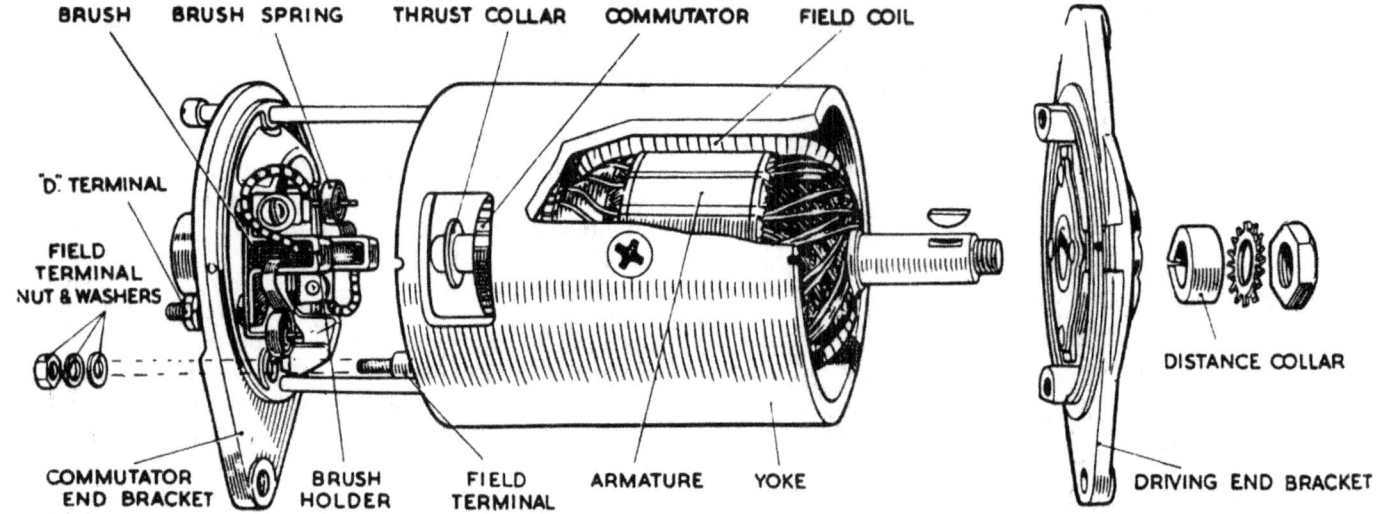

Exploded View of Generator (Early Cars).

gish, remove the brush from its holder and ease the sides by lightly polishing on a smooth file. Always replace brushes in their original positions. If the brushes are worn so that they no longer bear on the commutator, or if the brush flexible lead has become exposed on the running race, new brushes must be fitted. If the commutator is blackened or dirty, clean it by holding a petrol-moistened cloth against it while the engine is turned slowly by hand-cranking.

(9) Retest the generator; if there is still no reading on the voltmeter there is an internal fault and the complete unit should be renewed.

(10) If the generator is in good order, leave the temporary link in position between the terminals and restore the original connections, taking care to connect the generator terminal D to the control box terminal D and the generator terminal F to the control box terminal F.

(11) Remove the lead from the D terminal on the control box and connect the voltmeter between this cable and a good earthing point on the vehicle.

(12) Run the engine as before. The reading should be the same as that measured directly at the generator. No reading on the voltmeter indicates a break in the cable to the generator.

(13) Carry out the same procedure for the F terminal, connecting the voltmeter between cable and earth. Finally remove the link from the generator. If the reading is correct test the control box.

TO REMOVE AND INSTALL

(1) To remove the generator, disconnect the generator leads from the generator terminals.

(2) Slacken all attachment bolts and pivot the generator towards the cylinder block to enable the fan belt to be removed from the generator pulley. The generator can then be removed by completely removing the attachment bolts.

(3) Replacement of the generator is an exact reversal of this procedure.

TO DISMANTLE

(1) Take off the generator pulley.

(2) Remove the cover band, hold back the brush springs and remove the brushes from their holders.

(3) Unscrew the locknuts from the through bolts at the commutator end. Withdraw the two through bolts from the driving end.

(4) Remove the nut, spring washer and flat washer from the smaller terminal (i.e., field terminal) on the commutator end bracket and remove the bracket from the generator yoke.

(5) The driving end bracket, together with the armature, can now be lifted out of the yoke.

(6) The driving end bracket which, on removal from the yoke, has withdrawn with it the armature and armature shaft ball bearing, need not be separated from the shaft unless the bearing is suspected and requires examination, in which event the armature should be removed from the end bracket by means of a hand press.

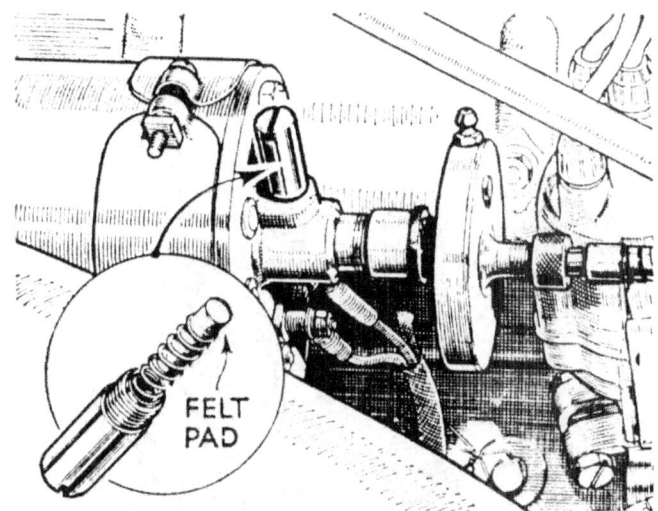

Generator lubricator and tachometer drive

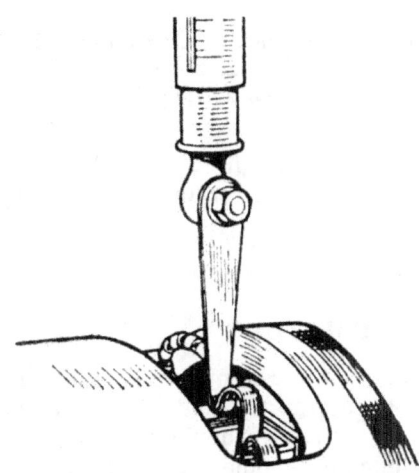

Testing the tension of brush springs

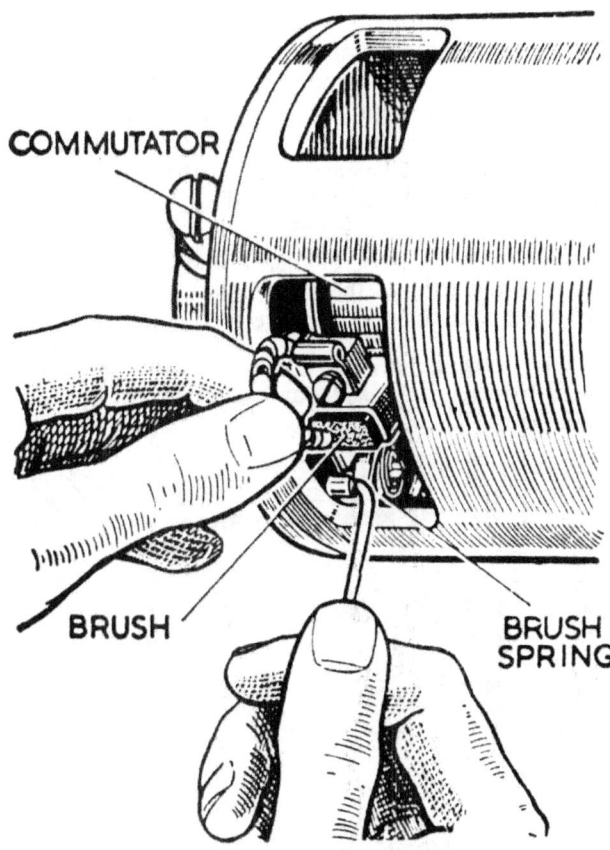

Releasing the generator brushes

TO SERVICE

(1) Test if the brushes are sticking. Clean them with petrol and, if necessary, ease the sides by lightly polishing with a smooth file. Replace the brushes in their original positions.

(2) Test the brush spring tension with a spring scale if available. The correct tension is 20 to 25 oz. Fit a new spring if the tension is low.

(3) If the brushes are worn so that the flexible lead is exposed on the running face, new brushes must be fitted. Brushes are pre-formed so that bedding to the commutator is unnecessary.

TO CHECK COMMUTATOR

A commutator in good condition will be smooth and free from pits or burned spots.

(1) Clean the commutator with a petrol-moistened cloth. If this is ineffective, carefully polish with a strip of fine glass-paper while rotating the armature.

(2) To remedy a badly worn commutator, mount the armature (with or without the drive end bracket) in a lathe, rotate it at high speed and take a light cut with a very sharp tool. Do not remove more metal than is necessary.

(3) Polish the commutator with very fine glasspaper.

(4) Undercut the mica insulation between the segments to a depth of $\frac{1}{32}''$ with a hacksaw blade ground down to the thickness of the mica.

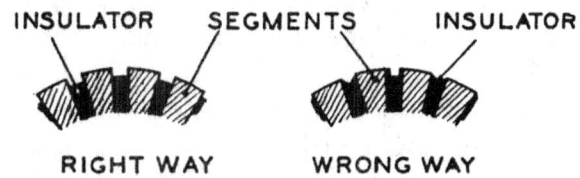

Correct Method of Undercutting Generator Commutator.

TO TEST FIELD COILS

Test the field coils, without removing them from the generator yoke, by means of an ohmmeter. The reading on the ohmmeter should be between 6.0 and

6.3 ohms. If this is not available, connect a 12-volt D.C. supply with an ammeter in series between the field terminal and the generator yoke. The ammeter readings should be approximately 2 amps. If no reading is indicated the field coils are open circuited and must be renewed. To test for earthed field coils, unsolder the end of the field winding from the earth terminal on the generator yoke and, with a test lamp connected from supply mains, test across the field terminal and earth. If the lamp lights, the field coils are earthed and must be renewed.

When fitting field coils, carry out the procedure outlined below, using an expander and wheel-operated screwdriver:

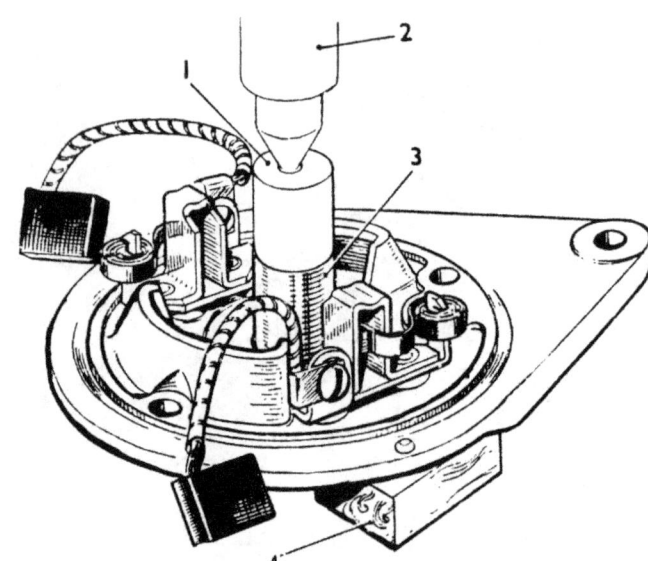

Fitting Bearing Bush to Commutator End Plate.
1. Shouldered Mandrel. 2. Hand Press. 3. Bearing Bush.
4. Supporting Block.

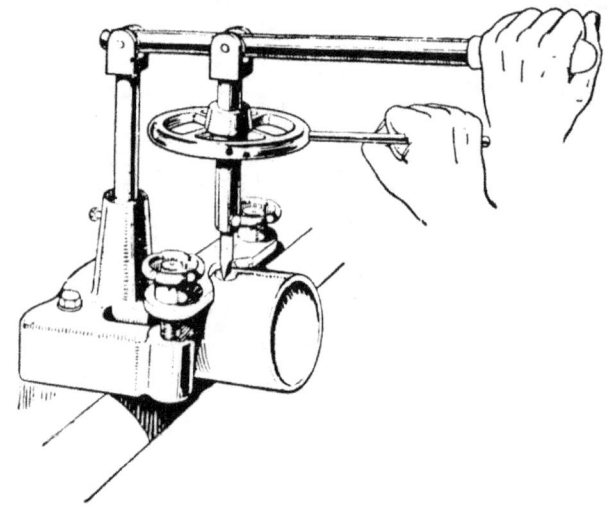

Showing use of Wheel Operated Screwdriver to remove Pole Shoe Attachment Screws.

(1) Remove the insulation piece which is provided to prevent the junction of the field coils from contacting the yoke.

(2) Mark the yoke and pole shoes in order that they can be installed in their original positions.

(3) Unscrew the two pole shoe retaining screws by means of the wheel-operated screwdriver.

(4) Draw the pole shoes and coils out of the generator yoke and lift off the coils.

(5) Fit the new field coils over the pole shoes and place them in position inside the yoke. Take care to ensure that the taping of the field coils is not trapped between the pole shoes and the yoke.

(6) Locate the pole shoes and field coils by lightly tightening the fixing screw.

(7) Insert the pole shoe expander, open it to the fullest extent and tighten the screws.

(8) Finally tighten the screws by means of the wheel-operated screwdriver and lock them by caulking.

(9) Replace the insulation piece between the field coil connections and the yoke.

TO TEST ARMATURE

The testing of the armature winding requires the use of a voltage drop test and growler. If these are not available, the armature should be checked by substitution. No attempt should be made to machine the armature core or to true a distorted armature shaft.

TO REPLACE BEARINGS

Bearings which are worn to such an extent that they will allow side movement of the armature shaft must be replaced by new ones.

To fit a new bearing at the commutator end of the generator, proceed as follows:

(1) Press the bearing bush out of the commutator end bracket.

(2) Press the new bearing bush into the end bracket, using a shouldered mandrel of the same diameter as the shaft which is to fit in the bearing.

Before fitting the new bearing bush allow it to stand completely immersed in thin engine oil for twenty-four hours, to fill the pores of the bush with lubricant.

The bearing at the driving end is renewed as follows:

(3) Knock out the rivets which secure the bearing retaining plate to the end bracket and remove the plate.

(4) Press the bearing out of the end bracket and remove the corrugated washer, felt washer and oil retaining washer.

(5) Before fitting the replacement bearing see that it is clean and pack it with high-melting-point grease.

(6) Place the oil retaining washer, felt washer and corrugated washer in the bearing housing in the end bracket.

(7) Locate the bearing in the housing and press it home by means of a hand press.

(8) Install the bearing retaining plate. Insert the new rivets from the inside of the end bracket and open the rivets by means of a punch to secure the plate rigidly in position.

TO REASSEMBLE

The reassembly of the generator is a reversal of the dismantling operations.

If the end bracket has been removed from the armature in dismantling, press the bearing end bracket on to the armature shaft, taking care to avoid damaging the end plate and armature winding.

Add a few drops of oil through the hole in the armature end cover.

4. STARTER

TO TEST ON VEHICLE

Switch on the lamps and operate the starter control. If the lights go dim, but the starter is not heard to operate, an indication is given that current is flowing through the starter windings but that the starter pinion is meshing permanently with the geared ring on the flywheel. This was probably caused by the starter being operated while the engine was still running. In this case the starter must be removed from the engine for examination.

Should the lamps retain their full brilliance when the starter switch is operated, check that the switch is functioning. If the switch is in order, examine the connections at the battery, starter switch and starter, and also check the wiring between these units. Continued failure of the starter to operate indicates an internal fault, and the starter must be removed from the engine for examination.

Sluggish or slow action of the starter is usually caused by a poor connection in the wiring which produces a high resistance in the starter circuit. Check as described above.

Damage to the starter drive is indicated if the starter is heard to operate but does not crank the engine.

TO DISMANTLE

(1) Take off the cover band (see illustration) at the commutator end, hold back the brush springs and take out the brushes from their holders.

(2) Withdraw the jump ring and shims from the armature shaft at the commutator end and remove the armature complete with drive from the commutator end bracket and starter frame.

(3) Remove the terminal nuts and washers from the terminal post at the commutator end bracket and also withdraw the two through bolts.

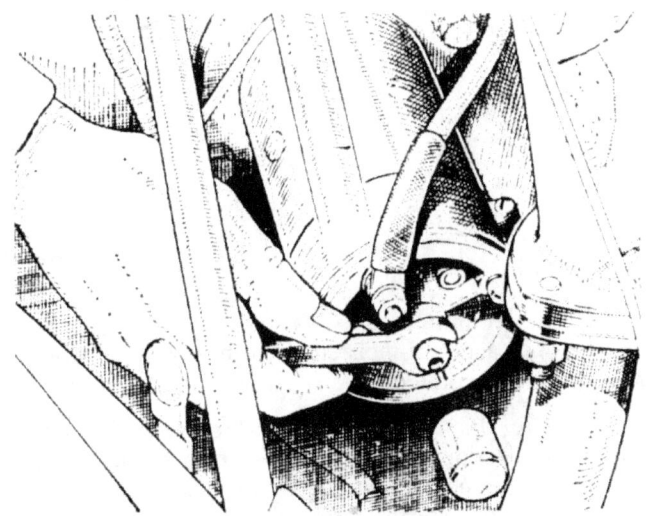

Freeing a jammed starter pinion

(4) Remove the commutator end bracket and the attachment bracket from the starter frame.

TO EXAMINE COMMUTATOR AND BRUSH GEAR

(1) Remove the starter cover band and examine the brushes and the commutator.

(2) Hold back each of the brush springs and move the brush by pulling gently on its flexible connector. If the movement is sluggish remove the brush from its holder and ease the sides by lightly polishing with a smooth file. Always replace brushes in their original positions. If the brushes are worn so that they no longer bear on the commutator, or if the brush flexible lead has become exposed on the running face, they must be renewed.

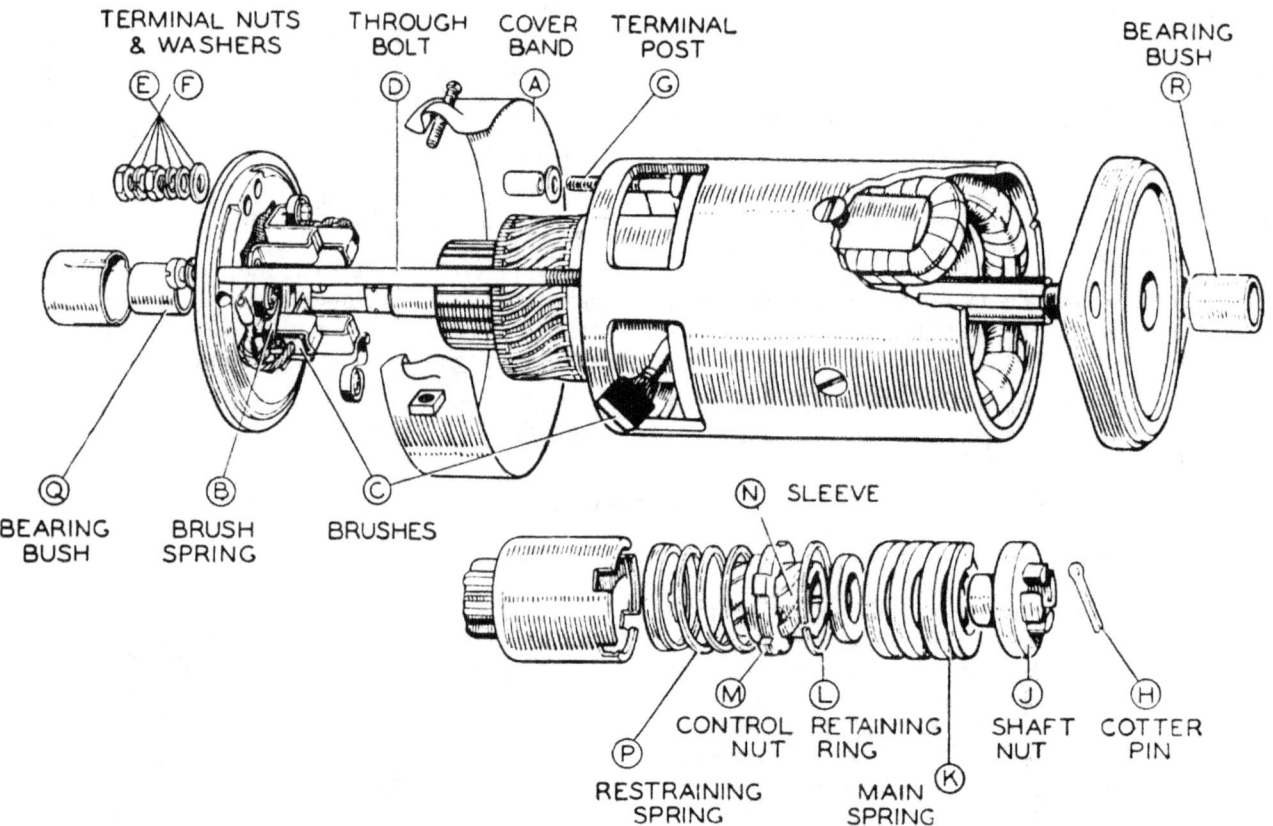

Exploded View of Starter and Drive.

(3) If the commutator is blackened or dirty, clean it by holding a petrol-moistened cloth against it while the armature is rotated.

(4) Secure the body of the starter in a vice and test by connecting it with heavy gauge cables to a battery of the correct voltage. One cable must be connected to the starter terminal and the other held against the starter body or end bracket. Under these light load conditions the starter should run at a very high speed.

If the operation of the starter is still unsatisfactory, the starter should be dismantled for detailed inspection and testing.

TO CHECK BRUSHES

(1) Test the brush springs with a spring scale. The correct tensions are given at the beginning of this section. Fit a new spring if the tension is low.

(2) If the brushes are worn so that they no longer bear on the commutator, or if the flexible connector has become exposed on the running face, they must be renewed. Two of the brushes are connected to terminal eyelets attached to the brush boxes on the commutator end bracket. The other two brushes are connected to tappings on the field coils.

(3) The flexible connectors must be removed by unsoldering and the connectors of the new brushes secured in place by soldering. The brushes are pre-formed, so that bedding of the working face to the commutator is unnecessary.

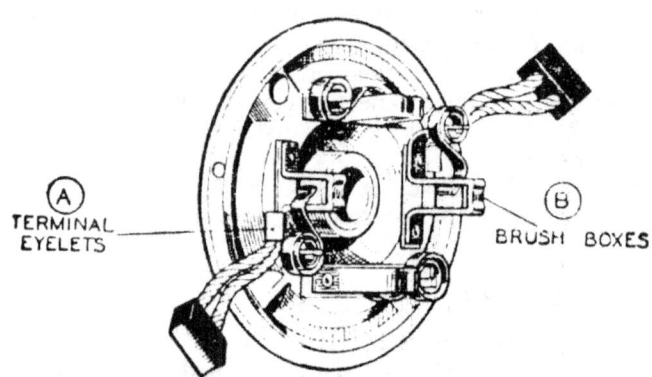

The starter end cover showing connections

TO SERVICE STARTER DRIVE

If the pinion is tight on the sleeve, wash in kerosene; replace any worn or damaged parts.

(1) To dismantle the drive, extract the split pin and remove the shaft nut; withdraw the main spring and collar.

(2) Rotate the barrel to push out the sleeve; remove the barrel and pinion.

(3) The barrel and pinion are supplied as an assembly but the parts may be separated by extracting the retaining ring.

NOTE: *Should either the control nut or screwed sleeve be damaged, a replacement assembly, consisting of a screwed sleeve and control nut, must be fitted. These components must not be fitted individually.*

Commutator

A commutator in good condition will be smooth and free from pits and burned spots. Clean the commutator with a cloth moistened with petrol. If this is ineffective, carefully polish with a strip of fine glasspaper, while rotating the armature. To remedy a badly worn commutator, dismantle the starter drive as described above and remove the armature from the end bracket. Now mount the armature in a lathe, rotate it at a high speed and take a light cut with a very sharp tool. Do not remove any more metal than is absolutely necessary, and finally polish with very fine glass-paper.

The mica on the starter commutator must not be undercut.

TO TEST FIELD COILS

The field coils can be tested for an open circuit by connecting a 12-volt battery, having a 12-volt bulb in one of the leads, to the tapping point of the field coils to which the brushes are connected, and the field terminal post. If the lamp does not light, there is an open circuit in the wiring of the field coils.

Lighting of the lamp does not necessarily mean that the field coils are in order, as it is possible that one of them may be earthed to a pole shoe or to the yoke. This may be checked by removing the lead from the brush connector and holding it on a clean part of the starter yoke. Should the bulb now light it indicates that the field coils are earthed.

Should the above tests indicate that the fault lies in the field coils, they must be renewed. When renewing field coils carry out the procedure detailed in To Service Generator.

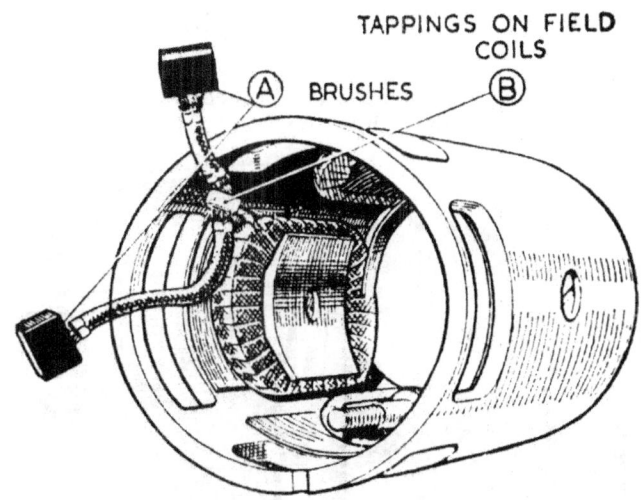

FIG 11:9 Field coil connections of starter motor

TO CHECK ARMATURE

Examination of the armature will in many cases reveal the cause of failure, e.g., conductors lifted from the commutator due to the starter being engaged while the engine is running and causing the armature to be rotated at an excessive speed. A damaged armature must in all cases be renewed—no attempt should be made to machine the armature core or to true a distorted armature shaft.

TO SERVICE BEARINGS (COMMUTATOR END)

Bearings which are worn to such an extent that they will allow excessive sideplay of the armature shaft, must be renewed. To renew the bearing bush, proceed as follows:

Press the new bearing bush into the end bracket, using a shouldered mandrel of the same diameter as the shaft which is to fit in the bearing.

The bearing bush is of the porous phosphor-bronze type, and before fitting, new bushes should be allowed to stand completely immersed for 24 hours in thin engine oil in order to fill the pores of the bush with lubricant.

5. CONTROL BOX

TC—TD—TF—TF 1500 SERIES

The regulator is carefully set before leaving the Works to suit the normal requirements of the standard equipment, and in general it should not be necessary to alter it. If, however, the battery does not keep in a charged condition, or if the generator output does not fall when the battery is fully charged, it may be advisable to check the setting and, if necessary, to re-adjust it.

It is important, before altering the regulator setting when the battery is in a low state of charge, to check that its condition is not due to a battery defect or to the generator belt slipping.

TO CHECK AND ADJUST ELECTRICAL SETTING

The regulator setting can be checked without removing the cover of the control box.

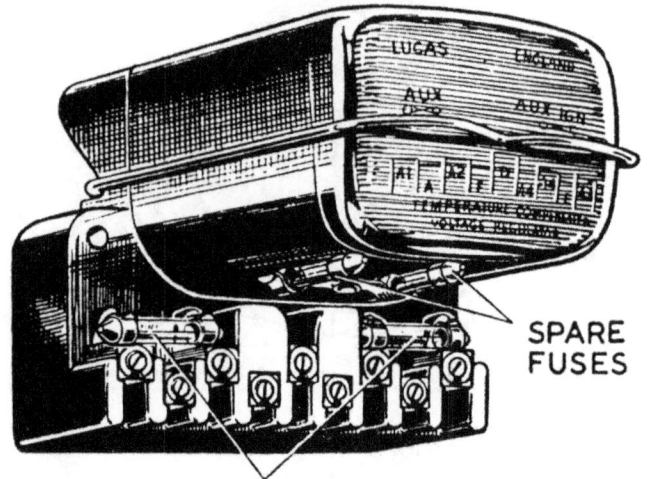

FUSES IN CIRCUITS OF ACCESSORIES

Control box with fuses, TC and early TD models

(1) Withdraw the cables from the terminals marked A and A.1 at the control box and join them together. Connect the negative lead of a moving coil voltmeter (0 to 20 volts full-scale reading) to the D terminal on the generator and connect the other lead from the meter to a convenient chassis earth.

(2) Slowly increase the speed of the engine until the voltmeter needle flicks and then steadies; this should occur at a voltmeter reading between the limits given below for the appropriate temperature of the regulator.

Setting at	10°C (50°F)	....	16.1 to 16.7 volts
,,	,, 20°C (68°F)	....	15.8 to 16.4 ,,
,,	,, 30°C (86°F)	....	15.6 to 16.2 ,,
,,	,, 40°C (104°F)	....	15.3 to 15.9 ,,

(3) If the voltage at which the reading becomes steady occurs outside these limits, the regulator must be adjusted.

(4) Shut off the engine, remove the control box cover, release the locknut A (see illustration) holding the adjusting screw B and turn the screw in a clockwise direction to raise the setting or in an anti-clockwise direction to lower the setting. Turn the adjusting screw a fraction of a turn and then tighten the locknut.

(5) When the generator is run at a high speed on open circuit, it builds up a high voltage. When adjusting the regulator, do not run the engine up to more than half-throttle or a false voltmeter reading will be obtained.

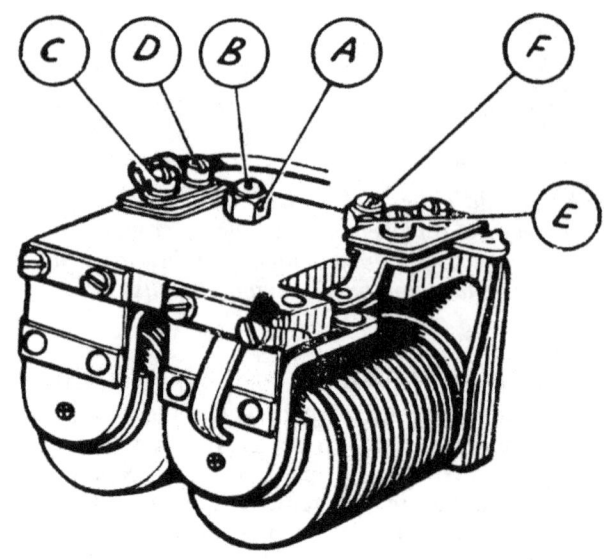

Cut-out and Regulator Assembly.

TO ADJUST MECHANICAL SETTING

The mechanical setting of the regulator is accurately adjusted before leaving the Works, and provided that the armature carrying the moving contact is not removed, the regulator will not require mechanical adjustment. If, however, the armature has been removed from the regulator for any reason, the contacts will have to be reset. To do this proceed as follows:

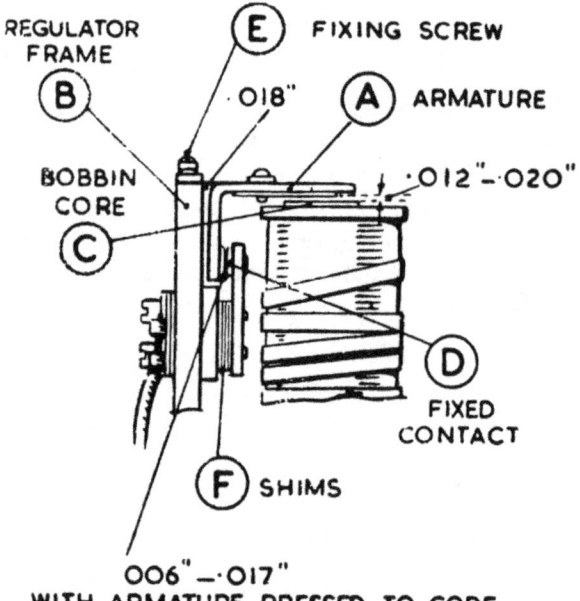

Regulator Mechanical Adjustment.

(1) Slacken the two armature fixing screws E (see illustration). Insert a .018" feeler gauge between the back of the armature A and the regulator frame.

(2) Press back the armature against the regulator frame and down on to the top of the bobbin core with the gauge in position and lock the armature by tightening the two fixing screws.

(3) Check the gap between the underside of the arm and the top of the bobbin core. This must be .012" to .020". If the gap is outside these limits correct by adding or removing shims F at the back of the fixed contact D.

(4) Remove the gauge and press the armature down, when the gap between the contacts should be between .006" and .017".

TO CLEAN REGULATOR CONTACTS

(1) To render the regulator contacts accessible for cleaning, slacken the screws securing the plate carrying the fixed contact. It will be necessary to slacken the upper screw C a little more than the lower screw D, so that the contact plate can be swung outwards.

(2) Clean the contacts by means of fine carborundum stone or fine emery cloth.

(3) Carefully wipe away all traces of dirt or other foreign matter.

(4) Finally tighten the securing screws.

TO ADJUST CUT-OUT

If it is suspected that the cutting-in speed of the generator is too high, connect a voltmeter between the terminals marked D and E at the control box and slowly raise the engine speed. When the voltmeter reading rises to between 12.7 and 13.3 volts the cut-out contacts should close.

If the cut-out has become out of adjustment and operates at a voltage outside these limits it must be reset. To make the adjustment, slacken the locknut E and turn the adjusting screw F a fraction of a turn in a clockwise direction to raise the operating voltage or in an anti-clockwise direction to lower the voltage. Tighten the locknut after making the adjustment.

TO CLEAN CUT-OUT CONTACTS

To clean the contacts remove the cover, place a strip of fine glass-paper between the contacts and then, closing the contacts by hand, draw the paper through. This should be done two or three times, with the rough side towards each contact.

TO INSTALL RADIO SUPPRESSORS

When it is desired to install suppressors for radio equipment, make sure that this is done only in accordance with recommended practice. Suppressors and capacitors wrongly fitted may cause damage to the electrical equipment.

6. HORN

The Lucas windtone horns, type WT 614 should give long periods of service without attention.

If adjustment should be necessary, remove the cover after removing the fixing screw. Disconnect and insulate the lead to the other horn, and short-circuit the fuse, otherwise it is liable to blow during adjustment.

Slacken the adjuster locknut and rotate the adjusting nut until the contacts are just separated, indicated by the horn failing to sound. Turn the adjustment half a turn in the opposite direction and tighten the locknut. If the horn note is still unsatisfactory, it should not be dismantled but returned to a Lucas service depot for examination.

7. FLASHING DIRECTION INDICATORS

Flashing indicators were not fitted as original equipment to **TC** (UK) or early **TD** models.

Flashing indicators in combination with the sidelamps and with the stop and tail lamps were fitted to **TC** (USA export) and to later **TD** and all **TF** models. Two systems were used, the **TC** (USA) cars having two relays, one for lefthand indicators, the other for the righthand indicators, while on the **TD** and **TF** systems a single relay unit was used. The circuitry for these systems of indicators will be found in the wiring diagrams for the appropriate models.

The flashing direction indicators are operated by a pneumatic time-switch through a flasher unit and a relay to the dual filament bulbs in the side and taillamps. In the event of failure, carry out the following procedure:

(1) Check the bulbs for broken filaments.

(2) Refer to the wiring diagram and check over the flasher circuit connections.

(3) Switch on the ignition and check that terminal B on the flasher is at 12 volts with respect to earth.

(4) Connect together terminals B and L at the flasher unit and operate the direction indicator switch.

If the flasher lights now work, the flasher unit is defective and must be replaced.

If the lights do not work the relay is defective and must be replaced.

The length of time the flasher is operating can be altered by screwing up the adjusting screw located in the small boss at the back of the time switch. Screw in to lengthen the time of operation and out to shorten the period.

8. WINDSCREEN WIPER

The majority of cars in the series covered by this manual are fitted with the Lucas type CW windscreen wiper motor, the arm and blade on the driver's side being geared directly to the armature spindle. The motor is shown with the cover removed.

The electrical feed to the wiper is taken from the ignition auxiliary circuit, so that the instrument only operates when the ignition is switched on. To start the wiper, pull the setting lever towards you and move the swich to the right. To park the wiper arms switch off the motor by moving the switch arm to the left, pulling the setting lever towards you and then turning it to engage the end of the switch arm.

If the wiper fails to operate, check whether current is passing through the instrument. This will be indicated by movement of the ammeter. If no current is indicated the trouble can be due to a faulty connection, a blown fuse or faulty switch contacts in the wiper itself. If the fuse has blown check for short-circuits in the wiring before renewing the fuse. If the fuse blows again the wiper motor should be removed for inspection. Faulty contacts, damage to the switch by a dented cover, or broken internal connections should be rectified.

Normally the windshield wiper will not require any servicing apart from the occasional renewal of the rubber blades.

TO DETACH CABLE RACK FROM MOTOR AND GEARBOX

(1) Unscrew the pipe union nut.

(2) Remove the gearbox cover.

(3) Remove the split pin and washer from the crankpin and final gear wheel.

(4) Lift off the connecting link.

TO SERVICE DIRTY COMMUTATOR

(1) Remove the connecting leads to the terminals, and withdraw the three screws securing the cover at the commutator end.

(2) Lift off the cover.

(3) Clean the commutator with a cloth moistened with petrol and carefully remove any carbon dust from between the commutator segments.

TO SERVICE STIFF BRUSH LEVER OR BRUSHES NOT BEARING ON COMMUTATOR

(1) Check that the brushes bear freely on the commutator. If they are loose and do not make contact, a replacement tension spring is necessary. The brush levers must be free on their pivots.

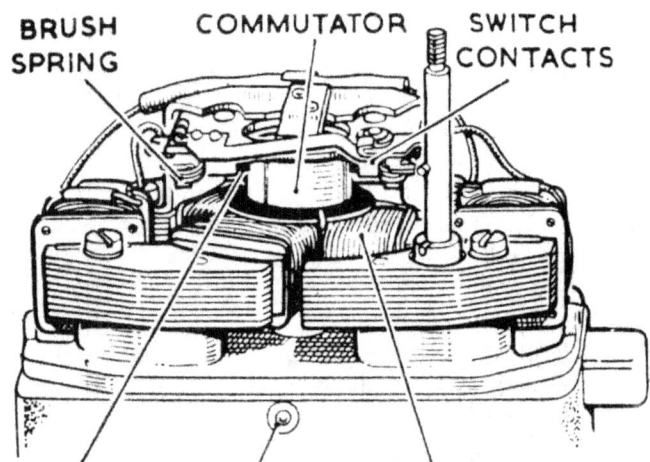

Windscreen wiper motor type CW with cover removed to show switch contacts

(2) If they are stiff they should be freed by working them backwards and forwards by hand and by applying a trace of thin machine oil. Packing shims are fitted beneath the legs of the brush to ensure that the brushes are central and that there is no possibility of the brush boxes fouling the commutator.

(3) If the brushes are considerably worn they must be replaced by new ones.

TO CHECK OPERATING MOTOR WHICH DOES NOT TRANSMIT MOTION TO SPINDLES

(1) Remove the cover of the gearbox. A push-pull motion should be transmitted to the inner cable of the flexible rack. If the cross-head moves sluggishly between the guides, lightly smear a small amount of medium grade engine oil in the groove formed in the die-cast housing.

(2) When overhauling, the gear must be lubricated by lightly packing the gearbox with a recommended lubricant.

TO ADJUST THRUST SCREW

The thrust screw is located on the top of the cross-head housing. To adjust, slacken the locknut, screw down the thrust screw until it contacts the armature and then turn back a fraction of a turn. Hold the thrust screw with a screwdriver and tighten the locknut.

TO REMOVE MOTOR

(1) Detach the cable rack from the motor and gearbox as detailed above.

(2) Disconnect the lead.

(3) Remove the two screws securing the mounting bracket to remove the motor.

9. FAULT LOCATION AND REMEDY

Although every precaution is taken to eliminate possible causes of trouble, failure may occasionally develop through lack of attention to the equipment, or damage to the wiring. The following pages set out the recommended procedure for a systematic examination to locate and remedy the causes of some of the more usual faults encountered.

The sources of trouble are by no means always obvious, and in some cases a considerable amount of deduction from the symptoms is needed before the cause is disclosed.

For instance, the engine might not respond to the starter switch; a hasty inference would be that the starter motor is at fault. However, as the motor is dependent on the batteries, it may be that the batteries are exhausted.

This, in turn, may be due to the generator failing to charge the batteries, and the final cause of the trouble may be, perhaps, a loose connection in some part of the charging circuit.

If, after carrying out an examination, the cause of the trouble is not found, the equipment should be checked by the nearest Lucas service depot or agent.

CHARGING CIRCUIT

1. Batteries in low state of charge

(a) This state will be shown by lack of power when starting, poor light from the lamps, and hydrometer readings below 1.200. It may be due to the generator not charging or giving low or intermittent output. The ignition warning light will not go out if the generator fails to charge, or will flicker on and off in the event of intermittent output.

(b) Examine the charging and field circuit wiring, tightening any loose connections or replacing broken cables. Pay particular attention to the battery connections.

(c) Examine the generator driving belt; take up any undue slackness by swinging the generator outwards on its mounting after slackening the attachment bolts.

(d) Check the regulator setting and adjust if necessary.

(e) If, after carrying out the above, the trouble is still not cured, have the equipment examined by a Lucas service depot or agent.

2. Batteries overcharged

This will be indicated by burnt-out bulbs, very frequent need for topping up the batteries, and high hydrometer readings. Check the charge reading with an ammeter when the car is running. It should be of the order of only 3 to 4 amps.

If the ammeter reading is in excess of this value, it is advisable to check the regulator setting and adjust if necessary.

STARTER MOTOR

1. Starter motor lacks power or fails to turn engine

(a) See if the engine can be turned over by hand. If not, the cause of the stiffness in the engine must be located and remedied.

(b) If the engine can be turned by hand, first check that the trouble is not due to a discharged battery.

(c) Examine the conections to the batteries, starter and starter switch, making sure that they are tight and that the cables connecting these units are not damaged.

(d) It is also possible that the starter pinion may have jammed in mesh with the flywheel, although this is by no means a common occurrence. To disengage the pinion, rotate the squared end of the starter shaft by means of a spanner.

2. The starter operates but does not crank engine

This fault will occur if the pinion of the starter drive is not allowed to move along the screwed sleeve into engagement with the flywheel, due to dirt having collected on the screwed sleeve. Remove the starter and clean the sleeve carefully with kerosene.

3. The starter pinion will not disengage from the flywheel when the engine is running

Stop the engine and see if the starter pinion is jammed in mesh with the flywheel, releasing it if necessary by rotation of the squared end of the starter shaft. If the pinion persists in sticking in mesh, have the equipment examined at a Service Depot. Serious damage may result to the starter if it is driven by the flywheel.

LIGHTING CIRCUITS

1. Lamps give insufficient illumination

(a) Test the state of charge of the battery, recharging it if necessary from an independent electrical supply.

(b) Check the setting of the lamps.

(c) If the bulbs are discolored as a result of long service, they should be renewed.

2. Lamps light when switched on but gradually fade out

As paragraph 1 (a).

3. Brilliance varies with speed of car

(a) As paragraph 1 (a).

(b) Examine the battery connections, making sure that they are tight, and renew any faulty cables.

10. DISTRIBUTOR

TO REMOVE

If the clamp plate pinch bolt is not slackened the distributor can be removed without disturbing the ignition timing. Proceed as follows:

(1) Crank the engine until the rotor finger points to the segment connected to the plug on No 1 cylinder.

(2) Unscrew the union and disconnect the suction advance unit from the tube to the inlet manifold.

(3) Disconnect the low tension lead.

(4) Remove the distributor cover.

(5) Unscrew the bolts securing the distributor clamp plate to the distributor housing.

(6) Remove the distributor.

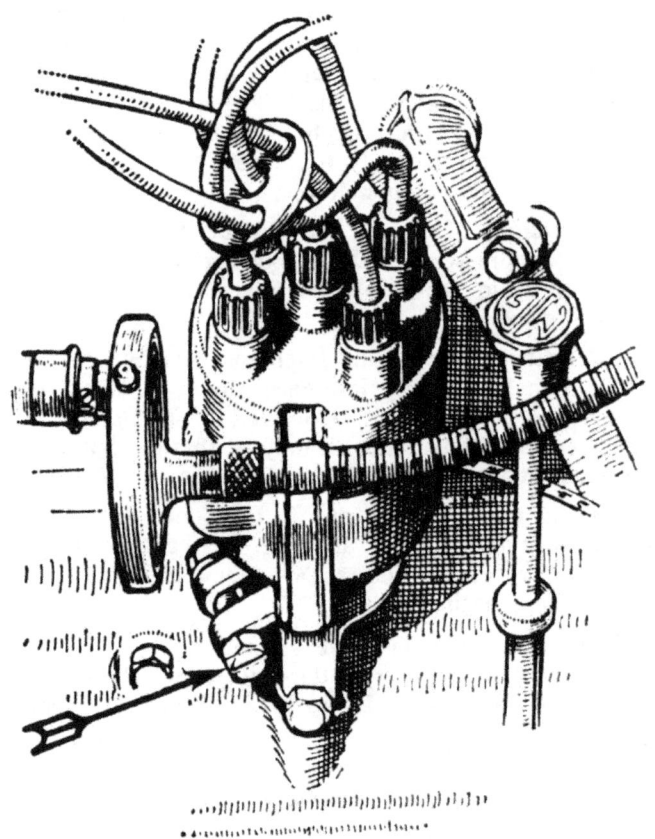

Distributor with clamp bolt fitting indicated by arrow. To withdraw the distributor the lower bolt with the lock wire is the only one that need be removed

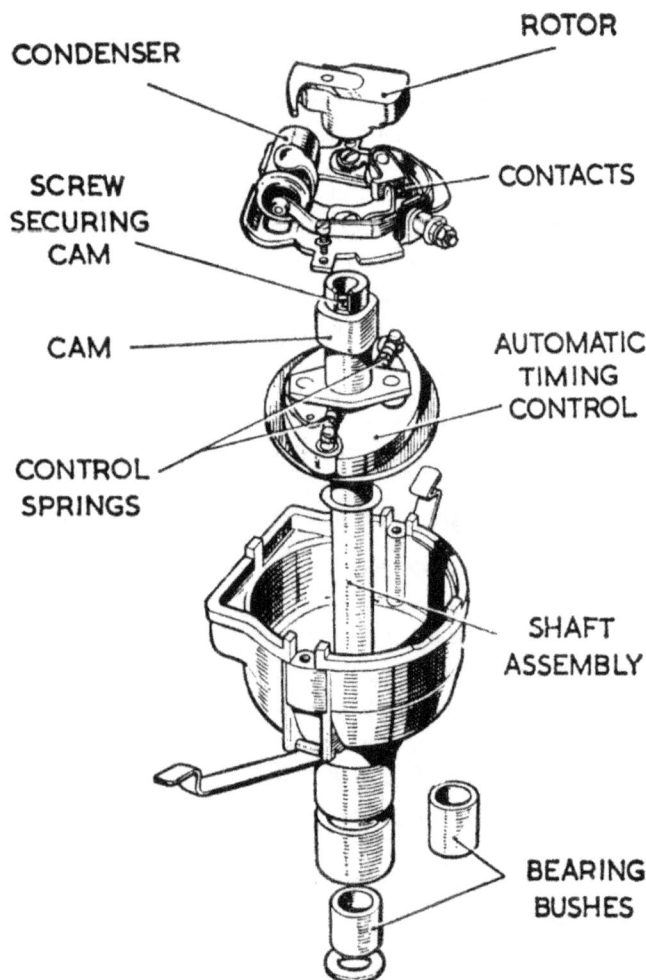

The component parts of the distributor

Attachment of distributor on later TD and all TF cars by cotter bolt (arrowed) engaging the distributor stem

144

TO DISMANTLE

(1) Remove the rotor arm.

(2) Slacken the low tension terminal nuts and withdraw the slotted connector from between the head of the terminal bolt and the insulating washer.

(3) Remove the spring clip securing the suction advance unit arm to the plate.

(4) Remove the two screws securing the plate assembly to the distributor body.

(5) Remove the plate assembly.

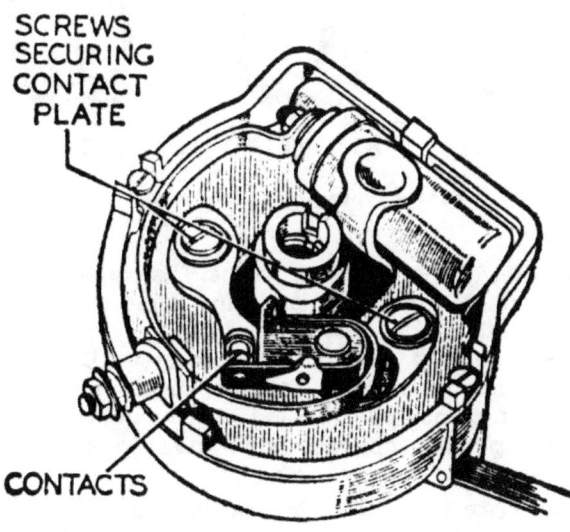

Distributor with cap and rotor arm removed, showing contact plate and other components

TO CHECK AND INSPECT

(1) Thoroughly clean all parts with cleaning solvent, taking care not to immerse the capacitor, contacts, or vacuum advance unit in solvent.

(2) Check and test the capacitor.

(3) Check the contacts for pitting and burning and if necessary renew as a set only.

(4) Check the low tension and earth wires for possible fractures.

(5) Check the distributor shaft or bush for wear and renew as necessary. Wear in excess of .002" between the shaft and bush, will necessitate shaft and/or bush renewal.

(6) Check the cams for wear or roughness. Variations in lift between any two cams in excess of .002" will necessitate renewing the cam and shaft assembly.

(7) Check the rotor arm and distributor cap for fine cracks or carbon tracking.

(8) Check the vacuum advance unit for a leaking diaphragm. To do this, push in on the diaphragm connecting link, place a finger over the pipe union and release the connecting link. The vacuum on the finger should hold for at least 30 seconds.

(9) Check the rubber O-ring seal and renew as necessary.

TO REASSEMBLE

Assembly is a reversal of the dismantling procedure but the following points should be observed.

(1) Lubricate the automatic timing control and the cam bearing with a few drops of thin oil. Lightly smear the cam with a little grease or clean engine oil.

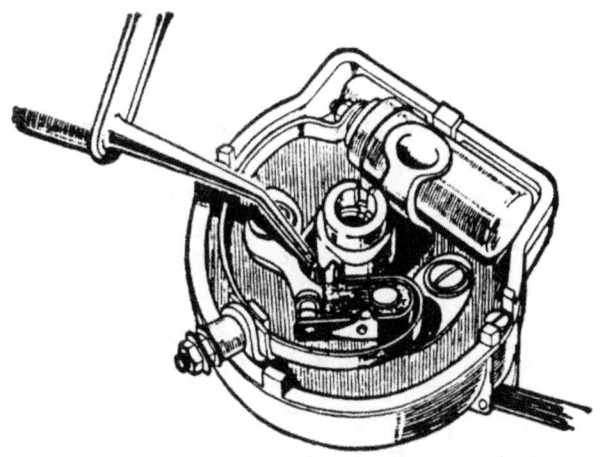

Lubrication of the automatic timing control through the aperture round the cam spindle

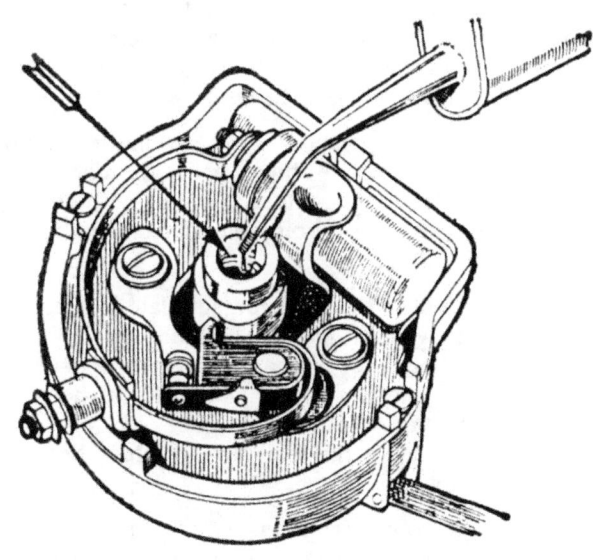

Lubrication of the distributor cam bearing

(2) Set the micro-adjuster to the centre position of adjustment.

(3) Set the contact breaker points to the recommended gap.

(4) Leave the clamp plate securing bolt slack.

TO INSTALL

(1) Insert the distributor into the distributor housing until the driving dog rests on the distributor drive shaft.

(2) Rotate the rotor arm slowly until the driving dog engages the recess in the distributor drive from the camshaft.

NOTE: The lugs on the dog are offset to ensure correct replacement.

(3) Turn the distributor body until the clamping plate holes align with the holes in the housing and replace the bolts.

(4) Now proceed to assemble in reverse order of dismantling.

NOTE: The rotor arm will point to the segment connected to No 1 cylinder as long as the crankshaft has remained in its original position as at the commencement of removal.

(5) Replace high tension leads in the firing order 1, 3, 4, 2, bearing in mind the direction of rotation of the rotor.

TO ADJUST CONTACT GAP

(1) Remove the distributor and rotor arm.

(2) If the contact points are serviceable, remove from the distributor, clean and reface them on a smooth oil stone or contact file. Wash in clean solvent to remove any traces of oil from the contact faces and re-instal them in the distributor.

(3) Turn the distributor in an anti-clockwise direction, as viewed from above, or, if the distributor is installed in the engine, turn the engine until the heel of the breaker arm rubbing block is on the highest point of a cam lobe.

(4) Slightly loosen the fixed contact plate lock screws and using a screwdriver, move the contact plate in the necessary direction until a clean feeler gauge blade of the specified thickness is a neat sliding fit in the point gap, then retighten the contact plate lock screws. Again check the fit of the feeler gauge blade between the contact points.

NOTE: If new points are being fitted, set the gap at the upper limit of the specification as the initial wear of a new breaker arm rubbing block will be rapid. If the points have been in use for some time, but are still serviceable, set the gap at approximately midway between the upper and lower limits of the specifications.

(5) Turn the engine or distributor and measure the contact point gap at each cam lobe, being sure that the heel of the breaker arm rubbing block is in the position of maximum lift on each cam.

NOTE: Variation in lift between any two cams should not exceed .002" when measured at the contact points.

SYMMETRIC   ASYMMETRIC   HIGH LIFT

The three types of distributor cam

Check the gap with a feeler gauge. The correct setting is .010 to .012 inch for distributors fitted on **TC** and earlier **TD** models with symmetric or asymmetric cams and .014 to .016 inch for later **TD** and **TF** models fitted with high lift cams. Distributors having high lift cams are denoted by the letter **E** or a following letter appearing after the service number.

(6) Place a smear of high melting point grease on the lobes of the cam assembly and install the rotor arm and distributor cap.

TO SET IGNITION TIMING (STATIC SETTING)

(1) Crank the engine until No 1 piston is at tdc on compression stroke. This position can be obtained by observing the valves on No 4 cylinder. The approximate position will be when the valves on No 4 cylinder are rocking (i.e. the exhaust just closing and the inlet just opening).

(2) Check the required setting from the specifications at the beginning of this section.

(3) Rotate the crankshaft (in the direction of rotation) until the notch on the crankshaft pulley is opposite the nearest pointer on the timing cover case to the required setting.

NOTE: the longer pointer indicates tdc the next 5° btdc and the last 10° btdc.

(4) Connect a 12-volt bulb in parallel with the contact breaker points, switch on the ignition and rotate the distributor body anti-clockwise until the bulb lights. At this instant the points have just opened.

(5) Slacken the clamp plate set bolts and secure the distributor body in this position by tightening the clamp plate bolt (or nut).

(6) Now adjust the vacuum control adjusting screw to obtain the correct setting.

NOTE: Approx 55 clicks on the screw will move the vacuum control barrel one graduation on the scale and each graduation is equal to approximately 5° on the moving plate.

(7) Check that the rotor arm is opposite the segment on the distributor cap connected to the plug on No 1 cylinder.

(8) Road test the vehicle and make any further adjustments with the micrometer adjusting nut as warranted by the condition of the engine and the grade of fuel being used.

TO SET IGNITION TIMING (WITH SYNCHROSCOPE/TIMING LIGHT)

NOTE: If the distributor drive gear assembly has been removed from the engine it should be installed as described in TO INSTALL (DISTRIBUTOR).

(1) Disconnect the vacuum advance connection to the induction manifold.

(2) Mark the notch in the pulley and the pointers with chalk.

(3) Connect the leads of the synchroscope to No 1 spark plug.

(4) Run the engine at a speed below that at which the centrifugal weights come into operation (400 rpm).

(5) Aim the synchroscope at the notch and pointers and note the position of the notch on the pulley in relation to the pointers. This should be as specified for the model being attended to.

(6) If adjustment is required slacken the clamp plate bolt (or nut) and carefully rotate the distributor body in the direction necessary to achieve the desired ignition setting and tighten the clamp plate bolt (or nut).

(7) Road test the vehicle and make any further adjustments with the micrometer adjusting nut.

11. SPARK PLUGS AND HIGH TENSION LEADS

TO SERVICE

The spark plugs should be removed for inspection, cleaning and resetting at intervals of 3000 to 4000 miles.

Spark plugs removed from an engine in good condition, operating under normal conditions should have a light powdery deposit ranging in colour from light brown to a greyish tan. After considerable service the electrodes will show signs of wear or normal burning.

Spark plugs showing a thick black oily deposit indicate an engine in poor mechanical condition or possibly, that a plug with too low a heat range has been fitted.

Spark plugs showing a white or yellowish deposit indicate sustained high speed driving or possibly that plugs of too high heat range have been fitted, particularly when these deposits are accompanied by blistering of the porcelain and burning of the electrodes. Check the recommended heat range for the engine, and select the correct heat range if operating conditions are abnormal.

If the heat range is correct, clean the plugs on a sandblast machine and blow clean with compressed air.

Set the electrode gap (see Specifications) by bending the earthing electrode and test the plugs on a reliable testing machine.

NOTE: Never attempt to set the electrode gap by bending the centre electrode or a cracked insulator will result.

Clean the spark plug threads and, using new gaskets, fit the plugs finger tight.

Using a torque wrench, tighten to the recommended torque figure.

Check the high tension wires between the plugs and distributor cap and the cap and coil for deterioration and sharp bends. When removing the wires, grasp the terminals or the wires as close to the ends as possible to avoid stretching or bending.

Renew any wires that are inclined to cracking or perishing.

Renew the high tension wire thimbles on the distributor cap and the one on the coil if deterioration or perishing is evident.

Plug terminals should incorporate radio/television suppressors.

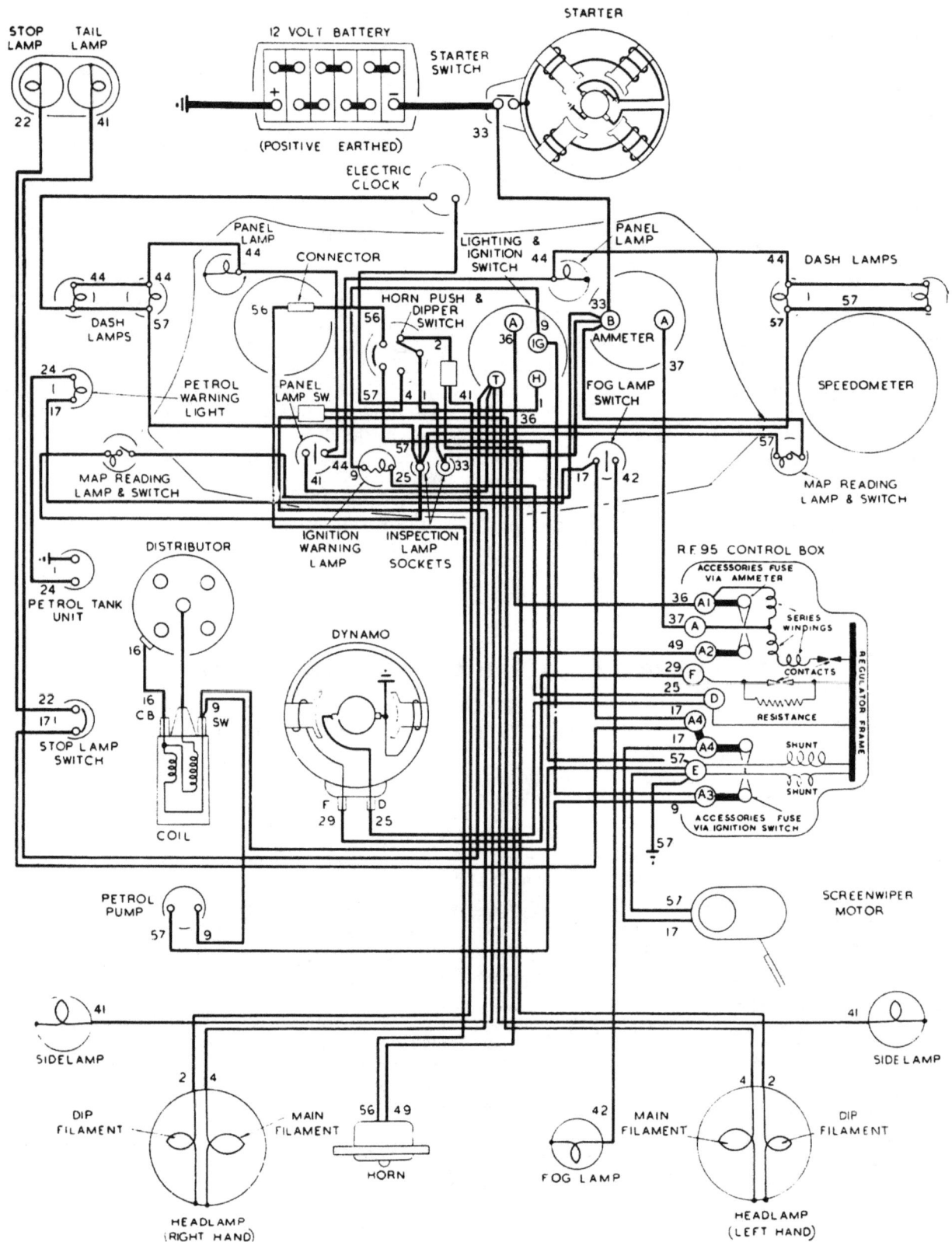

Wiring Circuit Diagram for TC Cars.

148

KEY TO CABLE COLORS—TC CARS

1. Blue.
2. Blue with Red.
3. Blue with Yellow.
4. Blue with White.
5. Blue with Green.
6. Blue with Purple.
7. Blue with Brown.
8. Blue with Black.
9. White.
10. White with Red.
11. White with Yellow.
12. White with Green.
13. White with Green.
14. White with Purple.
15. White with Brown.
16. White with Black.
17. Green.
18. Green with Red.
19. Green with Yellow.
20. Green with Blue.
21. Green with White.
22. Green with Purple.
23. Green with Brown.
24. Green with Black.
25. Yellow.
26. Yellow with Red.
27. Yellow with Blue.
28. Yellow with White.
29. Yellow with Green.
30. Yellow with Purple.
31. Yellow with Brown.
32. Yellow with Black.
33. Brown.
34. Brown with Red.
35. Brown with Yellow.
36. Brown with Blue.
37. Brown with White.
38. Brown with Green.
39. Brown with Purple.
40. Brown with Black.
41. Red.
42. Red with Yellow.
43. Red with Blue.
44. Red with White.
45. Red with Green.
46. Red with Purple.
47. Red with Brown.
48. Red with Black.
49. Purple.
50. Purple with Red.
51. Purple with Yellow.
52. Purple with Blue.
53. Purple with White.
54. Purple with Green.
55. Purple with Brown.
56. Purple with Black.
57. Black.
58. Black with Red.
59. Black with Yellow.
60. Black with Blue.
61. Black with White.
62. Black with Green.
63. Black with Purple.
64. Black with Brown.

KEY TO CABLE COLORS—TD, TF AND TF-1500 CARS

1. Blue.
2. Blue with Red.
3. Blue with Yellow.
4. Blue with White.
5. Blue with Green.
6. Blue with Purple.
7. Blue with Brown.
8. Blue with Black.
9. White.
10. White with Red.
11. White with Yellow.
12. White with Blue.
13. White with Green.
14. White with Purple.
15. White with Brown.
16. White with Black.
17. Green.
18. Green with Red.
19. Green with Yellow.
20. Green with Blue.
21. Green with White.
22. Green with Purple.
23. Green with Brown.
24. Green with Black.
25. Yellow.
26. Yellow with Red.
27. Yellow with Blue.
28. Yellow with White.
29. Yellow with Green.
30. Yellow with Purple.
31. Yellow with Brown.
32. Yellow with Black.
33. Brown.
34. Brown with Red.
35. Brown with Yellow.
36. Brown with Blue.
37. Brown with White.
38. Brown with Green.
39. Brown with Purple.
40. Brown with Black.
41. Red.
42. Red with Yellow.
43. Red with Blue.
44. Red with White.
45. Red with Green.
46. Red with Purple.
47. Red with Brown.
48. Red with Black.
49. Purple.
50. Purple with Red.
51. Purple with Yellow.
52. Purple with Blue.
53. Purple with White.
54. Purple with Green.
55. Purple with Brown.
56. Purple with Black.
57. Black.
58. Black with Red.
59. Black with Yellow.
60. Black with Blue.
61. Black with White.
62. Black with Green.
63. Black with Purple.
64. Black with Brown.
65. Dark Green.
66. Light Green.

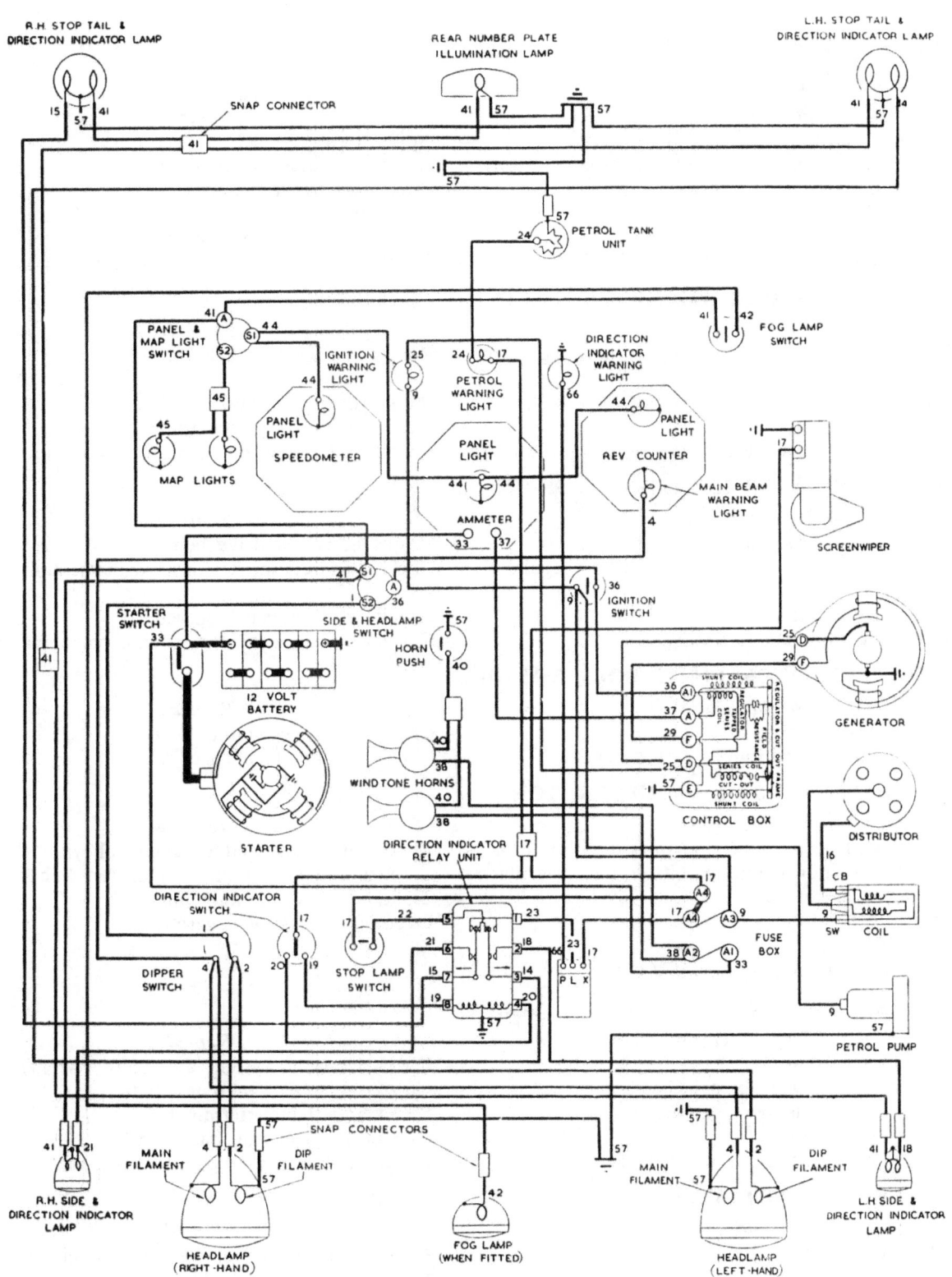

Wiring Circuit Diagram for TD, TF and TF-1500 Cars.

12. ELECTRICAL FAULT DIAGNOSIS

BATTERY AND GENERATOR SYSTEM:

(1) BATTERY UNDERCHARGED

Possible cause	*Remedy*
(a) Loose or broken generator drive belt.	— Adjust or renew belt.
(b) Faulty or incorrectly adjusted generator regulator.	— Renew or adjust regulator unit.
(c) Faulty battery.	— Renew or repair battery.
(d) Faulty generator.	— Overhaul or renew generator.
(e) Fault in charging circuit wiring.	— Check and repair or renew wiring.
(f) Faulty connections in charging circuit.	— Check and renew or repair component/s.

(2) BATTERY OVERCHARGED

Possible cause	*Remedy*
(a) Faulty or incorrectly adjusted generator regulator unit.	— Renew or adjust regulator.
(b) Faulty battery.	— Renew or repair battery.
(c) Faulty generator.	— Overhaul or renew generator.
(d) Faulty charging circuit wiring or connections.	— Check and renew or repair faulty components.

(3) CHARGE INDICATOR LIGHT REMAINS ON

Possible cause	*Remedy*
(a) Loose or broken generator drive belt.	— Adjust or renew drive belt.
(b) Faulty or incorrectly adjusted generator regulator unit.	— Check and renew or adjust regulator unit.
(c) Faulty generator.	— Check and overhaul generator.
(d) Low regulator voltage setting.	— Check and adjust voltage setting on regulator unit.

(4) CHARGE INDICATOR LIGHT DOES NOT OPERATE

Possible cause	*Remedy*
(a) Light bulb blown.	— Check and renew faulty bulb.
(b) Open circuit in wiring or bulb socket.	— Check and rectify open circuit.

(5) NOISE IN DRIVE BELT OR GENERATOR

Possible cause	*Remedy*
(a) Drive belt frayed or out of alignment with pulleys.	— Renew drive belt and/or align pulleys.
(b) Loose generator mounting bolts or worn bearings.	— Tighten mounting bolts and/or renew bearings.
(c) Loose generator pulley.	— Tighten pulley retaining nut.
(d) Faulty generator.	— Overhaul or renew generator.

BATTERY AND STARTING SYSTEM:

(1) STARTER LACKS POWER TO CRANK ENGINE

Possible cause	*Remedy*
(a) Battery undercharged.	— Check charging system and rectify as necessary.
(b) Battery faulty, will not hold charge.	— Check and repair or renew battery.
(c) Battery terminals loose or corroded.	— Clean and tighten terminals.
(d) Faulty starter motor.	— Check and overhaul starter motor.
(e) Faulty starter solenoid switch or contacts.	— Check and renew solenoid as necessary.

(2) STARTER WILL NOT ATTEMPT TO CRANK ENGINE

Possible cause	*Remedy*
(a) Open circuit in starting system.	— Check for: dirty or loose terminals, dirty commutator, faulty solenoid, faulty switch.
(b) Discharged battery.	— Check for fault or short circuit in system.
(c) Battery fully charged but will not crank engine.	— Check for: locked drive and ring gears, internal starter fault or seized engine.

HEADLAMP SYSTEM:

(1) LAMPS FAIL TO LIGHT

Possible cause

(a) Burnt out bulb/s.
(b) Open circuit in wiring or connections.
(c) Faulty light switch.
(d) Burnt out fuse, if fitted.

Remedy

— Check and renew.
— Check and rectify.
— Check and renew switch.
— Eliminate cause and renew fuse.

(2) LAMPS FLARE WITH ENGINE SPEED INCREASE

Possible cause

(a) Faulty battery.
(b) Battery in low state of charge.
(c) High resistance or faulty connections between generator and battery.
(d) Poor earth connection between battery and engine or generator.
(e) Voltage regulator setting too high or unit inoperative.

Remedy

— Check and renew or repair battery.
— Recharge battery and check charging system.
— Check circuit and rectify condition.
— Check battery earth lead and strap between engine and body.
— Check and adjust voltage regulator setting.

DIRECTION INDICATOR LIGHT SYSTEM:

(1) INDICATOR WARNING LIGHT DOES NOT BURN AND NO AUDIBLE CLICKING FROM FLASHER UNIT, WHEN TURN IS SELECTED ON SWITCH LEVER

Possible cause

(a) Fuse blown.
(b) Bulb blown on one or both sides.
(c) Faulty flasher unit.
(d) Faulty direction indicator switch.
(e) Fault in wiring circuit.

Remedy

— Rectify fault and renew fuse.
— Check system and renew bulb/s.
— Renew flasher unit. Do not attempt repair.
— Renew or repair switch.
— Check and repair fault.

(2) INDICATOR WARNING LIGHT DOES NOT FLASH BUT AUDIBLE CLICKING FROM FLASHER UNIT, WHEN TURN IS SELECTED ON SWITCH LEVER

Possible cause

(a) Warning light bulb blown.
(b) Front bulb blown on opposite side to turn selected.

Remedy

— Check and renew bulb.
— Check and renew bulb.

(3) BOTH WARNING LIGHTS FLASH WEAKLY AND AT GREATER THAN NORMAL SPEED WHEN TURN IS SELECTED ON SWITCH LEVER

Possible cause

(a) Front bulb blown on turn side.
(b) Rear bulb blown on turn side.
(c) Faulty flasher unit.

Remedy

— Check and renew bulb.
— Check and renew bulb.
— Check and renew flasher unit.

(4) BOTH INDICATOR WARNING LIGHTS BURN CONSTANTLY WHEN TURN IS SELECTED ON SWITCH LEVER

Possible cause

(a) Front and rear bulbs blown on turn side.
(b) Faulty flasher unit.

Remedy

— Check and renew bulbs.
— Check and renew flasher unit.

IGNITION SYSTEM:

(1) ENGINE WILL NOT START

Possible cause	Remedy
(a) Fault in ignition primary circuit wiring.	— Check circuit and repair as necessary.
(b) Faulty ignition switch.	— Renew ignition switch.
(c) Fault in coil primary winding.	— Renew coil.
(d) Burnt or dirty contact breaker points.	— Clean or renew and adjust points.
(e) Faulty capacitor or capacitor lead.	— Check and renew capacitor.
(f) Fused or broken low tension wire from breaker arm to low tension terminal.	— Renew low tension terminal block and wire.
(g) Fault in coil high tension circuit.	— Test and renew coil as necessary.
(h) Cracks in distributor cap.	— Renew distributor cap.
(i) Crack in distributor rotor.	— Renew distributor rotor.
(j) Faulty high tension leads.	— Check and renew leads.
(k) Faulty or incorrectly adjusted spark plugs.	— Renew or clean and adjust spark plugs.

(2) ENGINE STARTS BUT MISFIRES UNDER LOAD

Possible cause	Remedy
(a) Faulty, dirty or incorrectly adjusted spark plugs.	— Renew and/or clean and adjust spark plugs.
(b) Dirty or incorrectly adjusted contact points.	— Clean, adjust or renew points.
(c) Uneven wear on distributor cam.	— Check and overhaul distributor.
(d) Condensation moisture in distributor cap.	— Check and dry out and examine cap for cracks.
(e) Cracked spark plug insulator/s.	— Renew faulty spark plug/s.
(f) Faulty ignition coil.	— Check and renew coil.

(3) ENGINE RUNS BUT LACKS POWER

Possible cause	Remedy
(a) Ignition timing incorrectly set or contact points require adjusting.	— Check and readjust timing and/or contact points.
(b) Centrifugal advance mechanism seized or excessively worn.	— Overhaul distributor.
(c) Vacuum advance unit inoperative.	— Check for broken vacuum pipe or faulty unit.
(d) Vacuum advance unit operates, but ineffective.	— Advance unit link disconnected or broken.

APPENDIX

Body

Maintenance and Lubrication

Torque Wrench Settings

General Specifications

Performance Tuning

Exploded view of chassis, suspension, radiator, fuel tank and exhaust system components, model TD

BODY TC—TD—TF—TF 1500 SERIES

Care and repair of bodywork

The open body is of normal coachbuilt construction with metal panels on a wooden framework. It is attached to the chassis frame by a series of bolts and is removed without difficulty by following the directions given at the end of this chapter. Many aspects of body maintenance are within the capabilities of the enthusiastic owner, but the removal of dents in body panels should only be attempted by a skilled panel beater. Amateur attempts to knock out dents usually result in raising a worse one. Very small dents, however, can be filled using one of the catalytic fillers supplied for this purpose.

The finish is cellulose and in refinishing after repair it is better to have a larger area sprayed, such as a complete wing, than to repaint a small section. If the car is still finished in one of the maker's original colours, supplies of the correct shade of cellulose enamel can be obtained from an agent's Service Parts Department.

Hood and sidescreens

The hood should not be folded when it is wet or damp. Always wait until it dries. **FIG: 01** shows the correct method of folding on models TC, TD and TF. Before folding the hood back, release the press buttons at each side. Referring to the numbered illustrations:

1 Make sure that no hood material is trapped between the hood-sticks and that the rear panel of the hood is pulled forward.
2 Fold the hood-sticks right down and gently pull the hood material out as shown.
3 Fold the two corners at right angles and fold the back in once.
4 Fold the hood material over again and the hood is then ready for the tonneau cover to be fitted over it.

The sidescreens are fitted to the doors by socket fittings and slotted brackets which engage locking screws. When not in use the screens are stored in the special compartment at the back of the body behind the seat. As this compartment has been kept to minimum dimensions it is essential that the sidescreens are packed carefully so as to prevent damage. **FIG: 02** shows the method of stowing the earlier type of sidescreens fitted to Model TD. Referring to the numbered sections of the illustration, the operations are as follows:

1 Start with the righthand front sidescreen and lay it on a flat surface as shown, taking care that the stays are the right way up. Then place the lefthand front sidescreen on top of it, with its flap folded under and the stays at opposite ends.
2 Lay the righthand rear sidescreen on the other two as shown, tucking its front bracket under that of the lefthand front sidescreen.
3 Lay the lefthand rear sidescreen on the others in the opposite direction with its bracket slipped under the cranked stay of the righthand front sidescreen with which the pile was started.
4 Transfer the complete pile of sidescreens to the compartment provided, inserting them brackets first as shown.

Parts list

1 Chassis frame—complete
2 Extension—front R/H —frame
3 Extension—front L/H —frame
4 Bracket—engine steady
5 Bracket—engine mounting support
6 Anchor—stay tube
7 Bracket—frame stiffener R/H
8 Bracket—frame stiffener L/H
9 Bracket—engine mounting rear
10 Bracket—propeller shaft tunnel
11 Bracket—exhaust pipe
12 Bracket—exhaust pipe
13 Bracket—centre—body mounting
14 Bracket—front—rear spring R/H
15 Bracket—front—rear spring L/H
16 Bracket—rear—body mounting
17 Bracket—rear—rear spring
18 Mounting bracket—rear wing R/H
19 Mounting bracket—rear wing L/H
20 Mounting bracket—rear (valance)
21 Stiffener bracket R/H
22 Stiffener bracket—L/H
23 Stay tube assembly
24 Fork end
25 Dash stiffener assembly
26 Gusset plate—dash stiffener
27 Gusset plate—top—dash stiffener
28 Steering knuckle—R/H
29 Steering knuckle—L/H
30 Swivel pin—R/H
31 Swivel pin—L/H
32 Link—swivel pin—upper R/H
33 Link—swivel pin—upper L/H
34 Plate—link
35 Bush—link
36 Link—swivel pin—lower R/H
37 Link—swivel pin—lower L/H
38 Seal—swivel pin
39 Grease nipple ($\frac{1}{4}$ inch × 90°)—link
40 Nut—steering knuckle—R/H
41 Steering lever—R/H
42 Nut—Simmonds thin. $\frac{1}{2}$ inch B.S.F.
43 Key—Woodruff No. 8
44 Nut—steering knuckle—R/H
45 Nut—steering knuckle—L/H
46 Felt washer—hub
47 Grease retainer—hub
48 Bearing hub—inner
49 Bearing hub—outer
50 Distance-piece—hub
51 Distance washer—hub
52 Oil seal—hub
53 Hub and brake-drum assembly—front
54 Wheel studs
55 Damper complete—front
56 Bolt—wishbone to link
57 Link—distance tube
58 Thrust washer—link
59 Seal—link
60 Support—link
61 Spring coil
62 Spring pan assembly
63 Bottom wishbone assembly
64 Fulcrum pin
65 Bolt—wishbone to link
66 Spigot for spring
67 Check rubber
68 Bush—bottom wishbone
69 Washer—wishbone
70 Main leaf complete with bush
71 Bush—Silentbloc
72 Second leaf
73 Third leaf
74 Fourth leaf complete with clips
75 Leaf clips
76 Distance tube
77 Fifth leaf
78 Sixth leaf
79 Seventh leaf
80 Rubber pad
81 Rubber—spring clip
82 Bolt—$\frac{1}{4}$ inch B.S.F.
83 Locating bolt
84 Clip—rear spring
85 Bracket—L/H (damper to rear spring)
86 Bracket—R/H (damper to rear spring)
87 Pin—rear spring front end
88 Washer—Silentbloc
89 Seating pad—rear spring
90 Locating plate—rear spring
91 Shackle plate
92 Shackle pin
93 Bush
94 Damper complete—R/H
95 Damper complete—L/H
96 Radiator case (with medallion, grille and false nose)
97 Radiator filler cap
98 Medallion—M.G.
99 Radiator grille
100 Radiator film block complete (with tanks)
101 Drain tap
102 Filler cap—radiator
103 Ring—rubber—filler cap
104 Packing washer—radiator mounting
105 Support member—radiator
106 Stay tube—radiator R/H
107 Stay tube—radiator L/H
108 Yoke end—stay tube
109 Hose—bottom—radiator
110 Hose—top—radiator
111 Clip—bottom hose
112 Clip—top hose
113 Drain pipe
114 Exhaust system complete (welded assembly)—later models
115 Front exhaust pipe only
116 Silencer and rear pipe assembly
117 Gasket—exhaust pipe flange
118 Bracket—front support
119 Support—tail pipe
120 Fuel tank complete
121 Drain plug—fuel tank
122 Main feed adaptor
123 Washer (drain plug and main feed)
124 Filler cap (Westwood) complete
125 Trigger—cap
126 End cover—fuel tank R/H
127 End cover—fuel tank L/H
128 Special bolt—tank end cover
129 Pipe (between carburetters)
130 Pipe (tank to pump) complete with washer and union washer
131 Mounting bracket
132 Rubber for mounting bracket
133 Strap—fuel tank
134 Packing—tank strap
135 Rubber packing—tank to frame
136 Pipe—pump to carburetters
137 Fuel pump
138 Elbow—fuel pump
139 Check strap assembly—rear axle
140 Check strap
141 Buffer—checkstrap
142 Rebound rubber—rear axle
143 Spare wheel carrier bracket assembly
144 Clamp bracket—lower—carrier
145 Plug—spare wheel carrier
146 Clamp—rear number-plate
147 Mounting bracket—rear number-plate
148 Attachment plate—dash stiffener

157

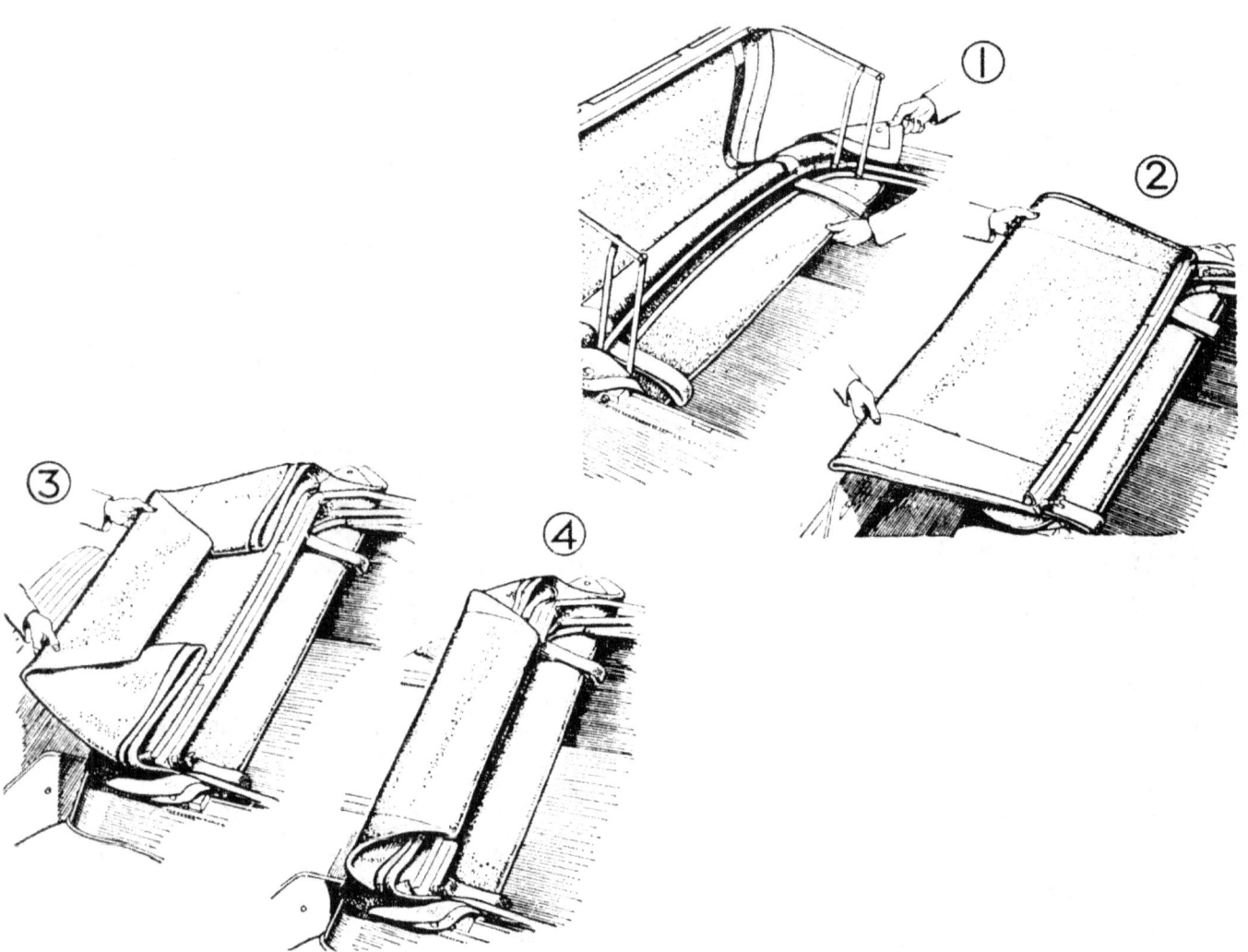

FIG: 01 Folding the hood, TC, TD, TF

FIG: 03 shows the method of stowing the deeper sidescreens which were fitted to later **TD** models. Procedure is as follows:
1 Place the lefthand rear sidescreen in the compartment as shown, with the attachment lugs facing the front of the car and the canvas part against the lefthand body panel.
2 Place the righthand rear sidescreen in front of the first one, again with the attachment lugs facing the front of the car, but with the canvas part against the righthand panel.
3 Insert the righthand front sidescreen with its lugs pointing downwards and its flap folded under towards the rear of the car. Make sure it is inserted as far down as it will go.
4 Insert the lefthand front sidescreen, again with its attachment lugs downwards and its flap folded under to the rear. The stowage compartment lid can now be closed and secured by means of the two press studs.

FIG: 04 shows the method of stowing the sidescreens on Model **TF**:
1 Start with the lefthand front sidescreen and stow it face downwards with the top edge against the rear of the stowage compartment and the front lower point against the lefthand wheel arch.
2 Place the righthand front sidescreen on top of the lefthand one with its face side uppermost and its rear edge against the righthand wheel arch.
3 Place the lefthand rear sidescreen on top of the other two, with the chromium-plated side uppermost and the front edge against the righthand wheel arch.
4 Place the righthand rear sidescreen with its chromium plated side uppermost and its front edge against the lefthand wheel arch. The lid of the stowage compartment should now close without difficulty.

Front wing removal and refitting

To remove the front wings from Model **TD** proceed as follows:
1 Disconnect the battery. Remove the headlamp and sidelamp fronts and disconnect and withdraw the cables through the wing clips and valance.
2 Remove the nuts, bolts and spring washers attaching the headlamp tie rod bracket to the radiator shell and

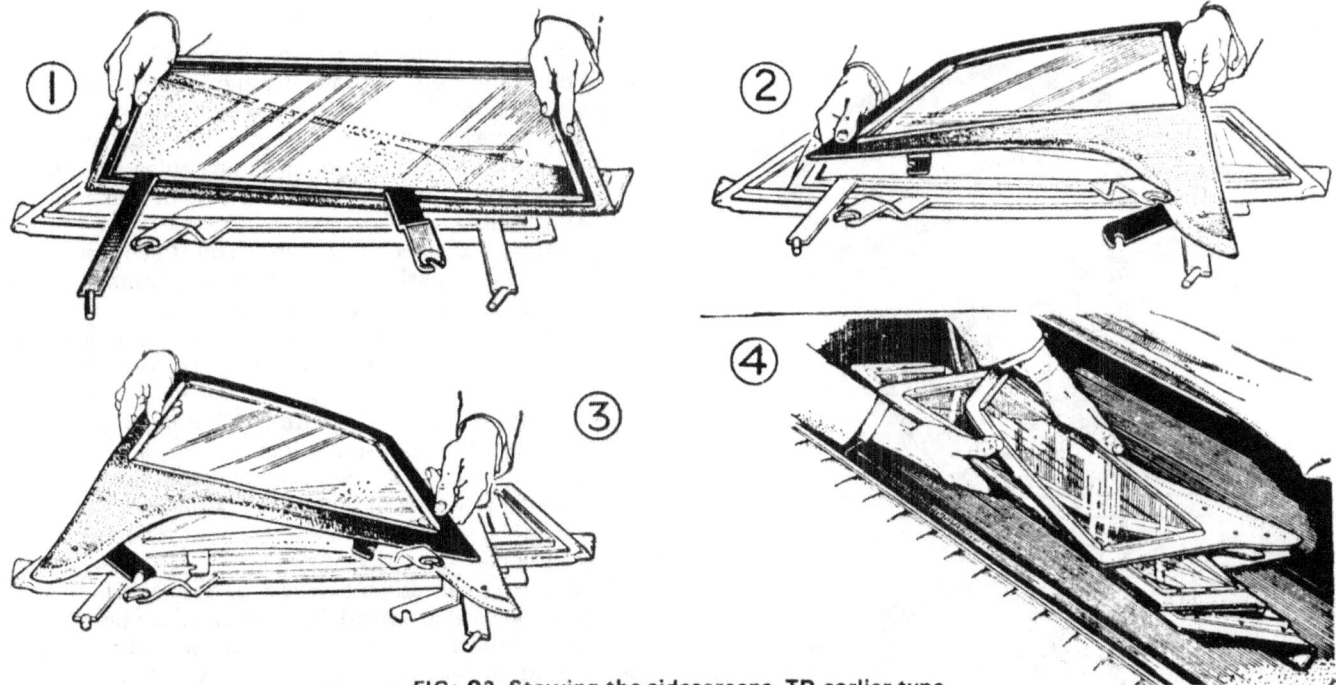

FIG: 02 Stowing the sidescreens, TD earlier type

the nuts, locknuts and flat washers securing the tie rod bracket to the wings.
3 Remove the bolts and spring washers securing the sidelamp and sidelamp cable clips to the wings.
4 Withdraw the two Phillips screws and flat washers securing each side of the front valance to the wings, and the bolt securing the leading edge of the valance below each bumper attachment bolt.

5 Remove the two nuts, bolts and spring and flat washers forward of the suspension unit and the four bolts with spring and flat washers to the rear of it securing the wing to the chassis frame.
6 Remove the two Phillips screws securing the wing to the body and the three nuts, bolts and spring and flat washers securing the wing to the running-board. Lift the wing clear of the car.

FIG: 03 Stowing the sidescreens, TD later type

159

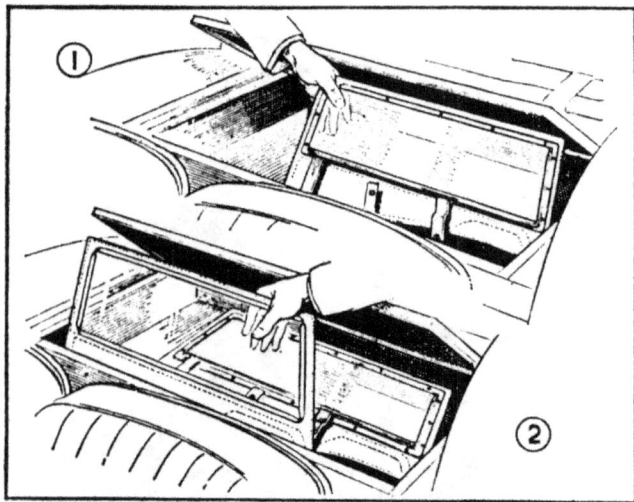

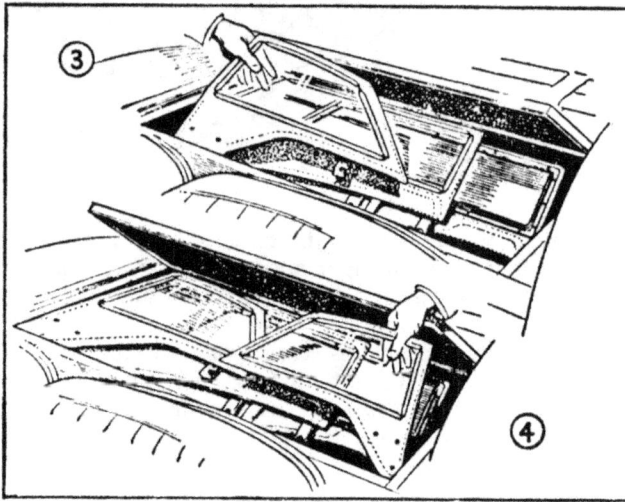

FIG: 04 Stowing the sidescreens, TF

Refitting is carried out in the reverse order to that given for removal. Detailed descriptions have been given of washers used, as the omission of any of these will prevent the rattle-free attachment of wings. Where holes in sheet metal have become enlarged, additional large diameter washers may be inserted to rectify this trouble. Although the detailed description given applies to **TD** models only, the basic instructions apply also to earlier cars.

To remove the front wings from **TF** models:
1 Disconnect the battery.
2 Remove the bolt securing each front bumper bracket.
3 Disconnect the sidelamp and headlamp wires at the snap connectors on the engine side of the valances. Pull the wires through the clips in the valances.
4 Unscrew the line of bolts under each wing securing it to the valance and the bolts at the end flange securing it to the running-board.
5 Unscrew the nuts below the running-boards and release the tread strips. The wings can now be removed from the car.

Refitting is carried out in the reverse order to that given for removal.

Rear wing removal and refitting

To remove the rear wings from **TD** models:
1 Remove the nuts, screws and flat washers securing the stop- and tail-lamps to the wings. On later models Phillips screws with flat and spring washers are used. Disconnect the stop- and tail-lamp cables, noting the respective connections to ensure correct operation on reassembly.
2 Remove the nut, bolt and two washers securing each wing to the chassis frame and the five bolts with flat washers securing the wing to the body.
3 Remove the nut, bolt, flat washers and rubber packing securing the wing to the running-board and lift off the wing.

To remove the rear wings from **TF** models:
1 Disconnect the tail-lamp wires.
2 Unscrew the bolts securing the wings to the running-boards and the line of bolts and screws securing each wing to the body. The wings can now be removed from the car.

Refitting is carried out in the reverse order to that given for removal. Detailed descriptions have been given of washers used, as the omission of any of these will prevent rattle-free attachment of the wings. The rubber packing between the wings and the running boards should be renewed if unserviceable.

Running-boards

To remove the running-boards from **TD** models:
1 Remove the three nuts, bolts and spring and flat washers securing each running-board to the front wing.
2 Remove the nut, bolt, flat washers and rubber packing securing each running-board to the rear wing.
3 Remove the three bolts and flat washers securing each running-board to the body. The running-boards can now be lifted clear of the car.

Refitting is carried out in the reverse order to that described for removal.

To remove the running boards from **TF** models:
1 Unscrew the nuts securing the tread strips to the running-boards and front wings.
2 Unscrew the bolts securing the running-boards to the wings and body. The running-boards can then be lifted clear of the car.

Refitting is carried out in the reverse order to that described for removal. Renewal of worn or scuffed tread-strips will greatly enhance the appearance of the bodywork.

Facia board and instrument panel

The following instructions are for the removal of the facia board and instrument panel from the **TD** model. Earlier cars differ in having the speedometer on the lefthand side of the facia, a position occupied on the **TD** model by the glove box. Individual instruments on the central instrument panel are also mounted in a slightly different order, but the same basic instructions will apply:

1. Disconnect the battery.
2. Extract the screws from the brackets and the rubber stop securing the instrument panel undershield to the lower edge of the facia board.
3. Insert a hand through the aperture provided in the undershield and disconnect the drives from the speedometer and revolution counter.
4. Withdraw the innermost screw from each hinge of the glove box lid. Remove the eight Phillips screws and cup washers securing the facia board.
5. Draw the facia board forward and disconnect the oil pressure gauge pipe and the instrument panel wiring. Refitting is carried out in the reverse order to that described for removal.

To remove the facia board and instrument panel from **TF** models:

1. Disconnect the battery.
2. Remove the eight Phillips screws securing the panel undershield and remove the shield.
3. Disconnect the speedometer and revolution counter drives and all controls and wiring.
4. Unscrew the six nuts securing the instrument panel and remove the panel from the facia board.
5. Unscrew the securing bolt at each end underneath the facia board, which can now be removed.

Refitting is carried out in the reverse order to that described for removal.

Body removal

All the cars covered by this manual have a separate body and chassis and if complete restoration or major overhaul of the vehicle is contemplated, removal of the body presents little difficulty. A block and tackle should be used for lifting in conjunction with a rope sling. The following detailed instructions are for the removal of the body from **TD** models, but the basic procedure will apply to both earlier and later cars:

1. Remove the two round-headed screws securing the rear bonnet support to the bulkhead and lift the bonnet clear of the car.
2. Disconnect both battery leads. Remove the battery.
3. Remove the front wings and the running-boards - see previous section. The rear wings may be left in position, but to avoid damage they should be removed.
4. Remove the bolts securing the rear bumper bar to the chassis frame and withdraw the bumper bar assembly and distance tubes. Remove the spare wheel and remove the bolts and two Phillips screws to release the rear valance.
5. Drain the petrol tank, disconnect the delivery pipe and the fuel gauge wire. Slacken the nut and locknut on the lower end of each petrol tank strap and the bolts clamping the spare wheel carrier to the chassis rear crossmember. Remove the four domed nuts securing the spare wheel carrier and petrol tank straps to the body. Swing the spare wheel carrier to the left and lift off the petrol tank.
6. Remove the number plate lamp cover, disconnect the cables, withdraw the rubber sleeve and thread the cables through the carrier tube. By removing the clamp bolts the spare wheel carrier can then be removed.
7. Withdraw the sidescreens from their stowage. Undo the wingnut locating each side of the backrest and lift it clear of the car. **Slide the seat cushions from their runners. Remove the carpets and underfelt.**
8. Remove the steering wheel - see previous section. and release the steering column from the support bracket.
9. Remove the screws from the brackets and rubber stop securing the instrument panel undershield to the lower edge of the facia board and remove the shield. Disconnect the starter pull cable from the switch and the mixture control cable from the carburetter. Disconnect the throttle pedal control and return spring from the carburetter and detach the revolution counter drive cable clip from the bulkhead. Disconnect the oil pressure gauge pipe, revolution counter and speedometer drive cables from the instruments.
10. Remove the innermost screw from each hinge of the glove box lid and the eight screws with cup washers securing the facia board and draw the facia forward. Disconnect the main wiring loom from the rear of the instrument panel and remove the facia board complete with instruments and starter and mixture control cables.
11. Remove the gearbox protecting cover, pedal draught excluder retaining plate and floorboards. Remove the trim panel beneath the scuttle. Slacken the draught excluder clip at the foot of the steering column and remove the three bolts securing the retainer plate to the toe-plate. Remove the bolts and nuts securing the toe-plate to the body, noting the position of the long bolt below the ignition coil.
12. Disconnect the horn leads and all cables from the starter motor switch and petrol pump. Remove the control box from the bulkhead. Draw all instrument panel wiring through the bulkhead and coil it over the engine, together with the control box and ignition coil.
13. Disconnect the flexible oil pipe from the engine and the revolution counter drive from the rear of the generator. Withdraw the speedometer cable from the bulkhead and coil it over the engine. Disconnect the pipes from the petrol pump. Slacken and remove the handbrake cable adjusting nuts and springs. Release the outer cables from the abutment bracket and thread them through the propeller shaft tunnel flange. Remove the five bolts securing the propeller shaft tunnel to the body and chassis frame.
14. Remove the two nuts and bolts from the attachment plates securing each side of the body to the stiffener tube below the bulkhead.
15. The body is secured to the chassis frame by eight bolts. The rear two are located in the rear corners of the sidescreen stowage compartment and the front

two are inserted through the bulkhead flanges into the A brackets on the chassis frame. The four remaining bolts are inserted through the body floor.

16 Carry out a final check to ensure that no cables connecting body and chassis have been overlooked, especially if modifications to the wiring have been carried out since the car was new. The body can now be lifted clear of the chassis. Note the position of any cork or felt packing pieces between the body and chassis.

17 If the body is to be stored while work is carried out on the chassis, it should be supported carefully on suitably placed blocks to avoid distortion.

Body refitting, door adjustment

When refitting the body, the following procedure will enable it to be remounted so that the bonnet, wings and doors fit correctly:

1 Some insulating material must be placed between all body support brackets secured to the chassis frame and the body. Usually this consists of cork or felt pads.
2 Register the body in a central position on the chassis frame.
3 Refit any additional packings in the same position as they were before the body was removed. If this is not known refer to operations 8 and 9.
4 Locate and fit the securing bolts, but do not tighten any until all the bolts are in place.
5 Tighten all bolts around the scuttle.
6 Tighten all bolts on either side of the body.
7 Secure the rear end of the body.
8 The correct fitting of doors depends on correct positioning of the packing pieces referred to in operation 3, and adjustments are carried out as follows. If the door is too high, sufficient packing must be fitted under the front end of the body forward of the door. This will necessitate slackening all bolts around the scuttle.
9 If the door is low, packing must be inserted under the hinge pillar.
10 The packing used for adjustment can be in the form of large flat washers or steel plates of suitable size and thickness. The success of this operation can only be judged when all body securing bolts have been tightened so that a certain amount of trial and error may be necessary.

From time to time it is advisable to check the tightness of all body mounting bolts, as well as those securing the wings and running-boards.

MAINTENANCE AND LUBRICATION   TC—TD—TF—TF 1500 SERIES

ENGINE CRANKCASE OIL

(1) Check level daily or every 500 miles and top up as necessary with engine oil as recommended.

(2) Drain and refill every 3,000 miles or sooner if vehicle is operating under very dusty conditions.

(3) Release the oil filter bowl, wash in petrol, fit a new element and change engine oil every 6,000 miles.

COOLING SYSTEM

(1) Check the water level in the radiator every 500 miles and top up as necessary.

NOTE: If the vehicle is at normal operating temperature, use care when removing the radiator pressurised cap to avoid scalding.

(2) Drain, flush and refill the cooling system every 10,000 miles.

FUEL SYSTEM

(1) Remove filter gauze on Electric fuel pump, clean, blow out and reinstal every 6,000 miles or more often if fuel supplied contains rust and other impurities.

(2) Every 1,000 miles remove the cap from the top of each carburettor suction chamber and add a few drops of light oil as recommended.

(3) The air filter casings should be removed and cleaned out periodically. Replace at 12,000 miles.

GEARBOX

Drain off the oil every 6,000 miles and refill with fresh oil.

REAR AXLE

Check oil level and top up at 3,000 miles. Drain off and refill with fresh oil, as recommended at 6,000 miles.

DRIVE SHAFT

Give the shaft couplings nipples three or four strokes with the grease gun and recommended lubricant every 1,000 miles. Also the sliding joint.

STEERING GEAR

(1) Every 1,000 miles give the nipples in the steering joints three or four strokes of the grease gun.

(2) Every 12,000 miles give the nipple on the steering box ten strokes of the oil gun and two strokes ONLY to the pinion shaft nipple.

FRONT SUSPENSION

Every 6,000 miles remove the grease retaining cap on each stub axle and refill the cap with the recommended grease. On wire type wheels unscrew the winged hub nut, remove and repack with grease.

TYRES

Test and inflate to the recommended pressures as required.

BATTERY

Check and top up electrolyte with distilled water as required or at least monthly.

BODY

(1) Check and lubricate the following components as required with a dry lubricant: door lock, bonnet catch, luggage compartment lock.

(2) Lubricate the following components as required with a few drops of engine oil: Door hinges, bonnet catch and hinges, door lock replacements, door lock cylinders, luggage compartment lock cylinder and handbrake linkage and pivots.

BRAKE FLUID RESERVOIR

(1) Check reservoir and top up with recommended hydraulic fluid, if necessary, every 1,000 miles.

(2) Flush and refill reservoir with new fluid at master cylinder overhaul.

GENERATOR

Every 12,000 miles add a few drops of recommended oil through the oil hole in the commutator end bearing. In the case of the C40-1 dynamo inject a few drops of clean engine oil into the hole marked oil at the rear bearing housing.

DISTRIBUTOR

Every 6,000 miles withdraw the rotor arm and add a few drops of engine oil to the cam bearing and to the advance mechanism through the gap round the cam spindle. Smear the cam lightly with grease and add a spot of oil to the contact breaker pivot.

HANDBRAKE CABLE

The grease nipple on the handbrake cable should be given three or four strokes with the grease gun and recommended grease every 1,000 miles.

SPEEDOMETER AND TACHOMETER CABLES

The inner cables must be given a light application of grease every 12,000 miles.

SUMMARY OF LUBRICATION TASKS

A. EVERY 250 MILES

Check engine oil and top up.

B. EVERY 1,000 MILES

Steering gear
Propeller shaft } Use grease gun and grease.
Handbrake cable

Gearbox (and overdrive where applicable)
Rear axle } Check and top up.

Carburettor Damper—Lubricate with light oil.

C. EVERY 3,000 MILES

In addition to tasks at B above:
Change engine oil.
Wash air cleaners in petrol, dry and replace.

D. EVERY 6,000 MILES

In addition to tasks at A and B above less GEARBOX AND REAR AXLE:

Distributor—
    Cam bearing
    Automatic timing control } Lubricate with a few drops of oil.
    Contact breaker pivot

Cam—smear with a light application of grease.

Gearbox
Rear axle } Change oils.

Front wheel hubs—
    Disc wheels—refill grease cup.
    Wire wheels—pack hubs with grease.

Engine oil filter—Replace.

Water pump—Lubricate sparingly with heavy oil.

E. EVERY 12,000 MILES

In addition to the tasks at B, C and D above.
Engine—drain, flush and refill with new oil.
    fit new filter thereafter.

Steering—gearbox nipple
    —pinion nipple
Speedo cable nipple } Grease.
Tachometer cable nipple

Dynamo—lubricate rear end bearing.

TORQUE WRENCH SETTINGS (See cautionary notes*)
TC—TD—TF—TF 1500 SERIES

Cylinder head (Up to Engine No. XPAG/TF/31727)	50 ft/lb
Cylinder head (From Engine No. XPEG/TF/31728)	42 ft/lb
Main bearing cap bolts:	
TC-TD-TF-TF 1500	62 ft/lb
Connecting rod big-end bolts:	
TC	33 ft/lb
TD-TF-TF 1500	27 ft/lb
Small end clamp bolt (All)	25 ft/lb
Rocker Shaft 8 mm bolts	25 ft/lb
Rocker Shaft 10 mm bolts	35 ft/lb
Timing cover bolts	21 ft/lb
Flywheel to crank bolts	50 ft/lb
Clutch cover bolts	25 ft/lb
Manifold nuts	19 ft/lb
Spark plugs	30 ft/lb
Sump Bolts (Engine block)	25 ft/lb
Sump bolts (Timing cover)*	20 ft/lb
Bell housing bolts (engine block)	25 ft/lb
Bell housing bolts (Sump)*	20 ft/lb

* CAUTION: Tightening into aluminium housings that may have been disassembled on a number of previous occasions will usually require less torque - proceed with extreme caution!

* CAUTION: Care should always be exercised when tightening nuts and bolts on a vehicle that may have been disassembled on a number of previous occasions - if in doubt replace old hardware with new!

TC SERIES
ENGINE

Type	XPAG
Bore	2.61" (66.5 mm)
Stroke	3.54" (90 mm)
Capacity	76.3 cu in (1250 cc)
Number of cylinders	4
Firing order	1, 3, 4, 2
Nominal hp	10.9
Compression ratio	7.25 to 1
BHP	55.4 at 5200 rpm
Maximum torque	64 ft/lb at 2600 rpm
Maximum Bmep	125 psi at 2600 rpm
Cylinder head gasket:	
Type	Copper asbestos
Normal thickness	.045"
Ignition timing	Tdc
Compression pressure, cranking	90 psi
Location of engine number	On flywheel housing

CYLINDER BLOCK

Material	Cast iron
Bore diameters (Standard)	2.610"
Bore for oversizes:	
First	.010"
Second	.030"
Third	.040"
Fourth	.050"

CYLINDER HEAD

Material	Cast iron
Type	Valve in line
Combustion space volume	45.5 cc
Maximum permissible reduction of metal (refacing head)	⅛" (stage 2 tune)
Valve seats:	
Angle, inlet	30°
Angle, exhaust	30°

CRANKSHAFT (Continued on next page)

Material	Forging
Type	Counter-balanced
Thrust taken at	Centre bearing
Number of journals	3
Main bearing journal diameter	2.0472"
Undersizes	.012", .020", .030", .040", .050"
Main bearing journal, length:	
Front	1.496"
Centre	1.496"
Rear	1.5748"
Method of sealing oil:	
Front end of shaft	Asbestos ring
Rear end of shaft	Scroll and cork

CRANKSHAFT (Continued)

Crankpin bearing journals:	
Length	1.1023"
Diameter	1.7716"
Undersizes	.012", .020", .030", .040", .050"

MAIN BEARINGS

Type	Thick steel with white metal thin shells
Number of main bearings	3
Length	1.496"
Clearance on crankshaft	.0005" to .002"
End play	.0015" to .004"

CONNECTING RODS

Type	H-section
Material	Steel
Length, centre to centre	7.00"
Small end type	Pin clamped
Big end bearings:	
Type	Thin wall, white metal lined
Diameter	1.7716"
Running clearance	.0005" to .002"
Length	1.1023"
End float on crankpin	.004" to .006"

GUDGEON PIN

Type	Clamped
Material	Steel
Method of securing	Screw and washer
Diameter, outer	.7086"
Fit in connecting rod	Clamped
Fit in piston	Double thumb

PISTONS

Type	Oval skirt
Material	Aluminium alloy
Removal	Downwards
Oversizes	.020", .030", .040", .050'
Clearance in bore	.0015" to .0025"
Weight of piston complete with rings and gudgeon pin	12¾ oz
Compression height (top of crown)	1.7716"

PISTON RINGS (Continued on next page)

Type	Rectangular compression and slotted oil control		
No of rings:			
Compression	2		
Oil control	1		
	Top Ring	2nd Ring	Oil Control
Nominal diameter	2.610"	2.610"	2.610"
Width	.0885"	.0885"	.1575"

PISTON RINGS (Continued)

Groove clearance	.001" to .002"	.001" to .002"	.001" to .002"
Ring gap (fitted):			
Minimum	.006"	.006"	.006"
Maximum	.010"	.010"	.010"

VALVES

Type	Poppet	
Position	In head	
Operation	Push rod	
Timing:		
Inlet opens	11° btdc	
Inlet closes	57° abdc	
Exhaust opens	52° bbdc	
Exhaust closes	24° atdc	
Markings	Timing wheels and chain	
Bounce speed	6000 rpm	
	Inlet	**Exhaust**
Head diameter	1.299"	1.2205"
Stem diameter	.315"	.315"
Clearance at tappets	Hot .019"	Hot .019"
Angle of face	30°	30°

VALVE SPRINGS

Type	Helical	
	Inner	**Outer**
Free length	2.565"	2.927"
Fitted length	1.438"	1.532"
At load	43 lb	80 lb

CAMSHAFT

Type	Side
Method of taking thrust	Plate behind sprocket
Number of bearing journals	3
Length of bearing journals:	
No 1	1.142"
No 2	.98425"
No 3	1.142"
Diameter of bearing journals:	
No 1	1.615"
No 2	.9055"
No 3	.9055"

CAMSHAFT BEARINGS

Type	White metal bushes
Clearance	.0015" to .004"

CAMSHAFT DRIVE

Type	Chain
Fit of gear on camshaft	Slide
How secured	Woodruff key and setscrew
Fit on crankshaft	Slide
How secured	Woodruff key & starter dog

LUBRICATION SYSTEM

Type	Forced feed
Type of pump	Gear
Type of pump drive	Skew gear
Normal pressure	50 to 70 psi
Clearance between gears and cover not to exceed	.003"
Filter:	
Type	Full flow
Location	Side of crankcase
Oil pressure relief spring:	
Free length	1.4767"
Loaded length	1.063"
At load	7 lb
Crankcase capacity	1⅛ gal

FUEL SYSTEM

Type	Twin H2
Size	1¼"
Needles:	
Standard	ES
Rich	EM
Lean	AP
Air cleaner	AC dry, No 1573577
Number of fuel filters	2
Location of fuel filters	At float chambers

SU FUEL PUMP

Make	SU
Type	Electric type L
Contact point gap	.030"

COOLING SYSTEM

Type	Pump, fan & thermosiphon
Radiator type	Pressurised
Top hose internal diameter	2 3/16"
Bottom hose internal diameter	1⅛"
Water pump type	Centrifugal
Water pump drive	V-belt
Water pump bearings	Ball
Number of fan blades	4

CLUTCH

Make	Borg and Beck
Type	Single dry plate
Diameter:	7¼"
Type of hub	Spring cushion
Number of pressure springs	6
Type of release bearing	Carbon ring
Clutch pedal free travel	1"

GEARBOX

Type	4 speed, synchromesh on 2nd, 3rd and top.
Overall ratios 5.125:1 final drive:	
Top	5.125 : 1
Third	6.93 : 1
Second	10.00 : 1
First and reverse	17.32 : 1

PROPELLER SHAFT

Type	Hardy Spicer
Number of universal joints	2
Type of joints	Needle roller

REAR AXLE

Type	¾ floating
Final drive	Spiral bevel
Side bearings	Ball semi-thrust
Number	2
Pinion bearings:	
Front	Double ball
Rear	Roller
Crownwheel and pinion:	
Method of adjustment	Pinion by shims—crownwheel by nuts
Normal backlash	.007" to .010"
Number of pinion teeth	8
Crownwheel teeth	41
Ratio	5.125 to 1
Capacity	2 pt

STEERING

Type of box	Bishop cam and lever
Number of turns from lock to lock	1½
End float, inner column	Nil
Toe-in	¼"
Caster	Early cars 8° Later cars 5½°
Camber	3°
King pin inclination	7½°
Angles taken at unladen weight, tyre pressures as specified	
Turning circle	37'0"

FRONT SUSPENSION

Type of axle	Reverse Elliott
Type of springing	Semi-elliptic
Number of leaves	6
Width of leaves	1¼″
Distance between eyes:	
Laden	26¾″
Load in lb	500 to 520
Free camber	1.85″
Laden camber	Nil
Track	45″

REAR SUSPENSION

Type of springing	Semi-elliptic
Number of leaves	9
Width of leaves	1¼″
Distance between eyes:	
Laden	36½″
Load in lb	385
Free camber	1.687″
Laden camber	Nil
Track	45″

BRAKES

Make	Lockheed
Type:	
Foot brake	Hydraulic
Hand brake	Cable
Drum diameter (front and rear)	9.00″
Drum to lining clearance	Minimum
Lining:	
Width	1½″
Thickness	3/16″
Length per shoe	8½″
Total area	102 sq in
Pedal free travel	½″

BATTERY

Make	Lucas
Voltage	12
Model	STXW9A
Capacity	51 amp/hr at 10 hour rate
Earth terminal	Positive
Number of plates per cell	9
Height	10⅛″
Width	6⅞″
Length	13¼″

GENERATOR

Make and model	Lucas C45YV
Service number	228334
Maximum output	13 amps at 13 volts
Cut-in speed	100 to 1100 rpm at 13 volts
Field resistance	6.3 to 6.5 ohm
Brush spring tension	15 to 25 oz

STARTER

Make and type	Lucas M418G
Service number	255378
Lock torque	17 ft/lb at 7.2 volts
Lock current draw	450 amps
Brush spring tension	32 to 40 oz

DISTRIBUTOR AND COIL

Make and model	Lucas DKY4A
Service number	40048B
Contact point gap	.010″ to .012″
Centrifugal advance:	
Starts	250 to 400 rpm
Intermediate advance	9° to 11° at 1020 rpm
Maximum advance	14° to 16° at 2220 rpm
Condenser capacity	.18 to .23 mfd
Contact spring tension	20 to 24 oz
Direction of rotation	Clockwise (at top)
Coil:	
Make	Lucas Q12
Service number	45020A
Current consumption	1.4 amps (running)
	2.7 amps (stalling)

SPARK PLUGS

Make and type	Champion L10S
Size	14 mm
Plug gap	.020″ to .022″
Firing order	1-3-4-2

WINDSCREEN WIPER

Make	Lucas
Model	SW4
Service number	734655
Current consumption	3.5 amps

HORN

Make	Lucas
Model	HF1234
Service number	70038A
Current consumption	2 amps

BULBS

	Volts	Watts
Headlamps	12	36/36
Side lamps	12	6
Stop, tail	12	6/24
Ignition warning light	2.5	.5
Panel illumination	12	2.4
Fog lamp:		
FT 27	12	36
SFT 462	12	36
Number plate illumination	12	6

FUSES

Number used	2
Rating	35 amps
Circuit	Aux and aux ign

GENERAL DIMENSIONS

Wheelbase	94"
Ground clearance	6"
Height	53"
Width	56"
Length	139½"
Weight	15½ cwt
Serial numbers	TC 0251 to TC 10,251
Year of manufacture	1946 to 1949

WHEELS AND TYRES

Type of wheel	Wire spoked—quick release
Make	Dunlop
Rim size	2.75 × 19"
Tyres:	
Make	Dunlop
Size	4.50-19"
Pressure:	
Front	24 lb
Rear	26 lb

CAPACITIES

Crankcase	1⅛ gal
Gearbox	1½ pt
Rear axle	2 pt
Fuel tank	13½ gal
Cooling system	1¾ gal

END OF TC SERIES SPECIFICATIONS

TD—TF SERIES
ENGINE

Type	XPAG/TD (XPAG/TF)
Bore	2.618″ (66.5 mm)
Stroke	3.543″ (90 mm)
Number of cylinders	4
Firing order	1, 3, 4, 2
Capacity	76 cu in (1250 cc)
Compression ratio	7.25 to 1 (8.1 to 1—TF)
Bhp	54 at 5200 rpm (57 at 5500 rpm on TF)
Maximum Bmep	125 at 2600 rpm
Cylinder head gasket:	
Type	Copper asbestos
Normal thickness	.045″
Ignition timing	Tdc
Location of engine number	On flywheel housing

CYLINDER BLOCK

Material	Cast iron
Bore diameter (standard)	2.618″
Bore for oversizes:	
First	2.6381″ (+.020″)
Second	2.6581″ (+.040″)
Number of main bearings	3
Location of No 1 cylinder	Front

CYLINDER HEAD

Material	Cast iron
Type	Valves in line
Combustion space volume	45.6 cc
Maximum permissible reduction of metal (refacing head)	2.8966″ (for stage 2 tuning)
Valve seats:	
Angle, inlet	30°
Angle, exhaust	30°
Valve throat diameter:	
Inlet	1.181″ (1.274″ on TF)
Exhaust	1.024″ (1.126″ on TF)

CRANKSHAFT

Material	Steel
Type	Forging
Thrust taken at	Centre bearing
Number of journals	3
Main bearing journals:	
Diameter	2.047″
Undersizes as follow	.012″, .020″, .030″, .040″ and .050″
Method of sealing oil:	
Front end of shaft	Asbestos washer
Rear end of shaft	Oil scroll and drain
Crankpin bearing journals:	
Diameter	1.772″
Undersizes permissible	.012″, .020″, .030″, .040″ and .050″

MAIN BEARINGS

Type	Shimless, steel backed
Material	White metal lined
Number of main bearings	3
Side clearance between bearing and shaft	.0014″ to .0037″
Clearance on crankshaft diameter	.0008″ to .003″

CONNECTING RODS

Type	H-section
Material	Steel
Length centre to centre	7.008″
Small end lubrication	Splash
Small end type	Clamped
Big end bearings:	
Type	Thin wall, white metal lined
Running clearance	.0005″ to .002″
End float on crankpin (nominal)	.004″ to .006″

GUDGEON PIN

Type	Semi-floating
Material	Steel
Method of securing	Pinch bolt
Diameter (outer)	.7087″ $\begin{cases} +.0004″ \\ +.0006″ \end{cases}$
Fit in piston	Double thumb (cold)

PISTONS

Type	Oval and tapered
Material	Aluminium alloy
Removal	Downwards
Oversizes available	+.020″, +.040″
Skirt clearance below oil ring	.0021″ to .0029″

PISTON RINGS

Type	Rectangular section compression; slotted scraper
Number of compression	2
Number of oil control	1
Nominal diameter	2.618″
Width:	
Compression	.0885″
Oil control	.1575″
Ring gap (fitted):	
Minimum	.006″
Maximum	.010″

VALVES

Type	Poppet
Position	In head
Operation	Push rod
Timing — Piston traverse (top of crown to face of block)	.055"
Timing:	
Inlet opens	11° btdc (5°—TF)
Inlet closes	57° abdc (45°—TF)
Exhaust opens	52° bbdc (45°—TF)
Exhaust closes	24° atdc (5°—TF)
Markings	Bright chain links and T marks on wheels.
Bounce speed	6,000 rpm

	Inlet	Exhaust
Amount of lift	.315"	.315"
Head diameter	1.299"	1.221"
	1.417"—TF	1.338"—TF
Stem diameter	.315"	.315"
Clearance at tappets	See —To Adjust Tappets	
Clearance for setting valve timing	.037"	
Angle of face	30°	30°

TAPPETS

Type	Hollow
Material	Cast iron
Type of adjustment	Screw and locknut at top of push rod

CAMSHAFT

Material	Steel
Method of taking thrust	Front end plate
End float	.005" to .013"
Number of bearing journals	3

CAMSHAFT BEARINGS

Type	White metal front — Zinc alloy centre and rear
Clearance	.0016" to .004" front; .0018" to .0037" centre and rear

CAMSHAFT DRIVE

Type	Chain
Fit of gear on camshaft	Slide
How secured	Woodruff key and setscrew
Fit of gear on crankshaft	Slide
How secured	Woodruff key and dog nut

CAMSHAFT CHAIN

Pitch	⅜" Duplex
Number of pitches	60

LUBRICATION SYSTEM

Type	Forced feed
Type of pump	Gear
Type of pump drive	Skew gear from camshaft
Idler gear:	
Overall diameter	1.2678″+.001″
Overall length	1.378″ {−.0016″ / −.0024″}
Driving gear:	
Overall diameter	1.2678″+.001″
Overall length	1.378″ {−.0016″ / −.0024″}
Clearance between gears and cover not to exceed	.0016″ to .0035″
Pressure lubrication to	Big ends, mains, camshaft and rockers
Leak lubrication to	Timing gears
Splash feed to	Pistons and cylinders
Crankcase capacity:	
TD	9 pt
TF	10 pt
TF 1500	10½ pt
Filter:	
Type	Full flow
Location	Crankcase side
Oil pressure relief spring:	
Number of free coils	13½
Pressure at fitted length	7 lb
Fitted length	1.063″
Free length	1.476″
Diameter of wire	.056″
External diameter	.500″
Relief valve opens at	50 to 70 psi

FUEL SYSTEM

Type	Twin H2, semi-downdraught
Size	1¼″
Jet	.090″
Needles:	
TD	Standard ES, Weak AP, Rich EM
TF and TF-1500	Standard GJ, Weak GL, Rich HI
Air cleaner	Oil bath (TD) Separate gauze (TF)
Number of fuel filters	2
Location of fuel filters	At float chambers

SU FUEL PUMP

Make	SU
Type	Electric type L
Contact point gap	.030″

COOLING SYSTEM

Type	Pump, fan & thermosiphon
Radiator type	Pressurised
Top hose internal diameter	$2\frac{3}{16}''$
Bottom hose internal diameter	$1\frac{1}{8}''$
Water pump type	Centrifugal
Water pump drive	V-belt
Water pump bearings	Ball
Number of fan blades	4

CLUTCH

Make	Borg and Beck
Type	Single dry plate
Diameter:	
TD	$7\frac{1}{4}''$
TD From engine No. 9408 - Engine type XPAG/TD/2	8''
TF and TF 1500	8''
Type of hub	Spring cushion
Number of pressure springs	6
Type of release bearing	Carbon ring
Clutch pedal free travel:	
TD-TF and TF 1500	$\frac{3}{4}''$

GEARBOX

Type	Synchromesh
Ratios:	
Top	1.00 to 1
Third	1.385 to 1
Second	2.07 to 1
First	3.5 to 1
Reverse	3.5 to 1
Mounting	Bolted to engine

PROPELLER SHAFT

Type	Hardy Spicer
Number of universal joints	2
Type of joints	Needle roller

REAR AXLE (Continued on next page)

Type	Semi-floating
Final drive	Hypoid gears
Side bearings	Ball thrust
Number	2
Pinion bearings:	
Front	Taper roller
Rear	Taper roller
Crownwheel and pinion:	
Method of adjustment	By means of spacers
Normal backlash	Set automatically by calculation, of spacer thickness

REAR AXLE (Continued)

Pinion bearing pre-load	6 to 8 in/lb		
Number of pinion teeth	8	8	9
Crownwheel teeth	41	39	41
Ratio	5.125	4.875	4.555
Capacity	2¼ pt		

STEERING

Type of box	Rack and pinion
Angles taken at unladen weight, tyre pressures as specified	
Toe-in	Nil
Caster	2° ± ½°
Camber	1° ± 1°
King pin inclination	9° to 10½° (full bump)
Turning circle	31'3"

FRONT SUSPENSION

Type	Independent
Type of springing	Coil
Mean coil diameter	3.238"
Wire diameter	.498"
Free height	9.59" ± $\frac{1}{16}$"
Number of free coils	7½
Maximum deflection	4.24"
Static laden length	6.44" ± $\frac{1}{32}$"
Load	1095 lb
Track	47⅜"
Shock absorbers	Double acting Girling-Luvax
Compression	20°/sec at 200 in/lb at 18°C Weight on arm 50 lb
Rebound	20°/sec at 400 in/lb at 18°C Weight on arm 25 lb

REAR SUSPENSION

Type	Half elliptic
Spring:	
Number of leaves	7
Width of leaves	1½"
Thickness	$\frac{7}{32}$"
Distance between eyes (free)	42.00"
Working load	500 lb (TD); 397 lb (TF)
Free camber	4.1" (TD); 2.85" (TF)
Laden camber	½" positive (TD); nil (TF)
Track	50"
Shock absorbers	Double acting Girling-Luvax
Compression	20°/sec at 250 in/lb at 18°C Weight on arm 41.7 lb
Rebound	20°/sec at 400 in/lb at 18°C Weight on arm 66.7 lb

BRAKES

Make	Lockheed
Type:	
Foot brake	Hydraulic (2LS)
Hand brake	Cable
Drum diameter: front and rear	9.00″
Lining:	
Material	Ferodo MR19
Width	1½″
Thickness	.187″
Length per shoe	8.75″
Total area	105 sq in
Pedal free travel	½″

BATTERY

Make	Lucas
Voltage	12
Model	GTW9A
Capacity	51 amp/hr at 10 hour rate
Earth terminal	Positive
Number of plates per cell	9
Height	9¼″
Width	6⅞″
Length	12¾″

GENERATOR

Make and Type:	
Early cars	Lucas C39PV
Later cars	Lucas C39PV2
Service number:	
C39PV	22257A
C39PV2	22265B
Maximum output:	
C39PV	17 amps
C39PV2	19 amps
Maximum output voltage	13.5 volts 1850 to 2100 rpm
Cut-in speed	1050 to 1200 rpm
Cut-in voltage	13 volts
Field resistance	6.10 ohms
Brush spring tension	22 to 25 oz

STARTER

Make and type	M35G
Service number	25022
Lock torque	9.30 ft/lb at 7.50 to 8 volts
Lock current draw	300 to 350 amps
Brush spring tension	30 to 40 oz

DISTRIBUTOR AND COIL

Make and model:	
Early TD cars	Lucas DKY4A
Later cars	Lucas D2A4
Service number:	
DKY4A	40162A
D2A4	40367A
DKY4A specifications:	
Centrifugal advance starts	250 to 400 rpm
Intermediate advance	9° to 11° at 1050 rpm
Maximum advance	14° to 16° at 2220 rpm
Contact point gap	.010" to .012"
D2A4 specifications:	
Centrifugal advance starts	300 to 500 rpm
Intermediate advance	5° to 7° at 980 rpm
Maximum advance	11° to 13° at 1150 rpm
Contact point gap	.014" to .016"
Condenser capacity	.18 to .23 mfd

SPARK PLUGS

Make and type:	
To Engine No XPAG/TD2/22735	Champion L10S
From Engine No. XPAG/TD2/22736	Champion NA8
Size	14 mm
Plug gap	.020" to .022"
Firing order	1-3-4-2

BULBS

	Volts	Watts
Headlamps	12	36/36
Side lamps	12	6
Stop, tail	12	6/24
Ignition warning light	2.5	.5
Panel illumination	12	2.4
Fog lamp:		
FT 27	12	36
SFT 462	12	36
Number plate illumination	12	6

FUSES

Number used	2
Rating	35 amps
Circuit	Aux and aux ign

GENERAL DIMENSIONS (Continued on next page)

Wheelbase	94"
Ground clearance	6"
Height	53"
Width	58⅝"
Length	145"
Weight	17¼ cwt

GENERAL DIMENSIONS (Continued)

Serial numbers	TD 0251 to TD 9087 (1950 to Aug 1951)
	TD 9088 to TD 20427 (Aug 1951 to Oct 1952)
	TD 20428 (Oct 1952 onwards)
	TF 501 to TF 6500
Location of serial number	On engine bulkhead
Year of manufacture	TD—1950-1953
	TF—1954-1955
	TF 1500—1955

WHEELS AND TYRES

Type of wheel	Wire	
Make	Dunlop	
Rim size	4J × 15″	
Tyre size	5.50-15″	
Pressure:	**Front**	**Rear**
Normal	18	18
Fast driving	24	24

CAPACITIES

Crankcase	9 pt (TD) 10 pt (TF) 10½ pt (TF 1500)
Gearbox	1¾ pt
Rear axle	2¼ pt
Fuel tank	12½ gal
Cooling system	12 pt

END OF TD—TF SERIES SPECIFICATIONS

ADDITIONAL DATA FOR THE TF 1500 CAN BE FOUND IN THE 'PERFORMANCE TUNING' SECTION

PERFORMANCE TUNING FOR ROAD AND COMPETITION

ENGINE TYPES
XPAG AS FITTED TO SERIES TC CARS
XPAG/TD AS FITTED TO SERIES TD CARS

SPECIFICATIONS

STANDARD ENGINE DATA

Bore	66.5 mm
Stroke	90 mm
Capacity	1250 cc
Firing order	1-3-4-2
Sparking plugs	Champion L10S
Compression ratio	7.25 to 1
Valve timing:	
Inlet	Opens 10° btdc; closes 57° abdc
Exhaust	Opens 52° bbdc; closes 24° atdc
Valve lift	8 mm inlet and exhaust
Tappet clearance	.019″ hot
Contact breaker points	.010″ to .012″
Ignition timing	Tdc
Octane rating	Minimum requirements for knock-free operation 74 octane. For maximum power—82 octane
Carburettors	Twin SU, 1¼″ bore
Carburettor jet	.090″
Type XPAG carburettor needles	Standard ES, richer DK, weaker EF
Type XPAG/TD carburettor needles	Standard ES, richer EM, weaker AP
Bmep	125 at 2600 rpm

POWER

Bhp	Rpm	Bhp	Rpm
11.00	1000	54.00	5000
23.50	2000	54.00	5200
36.00	3000	52.50	5500
47.00	4000	47.00	6000

Safe maximum rpm	5700
Valve crash rpm	6000
Capacity of combustion space	45.5 cc
Cylinder head depth	Top to bottom face 3.0177″
Thickness of cylinder head gasket	.045″
Capacity of cylinder head gasket	Approximately 4.5 cc compressed

CAR DATA TC SERIES

Gear	Overall Ratios	Mph per 1000 rpm
Top	5.125 to 1	15.84
3rd	6.93 to 1	11.74
2nd	10.00 to 1	8.13
1st	17.32 to 1	4.68
Rear axle ratio	5.125 to 1	

CAR DATA TD SERIES

Gear	Overall Ratios	Mph per 1000 rpm
Top	5.125 to 1	14.42
3rd	7.098 to 1	10.412
2nd	10.609 to 1	6.966
1st and reverse	17.938 to 1	4.12
Rear axle ratio	5.125 to 1	

STAGE 1

HIGH COMPRESSION RATIO TUNING (8.6 TO 1)

The engine is raised to 8.6 to 1 compression ratio by removing $\frac{3}{32}''$ from the cylinder head face.

The standard head is 3.0177″ thick; the finished thickness after machining would be 2.928″.

(1) Remove any burrs left, and polish, but do not grind out the combustion chambers, as there are already quite clean and are machined nearly all over.

(2) Make sure the gasket edges do not overlap the combustion spaces.

(3) The ports may be ground and polished, but should not be ground out so heavily that the shape or valve choke diameter is impaired.

(4) The inlet port outer separating stud boss may be ground away slightly—about $\frac{1}{16}''$ off each side (still maintaining its streamline shape)—so that oblong ports are obtained, $1\frac{3}{16}''$ high $\times \frac{21}{32}''$ wide (minimum).

Do not remove this boss completely or it will affect mixture distribution.

(5) Match up, by grinding, all the exhaust and inlet manifold ports with the cylinder head ports.

(6) Grind out and polish the inlet manifold, also matching the carburettor bores.

(7) Observe the following:

(a) Use standard cylinder head gasket.

(b) Use $\frac{3}{32}''$ thick $\times \frac{3}{4}''$ OD washers under the cylinder head nuts (to correct for reduced head thickness).

(c) Use four rocker shaft bracket packing pieces. (Fitted under the base of the bracket to correct the rocker adjustment.) MG part No MG 862/459—$\frac{1}{16}''$ thick mild steel with three holes to match the base of the bracket.

(d) Use fuel 50% petrol, 70 or 80 octane and 50% benzol, or for sustained power use 25% petrol and 75% benzol.

(e) Plugs:

For Series TC use Champion LA11 or Lodge R49.

For Series TD use Champion L10S for ordinary road work. For sustained power use Champion L11S or better Champion LA11 or Lodge R49.

(f) Use carburettor needles ES—jet .090″.

(g) Tappet setting: .022″.

(h) Ignition setting: Tdc—

(i) Use standard $1\frac{1}{4}''$ SU carburettors.

The engine should then give the following output.

Bhp	Rpm
11.3	1000
23.5	2000
38.0	3000
49.0	4000
58.0	5000
60.0	5500
60.0	6000

STAGE 1A

HIGH COMPRESSION RATIO TUNING (8.6 to 1) BUT PERMITTING USE OF LOW OCTANE FUEL

(1) Raise the compression ratio to 8.6 to 1 and polish the head, ports and manifold as for Stage 1.

(2) Install the larger inlet and exhaust valves as explained in Stage 2, using inlet valves (part No MG 862/460), but sodium-cooled exhaust valves (part No MG 862/466).

These exhaust valves have larger stems and require special bronze guides (part No MG 862/467), and special valve cotters (part No MG 862/468).

(3) Press the valve guides in so that they stand .945″ above the top of the cylinder head face. The bronze guides are longer than the standard ones and will protrude farther into the exhaust port. Due to the increase in valve weight fit the stronger 150 lb valve springs (part Nos MG 862/462 and 463) as described in Stage 2.

The 150 lb springs will prevent bounce up to 6000 rpm.

(4) To help compensate for the additional valve weight the valve stem shrouds may be cut off close to the top, leaving just the top collar and $\frac{1}{4}''$ of the tubular portion to locate the inner valve spring. The valve stem shrouds are cyanide hardened and will have to be cut off with a grinding wheel.

(5) Remove the thrust springs which are between

the rockers on the rocker shaft and replace them with steel distance tubes, leaving .003″ to .005″ end float. This removes some of the rocker friction.

(6) If trouble is experienced with the cylinder head gasket a competition gasket (part No MG 862/472) can be supplied or, if the car is used for racing purposes only, a gasket made from 20 SWG silver finishing auto body steel may be fitted. To accommodate this gasket it will be necessary to lap the cylinder head and block faces together with valve grinding compound. This makes a most reliable seal.

(7) Install the larger carburettors as described in Stage 3.

(8) Remove the thermostat bellows and valve completely and plug up or blank off the small by-pass pipe which goes from the lower radiator outlet pipe up the side of the thermostat body.

(9) Observe the following:

(a) Fuel of 70 octane may be used, some pinking will be experienced but will not be detrimental.

(b) Tappet setting: .025″ for maximum power; .022″ or .019″ may be used but up to 2 bhp may be lost.

(c) Ignition setting: Tdc.

(d) Use carburettor jets .090″ and needles LS1 or weaker EL, put in with the shoulder $\frac{1}{32}$″ below the face of the dashpot piston.

Screw the mixture adjusting nuts approximately seven flats down.

Remove the supplementary springs from the carburettor dashpots and remove the hydraulic damper pistons.

(e) Plugs: Use Champion L11S or for continuous high speed work use Champion LA11 or Lodge R49. For ordinary road work the standard L10S will do.

(f) Leave off the air cleaner and connecting branch pipe for high speed work, but if it is felt necessary to fit it for road work bore out the port holes to match the outer carburettor flanges.

(g) Fit a Lucas BR 12 coil.

(h) Plug setting: .018″ to .022″.

(j) As a safety factor for high speed work and to ensure sufficient fuel supply under all conditions, it is advisable to use two SU petrol pumps, as explained at item (j) in Stage 3. The engine on 70 octane fuel should give the following power:

Rpm	Bhp	Rpm	Bhp	Rpm	Bhp
2500	29.5	4000	50.0	5500	64.0
3000	40.5	4500	56.0	5700	64.5
3500	43.5	5000	61.0	6000	63.0

If the ordinary large exhaust valves, Part No MG 862/461 (as used in Stage 2), are used in place of the sodium-cooled exhaust valves the engine should be run on 80 octane petrol.

STAGE 2

HIGH COMPRESSION RATIO TUNING (9.3 TO 1), AND USING LARGER VALVES

The standard engine is raised to 9.3 to 1 compression ratio by removing $\frac{1}{8}$″ from the cylinder head face.

The finished thickness after machining should be 2.8966″. This is the absolute maximum to remove.

(1) Polish the head, ports and manifolds as in Stage 1.

(2) It will be noticed that a sharp edge is left on the combustion space profile at the end of the sparking plug hole. File this edge back vertically until it is a minimum of $\frac{3}{32}$″ thick at the centre.

(3) File this only locally at the plug hole (approximately $\frac{1}{4}$″ wide scoop) and blend into the combustion chamber shape with a radius each side. Do not file back too far. Check that the combustion space edge still extends safely over the gasket edge.

(4) Use larger inlet valves (part No MG 862/460), having 1.4173″ OD heads.

(5) In fitting these valves it is necessary to cut away part of the combustion space wall to clear the valve head. To do this use a 1.4961″ diameter (maximum) side and face cutter piloted off the valve guide.

The cutter corner should have a .040″ radius.

This may alternatively be done by careful grinding of the vertical wall until the valve head has a .040″ working clearance.

(6) Then cut or bore out the valve choke in a similar manner to 1.299″ diameter.

(7) Feather off by grinding any local ridge left in the valve port. Recut the seat to 30° × 1.3740″ top diameter.

(8) Fit larger exhaust valves (part No MG862/461), having 1.3386" OD heads.

(9) Follow the procedure as for the inlet valves, but cut away the combustion wall to clear the head with a 1.4173" diameter cutter, bore the valve choke to 1.1417" diameter and recut the seat 30° × 1.2913" top diameter.

(10) Fit stronger valve springs (150 lb open tension). Outer spring (part No MG 862/462) and inner spring (part No MG 862/463).

These are interchangeable with the standard springs, but one point should be noticed: they are staggered pitch springs and the closed coil ends should be fitted next to the cylinder head. Valve crash occurs with these springs around 6500 rpm.

(11) Observe the following:

(a) Use standard cylinder head gasket.

(b) Use $\frac{1}{8}$" thick × $\frac{3}{4}$" OD washers under the cylinder head nuts (to correct the reduced thickness).

(c) Use 4 rocker shaft bracket packing pieces (part No MG 862/459) to correct the rocker adjustment. These are $\frac{1}{16}$" mild steel with 3 holes to match the base of the bracket

(d) Plugs: Use Champion LA11 or Lodge R49.

(e) Tappet setting .022".

(f) Ignition setting: Tdc.

(g) Use standard 1$\frac{1}{4}$" SU carburettors.

Using fuel 75% benzol and 25% petrol, with carburettor needles ES, jet .090", the engine should then give the following output:

Bhp	Rpm
61.00	5000
65.00	5500
63.00	6000

Or using fuel 50% methanol, 20% petrol and 30% benzol, with carburettor needles RO, jet .090", the engine should give the following output:

Bhp	Rpm
62.5	5000
66.5	5500
64.0	6000

Alternative richer needle for above—RLS, or weaker—No 5.

An addition of 1% castor oil can be added to the methanol fuel.

When running on the above fuel, it is advisable to fit twin SU pumps, as explained at item (j) in Stage 3.

NOTE: The fan blades may be removed if the car is going to be used generally above 40 mph, but for trials work, slow hill-climbing and traffic work it should be retained.

The fan takes approximately 1 bhp to drive.

Tappet settings in all stages may be .019" if quietness is desired, with consequent loss of approximately 1 bhp.

In addition to the above, the 1$\frac{1}{2}$" diameter competition carburettors may be fitted, as described in Stage 3.

Using fuel 75% benzol and 25% petrol, with carburettor needles EL, jet .090", the engine should give the following output:

Bhp	Rpm
66.00	5000
70.00	5500
68.00	6000

Alternative richer needles for the above—CS2, or weaker—RO.

If richer needles are required, change to the .100" range.

STAGE 3

HIGH COMPRESSION RATIO TUNING (12 TO 1)

The standard engine, using the standard cylinder head with a depth of 3.0177", is raised to 12 to 1 compression ratio by the use of special pistons (part No MG 862/458). When ordering, the MG Car Company ask that the exact bore sizes be stated.

These pistons can only be fitted one way round— that is, with the flame groove on the sparking plug side.

When using this high compression ratio it is necessary to run on a high content methanol base fuel and to carry out the following alterations:

(a) Fuel:

80% dry blending methanol. Specific gravity: .796 at 60°F.

10% benzol (90). Specific gravity: .8758 at 60° F.
10% petrol. 70 octane or 80 octane.
1% castor oil.

187

(b) Use standard 1¼″ SU carburettors.

(c) Use carburettor jet size .100″.

(d) Use carburettor needles GK, or richer—RC, and weaker—RV.

(e) Sparking plugs: Use Champion LA14 or Lodge R49.

(f) Use carburettor float chamber needle and seat assemblies SU type T3.

(g) Tappet setting: .022″.

(h) Ignition setting 4° atdc (flywheel).

(j) Use two SU petrol pumps for increased fuel delivery. Do not couple the pumps together, but use duplicate fuel lines. Run an additional pipe from the tank to the extra pump. Run an additional flexible pipe from this pump to the carburettors. On the carburettors use a double-feed banjo union on each float chamber. One pump line to feed the rear float chamber, and one line to feed the front one.

Now run a flexible fuel pipe between the two float chamber banjo unions to balance the feed. The above arrangement will ensure getting sufficient discharge from the pumps.

The engine should then give the following output:

Bhp	Rpm
69.0	5000
73.0	5500
74.0	5800
73.0	6000

On Type XPAG/TD—Use competition cylinder head gasket (part No MG 862/472), to obtain the above figures.

These figures can now be increased by the fitting of the larger inlet and exhaust valves and 150 lb valve springs as in Stage 2.

The maximum output should then be 76 bhp at 5800 rpm.

To increase still further, fit the 1½″ diameter SU competition carburettors and grind out the inlet manifold at the outer bores to 1½″ diameter to match the carburettors.

It is not possible to grind right through the 1½″ diameter, but it is necessary to taper off in about a ¾″ length to 1⅜″ diameter. Maintain a minimum of 1⅜″ diameter or more right through. Otherwise aim at a minimum area of 1.5 inches squared.

These carburettors will be found to be fitted with light aluminium pistons, with additional return springs fitted above in the dashpots.

For absolute maximum power these springs may be removed, but for good pick-up and general carburation smoothness they should be left in position.

Fit the carburettors with .125″ jets and VE needles, or richer—VG, or weaker—VA.

On the same fuel and with other conditions as stated for Stage 3 (including large valves), the engine should give the maximum output of 80 bhp at 6000 rpm.

Run on a fuel of 100% methanol, using .125″ jets and VJ needles, or richer—VL, or weaker—VI. The engine should then give a maximum output of 83 bhp at 6000 rpm.

NOTE: When using methanol in the fuel it is necessary to clean out the whole of the carburettor and fuel system fairly frequently.

STAGE 4

INCREASING PERFORMANCE BY FITTING THE SHORROCK SUPERCHARGER KIT

The supercharger is an eccentric vane-type with balanced pressure lubrication system. It is mounted on the inlet manifold and driven by twin belts from the front end of the crankshaft. A large increase in power at the lower and medium engine speeds is obtained.

Details of the supercharger are:

Drive ratio: 1.16 to 1 step-up on engine speed.

Swept volume: .720 litre per revolution.
Boost pressures;

Rpm	Psi boost (approx)
1000	1.5
2000	2.5
3000	3.8
4000	5.5
5000	6.0

Oil metering pin: .304″ diameter, fitted in a reamed housing bore of .3125″ diameter.

Supercharger oil feed tank: Use SAE 30.

Type XPAG

Carburettor: SU 1⅜".
Standard needle: RA.
Jet size: .090".

Type XPAG/TD

Carburettor: SU 1½".
Standard needle RA.
Jet size: .100".

With:

(1) The supercharger kit fitted to a standard engine (see Standard Data).

(2) Petrol (70 octane).

(3) Plugs:

Type XPAG: Champion L11S or Lodge HNP.
Type XPAG/TD: Champion L10S or Lodge HNP.

(4) Tappet setting: .022".

The engine should give the following output:

Bhp	Rpm
18.5	1500
28.0	2000
45.0	3000
58.0	4000
69.0	5000
69.0	5500

or with 80 octane fuel, the following output:

Bhp	Rpm
19.0	1500
28.5	2000
45.5	3000
61.0	4000
70.0	5000
70.0	5500
70.0	6000

If required for special purposes the engine may be run on a fuel of 50% methanol, 20% petrol and 30% benzol.

Type XPAG—To do this, fit to the 1⅜" carburettor a .125" jet and use carburettor needle VE or richer—VB, or weaker—VA.

Type XPAG/TD—To do this, fit to the 1½" carburettor a .125" jet and use carburettor needle VG or richer—VI, or weaker—VE.

Fit the carburettor float chamber with a T3 needle and seat, and it is advisable to fit twin-coupled SU petrol pumps (see Stage 3).

Sparking plugs: Use Champion L11S or Lodge HNP, or if harder plugs are required, Champion LA11 or Lodge R49.

The engine should then give the following output:

Bhp	Rpm
20.5	1500
31.5	2000
52.0	3000
68.5	4000
75.0	5000
75.5	5500
75.0	6000

NOTE: If the carburettor vibration is such that it disturbs the mixture at high speeds, fit a ⅛" thick Neoprene gasket to the carburettor flange in place of the ordinary gasket.

Fit slotted nuts and double-coil spring washers to the carburettor fixing studs. Tighten these nuts only enough to grip the carburettor firmly, drill the studs through the nut slots, and lock with wire from one stud to the other around the carburettor body.

STAGE 5

FITTING THE SHORROCK SUPERCHARGER IN CONJUNCTION WITH A 9.3 TO 1 COMPRESSION RATIO

Fit the Shorrock supercharger kit and raise the compression ratio to 9.3 to 1, as explained in Stage 2. Fit the larger exhaust and inlet valves and 150 lb valve springs.

Fit a .125" jet to the carburettor and a T3 needle and seat to the float chamber.

Use carburettor needle VG (with ⅛" shank), or richer—V1 (with ⅛" shank), or weaker—VE (with ⅛" shank).

Use twin-coupled SU petrol pumps.

Sparking plugs: Use Champion LA11 or LA14 or Lodge R49 or R51.

Use a fuel 50% methanol, 20% petrol and 30% benzol.

1% castor oil may be added.

The engine should then give the following output:

Bhp	Rpm
55.5	3000
73.5	4000
85.5	5000
88.0	5500
88.0	6000

To obtain a further increase in power, fit a larger carburettor SU specification No 538, type H6, 1¾" diameter, to the supercharger.

It will be necessary to make a new elbow (steel or aluminium) between the carburettor and supercharger with an inside diameter of 1¾". Make sure the inlet port to the supercharger matches up and is of the same diameter.

Use a .1875" diameter jet in the carburettor and needle RM7, or richer—RM8, or weaker—RM6.

With a fuel of 80% methanol, 10% petrol and 10% benzol, the engine should give the following output:

Bhp	Rpm
74.5	4000
82.0	4500
89.0	5000
94.25	5500
97.5	6000

ENGINE TYPES
XPAG/TF AS FITTED TO TF CARS
XPEG AS FITTED TO TF 1500 CARS

SPECIFICATIONS

STANDARD ENGINE DATA

	Type XPAG/TF	Variations for Type XPEG
Bore	66.5 mm	72 mm
Stroke	90 mm	
Capacity	1250 cc	1466 cc
Firing order	1-3-4-2	
Sparking plugs	Champion NA8	
Compression ratio	8.1 to 1	8.3 to 1
Valve timing:		
Inlet opens	5° btdc	
closes	45° abdc	
Exhaust opens	45° bbdc	
closes	5° atdc	
Valve lift	8.3 mm, inlet and exhaust	
Valve springs	150 pounds, valve open	
Tappet clearance	.012" hot	
Contact breaker points	.014" to .016"	
Ignition timing	Tdc	
Octane rating:		
Minimum requirements for knock-free operation	76 octane	78 to 80 octane
For maximum power	82 octane	86 to 90 octane
Carburettors	Twin SU 1¼" bore	
Carburettor jet	.090"	
Carburettor needles	Standard GJ, Richer HI, Weaker GL	
Carburettor piston	For richer pick-up BY Part No AUC8015, SU No 3182/1	
Carburettor piston spring	Blue	
Bmep	125 at 3,400 rpm	131 at 3,000 rpm
Maximum torque	65 ft/lb at 3,400 rpm	78 ft/lb at 3,000 rpm
Bhp	57 at 5,500 rpm	63 at 5,000 rpm
Safe maximum rpm	5,700	
Valve crash rpm	6,000	
CC of combustion space	39.3 cc	
Cylinder head (large port type):		
Exhaust valve throat diameter	29 mm	
Inlet valve throat diameter	33 mm	

Cylinder head depth (top to bottom face)	75.16 mm	76.75 mm
Thickness of cylinder head gasket	.045" (part No 168423)	(part No AEF116)
CC of cylinder head gasket	Approx. 4.5 cc compressed	5.25 cc compressed
Inlet and exhaust manifold gasket	Part No 168433	
Clutch pressure springs	150 to 160 pounds, brown	

GEAR RATIOS

	Overall Ratios	mph per 1,000 rpm
Top	4.875 to 1	15.195
3rd	6.725 to 1	10.97
2nd	10.09 to 1	7.34
1st and reverse	17.06 to 1	4.34

GEARBOX RATIOS

Top	1 to 1
3rd	1.385 to 1
2nd	2.07 to 1
1st and reverse gear	3.5 to 1
Speedo reduction gear	6-tooth gear to 15-tooth pinion
Rear axle ratio	4.875 to 1

OPTIONAL EQUIPMENT

Optional rear axle ratio .... 8/41; crownwheel and pinion [part No 102258 (pair)]

	Overall Ratios	mph per 1,000 rpm
Top	5.125 to 1	14.42
3rd	7.098 to 1	10.412
2nd	10.609 to 1	6.966
1st and reverse	17.938 to 1	4.12

Speedo reduction for above:
  Speedo gear .... 5-tooth (part No AEG3110)
  Speedo pinion .... 13-tooth (part No X22797)

Optional rear axle ratio .... 9/41; crownwheel and pinion [part No 102262 (pair)]

	Overall Ratios	mph per 1,000 rpm
Top	4.555	16.259
3rd	6.309	11.81
2nd	9.429	7.85
1st and reverse	15.942	4.64

Speedo reduction for above:
  Speedo gear .... 6-tooth (part No AEG3109)
  Speedo pinion .... 14-tooth (part No X19101)

STAGE TF 1 (1250)

HIGH COMPRESSION RATIO TUNING (8.6 TO 1)

The engine is raised to 8.6 to 1 compression ratio by removing $\frac{1}{32}''$ from the cylinder head face.

The standard head is 75.16 mm thick; the finished thickness after machining should be 74.37 mm.

(1) Remove any burrs left, and polish, but do not grind out the combustion chambers as these are already quite clean and are machined nearly all over.

(2) Make sure the gasket edges do not overlap the combustion spaces.

(3) The ports may be lightly ground and polished, but should not be ground out so heavily that the shape or valve choke diameter is impaired.

(4) The inlet port outer separating stud boss may be ground away slightly—about $\frac{1}{16}''$ off each side (still maintaining its streamlined shape)—so that oblong ports are obtained $1\frac{3}{16}''$ high, $1\frac{1}{16}''$ wide (minimum).

Do not remove this boss completely or it will affect mixture distribution.

(5) Match-up, by grinding, all the exhaust and inlet manifold ports with the cylinder head ports.

(6) Grind out and polish the inlet manifold, also matching the carburettor bore.

(7) Observe the following:

(a) Use standard cylinder head gasket (part No 168423).

(b) Use $\frac{3}{32}''$ thick by $\frac{3}{4}''$ OD wasshers under the cylinder head nuts (to correct for reduced head thickness).

(c) Use fuel 80 octane.

(d) Plugs:
Use Champion NA8 for ordinary road work. For sustained power use NA10.

(e) Use carburettor needles GJ—jet .090″.

(f) Tappet setting: .012″.

(g) Ignition setting: Tdc.

(h) Use standard $1\frac{1}{2}''$ carburettors.

(j) Use standard $1\frac{1}{4}''$ SU carburettors.

The engine should then give approximately 61 brake horsepower at 5000 rpm.

STAGE TF 2 (1250)

HIGH COMPRESSION RATIO TUNING (9.3 TO 1)

The standard engine is raised to 9.3 to 1 compression ratio by removing $\frac{1}{16}''$ from the cylinder head face.

The finished thickness after machining should be 73.575 mm. This is the absolute maximum to remove.

(1) Polish the head, ports and manifolds as in Stage 1.

(2) It will be noticed that a sharp edge is left on the combustion space profile at the end of the sparking plug hole.

File this sharp edge back vertically until it is a minimum of $\frac{1}{32}''$ thick at the centre.

(3) File this only locally at the plug hole (approximately $\frac{3}{4}''$ wide scoop) and blend into the combustion chamber shape with a radius each side. Do not file back too far. Check that the combustion space edge still extends safely over the gasket edge.

(4) Observe the following:
(a) Use a standard cylinder head gasket.
(b) Use $\frac{1}{8}''$ thick by $\frac{3}{4}''$ OD washers under the cylinder head nuts (to correct reduced thickness).

(c) To allow for the cylinder head machining it is better to shorten the push rods $\frac{1}{16}''$, by drawing off one end in the extractor jig, machining $\frac{1}{16}''$ off the tube end, counterboring the end $\frac{1}{16}''$ deeper for the push rod to enter, refitting the push rod end and spot welding through to retain it in position.

Alternatively, use four rocker shaft bracket packing pieces (part No MG 862/459) to correct the rocker adjustment. These are $\frac{1}{16}''$ mild steel with three holes to match the base of the bracket.

(d) Plugs: Use Champion NA8, or for sustained power use Champion NA10 or Lodge RL49.

(e) Tappet setting: .012″.

(f) Ignition setting: Tdc.

(g) Use standard $1\frac{1}{2}''$ carburettors.

Using fuel 90 octane, with carburettor needles GJ, jet .090″, the engine should then give approximately 64 brake horsepower between 5500 and 6000 rpm.

If your car is not fitted with the high pressure SU fuel pump fitted at the rear of the car, it would be advantageous to fit one.

STAGE TF 3 (1250)

HIGH COMPRESSION (9.3 TO 1) SEMI-RACING TUNE USING SPECIAL CAMSHAFT

(1) Carry out the procedure of raising the compression ratio as Stage TF2.

(2) Fit a new camshaft (part No AEG 122).

This camshaft gives the following timing:

Inlet opens 13° btdc. Inlet closes 59° abdc. Exhaust opens 50° bbdc. Exhaust closes 22° atdc.

The tappet setting is .019" hot, inlet and exhaust, but they may be set down to minimum .015" for quietness.

The valves should not flutter until 6300 to 6400 rpm.

This camshaft may be described as semi-racing and some feeling of lost power at the lower revs may be felt, but the free-running of the engine at the higher revs in top and the intermediate gears should compensate for this. But be reasonable when using the revs available as, due to the design of the camshaft, the valve crashing point is not loudly audible, and the maximum revs could be considerably exceeded. A good driver is aware of this point of uselessly over-revving his engine (with resulting expensive noises) and drives on the rev counter with due respect.

The oil pressure should be raised to approximately 80 lb maximum by fitting a spigoted steel washer (part No SK 1039) on the lower end of the oil pump release valve spring. Or turn one up yourself to the following dimensions: .490" OD × .075" thick with spigot .368" OD, making the total thickness ⅛".

Insert the spigot into the lower end of the spring and this should hold the washer in position during assembly.

The standard distributor will be reasonably satisfactory, but a special distributor to suit the characteristics of this tuning is available (part No AJG 5035 or Lucas No 40441A).

Static ignition setting is tdc.

Use 80 octane fuel, or 90 octane may be used.

The engine should give approximately 66 brake horsepower between 5800 and 6300 rpm.

Use carburettor needles GJ, or richer—LS1.

STAGE TF 1

HIGH COMPRESSION RATIO TUNING (8.6 TO 1)

The engine is raised to 8.6 to 1 compression ratio by removing .020" from the cylinder head face.

The standard head is 76.75 mm thick; the finished thickness after machining should be 76.25 mm.

(1) Remove any burrs left, and polish, but do not grind out the combustion chambers, as these are already quite clean and are machined nearly all over.

(2) Make sure the gasket edges do not overlap the combustion spaces.

(3) The ports may be lightly ground and polished, but should not be ground out so heavily that the shape or valve choke diameter is impaired.

(4) The inlet port outer separating stud boss may be ground away slightly—about $\frac{1}{16}$" off each side (still maintaining its streamline shape)—so that oblong ports are obtained $1\frac{3}{16}$" high, $1\frac{1}{16}$" wide (minimum).

Do not remove this boss completely or it will affect mixture distribution.

(5) Match-up, by grinding, all the exhaust and inlet manifold ports with the cylinder head ports.

(6) Grind out and polish the inlet manifold, also matching the carburettor bore.

(7) Observe the following:

    (a) Use standard cylinder head gasket (part No AEF 116).

    (b) Use 90 octane fuel.

    (c) Plugs: Use Champion NA8.

    (d) Use carburettor needles CJ—jet .090".

    (e) Tappet setting: .012".

    (f) Ignition setting Tdc.

    (g) Use standard 1¼" carburettors.

The engine should then give approximately 65 brake horsepower between 5000 and 5500 rpm.

STAGE TF 2 (1500)

HIGH COMPRESSION RATIO TUNING (9.3 TO 1)

The standard engine is raised to 9.3 to 1 compression ratio by removing .050″ from the cylinder head face.

The finished thickness after machining should be 75.50 mm.

(1) Polish the head, ports and manifolds as in Stage 1.

(2) It will be noticed that a sharp edge is left on the combustion space profile at the end of the sparking plug hole.

File this sharp edge back vertically until it is a minimum of $\frac{1}{32}$″ thick at the centre.

(3) File this only locally at the plug hole (approximately $\frac{1}{4}$″ wide scoop) and blend into the combustion chamber shape with a radius each side. Do not file back too far. Check that the combustion space edge still extends safely over the gasket edge.

(4) Observe the following:
  (a) Use standard cylinder head gasket.
  (b) Plugs: Use Champion NA8, or for sustained power use Champion NA10 or Lodge RL49.
  (c) Tappet setting: .012″.
  (d) Ignition setting: Tdc.
  (e) Use standard 1¼″ carburettors.

Using 90 octane fuel, with carburettor needles GJ, jet .090″, the engine should then give approximately 67 brake horsepower between 5500 and 6000 rpm.

STAGE TF 3 (1500)

HIGH COMPRESSION (9.45 TO 1) SEMI-RACING TUNE USING SPECIAL CAMSHAFT

The standard engine is raised to 9.45 to 1 compression ratio by removing .068″ from the cylinder head face.

The finished thickness after machining should be 75.16 mm.

Polish the head, ports and manifolds as in Stage 1.

Fit a new camshaft (part No AEG122).

This camshaft gives the following timing:
Inlet opens 13° btdc. Inlet closes 59° abdc.
Exhaust opens 50° bbdc. Exhaust closes 22° atdc.

The tappet setting is .019″ hot, inlet and exhaust, but they may be set down to minimum .015″ for quietness.

The valves should not flutter until 6300 to 6400 rpm.

This camshaft may be described as semi-racing and some feeling of lost power at the lower revs may be felt, but the free-running of the engine at the higher revs in top and the intermediate gears should compensate for this. But be reasonable when using the revs available as, due to the design of the camshaft, the valve crash-point is not loudly audible, and the maximum revs could be considerably exceeded. A good driver is aware of this point of uselessly over-revving his engine (with resulting expensive noises) and drives on the rev counter with due respect.

The oil pressure should be raised to approximately 80 lb maximum by fitting a spigoted steel washer (part No SK1039) on the lower end of the oil pump release valve spring. Or turn one up yourself to the following dimensions: .490″ OD × .075″ thick with spigot .368″ OD, making the total thickness ⅛″.

Insert the spigot into the lower end of the spring and this should hold the washer in position during assembly.

The standard distributor will be reasonably satisfactory, but a special distributor to suit the characteristics of this tuning is available (part No AJG5035 or Lucas No 40441A).

Static ignition setting is tdc.

Use 90 octane fuel.

The engine should give approximately 70 brake horsepower between 5800 and 6300 rpm.

Use carburettor needles LS1.

STAGE TF 4

HINTS ON EXTRA TUNING FOR SPECIALS

A. Special Exhaust System for Use with Semi-Racing Camshaft

Carry out the procedure as for tuning to Stage TF3 (1250 or 1500).

Make up and fit a 4-pipe extractor exhaust system similar to that shown (see illustration).

This will increase the power 2 or 3 bhp all the way up the range, or alternatively, a twin exhaust system, with a branch from cylinders 1 and 4 and another branch from cylinders 2 and 3 running into separate pipes is partly effective.

B. Racing Tune for 1500 Engines

For racing purposes, the best way of improving performance is to use a high compression ratio, in conjunction with a special camshaft.

If run on 90 octane fuel the compression ratio can be put as high as 10.7 to 1.

The cylinder head depth should be 73.575 mm for this compression ratio. This is the absolute maximum to remove. When raising the compression ratio from the standard engine, shorten the push rods by the same amount as is removed from the cylinder head face. This can be done by drawing the push rod end in a small jig, machining the tube and pressing the push rod end on again. Check that the undercutting inside the push rod tube is deep enough to allow the push rod end to go right home.

Fit high overlap camshaft (part No 168551).

The timing of this camshaft is:

Inlet opens 32° btdc. Inlet closes 58° abdc.

Exhaust opens 60° bbdc. Exhaust closes 30° atdc.

Tappet setting: .012″ inlet, .019″ exhaust.

Make up an exhaust system similar to that illustrated.

It is most important this extractor-type system is fitted, otherwise the camshaft will not be at all effective.

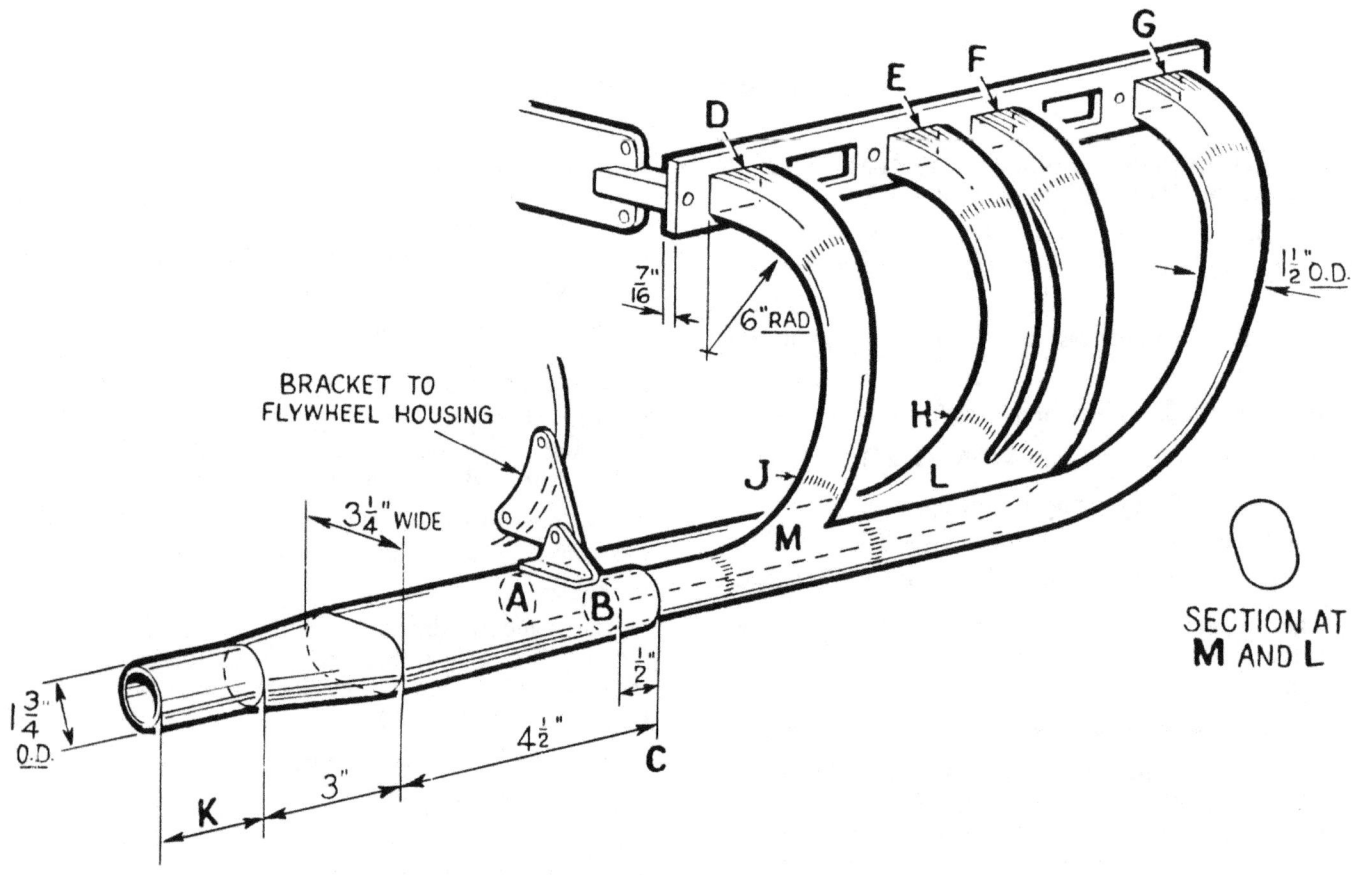

Special Four-pipe Extractor Exhaust.

Some erratic running may occur below 2000 rpm. The standard exhaust manifold is of no use. Variations to the system illustrated are no doubt possible, but this one has been proved successful, and it would be wise to follow it closely, unless you can prove your engine and its system on a test bed.

The camshaft will operate with the standard flat followers on this 1500 engine.

On the 1½″ carburettors the engine should give:

Rpm	Bhp
6300	78
6000	79
5500	78
5000	76

A further slight increase on these figures can be made:

Fit two 1¾″ carburettors (SU Spec 723).

They are fitted with needles CV. (If richer required use GK, or weaker required use BC or KTA.)

For maximum performance, blue springs are fitted to the carburettor pistons, but where acceleration only matters, it may prove better to fit heavier springs (red), with a slight loss of maximum power.

The TF inlet manifold (part No 168434) can be bored $\frac{25}{32}$″ diameter and an adapter plate fitted to accept the 1¾″ carburettors.

Taper grind the $\frac{25}{32}$″ diameter into the inlet manifold, making the passage through the manifold as large as possible.

The TF inlet manifold (part No 168434) used as suggested above with the adapter plate for the 1¾″ carburettors is rather heavy, and for the sake of lightness could be replaced with a sheet metal one, built directly into the exhaust manifold, following a similar design, with boxes up from main branch and ⅝″ ID steel balance tube across with a balance restrictor in the centre of this pipe having an 11 mm hole.

When fitting the large 1¾″ diameter carburettors it is advantageous to increase the width of the inlet ports in the cylinder head and the inlet manifold. It is just possible to remove a further $\frac{1}{16}$″ down each outer side of the inlet port, by grinding the wall and tapering into the port for approximately ⅝″. Do the same with the inlet manifold port, tapering out as far as possible. Grind the leading edge of the inlet port separating boss to a rather sharp edge and taper back as steeply as possible around the stud boss, do not thin down the walls of the stud boss excessively or the strength to clamp down the cylinder head will be impaired. Cut away the inlet manifold gasket to the shape of the enlarged port opening.

To prevent vibration of the carburettors, it is advisable to use a Neoprene gasket ¼″ thick and double coil spring washers under the bolt heads, so that the carburettors may be left not quite tightened solid. Wire the bolts in pairs to prevent them becoming slack.

The engine should then give the following:

Rpm	Bhp
6300	82
6000	81.5
5500	81
5000	78.5
4500	73
4000	66
3500	57
3000	49
2500	41

Use plugs KLG FE280/4, or softer KLG FE250/4, or harder KLG FE290/4, or alternative Champion NA10 or NA12, or Lodge RL47, or Lodge RL49.

As the carburettor float chamber will come close to the exhaust pipes, it will be necessary to fit a large asbestos-lined black steel sheet heat-deflector plate between the pipes and carburettors. Also if cold air can be arranged to blow on the float chambers this will prevent any chance of fuel boiling.

As the exhaust manifold (see illustration) has a large area of hot pipes under the carburettors, hot air rises and enters the carburettor chokes and seriously impairs the efficiency. The carburettor chokes must be in, or fed with, a cold air stream.

If the engine is fully enclosed, especially when in a streamlined body, it may be necessary to fit an airbox to the carburettors (see illustration) with an extension pipe to a cool air position such as at the nose of the car, although not essentially head on into the main air stream. A quiet spot behind the body nose adjacent to the grill will do. If the pipe is put head on into the main air stream, it may be necessary to connect (by unions in the air box) the float chamber top air vent pipes to the air box to balance the pressures, or alternatively, drill three ⅜″ holes in the centre bottom of the air box to prevent any pressure variation building up.

A satisfactory alternative method to the above is to use a length of 4″ car heater hose, fitted with the front open end in the main air stream at the body nose and the end supported 3″ or 4″ ahead of the front carburettor, with the direction of the air stream crossing the carburettor intakes.

If maximum overall car performance is required, do not overgear these engines. Let them attain 6300 rpm in top gear. There is a potential for valves to crash between 6500 and 6800 rpm.

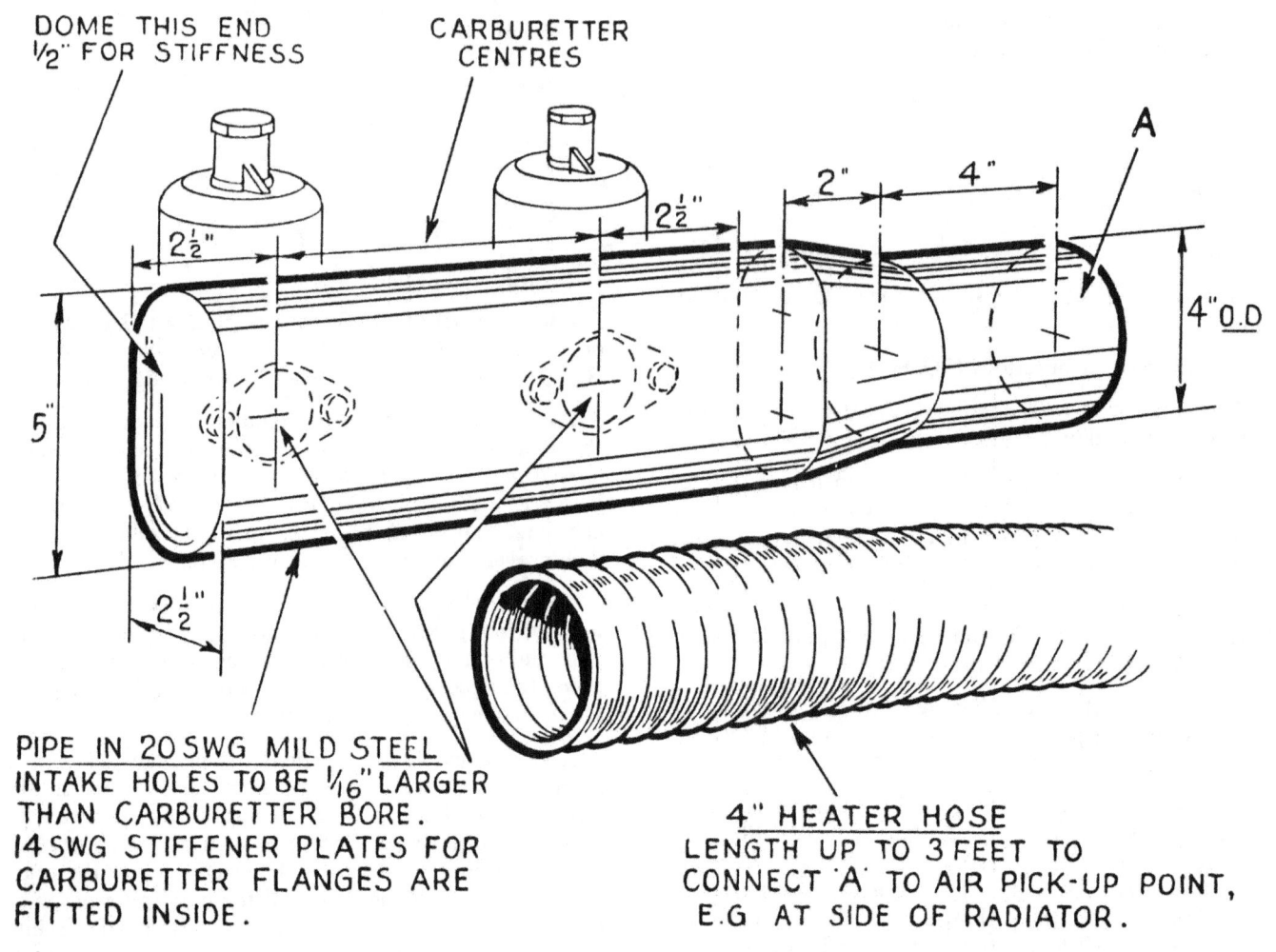

Details of Carburettor Intake Air Box.

AUTOBOOKS WORKSHOP MANUALS

ALFA ROMEO GIULIA 1300, 1600, 1750, 2000 1962-1978 WSM
BMW 1600 1966-1973 WSM
BMW 2000 & 2002 1966-1976 WSM
BMW 2500, 2800, 3.0 & 3.3 1968-1977 WSM
BMW 316, 320, 320i 1975-1977 WSM
BMW 518, 520, 520i 1973-1981 WSM
FIAT 1100, 1100D, 1100R & 1200 1957-1969 WSM
FIAT 124 1966-1974 WSM
FIAT 124 SPORT 1966-1975 WSM
FIAT 125 & 125 SPECIAL 1967-1973 WSM
FIAT 126, 126L, 126 DV, 126/650 & 126/650 DV 1972-1982 WSM
FIAT 127 SALOON, SPECIAL & SPORT, 900, 1050 1971-1981 WSM
FIAT 128 1969-1982 WSM
FIAT 1300, 1500 1961-1967 WSM
FIAT 131 MIRAFIORI 1975-1982 WSM
FIAT 132 1972-1982 WSM
FIAT 500 1957-1973 WSM
FIAT 600, 600D & MULTIPLA 1955-1969 WSM
FIAT 850 1964-1972 WSM
JAGUAR E-TYPE 1961-1972 WSM
JAGUAR MK 1, 2 1955-1969 WSM
JAGUAR S TYPE, 420 1963-1968 WSM
JAGUAR XK 120, 140, 150 MK 7, 8, 9 1948-1961 WSM
LAND ROVER 1, 2 1948-1961 WSM
MERCEDES-BENZ 190 1959-1968 WSM
MERCEDES-BENZ 220/8 1968-1972 WSM
MERCEDES-BENZ 220B 1959-1965 WSM
MERCEDES-BENZ 230 1963-1968 WSM
MERCEDES-BENZ 250 1968-1972 WSM
MERCEDES-BENZ 280 1968-1972 WSM
MG MIDGET TA-TF 1936-1955 WSM
MINI 1959-1980 WSM
MORRIS MINOR 1952-1971 WSM
PEUGEOT 404 1960-1975 WSM
PORSCHE 911 1964-1973 WSM
PORSCHE 911 1970-1977 WSM
RENAULT 16 1965-1979 WSM
RENAULT 8, 10, 1100 1962-1971 WSM
ROVER 3500, 3500S 1968-1976 WSM
SUNBEAM RAPIER, ALPINE 1955-1965 WSM
TRIUMPH SPITFIRE, GT6, VITESSE 1962-1968 WSM
TRIUMPH TR2, TR3, TR3A 1952-1962 WSM
TRIUMPH TR4, TR4A 1961-1967 WSM
VOLKSWAGEN BEETLE 1968-1977 WSM

VELOCEPRESS AUTOMOBILE BOOKS & MANUALS

ABARTH BUYERS GUIDE
AUSTIN-HEALEY 6-CYLINDER WSM
AUSTIN-HEALEY SPRITE & MG MIDGET 1958-1971 WSM
BMW 600 LIMOUSINE FACTORY WSM
BMW 600 LIMOUSINE OWNERS HAND BOOK & SERVICE MANUAL
BMW ISETTA FACTORY WSM
BOOK OF THE CARRERA PANAMERICANA - MEXICAN ROAD RACE
COMPLETE CATALOG OF JAPANESE MOTOR VEHICLES
CORVAIR 1960-1969 OWNERS WORKSHOP MANUAL
CORVETTE V8 1955-1962 OWNERS WORKSHOP MANUAL
DIALED IN - THE JAN OPPERMAN STORY
FERRARI 250/GT SERVICE AND MAINTENANCE
FERRARI 308 SERIES BUYER'S AND OWNER'S GUIDE
FERRARI BERLINETTA LUSSO
FERRARI BROCHURES AND SALES LITERATURE 1946-1967
FERRARI BROCHURES AND SALES LITERATURE 1968-1989
FERRARI GUIDE TO PERFORMANCE
FERRARI OPP, MAINTENANCE & SERVICE H/BOOKS 1948-1963
FERRARI OWNER'S HANDBOOK
FERRARI SERIAL NUMBERS PART I - ODD NUMBERS TO 21399
FERRARI SERIAL NUMBERS PART II - EVEN NUMBERS TO 1050
FERRARI SPYDER CALIFORNIA
FERRARI TUNING TIPS & MAINTENANCE TECHNIQUES
HENRY'S FABULOUS MODEL "A" FORD
HOW TO BUILD A FIBERGLASS CAR
HOW TO BUILD A RACING CAR
HOW TO RESTORE THE MODEL 'A' FORD
IF HEMINGWAY HAD WRITTEN A RACING NOVEL
JAGUAR E-TYPE 3.8 & 4.2 WSM
LE MANS 24 (THE BOOK THAT THE FILM WAS BASED ON)
MASERATI BROCHURES AND SALES LITERATURE
MASERATI OWNER'S HANDBOOK
METROPOLITAN FACTORY WSM
MGA & MGB OWNERS HANDBOOK & WSM
MG MIDGET TC, TD, TF & TF1500 WORKSHOP MANUAL
OBERT'S FIAT GUIDE
PERFORMANCE TUNING THE SUNBEAM TIGER
PORSCHE 356 1948-1965 WSM
PORSCHE 912 WSM
SOUPING THE VOLKSWAGEN
SOLEX CARBURETORS (EMPHASIS ON UK & EU AUTOMOBILES)
SU CARBURETORS (EMPHASIS ON UK AUTOMOBILES)
TRIUMPH TR2, TR3, TR4 1953-1965 WSM
TUNING FOR SPEED (P.E. IRVING)
VEDA ORR'S NEW REVISED HOT ROD PICTORIAL
VOLKSWAGEN TRANSPORTER, TRUCKS, STATION WAGONS WSM
VOLVO 1944-1968 ALL MODELS WSM
WEBER CARBURETORS (EMPHASIS ON ALFA & FIAT)

BROOKLANDS BOOKS & ROAD TEST PORTFOLIOS (RTP)

AC CARS 1904-2009
ALFA ROMEO 1920-1933 ROAD TEST PORTFOLIO
ALFA ROMEO 1934-1940 ROAD TEST PORTFOLIO
BRABHAM RALT HONDA THE RON TAURANAC STORY
BUGATTI TYPE 10 TO TYPE 40 ROAD TEST PORTFOLIO
BUGATTI TYPE 10 TO TYPE 251 ROAD TEST PORTFOLIO
BUGATTI TYPE 41 TO TYPE 55 ROAD TEST PORTFOLIO
BUGATTI TYPE 57 TO TYPE 251 ROAD TEST PORTFOLIO
DELAHAYE ROAD TEST PORTFOLIO
FERRARI ROAD CARS 1946-1956 ROAD TEST PORTFOLIO
FIAT 500 1936-1972 ROAD TEST PORTFOLIO
FIAT DINO ROAD TEST PORTFOLIO
HISPANO SUIZA ROAD TEST PORTFOLIO
HONDA ST1100/ST1300 PAN EUROPEAN 1990-2002 RTP
JAGUAR MK1 & MK2 ROAD TEST PORTFOLIO
LOTUS CORTINA ROAD TEST PORTFOLIO
MV AGUSTA F4 750 & 1000 1997-2007 ROAD TEST PORTFOLIO
TATRA CARS ROAD TEST PORTFOLIO

VELOCEPRESS MOTORCYCLE BOOKS & MANUALS

AJS SINGLES & TWINS 250cc THRU 1000cc 1932-1948 (BOOK OF)
AJS SINGLES 1955-65 350cc & 500cc (BOOK OF)
AJS SINGLES 1945-60 350cc & 500cc MODELS 16 & 18 (BOOK OF)
ARIEL 1939-1960 4 STROKE SINGLES (BOOK OF)
ARIEL LEADER & ARROW 1958-1964 (BOOK OF)
ARIEL MOTORCYCLES 1933-1951 WSM
ARIEL PREWAR MODELS 1932-1939 (BOOK OF)
BMW M/CYCLES R26 R27 (1956-1967) FACTORY WSM
BMW M/CYCLES R50 R50S R60 R69S (1955-1969) FACTORY WSM
BSA BANTAM (BOOK OF)
BSA ALL FOUR-STROKE SINGLES & V-TWINS 1936-1952 (BOOK OF)
BSA OHV & SV SINGLES - 250cc 1954-1970 (BOOK OF)
BSA OHV & SV SINGLES 1945-54 250-600cc (BOOK OF)
BSA OHV SINGLES 350 & 500cc 1955-1967 (BOOK OF)
BSA PRE-WAR MODELS TO 1939 (BOOK OF)
BSA TWINS 1948-1962 (BOOK OF)
BSA TWINS 1962-1969 (SECOND BOOK OF)
CATALOG OF BRITISH MOTORCYCLES (1951 MODELS)
DOUGLAS PRE-WAR ALL MODELS 1929-1939 (BOOK OF)
DOUGLAS POST-WAR ALL MODELS 1948-1957 FACTORY WSM
DUCATI 160cc, 250cc & 350cc OHC MODELS FACTORY WSM
HONDA 50 ALL MODELS UP TO 1970 INC MONKEY & TRAIL (BOOK OF)
HONDA 90 ALL MODELS UP TO 1966 (BOOK OF)
HONDA MOTORCYCLES 125-150 TWINS C/CS/CB/CA WSM
HONDA MOTORCYCLES 250-305 TWINS C/CS/CB WSM
HONDA MOTORCYCLES C100 SUPER CUB WSM
HONDA MOTORCYCLES C110 SPORT CUB 1962-1969 WSM
HONDA TWINS & SINGLES 50cc THRU 305cc 1960-1966 (BOOK OF)
HONDA TWINS ALL MODELS 125cc THRU 450cc UP TO 1968 (BOOK OF)
INDIAN PONYBIKE, BOY RACER & PAPOOSE ILL PARTS LIST & SALES LIT
J.A.P. ENGINES 1927-1952 & MOTORCYCLES 1934-1952 (BOOK OF)
LAMBRETTA ALL 125 & 150cc MODELS 1947-1957 (BOOK OF)
LAMBRETTA LI & TV MODELS 1957-1970 (SECOND BOOK OF)
MATCHLESS 350 & 500cc SINGLES 1945-1956 (BOOK OF)
MATCHLESS 350 & 500cc SINGLES 1955-1966 (BOOK OF)
MOTORCYCLE ENGINEERING (P. E. Irving)
NORTON 1932-1947 (BOOK OF)
NORTON 1938-1956 (BOOK OF)
NORTON DOMINATOR TWINS 1955-1965 (BOOK OF)
NORTON MODELS 19, 50 & ES2 1955-1963 (BOOK OF)
NORTON MOTORCYCLES 1957-1970 FACTORY WSM
NORTON PREWAR MODELS 1932-1939 (BOOK OF)
NSU PRIMA ALL MODELS 1956-1964 (BOOK OF)
NSU QUICKLY ALL MODELS 1953-1963 (BOOK OF)
RALEIGH MOPEDS 1960-1969 (BOOK OF)
ROYAL ENFIELD SINGLES & V TWINS 1934-1946 (BOOK OF)
ROYAL ENFIELD SINGLES & V TWINS 1937-1953 (BOOK OF)
ROYAL ENFIELD SINGLES 1946-1962 (BOOK OF)
ROYAL ENFIELD 736cc INTERCEPTOR FACTORY WSM
ROYAL ENFIELD 250cc & 350cc SINGLES 1958-1966 (SECOND BOOK OF)
SPEED AND HOW TO OBTAIN IT
SUNBEAM MOTORCYCLES 1928-1939 (BOOK OF)
SUNBEAM S7 & S8 1946-1957 (BOOK OF)
SUZUKI 50cc & 80cc UP TO 1966 (BOOK OF)
SUZUKI T10 1963-1967 FACTORY WSM
SUZUKI T20 & T200 1965-1969 FACTORY WSM
TRIUMPH PRE-WAR MOTORCYCLE 1935-1939 (BOOK OF)
TRIUMPH MOTORCYCLES 1935-1949 (BOOK OF)
TRIUMPH MOTORCYCLES 1937-1951 WSM
TRIUMPH MOTORCYCLES 1945-1955 FACTORY WSM
TRIUMPH TWINS 1945-1958 (BOOK OF)
TRIUMPH TWINS 1956-1969 (BOOK OF)
VELOCETTE ALL SINGLES & TWINS 1925-1970 (BOOK OF)
VESPA 1951-1961 (BOOK OF)
VESPA 125 & 150cc & GS MODELS 1955-1963 (SECOND BOOK OF)
VESPA 90, 125 & 150cc 1963-1972 (THIRD BOOK OF)
VESPA GS & SS 1955-1968 (BOOK OF)
VILLIERS ENGINE (BOOK OF)
VINCENT MOTORCYCLES 1935-1955 WSM

PLEASE VISIT OUR WEBSITE
www.VelocePress.com
FOR A DETAILED DESCRIPTION OF ANY OF THESE TITLES

Please check our website:

www.VelocePress.com

for a complete
up-to-date list of
available titles

www.ingramcontent.com/pod-product-compliance
Lightning Source LLC
Chambersburg PA
CBHW060250240426
43673CB00047B/1903